Computer Language Engineering

Computer Language Engineering

Editor:

Nelson Bolívar, Ph.D

ArclerPress

www.arclerpress.com

Computer Language Engineering

Editor: Nelson Bolívar, Ph.D

708 3rd Avenue, 6th Floor
New York
NY 10017
United States of America
www.arclerpress.com

ISBN: 978-1-68094-445-7

Library of Congress Control Number: 2016951162

About the Editor

Nelson Bolívar, Ph.D

Nelson Bolivar has a PhD. in physics from the University of Lorraine in France finished in 2014. His expertise is in quantum systems and condensed matter. His interest includes spintronic devices and correspondences between general relativity and condensed matter. He is currently an associate professor at the Central University of Venezuela

Contents

List of Contributors ... *xi*
Preface ... *xv*
Introduction ... *xvii*

Chapter 1 Software Engineering Principles ... 1
1. Introduction ... 1
2. Related Work on Software Engineering Principles ... 1
3. Phase 1: Identification of Engineering Criteria ... 3
4. Phase 2: Verification against the Two Sets of Criteria ... 5
5. Phase 3: Analysis and Consolidation Using Both Sets of Criteria ... 6
6. Work Limitations ... 7

Conclusions ... 8
References ... 8

Chapter 2 Lightweight Behavior-Based Language for Requirements Modeling ... 9
1. Introduction ... 9
2. Behavior Based Requirements Modeling Language ... 9
3. Behavior Based Requirements Description Model ... 11
4. Case Study ... 12
5. Related Works ... 15

Conclusions and Future Work ... 16
Acknowledgements ... 16
References ... 16

Chapter 3 A Massively Parallel Re-Configurable Mesh Computer Emulator: Design, Modeling and Realization ... 19
1. Introduction ... 19
2. Parallel Computational Model ... 20
3. Object Modeling of the RMC ... 22
4. Applications ... 28

Conclusions ... 33
References ... 33

Chapter 4 Semantic Analysis of Natural Language Queries for an Object Oriented Database ... 35
1. Introduction ... 35
2. Natural Language Database ... 36
3. Query Semantic Validation ... 37
4. Experimental Results ... 39

Conclusions ... 39
References ... 39

Chapter 5 Integrating Acad With GIS For Civil Engineering Applications ... 41
1. Introduction ... 41
2. Historical Background ... 41
3. GIS and CAD ... 42
4. GIS Technology ... 42
5. Benefits of GIS ... 43

6. GIS Applications in Civil Engineering 43
7. Integrating Acad With GIS 43
8. Developing GIS Maps by Using Acad Software 44
9. Developing GIS Maps by Using Arcview Software 44
Conclusions 45
References 48

Chapter 6 C-Language Programming for Development of Conventional Water Treatment Plants Decision Support System 49
1. Introduction 49
2. Methodology 49
3. Results and Discussions 54
Conclusion 55
References 55

Chapter 7 PGQL: A Probabilistic Graphical Query Language For Gene Expression Time Courses 57
1. Background 57
2. Testing 60
3. Discussion 61
Conclusions 62
Authors' Contributions 62
References 62

Chapter 8 Bamql: A Query Language For Extracting Reads From Bam Files 63
1. Background 63
2. Implementation 63
3. Results 64
4. Discussion 67
Conclusions 67
Funding 67
Authors' Contributions 67
References 67

Chapter 9 High-Level Portable Programming Language for Optimized Memory Use of Network Processors 69
1. Introduction 69
2. Related Work 70
3. Packet-Processing Language 71
4. Implementation Method 72
5. Prototyping 75
6. Evaluation 76
Concluding Remarks 77
Acknowledgements 78
References 78

Chapter 10 A Comparison of Common Programming Languages Used in Bioinformatics 81
1. Background 81
2. Results 82
3. Discussion 83
4. Conclusion 85
5. Methods 85

6. Algorithms ... 86
Acknowledgements ... 87
Authors' Contributions ... 87
References ... 87

Chapter 11 An Introduction to Scripting in Ruby for Biologists ... 89
1. Background ... 89
2. Conclusion ... 94
3. Further Information ... 94
Acknowledgements ... 95
Authors' Contributions ... 95
References ... 95

Chapter 12 S3ql: A Distributed Domain Specific Language For Controlled Semantic Integration of Life Sciences Data ... 97
1. Background ... 97
2. Methods ... 99
3. Results ... 101
4. Discussion ... 104
Conclusions ... 106
Acknowledgements and Funding ... 107
Competing Interests ... 107
Authors' Contributions ... 107
References ... 107

Chapter 13 Rgg: A General Gui Framework For R Scripts ... 109
1. Background ... 109
2. Simple Example ... 112
3. Results and Discussion ... 113
4. Perspectives ... 114
Conclusion ... 114
Acknowledgements ... 114
Authors' Contributions ... 114
References ... 114

Chapter 14 Improving Type Error Messages For Generic Java ... 117
1. Introduction ... 117
2. An Overview of Java Generics ... 118
3. Examples ... 119
4. The Type Checking Process ... 128
5. The Modified Type Checking Process ... 130
6. Implementation ... 138
7. Related Work ... 138
Conclusions, Reflections and Future Work ... 139
Acknowledgements ... 140
Appendix: Using The System ... 140
References ... 140

Chapter 15 Ete: A Python Environment For Tree Exploration ... 143
1. Background ... 143
2. Results ... 144

3. Discussion 147
Conclusions 147
Acknowledgements 147
Authors' Contributions 147
References 147

Chapter 16 Evaluation of Xis-Mobile, A Domain Specific Language For Mobile Application Development 149
1. Introduction 149
2. Related Work 150
3. Case Study—The Flight Reservation App 150
4. Xis-Mobile Language 150
5. Xis-Mobile Framework 155
6. Evaluation 155
Conclusions 157
Acknowledgements 157
References 157

Chapter 17 Bio:: Phylo-Phyloinformatic Analysis Using Perl 159
1. Background 159
2. Implementation 160
3. Nexml 160
4. Results and Discussion 161
Conclusions 163
Installation 165
Acknowledgements 165
Authors' Contributions 165
References 165

Chapter 18 R/Parallel – Speeding Up Bioinformatics Analysis With R 169
1. Implementation 170
2. Results 170
Conclusion 172
Acknowledgements 172
Authors' Contributions 172
References 172

Chapter 19 Owlcpp: A C++ Library For Working With Owl Ontologies 175
1. Background 175
2. Implementation 176
3. Results 179
4. Discussion 180
Conclusions 181
Acknowledgements 181
Authors' Contributions 181
References 181

Index 183

List of Contributors

Kenza Meridji

École de Technologie Supérieure (ÉTS)—University of Québec, Montréal, Québec, Canada

Alain Abran

École de Technologie Supérieure (ÉTS)—University of Québec, Montréal, Québec, Canada

Zhengping Liang
College of Computer and Software Engineering, Shenzhen University, Shenzhen, China;
State Key Laboratory of Software Engineering, Wuhan, China;

Guoqing Wu
School of Computer, Wuhan University, Wuhan, China.

Li Wan
School of Computer, Wuhan University, Wuhan, China.

Mohamed YOUSSFI
Faculté Des Sciences Université Mohamed V Agdal Rabat Morocco.

Omar BOUATTANE
E. N. S. E. T, Bd Hassan II, BP, Mohammedia Morocco

Mohamed O. BENSALAH
Faculté Des Sciences Université Mohamed V Agdal Rabat Morocco.

Bentamar Hemerelain
Oran University, Wilaya of Oran, Algeria

Hafida Belbachir
University of Science and Technologie of Oran (USTO), Wilaya of Oran, Algeria.

Asma Thamir Ibraheem
Civil Engineering Department, College of Engineering, Nahrain University, Baghdad, Iraq.

Haidar Alaa Hassan
Civil Engineering Department, College of Engineering, Nahrain University, Baghdad, Iraq.

Mustefa Husam Abd Al-Husain
Civil Engineering Department, College of Engineering, Nahrain University, Baghdad, Iraq.

Thogare N. Shridhara
Department of Civil Engineering, NMAM Institute of Technology, Udupi District, India

Samson O. Ojoawo
Department of Civil Engineering, NMAM Institute of Technology, Udupi District, India

Pilli V. Mahaganesha
Department of Civil Engineering, NMAM Institute of Technology, Udupi District, India

Mallaura R. Thippeswary
Department of Civil Engineering, NMAM Institute of Technology, Udupi District, India

Rahul Anand
Department of Civil Engineering, NMAM Institute of Technology, Udupi District, India

Bevinahalli P. Sharath
Department of Civil Engineering, NMAM Institute of Technology, Udupi District, India

Ruben Schilling
Max Planck Institute for Molecular Genetics, Department of Computational Biology, Ihnestr. 63-73, 14195 Berlin, Germany.

Ivan G Costa
Center of Informatics, Federal University of Pernambuco, Av. Prof. Luiz Freire, s/n, Recife - Pernambuco - Brazil.

Alexander Schliep
Department of Computer Science and BioMaPS Institute for Quantitative Biology, Rutgers, The State University of New Jersey, 110 Frelinghuysen Rd, Piscataway, NJ 08854-8019, USA.

Andre P. Masella
Ontario Institute for Cancer Research, Suite 510, 661 University Avenue, M5G 0A3, Toronto, Canada.

Christopher M. Lalansingh
Ontario Institute for Cancer Research, Suite 510, 661 University Avenue, M5G 0A3, Toronto, Canada.

Pragash Sivasundaram
Ontario Institute for Cancer Research, Suite 510, 661 University Avenue, M5G 0A3, Toronto, Canada.

Michael Fraser
Ontario Cancer Institute, Princess Margaret Cancer Centre/University Health Network, Toronto, Canada.

Robert G. Bristow
Ontario Cancer Institute, Princess Margaret Cancer Centre/University Health Network, Toronto, Canada
Department of Medical Biophysics, University of Toronto, Toronto, Canada.
Department of Radiation Oncology, University of Toronto, Toronto, Canada

Paul C. Boutros
Ontario Institute for Cancer Research, Suite 510, 661 University Avenue, M5G 0A3, Toronto, Canada.
Department of Pharmacology & Toxicology, University of Toronto, Toronto, Canada.
Department of Medical Biophysics, University of Toronto, Toronto, Canada.

Yasusi Kanada
Central Research Laboratory, Hitachi, Ltd., Yokohama, Japan

Mathieu Fourment
Department of Biological Sciences, Macquarie University, Sydney, NSW 2109, Australia

Michael R Gillings
Department of Biological Sciences, Macquarie University, Sydney, NSW 2109, Australia

Jan Aerts
Genome Dynamics and Evolution Group, Wellcome Trust Sanger Institute, Wellcome Trust Genome Campus, Hinxton, CB10 1SA, UK

Andy Law
Division of Genetics and Genomics, The Roslin Institute and Royal (Dick) School of Veterinary Studies, University of Edinburgh, Roslin,EH25 9PS, UK

Helena F Deus
Digital Enterprise Research Institute, National University of Ireland at Galway, IDA Business Park, Lower Dangan, Galway, Ireland
Biomathematics, Instituto de Tecnologia Química e Biológica, Universidade Nova de Lisboa, Av. da República, Estação Agronómica Nacional, 2780-157 Oeiras, Portugal

Miriã C Correa
Laboratório Nacional de Computação Cientifica, Av. Getúlio Vargas, 333, Quitandinha, 25651-075 Petrópolis, Brasil.

Romesh Stanislaus
Sanofi Pasteur, 38 Sidney Street, Cambridge, MA 02139, USA

Maria Miragaia
Laboratory of Molecular Genetics, Instituto de Tecnologia Química e Biológica, Universidade Nova de Lisboa, Av. da República, Estação Agronómica Nacional, 2780-157 Oeiras, Portugal.

Wolfgang Maass
Research Center for Intelligent Media, Furtwangen University, Furtwangen, Germany

Hermínia de Lencastre
Laboratory of Molecular Genetics, Instituto de Tecnologia Química e Biológica, Universidade Nova de Lisboa, Av. da República, Estação Agronómica Nacional, 2780-157 Oeiras, Portugal.
Laboratory of Microbiology, The Rockefeller University, 10021 New York, USA

Ronan Fox
Digital Enterprise Research Institute, National University of Ireland at Galway, IDA Business Park, Lower Dangan, Galway, Ireland

Jonas S Almeida
Division of Informatics, Department of Pathology, University of Alabama at Birmingham, 619 South 19th Street, Birmingham, Alamaba, USA

Ilhami Visne
Austrian Research Centers GmbH – ARC, Molecular Diagnostics, A-2444 Seibersdorf, Austria and

Erkan Dilaveroglu
Austrian Research Centers GmbH – ARC, Molecular Diagnostics, A-2444 Seibersdorf, Austria and

Klemens Vierlinger
Austrian Research Centers GmbH – ARC, Molecular Diagnostics, A-2444 Seibersdorf, Austria and

Martin Lauss
Austrian Research Centers GmbH – ARC, Molecular Diagnostics, A-2444 Seibersdorf, Austria and

Ahmet Yildiz
Austrian Research Centers GmbH – ARC, Molecular Diagnostics, A-2444 Seibersdorf, Austria and

Andreas Weinhaeusel
Austrian Research Centers GmbH – ARC, Molecular Diagnostics, A-2444 Seibersdorf, Austria and

Christa Noehammer
Austrian Research Centers GmbH – ARC, Molecular Diagnostics, A-2444 Seibersdorf, Austria and

Friedrich Leisch
Institut für Statistik, LudwigMaximilians-Universität, Ludwigstraße 33, D-80539 München, Germany

Albert Kriegner
Austrian Research Centers GmbH – ARC, Molecular Diagnostics, A-2444 Seibersdorf, Austria and

Nabil el Boustani
Center for Software Technology, Department of Information and Computing Sciences, Universiteit Utrecht, P.O. Box 80.089, 3508 TB Utrecht, The Netherlands

Jurriaan Hage
Center for Software Technology, Department of Information and Computing Sciences, Universiteit Utrecht, P.O. Box 80.089, 3508 TB Utrecht, The Netherlands

Nabil el Boustani
Center for Software Technology, Department of Information and Computing Sciences, Universiteit Utrecht, 3508 TB Utrecht, The Netherlands

Jurriaan Hage
Center for Software Technology, Department of Information and Computing Sciences, Universiteit Utrecht, 3508 TB Utrecht, The Netherlands

Jaime Huerta-Cepas
Comparative Genomics group, Bioinformatics and Genomics Programme, Centre for Genomic Regulation (CRG), Dr. Aiguader, 88 08003 Barcelona, Spain.

Joaquín Dopazo
Bioinformatics Department, Centro de Investigación Príncipe Felipe, València, Spain

Toni Gabaldón
Comparative Genomics group, Bioinformatics and Genomics Programme, Centre for Genomic Regulation (CRG), Dr. Aiguader, 88 08003 Barcelona, Spain.

André Ribeiro
INESC-ID/Instituto Superior Técnico, Lisbon, Portugal

Alberto Rodrigues da Silva
INESC-ID/Instituto Superior Técnico, Lisbon, Portugal

Rutger A Vos
School of Biological Sciences, University of Reading, UK.

Jason Caravas
Department of Biological Sciences, Wayne State University, Detroit, MI, USA.

Klaas Hartmann
Tasmanian Aquaculture and Fisheries Institute, University of Tasmania, Australia.

Mark A Jensen
Fortinbras Research, Rockville, MD, USA.

Chase Miller
Center for Infection and Immunity, Columbia University, New York, NY, USA.

Gonzalo Vera
Groningen Bioinformatics Centre (GBiC), Groningen Biomolecular Sciences and Biotechnology Institute, University of Groningen, Haren, The Netherlands
Computer Architecture and Operating Systems Department (CAOS), Universitat Autònoma de Barcelona, Bellaterra, Spain

Ritsert C Jansen
Groningen Bioinformatics Centre (GBiC), Groningen Biomolecular Sciences and Biotechnology Institute, University of Groningen, Haren, The Netherlands

Remo L Suppi
Computer Architecture and Operating Systems Department (CAOS), Universitat Autònoma de Barcelona, Bellaterra, Spain

Mikhail K. Levin
Department of Clinical Sciences, University of Texas Southwestern Medical Center, 5323 Harry Hines Boulevard, Dallas, TX, USA

Lindsay G. Cowell
Department of Clinical Sciences, University of Texas Southwestern Medical Center, 5323 Harry Hines Boulevard, Dallas, TX, USA

Preface

Computer programming language is any of various languages for expressing a set of detailed instructions for a digital computer. Such instructions can be executed directly when they are in the computer manufacturer-specific numerical form known as machine language.

Computer Language Engineering addresses the implementation of high-level programming languages into specifics fields, from science to civil engineering. Students, scientist and engineers will find this book to be a good comprehensive resource for learning about the construction and application of some relevant languages, focusing on specific applications that are also novel research material in the area. The aim of first chapter is to provide basic principles of software engineering. Second chapter presents a lightweight behavior based language for requirements modeling. The goal of third chapter is to present an elaborated emulator of a 2-D massively parallel re-configurable mesh computer of size n x n processing elements (PE). Fourth chapter deals with the semantic analysis of queries written in natural language and dedicated to the object oriented data bases. Fifth chapter focuses on integrating auto computer-aided design (ACAD) with geographic information system (GIS) for civil engineering applications. In sixth chapter, C-language programming for development of conventional water treatment plants decision support system has been studied. The purpose of seventh chapter is to deal with probabilistic graphical query language for gene expression time courses and eighth chapter discusses about the application of binary alignment/map query language (BAMQL) for extracting reads from binary alignment/map (BAM) files. Ninth chapter proposes an open, high-level, and portable programming language called "Phonepl", which is independent from vendor-specific proprietary hardware and software but can be translated into a network processor (NP) program with high performance especially in the memory use. Tenth chapter deals with common programming languages used in bioinformatics and eleventh chapter introduces Ruby as a highly suitable scripting language for biologists to learn and use. Twelfth chapter presents a domain specific language, the S3DB query language (S3QL), to operate on its underlying core model and facilitate management of linked data. Thirteenth chapter provides a generic concept that allows R users to extend their statistical and bioinformatical procedures, which are relying on commands in the R prompt, with standard graphical user interfaces. Fourteenth chapter describe how to re-architect the Java type checking process in order to obtain more informative error messages. Fifteenth chapter highlights on the environment for tree exploration (ETE), a python programming toolkit that assists in the automated manipulation, analysis and visualization of hierarchical trees. In sixteenth chapter, XIS-Mobile, a domain specific language, focused on the development of mobile applications and on mitigating the problems related to the complexity of software development and mobile platform fragmentation were studied. Seventeenth chapter presents a Perl5 toolkit for phyloinformatic analysis and eighteenth chapter introduces the application of R/parallel in speeding up bioinformatics analysis with R. Last chapter deals with development of owlcpp, a library for storing and searching RDF triples, parsing RDF/XML documents, converting triples into OWL axioms, and reasoning.

Editor
Nelson Bolívar, Ph.D

INTRODUCTION

A computer language is a "language" made up of formal syntax and semantics that allow users to communicate instructions to computer systems. Programming languages are by far the most common examples of computer languages, so the terms "computer language" and "programming language" are often used interchangeably. A computer cannot work with human language and, in most cases, a human cannot efficiently work in computer binary, so a higher-level language is necessary to allow programmers to give instructions to computer systems. There are several types of computer languages. Different programmers choose to use one or more languages because of personal preference, the particular capabilities of a given language, and the demands of the project at hand.

Syntax and semantics, or structure and meaning, are the two defining characteristics of computer language and can be compared to the grammar and vocabulary of human languages. Different programming terms must be placed in particular orders and marked by specific punctuation and spacing to be understood by the computer. In general, these restraints on computer language are much stricter than those on human languages. A human language can often still be understood even with grammar and word usage problems, but the interpretive powers of computers are comparatively limited; even minor spacing issues will, in many languages, result in an error message, as the computer will not be able to follow the instructions as given.

Human languages are intended to allow individuals to communicate with each other. This can involve discussion, command, interrogation, declaration, and many other forms of communication. The purpose of computer language, on the other hand, is generally to provide explicit instructions for the computer to follow, so such languages are generally imperative in nature. Some computer languages, however, are based primarily on the use of logical expressions or mathematical formulas. Reducing computer language to mathematical or logical expressions can help to reduce the possibilities of side effects that can result from some imperative expressions, but it can also make programming more difficult for those without extensive mathematical skills.

Computer languages are modified and developed over time to better meet the needs of their users and to keep up with technological advancements. Modifications include changes in syntax and semantics as well as increases and additions to overall functionality. A modern computer language may, for instance, be updated from an older version to make use of processors with multiple cores. Languages are also optimized for programming applications for mobile devices.

What is Assembly Language?

An assembly language is a low-level way to instruct a computer to carry out a task. Computers do not inherently understand instructions from people. At the most basic level, computers understand instructions in binary language, that is, sequences of zeroes and ones. Binary language or machine language is extremely cumbersome to program in, however. Assembly language was invented as a symbolic representation of the underlying sequences of zeroes and ones.

Suppose we were to program a game which, upon a certain action, awards the player with five points. The computer keeps the score in a certain location; the locations are either a storage place within the CPU, called a "register," or in some space in the memory. The computer understands locations and low-level actions called operations. So if the score is kept at register RA, then it understands the command, 0101 1100 0000 0101, where the first four numbers indicate the operation ADD, the next four indicate the register RA, and the last eight indicate the number 5.

Originally computers had to be coded this way; machine language is slow, error-prone, and it can be very hard for one person to understand what another person is trying to code. So computer programmers created a language in which the operations, locations, numbers, etc., can be better understood. Thus the equivalent command for the above example would be ADD RA 5. In this hypothetical example, mnemonics are used for the ADD operation and the register RA, and the number 5 is written in digits.

A program called an assembler converts assembly language code into the underlying machine language. In earlier days, even this conversion used up expensive computing resources, so the operation codes, opcodes in short, such as Subtract were abbreviated as SUB, Copy-Move was abbreviated as MOV and in some cases even ADD was abbreviated to A.

Assembly language is mostly a thin layer above the machine structure. Hence the opcodes, registers, and the whole language is very much dependent on the CPU family. So, the Intel x86 family has opcodes such as MOV, MOVSX, and MOVZX, whereas IBM 360 has opcodes such as MVI, MVC, MVZ. When designing a computer or CPU, the designers specify the machine language including the opcodes. Programmers soon moved to "high-level" languages such as COBOL, Pascal, C++, and SQL. Compilers convert code written in these languages into machine language. Assembly code is still used for specialized CPUs, however, or for ensuring speed from game consoles to car systems.

What are some of the Different Computer Programming Languages?

There are thousands of computer programming languages. These languages are used to control the way computers behave, process information, express algorithms, and handle tasks. Some computer programming languages have been around for many years while new languages, or variations on old ones, are developed every year. Computer programming languages range from the simple and easy to use to very complicated languages used by only the most technologically proficient programmers.

One well-known computer programming language is called Visual BASIC. Microsoft Visual BASIC is considered a high level programming language. It is descendant from Beginners' All-purpose Symbolic Instruction Code (BASIC), a Disk Operating System (DOS) programming language. Visual BASIC is considered simple to learn, featuring codes that bear a similarity to written English. Visual BASIC is both visual and events driven, featuring a graphical environment for programming.

Pascal is also well known among those with interest in computer programming languages. Developed in 1970, by Professor Niklaus Wirth, Pascal is an imperative language. An imperative language is one that uses computations as statements, changing program states through sequences of commands. Professor Wirth developed Pascal to fill feature gaps left by other computer programming languages. His development goals included designing a programming language that would facilitate the creation of well-structured programs, allow for implementation efficiency, and prove helpful in teaching computer-programming concepts.

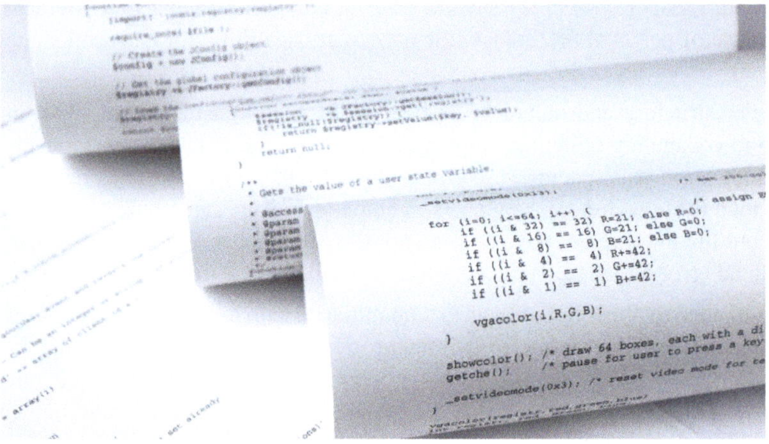

Fortran is a general-purpose computer programming language that was first introduced by IBM in the early 1950s. It is one of the most frequently used computer programming languages for numerical-based and scientific-computing applications. Fortran fits into categories reserved for general purpose and imperative computer programming languages; it is also considered procedural. It is frequently used in computation-heavy areas, such as computational sciences and climate modeling.

C++ is a high-level computer programming language. It is considered general purpose and is widely used for modern computers. Developed by Bjarne Stroustrup, at Bell Labs, C++ was first introduced in 1985. This programming language was developed for the UNIX environment, allowing programmers to enjoy an easier process for writing code and improving code quality. Additionally, C++ makes it possible to modify existing code without changing it.

Often considered a superset of the C programming language, C++ includes some features of the earlier language. It also boasts compilers capable of running C programs. However, there are major differences. For example, the C programming language, developed in the early 1970s, employs structured programming concepts while C++ is object oriented. C++ was designed with the goal of enhancing the C programming language.

What is COBOL Language?

Common Business-Oriented Language, more commonly known as COBOL Language, is one of the oldest programming languages in existence. COBOL languages can primarly be found in areas like business and finance for the government, as well as many companies. COBOL Language first appeared in late 1959, after a short-range committee, formed during a meeting at the Pentagon, was asked to recommend a new approach to a common business language.

The written description of COBOL, as well as the specifications for it, were influenced by another language, called FLOW-MATIC. Other languages were also influential in the development of COBOL. One, invented by Bob Bemer, was the IBM COMTRAN language. Another was the FACT language from Honeywell. It's Grace Hopper, however, who is often called "the mother of the COBOL language."

FLOW-MATIC, a data processing language, was invented by Grace Hopper, an American computer scientist and United States Naval officer. File separation (INPUT/OUTPUT), qualification of data-names, and figurative constant ZERO, are just some of the elements that were incorporated into the design of COBOL. Naturally, COBOL has undergone several enhancements, and even continues to evolve, but there has been a standard form of the language developed to prevent incompatibility between different versions. The version is known ANS COBOL, named for the American National Standards Institute (ANSI).

ANSI produced several revisions of the COBOL standard, including the Corrections Amendment - 1991. The development and ownership was eventually taken over by the International Organization for Standardization (ISO), which released several editions and technical reports. The ISO standard became available to the public in 2002. It can be found on the COBOL standards website, coded as ISO/IEC 1989.

COBOL's significant feature variables and file records are described in great detail, so names become truly connotative. Visual programming environments become accessible. It also allows integration with the World Wide Web.

In 2002, the 4th revision of the COBOL computer language came out. This version added many new features, such as national language support, floating-point support, XML generation and phrasing, and much more. The COBOL language is the main language that automated businesses, and solving business problems is exactly what it does.

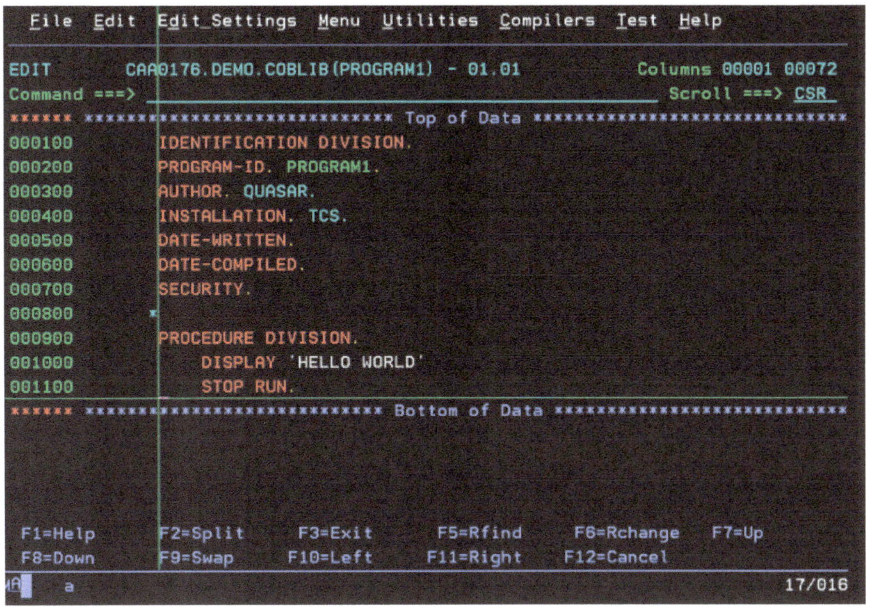

What is Prolog Language?

Prolog is a computer programming language that is based on logic. Most computer languages are based on the steps needed to solve a problem. The Prolog language, on the other hand, is a "declarative" language which indicates the logical relationships between entities. The way to solve the problem is left to the computer. The name Prolog comes from the French Programmation en Logique, that is, Programming Logic.

The following is a simple Prolog program:

```
ancestor(F, C) :- father(F, C)

ancestor(P, Q) :- father(P, R), ancestor(R, Q)

father(john, jim).

father(jim, jerry).

father(jerry, jason).
```

```
father(jerry, jeff).

father(jason, joshua).
```

The above program indicates truisms. If F is father of C, then F is an ancestor of C. If P is the father of some person R who is an ancestor of Q, then P is an ancestor of Q. A number of true facts are then given, such as john being the father of jim.

What Are the Different Types of Computer-Assisted Language Learning?

Computer-assisted language learning is a rapidly growing field. As new software and technologies continue to improve, online courses have become increasingly popular. Common modes of online language learning include online remote instruction, study software, and online tools for language students.

Many universities, private companies, and cultural organizations offer online computer-assisted language learning by means of distance education classes. These classes can generally be taken independently or as part of an online degree. Costs and quality of online degree programs vary wildly. Some programs are accredited, but others are not. Accreditation can be a good indicator of the quality of a course and will help ensure that the course can be used towards a university degree.

The two main varieties of online distance education classes are synchronous and asynchronous. Both are computer-assisted language learning, but the use of the computer varies somewhat. Asynchronous courses frequently use a computer to deliver texts or pre-recorded lectures. These courses also frequently employ some degree of computer graded assessment.

Synchronous online language learning courses require students to participate in real time or near real time classroom activities. Computer-assisted language learning technologies employed in these courses include student forums, live multicast lectures with student interaction, and one-on-one or group video chat. The additional human involvement required to run these courses can make them more expensive, but they can provide more extensive student feedback than asynchronous courses.

Another major area of computer-assisted language learning is note taking and study software. Note taking software allows students to record portions of live or online lectures and write associated notes to be stored with the recording. This can be especially helpful when studying pronunciation.

Study software includes flash card software, character recognition software, and computer-based dictionaries and translators. Flash card software is helpful for students learning new vocabulary. Many flash card programs use a spaced repetition algorithm to improve memorization by detecting which words are hardest for each student and showing those words most often. Various flash card programs are available at a variety of price points, ranging from a moderate monthly fee to a free download.

Students learning languages which use different writing systems may benefit from character recognition software. When combined with flash card software, this allows students to use a spaced repetition algorithm while learning new characters. It can also help students move from recognizing characters to easily writing them.

Advanced students studying texts often use computer based dictionaries to look up unknown words. These dictionaries can be much faster to use than traditional paper dictionaries. Online translation tools are generally not reliable for detailed translations but can help students who are not very familiar with a language confirm that they have not used incorrect words in their compositions.

What is Natural Language Processing?

Natural language processing (NLP) is a way of translating between computer languages and human languages. The goal of this field is to allow computers to understand what a text says without being given precise values and equations for the data that the text contains. In essence, natural language processing automates the translation process between human and computer languages. While much of this field relies on statistics and models to determine likely meanings of a phrase, there are and have been many different approaches to this problem. Findings in this field have applications in the areas of speech recognition, human language translation, information retrieval, and even artificial intelligence.

Evolving out of a background in computer science and linguistics, natural language processing faces many problems because language is not always consistent and not all clues to meaning are contained in language itself. Even a complete account of the entire grammar of a language including all exceptions does not always allow a computer to parse the information contained in a text. Some sentences are syntactically ambiguous, words often have more than one meaning, and some combinations of sounds or symbols change their meaning depending on the boundaries of the words — all of which can be problems for a computer that does not understand context. More importantly, much of language depends on a connection to the physical and social universe — some sentences, such as speech acts, do not convey information as much as act on the world. Even if a computer has a perfect understanding of human language syntax and semantics, the text to be analyzed must be free of human devices, such as sarcasm or passive aggression, for the computer to correctly ascertain what the text means.

Ideologically, natural language processing is a system of human-computer interaction that is governed by the idea that most computer users are more comfortable working with computers in a human language they already know than adapting to a computer's language. It also capitalizes on the fact that much of human knowledge is already encoded in human language, and the texts that contain that knowledge can be translated into logical structures that can be streamlined for a computer. While many projects in this field work to extract computer-readable data from human language texts, natural language processing is also used to generate human-readable texts from computer data. Both these understanding and generating facilities can be used by the same technology, such as in the case of applications that translate from one human language to another by first decoding the text into a computer language, then encoding it in another human language. The innovations obtained in natural language processing endeavors are also strikingly applicable to artificial intelligence projects because of the degree to which human-like intelligence is defined by a mastery of the complexities of human language.

CHAPTER 1 SOFTWARE ENGINEERING PRINCIPLES

Kenza Meridji, Alain Abran

Keywords: Engineering Criteria, Software Engineering Principles, Vincenti, Engineering Verification Criteria

INTRODUCTION

Software engineering is defined by the IEEE as:

- The application of a systematic, disciplined, quantifiable approach to the development, operation and maintenance of software, i.e. the application of engineering to software.
- The study of approaches as in 1" [1].

The intended goals of software engineering are different from those of computer science. In software engineering, artifacts are designed, produced and put into operation, while in computer science the theoretical foundations of information and computation are the object of study. Computer science deals with the investigation and analysis of algorithms and their related problems, in order to enable the computer perform the task [2]. Computer science is the discipline that underlies software engineering, and it is to be expected that the principles for computer science will be different from the principles of software engineering. For example, a principle proposed in computer science, "Use coupling and cohesion" [3], deals with the underlying science, while software engineering principles are more general, like "Apply and use quantitative measurements in decision making" [3]. Of course, software engineering is still an emerging engineering discipline and is not yet as mature as other traditional engineering disciplines such as mechanical and electrical engineering. Much of the research conducted to date in software engineering has focused on developing methods, techniques, and tools, and considerably less on exploring the engineering foundations of software engineering, including identifying the software engineering fundamental principles, or how to apply them in research and practice. A significant amount of the work carried out to date on software engineering principles has been based on expert opinion, with a few exceptions in which defined research methodologies have been used, such as in [4] and [5], where Delphi rounds are applied to develop an initial consensus among a group of 12 experts on a set of candidate principles for software engineering. In a 2006, literature survey on this topic, covering the previous 20 years [3], 308 separate proposals for candidate software engineering principles was identified. These were then analyzed against a set of criteria related to the specific concept of a 'principle', following which only 34 were recognized as bona fide 'candidate' fundamental principles (FPs) [3]. However, the research scope of that study did not, include within its research scope an analysis of these candidates from an engineering perspective.

In this paper, we perform that analysis. One of the challenges, of course, is to figure out what criteria should be verified from an engineering perspective, since, in the traditional engineering literature, such criteria are not explicitly described. This paper documents the methodology to make that determination, as well as what we found when we applied them to the set of 34 candidate FPs. The paper is organized as follows: Section 2 presents related work on software engineering principles. Section 3 presents the analysis methodology selected. Section 4 identifies the software engineering verification criteria. Section 5 describes the application of these criteria. Section 6 presents the analysis results. Section 7 points out the limitations of that work. Section 8 presents our conclusion.

RELATED WORK ON SOFTWARE ENGINEERING PRINCIPLES

The expression "fundamental principle" is composed of two terms. According to the Cambridge University Dictionary, the term "fundamental" means "forming the base, from which everything else originates; more important than anything

Citation: K. Meridji and A. Abran, "Software Engineering Principles," Journal of Software Engineering and Applications, Vol. 3 No. 10, 2010, pp. 972-982. doi: 10.4236/jsea.2010.310114.

else", and "principle" means "a basic idea or rule that explains or controls how something happens or works". From the literature on software engineering principles, the authors of [3] inventoried 308 principles that had been proposed by individuals (for instance [6-8]) or as part of a collaborative effort [9-12]. With the exception of [11] and [3], the authors involved proposed only nominative principles, without including either formal definitions or procedures for implementing them. To verify whether or not each of these was indeed a candidate 'fundamental' principle, in our sense of the terms, a two-step verification process was used in [3-11,13,14]:

1) Identification of seven verification criteria Five criteria applicable to each proposed principle were derived from [4]:

A principle is a proposal formulated in a prescriptive way;

- A principle should not be directly associated with, or arise from, a technology, a method, or a technique, or itself be an activity of software engineering;
- The principle should not dictate a compromise (or a proportioning) between two actions or concepts;
- A principle of software engineering should include concepts connected to the engineering discipline;
- It must be possible to test the formulation of a principle in practice, or to check its consequences.

Two additional criteria were identified as applicable across the full set of proposed principles:

- The principles should be independent, e.g. not deduced [6];
- A principle should not contradict another known principle [4].

2) Verification of each of the proposed 308 principles surveyed against these criteria

In [3] it is reported that only 34 of the 308 proposals met the full set of criteria to be recognized as candidate FPs. Table 1 lists them, in alphabetical order [3]. In their paper "Fundamental Principles of Software Engineering–A Journey" [4], the authors identified a set of fundamental principles through a well documented research methodology. They defined the relationships between principles, standards and implemented best practices as illustrated in Figure 1.

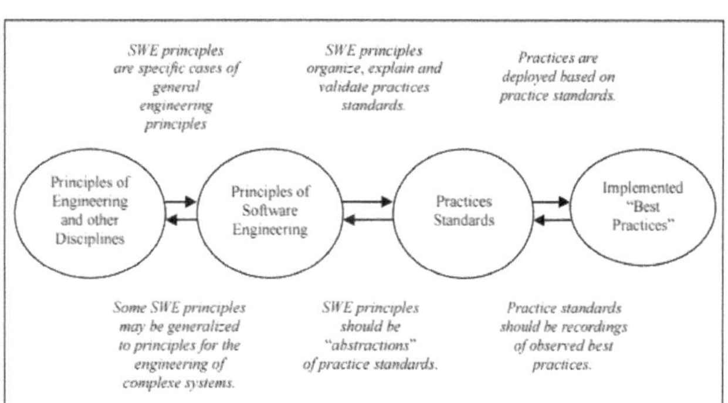

Figure 1: Relationships between principles, standards and practices [4].

This figure illustrates the relationships sought among principles standards and practices. It is believed that a body of fundamental principles has been recorded for some branches of engineering, e.g. [15]. Most of the engineering branches have a history far longer than that of software engineering and software engineering principles (SWE principles in Figure 1) would, in general, be regarded as specializations of these principles. The software engineering principles would play the role of organizing, motivating, explaining, validating the practice standards and implemented practices should be based on those practice standards [4]. Working from the specific toward the general, practice standards would be recordings and idealizations of observed and validated "best practices". The software engineering principles would be abstractions of the practice standards. Furthermore, software engineering principles might be candidates for generalization to the status of general engineering principles, particularly when complexity is a concern [4].

Analysis Methodology

The scope of the criteria used in [3] was limited to the concept of 'principles', and did not include the specific features of the engineering concepts themselves. This is the focus of the work reported here: the list of 34 candidate principles in Table 1 constitutes the input to the analysis process required to verify whether or not they conform to engineering criteria. This will make it possible to narrow the number of principles. More specifically, the research issue addressed in this paper is, which of these 34 candidate FPs conform to engineering criteria? Of course, engineering criteria are required for this verification and must be available, but no related work could be identified. So, the first challenge was to determine verification criteria from an engineering perspective.

To tackle this issue, it was necessary to study the epistemology of engineering. For that purpose, two sources, Vincenti, the author of the book, What Engineers Know and How They Know It [15], and the joint IEEE-ACM software engineering curriculum [16] were selected:

- Vincenti has identified a number of engineering knowledge types as key to the engineering disciplines and from which engineering criteria can be derived;
- The IEEE and the ACM have documented a set of topics within their joint software engineering curriculum from which engineering criteria can be derived.

The approach designed for identifying relevant criteria and applying them to the set of 34 candidate FPs consists of three phases—see Figure 2.

Phase 1: Identification of two Sets of Verification Criteria

This phase consists of the identification of criteria which would be relevant to any engineering discipline. Such criteria could have been taken either as is, when expressly identified and defined, or derived, when documented only implicitly. The inputs to this phase are the two sources of information identified from the related work. The outputs of this phase are the two sets of criteria derived from Vincenti and from the IEEE-ACM joint software engineering curriculum. The criteria identification phase based on Vincenti is summarized in Figure 3, which shows its inputs and outputs. The criteria identification phase based on the IEEE-ACM criteria is summarized in Figure 4, which shows its inputs and outputs. This phase is presented in greater detail in Section 4.

Phase 2: Verification execution:

The 34 candidate FPs will be taken as inputs in the second phase and analyzed next with respect to the two sets of engineering criteria identified in Phase 1. The output will be the FPs that have at least one direct mapping, and those that have only an indirect mapping to either Vincenti or to the IEEE-ACM engineering criteria. This phase is illustrated in Figure 5 and is presented in greater detail in Section 5. Phase 3: Analysis and selection: In Phase 3, the analysis across each set of engineering criteria is performed. This phase identifies the candidate FPs that meet engineering criteria from both sets of criteria and those that do not. For instance, the candidate FPs that meet only the Vincenti criteria [15] and the candidate FPs that only meet the IEEE-ACM criteria [14] are then be analyzed to check whether or not they can be identified from the FP that are recognized as engineering FPs. This phase is described in greater detail in Section 6.

Table 1: Inventory of Candidate FPs [3].

No	Proposals–in alphabetical order
1	Align incentives for developer and customer
2	Apply and use quantitative measurements in decision making
3	Build software so that it needs a short user manual
4	Build with and for reuse
5	Define software artifacts rigorously
6	Design for maintenance
7	Determine requirements now
8	Don't overstrain your hardware
9	Don't try to retrofit quality
10	Don't write your own test plans
11	Establish a software process that provides flexibility
12	Fix requirement specification errors now
13	Give product to customers early
14	Grow systems incrementally
3	Implement a disciplined approach and improve it continuously
16	Invest in understanding the problem
17	Involve the customer
18	Keep design under intellectual control
19	Maintain clear accountability for results
20	Produce software in a stepwise fashion
21	Quality is the top priority; long-term productivity is a natural consequence of high quality
22	Rotate (top performing) people through product assurance
23	Since change is inherent to software, plan for it and manage it
24	Since tradeoffs are inherent to software engineering, make them explicit and document them
25	Strive to have a peer find a defect, rather than a customer

PHASE 1: IDENTIFICATION OF ENGINEERING CRITERIA

Vincenti

Vincenti [17] studied the epistemology of engineering based on the historical analysis of five case studies in aeronautical engineering covering a roughly fifty-year period and proposed a taxonomy of engineering knowledge. He identified different types of engineering knowledge and classified them into six categories:

- Fundamental design concepts,
- Criteria and specifications,
- Theoretical tools,
- Quantitative data,
- Practical considerations, and
- Design instrumentalities.

26	Tailor cost estimation methods
27	To improve design, study previous solutions to similar problems
28	Use better and fewer people
29	Use documentation standards
30	Write programs for people first
31	Know software engineering techniques before using development tools
32	Select tests based on the likelihood that they will find faults
33	Choose a programming language to ensure maintainability
34	F aced with unstructured code, rethink the module and redesign it from scratch

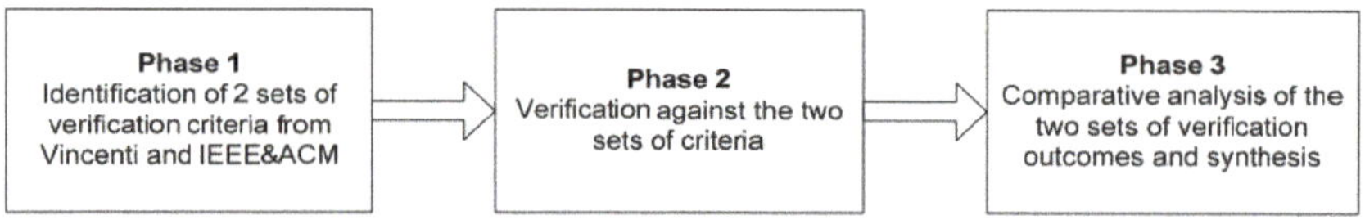

Figure 2. The three-phase verification process.

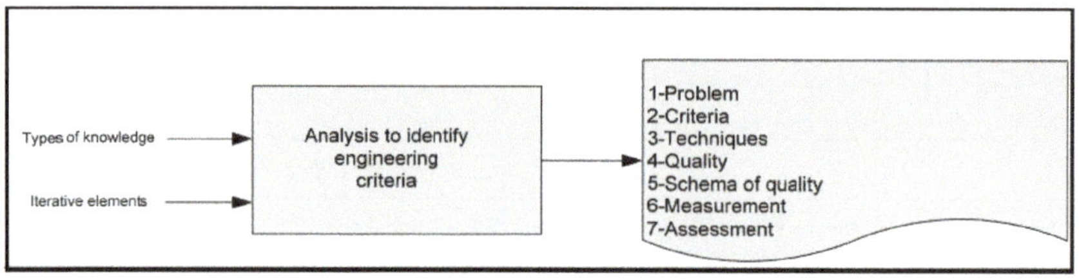

Figure 3. Identification of Vincenti engineering criteria.

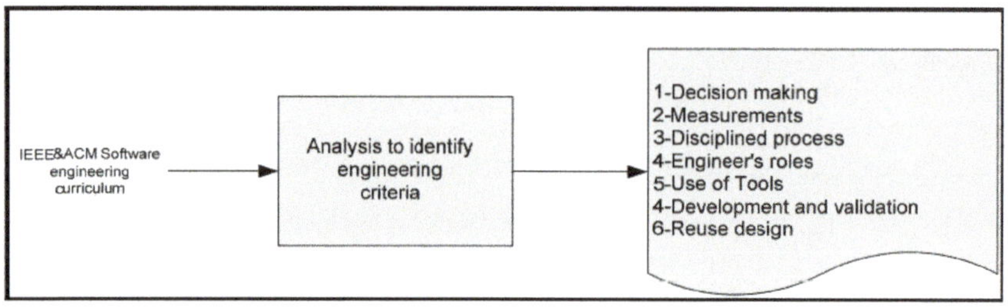

Figure 4: Identification of the IEEE-ACM engineering criteria.

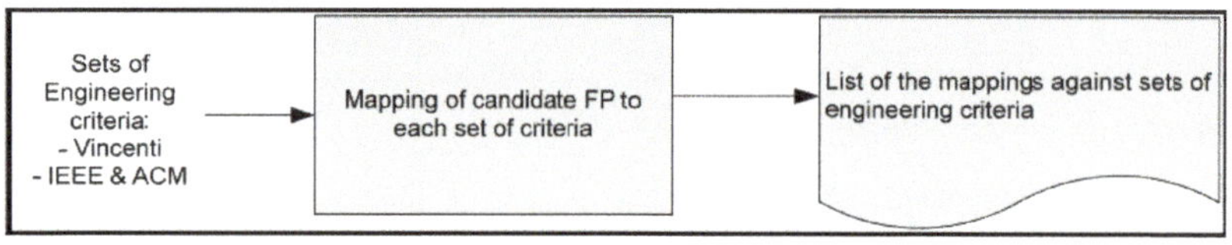

Figure 5: Phase 2: Process of verification against sets of engineering criteria.

According to Vincenti, this classification is not specific to aeronautical engineering, but can be transferred to other engineering domains. For instance, a detailed analysis of engineering knowledge types was used in [18] to analyze the content of the Software Quality Knowledge Area of the Guide to the Software Engineering Body of Knowledge–SWEBOK [15]. Vincenti has distinguished seven elements for engineering, which he refers to as "interactive elements", and which he selected prior to categories of engineering knowledge types. These elements show the epistemological structure of the engineering learning process based on the analysis of the five aeronautical case studies. These seven elements represent, in Vincenti's opinion, a necessary set of different elements that interact with each other for the completion of an engineering activity. These seven interactive elements are referred to here as the Vincenti engineering criteria, and are listed in Table 2. The abbreviations we have selected to represent each of these criteria are listed in the right-hand column of Table 2.

IEEE and ACM Joint Curriculum

The IEEE Computer Society (IEEE-CS) and the Association for Computing Machinery joined forces to develop a joint set of computer curricula, including one on software engineering. More specifically, chapter 2 of the joint software engineering curriculum lists the characteristics of an engineering disc pline (see i Table 3).

Table 2: Engineering criteria identified in Vincenti

ID.	Vincenti Engineering Criteria	Abbreviation
1	Recognition of a problem	Problem
2	Identification of concepts and criteria	Criteria
3	Development of instruments and techniques	Techniques
4	Growth and refinement of opinions regarding desirable qualities	Quality
5	Combination of partial results from 2, 3 and 4 into practical schema for research	Testing
6	Measurement of characteristics	Measurement
7	Assessment of results and data	Assessment

Table 3: Identification of IEEE & ACM engineering criteria

ID.	Engineering Criteria Identified	Abbreviation
1	Engineers proceed by making a series of decisions, carefully evaluating options, and choosing an approach at each decision point that is appropriate for the current task in the current context. Appropriateness can be judged by tradeoff analysis, which balances costs against benefits.	Decision making
2	Engineers measure things, and, when appropriate, work quantitatively; they calibrate and validate their measurements; and they use approximations based on experience and empirical data.	Measurements
3	Engineers emphasize the use of a disciplined process when creating a design and can operate effectively as part of a team in doing so.	Disciplined process
4	Engineers can have multiple roles: research, development, design, production, testing, construction, operations, management, and others, such as sales, consulting, and teaching.	Engineer's roles
5	Engineers use tools to apply processes systematically. Therefore, the choice and use of appropriate tools is key to engineering.	Use of Tools
6	Engineers, via their professional societies, advance by the development and validation of principles, standards, and best practices.	Development and validation
7	Engineers reuse designs and design artifacts.	Reuse design

These characteristics are adopted here as engineering verification criteria. The abbreviations we have selected to represent each of these criteria are listed in the right-hand column of Table 3.

PHASE 2: VERIFICATION AGAINST THE TWO SETS OF CRITERIA

The set of 34 candidate FPs is next mapped to the two sets of engineering criteria: each candidate FP is taken as input and analyzed using each of Vincenti's seven criteria and, again, each of the seven IEEE-ACM software engineering criteria. The output of the mapping to Vincenti's engineering criteria, where the letter D represents a direct mapping, and the letter I an indirect one. For instance:

- Candidate FP #2 (Apply and use quantitative measurements in decision making) maps directly to Vincenti's criterion #6 and indirectly to Vincenti's criterion #4.
- Candidate FP #31 (Know software engineering techniques before using development tools) has only an indirect mapping to criterion #3 and to criterion #7 (Assessment).
- Finally, there are candidate FPs with no mapping to any engineering criteria: for instance, candidate FP #13 (Give product to customers early). \

This first verification against the Vincenti criteria leads to the following results:

- 12 candidate FPs have at least one direct mapping to a Vincenti engineering criterion; · 21 candidate FPs have only indirect mappings to Vincenti engineering criteria;
- 1 candidate FP has no direct or indirect mapping to any Vincenti engineering criteria.

The second verification against the seven IEEE & ACM engineering criteria is presented.

For instance:

- Candidate FP #2 (Apply and use quantitative measurements…) has a direct mapping to criteria #1 (Decision making) and #2 (Measurements). Candidate FP #16 (Invest in the understanding of the problem) is mapped indirectly to criteria #1 (Decision making) and #3 (Disciplined process).
- Candidate FP #4 (Build with and for reuse) is mapped directly and indirectly to criteria #7 (Reuse) and #3 (Disciplined process).
- Finally, candidate FP #13 (Give products to customers early) is not related to any engineering criteria.

This second verification against the IEEE and ACM criteria leads to the following results:

- 15 candidate FPs have at least one direct mapping to an IEEE-ACM engineering criterion;
- 16 candidate FPs have only indirect mappings to an IEEE-ACM engineering criterion;
- 3 candidate FPs have neither direct nor indirect mappings to any IEEE-ACM engineering criteria.

Table 4: Candidate FPs that directly meet criteria from either set

#	Vincenti Mapping	#	IEEE-ACM Mapping
2	Apply and use quantitative measurements in decision making	2	Apply and use quantitative measurements in decision making
4	Build with and for reuse	4	Build with and for reuse
		5	Define software artifact rigorously
		6	Design for maintenance
7	Determine requirements now		
9	Don't try to retrofit quality		
		10	Don't write your own test plans
11	Establish a software process that provides flexibility	12	Fix requirements specification error now
14	Grow systems incrementally		
15	Implement a disciplined approach and improve it continuously	15	Implement a disciplined approach and improve it continuously
16	Invest in understanding the problem		
		18	Keep design under intellectual control
21	Quality is the top priority; long term productivity is a natural consequence of high quality	21	Quality is the top priority; long term productivity is a natural consequence of high quality
		22	Rotate (high performing) people through product assurance
23	Since change is inherent to software, plan for it and manage it		
24	Since tradeoffs are inherent to software engineering, make them explicit and document them	24	Since tradeoffs are inherent to software engineering, make them explicit and document them
		25	Strive to have a peer, find a defect rather than a customer
		26	Tailor cost estimation methods
27	To improve design, study previous solutions to similar problems	27	To improve design, study previous solutions to similar problems
		31	Know software engineering techniques before using development tools

PHASE 3: ANALYSIS AND CONSOLIDATION USING BOTH SETS OF CRITERIA

Analysis across Each Set of Engineering Criteria

The candidate FPs with a direct mapping to either the Vincenti or IEEE-ACM criteria are listed in Table 4. From a comparison of the two columns in this table, the candidate FPs with direct mappings can be grouped into three sets:

- Candidate FPs with a Vincenti mapping similar to the IEEE-ACM mapping;
- Candidate FPs with a Vincenti mapping with no equivalent IEEE-ACM mapping;
- Candidate FPs with an IEEE-ACM mapping with no equivalent Vincenti mapping.

Set A: From Table 4, we can see that six candidate FPs (#2, #4, #15, #21, #24, #27) are present in both columns (the highlighted ones) and therefore satisfy at least one engineering criterion in each set of criteria (Vincenti and IEEE-ACM): these six could reasonably be considered as FPs that conform to engineering criteria.

Set B: From Table 4, we note that there are 6 other candidate FPs that meet the Vincenti criteria, but no IEEE-ACM criteria, and 9 candidate FPs that meet the IEEE-ACM criteria, but no Vincenti criteria. Can these still be considered as FPs, or are they merely instances of more fundamental principles?

To answer this question, we could reasonably argue from the Vincenti subset that:

- Candidate FP #7 (Determine requirements now) can be deduced from candidate FP #16 (Invest in understanding the problem);
- Candidate FP #9 (Don't try to retrofit quality) can be deduced from candidate FP #21 (Quality is the top priority; long-term productivity is a natural consequence of high quality);
- Candidate FP #11 (Establish a software process that provides flexibility) can be deduced from FP #9 (Don't try to retrofit quality).

This would eliminate candidates FPs #7, #9, and #11 from the list of FPs, since they represent specific instantiations of more general FPs, while principles #16, #14, and #23 would be retained on the list of FPs.

Set C: From Table 4, there remain 9 candidate FPs without a corresponding direct mapping to the Vincenti criteria. We could reasonably argue that these 9 can be deduced from those with direct Vincenti mappings: for instance FP #18 (Keep design under intellectual control) and FP #31 (Know software engineering techniques before using development tools) can be deduced from FP #15 (Implement a disciplined approach and improve it continuously).

This would eliminate candidate FPs #5, #6, #10, #12, #18, #22, #25, #26, and #31 from the list of FPs, since they represent specific instantiations of more general FPs, while retaining principle #15. In summary, this analysis has allowed us to refine the list of 34 candidate principles to 9 software engineering principles based on engineering criteria. This analysis has also eliminated the overlap between the various principles; as a consequence, a subset of only 9 (see Table 5) from the list of 34 candidates identified in Seguin 2006 are recognized as principles that conform to engineering criteria, the remaining 25 being specific instantiations of those 9. In Table 5, these software engineering FPs are sequenced from 1 to 9, along with their original sequence number (right-hand column) assigned when the initial list of 34 candidates was compiled.

Identification of a Hierarchy

Table 6 presents next the outcome of our analysis of the 25 remaining candidate FPs as instantiations of the 9 principles in Table 5 that conform to engineering criteria.

WORK LIMITATIONS

The initial list of 34 candidates taken as input for this research is not necessarily exhaustive: to summarize, these 34 candidates have been refined from 304 proposed principles identified in the literature over a period of 20 years, up to 2006 [19]. The methodology used engineering

Table 5: List of 9 software engineering principles

#	Vincenti, IEEE-ACM mapping	
1	Apply and use quantitative measurements in decision making	2
2	Build with and for reuse	4
3	Grow systems incrementally	14
4	Implement a disciplined approach and improve it continuously	15
5	Invest in the understanding of the problem	16
6	Quality is the top priority; long term productivity is a natural consequence of high quality	21
7	Since change is inherent to software, plan for it and manage it	23
8	Since tradeoffs are inherent to software engineering, make them explicit and document it	24
9	To improve design, study previous solutions to similar problems	27

Table 6: Hierarchy of candidate principles for software engineering

#	Direct mapping to Vincenti criteria		Derived instantiation (= Indirect mapping)
2	Apply and use quantitative measurements in decision making	26	Tailor cost estimation methods
		8	Don't overstrain your hardware
4	Build with and for reuse		
14	Grow systems incrementally	5	Define software artifacts rigorously
		20	Produce software in a stepwise fashion
15	Implement a disciplined approach and improve it continuously	1	Align incentives for developer and customer
		10	Don't write your own test plans
		17	Involve the customer
		18	Keep design under intellectual control
		20	Produce software in a stepwise fashion
		31	Know software engineering's techniques before using development tools
		19	Maintain clear accountability for results
		29	Use documentation standards
		10	Don't write your own test plans
16	Invest in understanding the problem	7	Determine requirements now
		12	Fix requirements specification error now
		17	Involve the customer
21	Quality is the top priority; long term productivity is a natural consequence of high quality	9	Don't try to retrofit quality
		22	Rotate (high performing people through product assurance
		25	Strive to have a peer find a defect rather than a customer.
		30	Write programs for people first
		3	Build software so that it needs a short user manual
		11	Establish a software process that provides flexibility
		28	Use better and fewer people
23	Since change is inherent to software, plan for it and manage it	6	Design for maintenance
		33	Choose a programming language to ensure maintainability
		32	Select tests based on the likelihood that they will find faults
		34	In the face of unstructured code, rethink the module and redesign it from scratch
24	Since tradeoffs are inherent to software engineering, make them explicit and document them		
27	To improve design, study previous solutions to similar problems		

criteria from Vincentia and the joint IEEE & ACM software engineering curriculum to identify the 9 candidate principles that conform to these engineering criteria; however, this list of criteria is not necessarily exhaustive, and more criteria could eventually be added. Furthermore, most of the authors who proposed these principles did not provide operational descriptions of their proposals, and did not provide research experimentation for each principle identified

CONCLUSIONS

Software engineering, as a discipline, is certainly not yet as mature as other engineering disciplines, and, while a number of authors have proposed over 300 distinct FPs, a consensus on a set of well-recognized FPs has been lacking. This research report has taken as input, or as its object of study, the set of 34 statements identified in [19] as candidate FPs of software engineering. This set has been analyzed from an engineering perspective using the engineering criteria identified by either Vincenti or the IEEE-ACM joint effort on developing a software engineering curriculum. The 34 candidate FPs were divided into three categories: A) candidate FPs that are directly linked to engineering, B) candidate FPs that are indirectly linked to engineering, and C) candidate FPs with no specific link to engineering. In the next step, the candidate FPs that were generic were distinguished from the more specific ones: this distinction was based on the type of mapping (direct or indirect). In the final step, candidate FPs from both lists were analyzed and compared. Our proposed reduced list of 9 software engineering principles now needs to be further discussed by the software engineering community Of course, this list depends on the methodology used, and is being proposed to the engineering community for discussion and scrutiny with the aim of improving it and developing a consensus over time. There is no claim that this list is exhaustive or that it covers the whole software engineering discipline. Even though the inputs to this analysis were derived from an extensive literature survey, this does not guarantee that those authors have indeed provided full coverage of the software engineering discipline. Similarly, the hierarchy proposed in Table 6 is derived from the engineering criteria in our analytical approach. Further research should be carried out to verify the completeness of the criteria used.

REFERENCES

1. IEEE Std 610.12, IEEE Standard Glossary of Software Engineering Terminology. Corrected Edition, February 1991.
2. K. E. Wiegers, "Creating a Software Engineering Culture," Dorset House Publishing, New York, USA, 1996.
3. N. Séguin, "Inventaire, Analyse et Consolidation des Principes Fondamentaux du Génie Logiciel," École de technologie supérieure, Université du Québec, Québec, Canada, 2006.
4. P. Bourque, R. Dupuis, A. Abran, J. W. Moore, L. Tripp and S. Wolff, "Fundamental Principles of Software Engineering–A Journey," Journal of Systems and Software, Vol. 62, No. 1, 2002, pp. 59-70.
5. Jabir and J. W. Moore, "A Search For Fundamental Principles of Software Engineering," Report of a Workshop Conducted at the Forum on Software Engineering Standards Issues, Computer Standards & Interfaces–In- ternational Journal on the Development and Application of Standards for Computers, Data Communications and Interfaces, Elsevier, Amsterdam, North Holland (the participants at this workshop names their group "Jabir"), Vol. 19, No. 2, 1998, pp. 155-160.
6. B. W Boehm, "Seven Basic Principles of Software Engineering," Journal of Systems and Software, Vol. 3, No. 1, 1983, pp. 3-24.
7. A. M. Davis, "201 Principles of Software Development," McGraw-Hill, New York, USA, 1995.
8. K. E. Wiegers, "Creating a Software Engineering Culture," Dorset House Publishing, New York, 1996.
9. P. Bourque and R. Dupuis, "Fundamental Principles of Software Engineering," Third International Symposium and Forum on Software Engineering Standards, Walnut Creek, CA, USA, 1997.
10. F. Buschmann, R. Meunier, H. Rohnert, P. Sommerlad, and M. Stal, "Pattern Oriented Software Architecture," John Wiley & Sons, England, 1996.
11. C. Ghezzi, M. Jazayeri and D. Mandrioli, "Fundamentals of Software Engineering," Prentice Hall, New Jersey, 2003.
12. P. Bourque and R. Dupuis, "Fundamental Principles of Software Engineering," 3rd International Symposium and Forum on Software Engineering Standards, Walnut Creek, CA, 1997.
13. A. Abran, N. Seguin, P. Bourque and R. Dupuis, "The Search for Software Engineering Principles: An Overview of Results," Conference on the Principles of Software Engineering, Buenos Aires, Argentina, 2004.
14. N. Séguin and A. Abran, "Inventaire des principes du génie logiciel," Revue Génie Logiciel, Numéro 80, Paris, France, 2007, pp. 45-51.
15. W. G. Vincenti, "What Engineers Know and How They Know It—Analytical Studies from Aeronautical History," Johns Hopkins University, Baltimore, MD, USA, and London, UK, 1990.
16. IEEE and ACM, "IEEE Computer Society and Association for Computing Machinery," Curriculum Guidelines for Undergraduate Degree Programs in Software Engi neering, A Volume of the Computing Curricula Series, 2004.
17. A. Abran, J. W. Moore, P. Bourque and R. Dupuis, "Guide to the Software Engineering Body of Knowledge," 4th Edition, In: P. Bourque and R. Dupuis, Eds., IEEE Computer Society, Los Alamitos, CA, USA, 2005.
18. A. Abran and K. Meridji, "Analysis of Software Engineering from an Engineering Perspective," European Journal for the Informatics Professional, Vol. 7, No. 1, February 2006, pp. 46-52.
19. SO-TR-19759, "Software Engineering—Guide to the Software Engineering Body of Knowledge (SWEBOK)," International Organization for Standardization, Switzerland, 2005.

CHAPTER 2

LIGHTWEIGHT BEHAVIOR-BASED LANGUAGE FOR REQUIREMENTS MODELING

Zhengping Liang, Guoqing Wu, Li Wan

Keywords: Behavior Description Language (BDL), Scenario, Viewpoint, Behavior Requirements Model (BRM)

INTRODUCTION

Software requirements modeling is an important phase of software development process. To obtain high quality requirements model, an effective and well-defined requirements modeling language and technique, which both has formal semantic and can be easily understood and used by all kinds of stakeholders, is needed. The existing requirements modeling languages and techniques can be roughly divided into two categories. One is the semi-formal style based on graph symbol, the most famous representative of which is UML [1]. The other is the formal style based on mathematics symbol, such as Automata [2], Z [3], E-LOTOS [4], Petri net [5], Pi-calculus [6], etc. The former has the advantage of strong intuition, of being easy to be understood and used, but it usually lacks rigorous semantics and easily leads to an inconsistent and incomplete requirements model. On the contrary, the latter has rigorous semantics basis and is convenient to deduce and verify some properties, but it has poor practicability, and requires the user and analyzer with advanced skills.

How to deal with the gap between practicability and rigorousness of formal requirements modeling language and technique is a big challenge [7]. Some researches suggest to designating formal semantic for semi-formal language [8], and others believe the combination of graph symbol and formal language are more positiveness [9]. Although all of those approaches have some effect to bridge the gap, there are still inconvenient to put them into practice. At the same time, whether or not a software system satisfies the anticipated user requirements is ultimately determined by the behaviors of the software. That is to say, the requirements modeling language and technique need to support the description and validation of behavior. So it is necessary and valuable to research software requirements modeling language and technique both has practicability and rigorousness from the perspective of software behavior.

Due to lightweight formal style can help to bridge the gap between practicability and rigorousness [10], we established a lightweight formal language BDL (Behavior Description Language) to modeling user's requirements, which is based on the identifiable behaviors of software system. What should be emphasized is that the behaviors not only include the observable behaviors from the system external interface but also consist of the behaviors resided in the internal of the system. In addition, in order to support the requirements modeling of large and complex software, a general-purpose requirements description model BRM (Behavior Requirements Model) is proposed, which partly synthesizes some ideas of viewpoint-oriented requirements engineering [11] and scenario-oriented requirements engineering [12].

The structure of this paper is organized as follows: Section 2 introduces the formal syntax of BDL and its structural operational semantics. Section 3 introduces the requirements description model BRM and Section 4 demonstrates the modeling process through the case study On-line Campus Management System. Finally, the related works are discussed in Section 5 and the conclusions and future works are discussed in Section 6.

BEHAVIOR BASED REQUIREMENTS MODELING LANGUAGE

A behavior is a certain interaction among two or more entities. For easy discussion, this paper presumes a behavior is an interaction only between two entities. We define a software behavior as a process during which a subject implements an

Citation: Z. Liang, G. Wu and L. Wan, "Lightweight Behavior-Based Language for Requirements Modeling," Journal of Software Engineering and Applications, Vol. 3 No. 3, 2010, pp. 245-254. doi: 10.4236/jsea.2010.33030.

operation, service, or action to an object. The subject and the object which may be physical or logistic, can be a person, a software or hardware component of system, or certain element of environment. The structure of each behavior consists of a subject, an object, some properties, some inputs, some outputs, and an operation, service, or action. If a behavior can't be divided into two or more sub-behaviors, it is an atomic behavior. An atomic behavior is a simple behavior. Two or more simple behaviors form a composite behavior. In addition, according with the interact mode of software behaviors, the combine pattern of simple behaviors can be divided into five categories: sequence, certainty choice, uncertainty choice, parallel and shielding. Based on the above consideration about software behavior, the followings are the syntax and structural operational semantics of behavior based requirements modeling language BDL.

Syntax of BDL

Suppose , (ABehID ABehID $(i \in N)$ are atomic behavior identifier $BehID, BehID_i (i \in N)$ are behavior identifier.

Atomic Behavior Expression

$ABehID : f(sub, obj\,[\&\ obj'\,s\ additional\ remarks])$

[When *prepositive conditions*]

$[\text{INFrom}(ID)(u_1,\dots,u_n)]^*$

$[\text{OUTTo}(ID)(v_1,\dots,v_m)]^*$

where,

f is an operation or an action; sub and obj are the behavior's subject and object respectively;

When clause denotes the according to which the behavior can execute; prepositive conditions

INFrom and OUTTo clause denote the behavior's input data and output data respectively;

ID denotes a certain atomic behavior identifier, a external entity or a viewpoint identifier related to INFrom or OUTTo

$u_i (i \in \{1...n\})$ and $v_i (i \in \{1...m\})$ are described with the format of dataname or dataname = value ;

The superscript * denotes there are 0 or multiple items that belong to the same category. Besides, there are two kinds of special atomic behavior:

1) Null action: $ABehID : Idle$;

2) End action of composite behavior:

a) $ABehID : Return(ABehID_i)$

//jump to execute atomic behavior $ABehID_i$;

b) $ABehID : Return()$

//end of execute composite bahavior .

Simple Behavior

$\vdash$ ABehID //atomic behavior act as simple behavior

Composite Behavior

1) Sequence behavior:

a) $$\frac{\vdash ABehID \,\&\, \vdash BehID}{\vdash ABehID; BehID}$$

b) $$\frac{\vdash BehID \,\&\, \vdash ABehID}{\vdash BehID; ABehID}$$

c) $$\frac{\vdash BehID_1 \,\&\, \vdash BehID_2 \,\&\dots\&\, \vdash BehID_n}{\vdash BehID_1; BehID_2;\dots; BehID_n}$$

2) Certainty choice behavior:

$$\frac{\vdash BehID_1 \,\&\, \vdash BehID_2 \,\&\, b \text{ is a boolean expression}}{\vdash If\ b\ Then\ BehID_1\ Else\ BehID_2\ Fi}$$

3) Uncertainty choice behavior:

$$\frac{\vdash BehID_1 \,\&\, \vdash BehID_2 \,\&\dots\&\, \vdash BehID_n}{\vdash BehID_1 + BehID_2 + \dots + BehID_n}$$

4) Parallel behavior:

$$\frac{\vdash BehID_1 \,\&\, \vdash BehID_2 \,\&\dots\&\, \vdash BehID_n}{\vdash BehID_1 \,\|\, BehID_2 \,\|\dots\|\, BehID_n}$$

5) Shielding behavior:

a) $$\frac{\vdash BehID \,\&\, \vdash ABehID}{\vdash BehID \,/\, ABehID}$$ //shielding atomic behavior

b) $$\frac{\vdash BehID \,\&\, \vdash BehID_1}{\vdash BehID \,/\, BehID_1}$$ //shielding composite behavior

Structural Operational Semantics of BDL

Definition1: Suppose B is a behavior expression, s is a state of system, then < B,s > is a configuration. < B,s > denotes the current state is s and the behavior expression to be executed is B. < > s is also a configuration, which denotes the current state is s and there are no behavior expression need to be executed.

Definition2: Suppose b is a Boolean expression, s is a state, eval < b, > s denotes the Boolean value of b ats .

Suppose $\alpha, \alpha_i (i \in N)$ are atomic behavior, $B, B_i\ (i \in N)$ are behavior expression. The structural operational semantics of BDL can be defined in this way:

1. Semantic of atomic behavior expression:

$$<\alpha,\sigma> \rightarrow <\sigma'>$$

2. Semantic of Null action:

$$<Idle,\sigma> \rightarrow <\sigma>$$

3. Semantic of End action of composite behavior: Suppose a is the first atomic behavior of B.

$$<Return(\alpha),\sigma> \rightarrow <B,\sigma>$$

$$<Return(),\sigma> \rightarrow <\sigma>$$

4. Semantic of sequence behavior:

$$\frac{<B_1,\sigma> \rightarrow <\sigma'>}{<B_1;B_2,\sigma> \rightarrow <B_2,\sigma'>}$$

$$\frac{<B_1,\sigma> \rightarrow <B_1',\sigma'>}{<B_1;B_2,\sigma> \rightarrow <B_1';B_2,\sigma'>}$$

5. Semantic of certainty choice behavior:

$$\frac{eval < b,\sigma >= TRUE}{< If\ b\ Then\ B_1\ Else\ B_2\ Fi,\sigma > \to < B_1,\sigma >}$$

$$\frac{eval < b,\sigma >= FALSE}{< If\ b\ Then\ B_1\ Else\ B_2\ Fi,\sigma > \to < B_2,\sigma >}$$

6. Semantic of uncertainty choice behavior:

$$\frac{< B_1,\sigma > \to < B_1',\sigma' >}{< B_1 + B_2,\sigma > \to < B_1',\sigma' >}$$

$$\frac{< B_2,\sigma > \to < B_2',\sigma' >}{< B_1 + B_2,\sigma > \to < B_2',\sigma' >}$$

6. Semantic of parallel behavior:

$$\frac{< B_1,\sigma > \to < B_1',\sigma' >}{< B_1 \| B_2,\sigma > \to < B_1' \| B_2,\sigma' >}$$

$$\frac{< B_2,\sigma > \to < B_2',\sigma' >}{< B_1 \| B_2,\sigma > \to < B_1 \| B_2',\sigma' >}$$

7. Semantic of shielding behavior:

Suppose B = a';B'.

$$\frac{< B,\sigma > \to < B',\sigma' >}{< B / \alpha,\sigma > \to < B' / \alpha,\sigma' >} \quad (\alpha' \neq \alpha)$$

//shielding atomic behavior

BEHAVIOR BASED REQUIREMENTS DESCRIPTION MODEL

As to small and simple software system, BDL can be used to describe its requirements model directly due to BDL's syntax is also simple and small. But it is hard to describe requirements model of large and complex software system using BDL directly because on the one side the software scale and structure may be very complicated, and on the other side many kinds of stakeholders who reside in different time zone and space, may be involved. To deal with large and complex problems, people often employ the strategy of divide-and-rule. Based on this method, we propose a general-purpose requirements description model BRM, which synthesizes the concepts of viewpoint and scenario. The model process of BRM consists of five steps: first, to identify the scope of the whole problem domain of the software system, next, to divide the problem domain into some interrelated sub-domains. After that, to list all potential viewpoints and their sequence or overlap relationships of each sub-domain based on the viewpoint identifying methods of viewpoint-oriented requirements engineering [11]. Later on, to look for different scenarios and their sequence or overlap relationships of each viewpoint. Finally, to adopt the scenario describing way of scenario-oriented requirements engineering [12] to establish each scenario model using BDL. BRM is composed of three kinds of model. One is the scenario behavior model, another is viewpoint behavior model, and the last is system behavior model. The followings are the formal definition of them.

Definition3 (Scenario behavior model): A scenario's behavior model is a 6-tuple:

M_s=(B, ;, If, +, ||, /)

where,

B is the set of behaviors within the scenario, and each behavior in B has a corresponding behavior expression; ;, If, +, ||, respectively denotes the relationship of sequence, certainty choice, uncertainty choice, parallel and shielding between behaviors.

The syntax structure of scenario behavior model is defined as Figure 1, where, is a certain atomic behavior expression; is one of the relation symbol between behaviors, that is ;, If, +, ||,

Definition4 (Viewpoint behavior model): A viewpoint's behavior model is a 4-tuple

M_v=(S, ∘, ◊, ⊥)

where,

S is the set of scenarios within the viewpoint, and each scenario in S has a corresponding scenario behavior model;

o is a 2-tuple operator, which denotes two scenarios have the sequence relationship in terms of execution; have the sequence relationship in terms of execution;

◊ is also a 2-tuple operator, which denotes two scenarios have overlaps in content, that is, they have common behaviors;

⊥ denotes two or more scenarios are independent of each other in execution order and in domain. each other in execution order and in content.

These relation operators can be use to assisting analyze and check requirements model's properties from the aspect of syntax and semantic at the phase of requirements analysis. The syntax structure of system behavior model is defined as Figure 3, where, View point Operator is the viewpoint's relation symbol o or ◊ .

Definition 5 (System behavior model)

A software system's behavior model is a 4-tuple:

M=(V, ∘, ◊, ⊥)

where, V is the set of viewpoints related to the system, and each viewpoint in has a corresponding viewpoint behavior model;

o is a 2-tuple operator, which denotes two view points have the sequence relationship in terms of execution;

◊ is also a 2-tuple operator, which denotes two viewpoints have overlaps in domain, that is, the sub-domains where they belong to have common elements;

⊥ denotes two or more viewpoints are independent of each other in execution order and in domain.

These relation operators can also be use to assisting analyze and check requirements model's properties from the aspect of syntax and semantic at the phase of requirements analysis.

The syntax structure of system behavior model is defined as Figure 3, where, View point Operator is the viewpoint's relation symbol o or ◊ .

Obviously, because the structure and relationship of above models are very clear, people can smoothly transfer the user requirements expressed by natural languages to formal requirements model expressed by BDL based on BRM. Hence, BDL & BRM make a moderate balance between practicability and rigorousness.

```
ScenarioID
SCBEGIN
  [ABEH:   //list of atomic behaviors, it also can be given in BEH directly
    ABehID : atomic behavior
    [, ABehID : atomic behavior]* ;;]
  BEH :    //list of behaviors
    BehID = AbehID | atomic behavior | BehID |
      (AbehID | atomic behavior | BehID) BehaviorOperator (AbehID | atomic behavior | BehID)
      [BehaviorOperator (AbehID | atomic behavior | BehID)]*  //at lease one behavior in a scenario
    [, BehID = AbehID | atomic behavior | BehID |
      (AbehID | atomic behavior | BehID) BehaviorOperator (AbehID | atomic behavior | BehID)
      [BehaviorOperator (AbehID | atomic behavior | BehID)]* ]* ;;
    SBehID =    //scenario behavior expression
      (BehID | BehID BehaviorOperator BehID [BehaviorOperator BehID]* );;
SCEND
```

Figure 1: Syntax of scenario behavior model.

```
ViewpointID
VPBEGIN
  [data storage pool ID];; //used to store data input from other viewpoint and data
                           //shared by different scenarios within the viewpoint
  ScenarioID               //at lease one scenario in a viewpoint
  [, ScenarioID]* ;;
  SC_Relationship =        //set of relationship between scenarios
    {[< ScenarioID ScenarioOperator ScenarioID >
     [, < ScenarioID ScenarioOperator ScenarioID >]* ]};;
VPEND
```

Figure 2: Syntax of viewpoint behavior model.

CASE STUDY

On-line Campus Management System (OCMS) consists of several subsystems related each other, which used for the daily management of education administrative unit and schools. Its user requirements have modeled using BDL & BRM. In this section, we demonstrate a partial of function requirements model of OCMS. The following is part of the functions of Student Information Management Subsystem:

- Student needs to scan his or her IC card at the door-control reader when he or she enters or leaves schoolyard, at the same time, a correlative short message will be automatically sent to the student's parents' mobile phone;
- Teachers can process students' all kinds of information and send student's information to his or her parents by the way of short message and E-mail;
- Administrator distributes IC cards and manages its authorization. Besides, Administrator sets the students attendance rules and the system automatically creates the students attendance reports;
- Parents can query his or her child's all kind of information at school by the way of short message, automatic voice and webpage.

The logic structure of above functions as Figure 4.

Although the above function requirements look very simple, there are many complicated and redundant details. For example, how long and how to does the attendance report is created, how to manage the input, modification, processing, storage, transmission, respondence, etc. of all kinds of students' information among different domain elements. Due to space limitations, we directly give the analysis result of above requirements and only demonstrate a partial of requirements model using BDL & BRM.

The problem domain boundary of above user requirements is clear. The followings are the five sub-domains of it: Sub-domain 1: student, IC card, IC reader, mainframe, door and swivel of door; Sub-domain 2: administrator, attendance rules, terminal, mainframe, IC card, IC reader; Sub-domain 3: teacher, all kinds of student's information at school, terminal, mainframe; Sub-domain 4: parents, mobile phone, telephone, terminal, mobile phone networks, telephone networks, Internet, all kinds of student's information at school; Sub-domain 5: mainframe, IC reader, terminal, mobile phone networks, telephone networks, Internet, attendance report, all kinds of student's information at school, list of IC card information.

$SystemID$
SYBEGIN
  $ViewpointID$ //at lease one viewpoint in a system
  $[,ViewpointID]^*$;;
  $VP\_Relationship =$ //set of relationship between viewpoints
    $\{[<ViewpointID\ ViewpointOperator\ ViewpointID>$
    $[,<ViewpointID\ ViewpointOperator\ ViewpointID>]^*]\}$;;
SYEND

Figure 3: Syntax of system behavior model

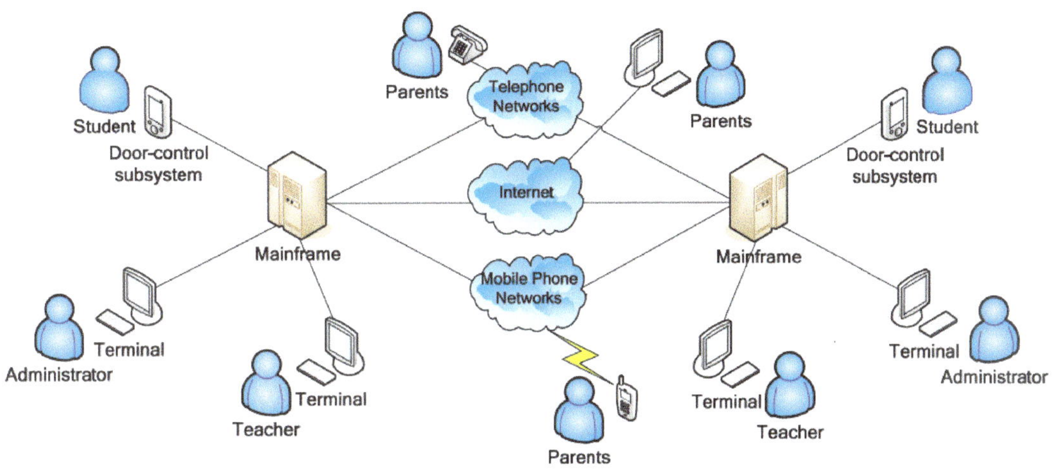

Figure 4: Logic structure of student information management subsystem

Table 1: Relationships of viewpoints belong to Sub-domain 5

Relationships	VP_ICInfo_Manage	VP_AttenRep_Create	VP_Query_Respond	VP_Info_Send	VP_Info_Edit
VP_ICInfo_Manage	\	◊	⊥	⊥	⊥
VP_AttenRep_Create	\	\	∘	⊥	⊥
VP_Query_Respond	\	\	\	◊, ∘	◊, ∘
VP_Info_Send	\	\	\	\	◊, ∘
VP_Info_Edit	\	\	\	\	\

(1) ICreaderDisp1 : display(ICreader, screen)
  OUTTo(screen)(*Prompt*="Please scanning card!")
(2) DoorConWait:idle()   //waiting user to scan card
(3) ScanC:scancard(person, IC)
(4) ReadC:read(ICreader, IC)
  OUTTo(SendCInfo)(*ICNo*, *username*),
(5) SendCInfo:send(ICreader, Mainframe)   //send the username to viwepoint VP_ICInfo_Manage
  OUTTo(VP_ICInfo_Manage)(*ICNo*, *username*)
(6) RecVerInfo:receive(ICreader, Mainframe)   //receive the verification result of IC
  INFrom(datapool)(*result*)   //the result is store in the viewpoint's data pool
(7) ICReaderDisp2:display(ICreader, screen)
  OUTTo(screen)(*username*, *Prompt*="Coming Please!")
(8) AllowOpen:allow(ICreader, swivel)
  OUTTo(swivel)(*signal*)
(9) OpenDoor:open(swivel, door)   //the action of open the door
(10) CloseDoor:close(swivel, door)

Figure 5: Atomic behavior expressions of the scenario with the right to open the door

These sub-domains related each other through common elements. For example, Sub-domain 1 and Sub-domain 5 has the common element IC reader, which hints some viewpoints of them may have the relationship " à " defined in Definition 5. As to Sub-domain 5, we can identify five viewpoints: VP_ ICInfo_Manage, VP_AttenRep_Create, VP_Query _Respond, VP_Info_Send, VP_Info_Edit. The relationships of them as Table 1 using the shape of strictly upper triangular matrix. As to Sub-domain 1, there is only one viewpoint VP_ScanCard, which have the following relationships with the viewpoints belong to Sub-domain 5, etc.

<VP_ScanCard ◊ VP_ICInfo_Manage>, <VP_Scan Card ∘ VP_Info_Send>, etc.

Now, we give a demonstration of VP_ScanCard's modeling process and its behavior model. The followings are the detailed user requirements of this viewpoint: When a student wants to enter or leave school, she or he needs to scan her or his IC card at the IC reader firstly. If the IC-holder is authorized to enter or leave the school, the door-control system will display the IC-holder's name on the IC reader's screen and open the door. Otherwise, a warning sound will be played in the IC reader's speaker, and the reason why the person is not permitted to enter or leave will be displayed on the screen. In this viewpoint, there are two scenarios: one is the IC-holder has the right to enter or leave school SC_ValidScanCard, the other is the opposite SC_InvalidScanCard.

First, we list all atomic behavior expressions belong to SC_ValidScanCard according to above requirements as Figure 5.

Then, the scenario behavior model of SC_ValidScanCard can be established as Figure 6 according to the interrelated relationship of above atomic behavior expressions and Definition 3. Next, the scenario behavior model of SC_Invalid ScanCard as Figure 7 can be established similarly. After that, due to SC_ValidScanCard and SC_ InvalidScanCard have the common elements in domain, the viewpoint behavior model of VP_ScanCard is established as Figure 8.

Here, the behavior model of VP_ScanCard is established successfully. Behavior model of other user requirements can be established similarly.

```
SC_ValidScanCard
SCBEGIN
  ABEH:
    ICreaderDisp1: display(ICreader, screen)
                  OUTTo(screen)(Prompt="Please scanning card!"),
    DoorConWait:idle(),
    ScanC:scancard(person, IC),
    ReadC:read(ICreader, IC)
           OUTTo(SendCInfo)(ICNo, username),
    SendCInfo:send(ICreader, Mainframe)
               OUTTo(VP_ICInfo_Manage)(ICNo, username),
    RecVerInfo:receive(ICreader, Mainframe)
                INFrom(datapool)(result),
    ICReaderDisp2:display(ICreader, screen)
                  OUTTo(screen)(username, Prompt="Coming Please!"),
    AllowOpen:allow(ICreader, swivel)
                OUTTo(swivel)(signal),
    OpenDoor:open(swivel, door),
    CloseDoor:close(swivel, door);;
  BEH:
```

```
    BehValidUResp=ICReaderDisp2 AllowOpen,
    BehValidU=
      ICreaderDisp1;
      DoorConWait;
      ScanC;
      ReadC;
      SendCInfo;
      RecVerInfo;
      BehValidUResp;  //if the IC is valid, open the door
      OpenDoor;
      CloseDoor;
      Return(ICreaderDisp1);;
    SBehID=BehValidU;;
SCEND
```

Figure 6: Scenario behavior model with the right to open the door

RELATED WORKS

The semi-formal and formal requirements modeling language and technique both have achieved prominent outcomes in the past twenty years. As to the behavior based requirements modeling, the importance and validity of it has also recognized by many researchers from academia and industry [13-20]. Ayaz et al. propose a behavioral specification language for complex systems—Viewcharts, which extends Statecharts to include behavioral views and their compositions [13]. And they define the syntax of viewcharts as attributed graphs and describe dynamic semantics of viewcharts by object mapping automata [14]. Viewcharts notation allows views to be specified independent of each other, which is similar to BDL. A difference between this work and ours is that View charts does not consider behaviors reside in the internal of system, but only observable behaviors from the external system.

Assem proposes an event-oriented requirements definition approach named Behavioral Pattern Analysis Approach (BPA) [15]. In BPA, Event is the primary object of the world model. And it use the so-called BPA Behavioral Pattern, which is the template that one uses to model and describe an event, takes the place of the use case in the UML. BPA is a more effective alternative to use cases in modeling and understanding the function requirements. However, BPA is special for real-time systems, multi-agent systems and safety-critical systems. Besides, it lacks clear links among Behavioral Patterns and can't be used for modeling complex system and is not convenient for requirements verification. On the contrary, our approach definitely labels the relationships of scenarios, viewpoints, and sub-domains, can effectively support the modeling and verification of large and complex system.

```
SC_InvalidScanCard
SCBEGIN
  ABEH:
    ICreaderDisp1:display(ICreader, screen)
                 OUTTo(screen)(Prompt="Please scanning card"),
    DoorConWait:idle(),          //waiting user to scan card
    ScanC:scancard(person, IC),
    ReadC:read(ICreader, IC)
           OUTTo(SendCInfo)(ICNo, username),
    SendCInfo:send(ICreader, Mainframe)
               OUTTo(VP_ICInfo_Manage)(ICNo, username),
    //receive the verification result of IC, and the result is store in the viewpoint's data pool
    RecVerInfo:receive(ICreader, Mainframe)
                INFrom(datapool)(result),
    PlayWarnSound:play(ICreader,speaker)
                  OUTTo(speaker)(soundfile),
    ICReaderDisp2:display(ICreader, screen)
                  OUTTo(screen)(Prompt="Overdue IC card!"),
    ICReaderDisp3:display(ICreader,screen)
                 OUTTo(screen)(Prompt="The IC card has reported be lost!"),
    ICReaderDisp4:display(ICreader,screen)
                  OUTTo(screen)(Prompt="Invalid user, unknown reason!");;
  BEH:
```

```
    BehInvalidUResp=
      PlayWarnSound□
      If result="overdue"
      Then ICReaderDisp2
      Else If result="lost"
           Then ICReaderDisp3
           Else ICReaderDisp4
           Fi
       Fi,
    BehInvalidU=
      ICreaderDisp1;
      DoorConWait;
      ScanC;
      ReadC;
      SendCInfo;
      RecVerInfo;
      BehInvalidUResp;   //if the IC is invalid, don't open the door
      Return(ICreaderDisp1);;
    SBehID=BehInvalidU;;
SCEND
```

Figure 7: Scenario behavior model without the right to open the door.

```
VP_ScanCard
VPBEGIN
  datapool;;     //the data pool of this viewpoint
  SC_ValidScanCard,
  SC_InvalidScanCard;;
  SC_Relationship={<SC_ValidScanCard ◊ SC_InvalidScanCard>};;
VPEND
```

Figure 8: Viewpoint behavior model of the scanning card

Khairuddin et al. propose a requirements notation RNSMA and a behavioral approach to specify interactive multimedia applications [16]. RNSMA is based on Petri Net, but its semantics are extended to support reactive systems. In RNSMA, transitions due to events are subdivided into automatic, user and clock. The transitions due to tasks to be done are subdivided into animate, image, sound, text and video. RNSMA uses an extremely simple syntax, which can be read even by novices as a form of pseudo-code. Compared with RNSMA, our work can support general-purpose requirements modeling, not special for stand-alone multimedia applications. UML is a general-purpose and most famous modeling language for software engineering, which is standardized by OMG [1]. Requirements modeling manner in UML consists of the use case diagram, sequence diagram, state diagram and activity diagram. UML provides standard notation for modeling software analysis and design. But a common and fair criticism of UML is that it is gratuitously large and complex, imprecise semantics, and a dysfunctional diagram interoperability standard (XMI). As another OMG standard, SysML acts as a general-purpose modeling language for systems engineering applications [17]. SysML is based on UML, and it reduces UML's size and software bias while extending its semantic to model requirements and parametric constraints. These capabilities are essential to support requirements engineering and performance analysis. Besides, there are some researches based on UML and SysML. Luigi et al. propose combining problem frames and UML to describe software requirements in order to improve the linguistic support for problem frames and the UML development practice by introducing the problem frames approach [18]. Pietro et al. propose the integration of SysML and problem frames by presenting how a set of well known problem frames can be represented by means of SysML [19]. Atle et al. propose to extend UML sequence diagrams to model trust-dependent behavior with the aim to support risk analysis [20]. All of these researches are good for the enhancement of behavior modeling. In addition, there are many kinds of formal languages and techniques for requirements modeling, especially for behavior requirements. Most of them are based on state or event. Some are standardized by different international organization, such as Z [3], E-LOTOS [4]. Others may be very famous in industry, such as B [21], VDM [22]. Although formal languages and techniques have many advantages, it is difficult to put into practices totally. On the contrary, our approach can be easily used to transform natural language requirements to formal requirements model because the syntax of BDL and the structure of BRM are very simple and clear.

CONCLUSIONS AND FUTURE WORK

Software requirements modeling from the perspective of behavior can not only supports the description and modeling of function requirements but also supports the analysis and deduction of non-function requirements. As a lightweight formal requirements description language and model, BDL & BRM can help to smoothly transfer the user requirements expressed by natural languages to formal requirements model expressed by BDL. And the formal model BRM is also good for subsequent requirements verification and validation. Hence, BDL & BRM can effectively bridge the gap between practicability and rigorousness of formal requirements modeling language and technique. Several completed case studies also testified this kind of feature of BDL & BRM. Currently, we have realized the prototype requirements modeling tool and experimented some case studies. Future works will mainly focus on to define all kinds of requirements properties based on BDL&BRM, and to design and implement corresponding automatic analyzing and deducing methods.

ACKNOWLEDGEMENTS

This work is supported by the National High Technology Research and Development Program of China under contract 2007AA01Z185, the Open Research Foundation of Chinese State Key Laboratory of Software Engineering under grant SKLSE20080702, and the SZU R/D Fund 200747.

REFERENCES

1. Object Management Group, "OMG Unified Modeling Language (OMG UML) Version 2.0," 2005.
2. J. E. Hopcroft, R. Motwani, and J. D. Ullman, "Introduction to automata theory, languages, and computation," 2nd Edition, Pearson Education, 2000.
3. "Information technology—Z formal specification notation — Syntax, type system and semantics," ISO/IEC 13568, 2002.
4. "Information processing systems—Open systems interconnection—Enhancements to LOTOS—A formal

description technique based on the temporal ordering of observational behavior," ISO/IEC 15437, 2001.

5. J. L. Peterson, "Petri net theory and the modeling of systems," Prentice Hall, 1981.
6. R. Milner, "Communicating and mobile systems: The Pi-calculus," Cambridge University Press, 1999.
7. J. P. Bowen and M. G. Hinchey, "Ten commandments of formal methods... ten years later," IEEE Computer, Vol. 39, No. 1, pp. 40 48, January 2006.
8. J. Kong, K. Zhang, J. Dong, and D. Xu, "Specifying behavioral semantics of UML diagrams through graph transformations," Journal of Systems and Software, Vol. 82, No. 2, pp. 292–306, April 2009.
9. C. Attiogbe, P. Poizat, and G. Salaun, "A formal and tool-equipped approach for the integration of state diagrams and formal datatypes," IEEE Transactions on Software Engineering, Vol. 33, No. 3, pp. 157–170, March 2007.
10. M. Hinchey, M. Jackson, and P. Cousot, J. P. Bowen, and T. Margeria, "Software engineering and formal methods," Communications of the ACM, Vol. 51, No. 9, pp. 54–59, September 2008.
11. G. Kotonya and I. Sommerville, "Requirements engineering with viewpoints," Software Engineering Journal, Vol. 11, No. 1, pp. 5–18, January 1996.
12. A. Sutcliffe, "Scenario-based requirements engineering," in Proceedings of the 11th IEEE International Conference on Requirements Engineering, Monterey, California, pp. 320–329, September 2003.
13. A. Isazadeh, D. A. Lamb, and G. H. MacEwen, "Viewcharts: A behavioral specification language for complex systems," Proceedings of the 4th International Workshop on Parallel and Distributed Real-Time Systems, Honolulu, Hawaii, pp. 208–215, April 1996.
14. A. Isazadeh and J. Karimpour, "Viewcharts: Syntax and semantic," Informatica, Vol. 19, No. 3, pp. 345–362, March 2008.
15. A. E. Ansary, "Requirements definition of real-time system using the Behavioral Patterns Analysis (BPA) approach: The elevator control system," Proceedings of the Second International Conference on Software and Data Technologies, Barcelona, pp. 371–377, July 2007.
16. K. Hashim and J. Yousoff, "A behavioral requirements specification approach for interactive multimedia applications," Proceedings of the 19th Australian Conference on Software Engineering, Perth, West Australia, pp. 696–699, March 2008.
17. "OMG Systems Modeling Language (OMG SysML) Version 1.1," Object Management Group, 2008.
18. L. Lavazza and V. D. Bianco, "Combining problem frames and UML in the description of software requirements," In: B. Luciano, H. Reiko, Ed., Lecture Notes in Computer Science, Vol. 3922, pp. 199–213, 2006.
19. P. Colombo, V. del Bianco, and L. Lavazza, "Towards the integration of sysml and problem frames," Proceedings of the 3rd International Workshop on Applications and Advances of Problem Frames, Leipzig, pp. 1–8, May 2008.
20. A. Refsdal and K. Stolen, "Extending UML sequence diagrams to model trust-dependent behavior with the aim to support risk analysis," Science of Computer Programming, Vol. 74, No. 1–2, pp. 34–42, January 2008.
21. S. Schenider, "The B-method: An introduction," Palgrave, 2001.
22. C. B. Jones, "Systematic software development using VDM," Prentice Hall, 1990.

CHAPTER 3

A MASSIVELY PARALLEL RE-CONFIGURABLE MESH COMPUTER EMULATOR: DESIGN, MODELING AND REALIZATION

Mohamed Youssfi, Omar Bouattane, Mohamed O. Bensalah

Keywords: Parallel processing, Object Modeling, Re-Configurable Mesh Computer, Emulation, XML, Parallel Virtual Machine

INTRODUCTION

Recently, in the data analysis and signal processing domain, the analysis tools, the computation methods and their technological computational models, have known a very high level of progress. This progress has oriented the scientists toward new computation strategies based on parallel approaches. Due to the large volume of data to be processed and to the large amount of computations needed to solve a given problem, the basic idea is to split tasks and data so that we can easily perform their corresponding algorithms concurrently on different physical computational units. Naturally, the use of the parallel approaches implies important data exchange between computational units. Subsequently, this generates new problems of data exchange and communications. To manage these communications, it is important to examine how the data in query are organized. This examination leads to several parallel algorithms and several corresponding computational architectures. Actually, we distinguish several computer architectures, starting from a single processor computer model, until the massively fine grained parallel machines having a large amount of processing elements interconnected according to several topological networks. Indeed, the analysis of the performance enhancement in terms of processing ability and execution speed must take into account the data computation difficulties and addressing management problem of these data. With relation to the last problem, it seems that the classical VON NEUMANN processor model is not able to respond to all the mentioned constraints. Furthermore, the optimized software realized for some cases have quickly demonstrated the limits of this model. The need of the new architectures and the processor efficiency improvement has been excited and encouraged by the VLSI development. As a result, we have seen the new processor technologies (e.g. Reduced Instruction Set Computer "RISC", Transputer, Digital Signal Processor "DSP", Cellular automata etc.) and the parallel interconnection of fine grained networks (e.g. Linear, 2-D grid of processors, pyramidal architectures, cubic and hyper cubic connexion machines, etc.) In this paper, our study is focused on a fine grained parallel architecture that has been largely studied in the literature and for which several parallel algorithms for scientific calculus were developed. From the theoretical point of view, each computational model has its motivations and its exciting proofs. In the practice, some models were technologically realized and served as real computational supports, but some others remain in their theoretical proposition state. They are not realized because of their technological complexities and to their very high production cost. The computational model that is concerned in our work has known a very large technological progress. At first, it was viewed as a simple grid of cellular automata, after some technological enhancement, the cellular automaton became a fine grained processing element and the resulted grid became the mesh connected computer MCC [1]. Using some additional communication Buses, the MCC became the mesh with multiple broadcast [2] and polymorphic torus [3]. Finally, we speak about the reconfigurable mesh computer (RMC) that integrates a reconfiguration network at each processing element [4,5].

From the algorithmic point of view, several authors were developed new parallel algorithms for data processing and scientific calculus. These algorithms were assigned to be implemented in the architectures mentioned above. Also, they are established using parallel approaches in order to reduce their complexities in term of execution times. In order to facilitate for each parallel programmer the task of validation and program tests (even if he has not a real parallel machine

Citation: M. Youssfi, O. Bouattane and M. Bensalah, "A Massively Parallel Re-Configurable Mesh Computer Emulator: Design, Modeling and Realization," Journal of Software Engineering and Applications, Vol. 3 No. 1, 2010, pp. 11-26. doi: 10.4236/jsea.2010.31002.

that supports his algorithms), the emulating solutions were proposed in the literature to elaborate some virtual systems to perform the algorithms. The emulated systems may be specific as in [21,22] or of general behaviors as in [19,20]. In this context, we present in this paper a virtual tool to emulate an RMC, in which we can easily implement parallel SIMD algorithms. It is a virtual RMC platform of size (n x m) processing elements (PE), where n is the number of rows in the matrix an m is the number of columns. Without loss of generality, we consider n = m and we speak about a squared matrix of n^2 PE's.

This emulator allows the scientists to overflow the problem of real RMC availability. (i.e. at this time the RMC machine is not yet popular due to its high cost). Using this emulator, we propose an extended virtual RMC model, which translates all the functionalities of a real machine. This model can be easily extended to perform other advanced functionalities required by the multiplicity of the algorithmic techniques. In order to reach this virtual machine result, we started by the object modeling of all the components of the RMC such as the n x n grid, its processing element PE, its connexion buses and so. To describe in more details the different steps of this emulator realization, we organize this paper as follows: Section II presents the real RMC model and the essential properties of its components. The object modeling of the RMC and some related details are given in section III. The next section, presents some parallel programs and their implementation on our virtual machine to illustrate the use of some established parallel instructions. Notice that, to avoid the upload of this paper, the complete set of instructions established for our platform is not presented in more details. We present just some examples of testing programs that involve some scientific computations such as basic matrix computation, data processing and image processing. Finally, the last section gives some concluding remarks and some exploiting perspectives of our virtual machine.

PARALLEL COMPUTATIONAL MODEL

Presentation

The parallel architectures have known a large development these recent years. They are presented in numerous topological shapes, such as, linear, planar, pyramidal, cubic and hyper cubic networks. This large number of architectures requires an adequate classification taking into account several criteria. Among these criteria, we distinguish for example, the size of the machine, its autonomy of addressing and connexion, data type used etc. This classification allows the programmer to choose an appropriate computational model to perform the programs. Several proposed classifications were described in the literature; the diversity of the architectural solutions makes difficult the establishment of a general taxonomy. The well known classification is based on multiplicity of the instruction and data flows. It proposed four types of data machines, they are: the Single Instruction Single Data (S.I.S.D), single Instruction Multiple Data (S.I. M.D), multiple Instruction Single Data (M.I.S.D) and multiple Instruction Multiple Data (M.I.M.D) machines. Throughout this classification, the concerned model in this work is the Re-configurable Mesh Computer. It is the 2-D planar grid or matrix of n x n processing elements (PE). It is an S.I.M.D structure where in the word model the PE's use data buses of width at most log2 n bits. Also, in this model, the PE's has the autonomy of operation, addressing and connexion.

Topology and Structure

A Re-configurable Mesh Computer (RMC) of size n x n, is a parallel machine having n2 Processing elements (PE's) arranged on a 2-D matrix as shown in Figure 1. It is a "Single Instruction Multiple Data (SIMD)" structure, in which each PE(i, j) is localized in row i and column j. It has an identifier defined by ID = n x i + j. Each PE of the mesh is connected to its four neighbors (if they exist) by communication channels. It has a finite number of registers of size ($\log_2$ n) bits. The PE's can carry out arithmetic and logical operations. They can also carry out reconfiguration operations to exchange data over the mesh.

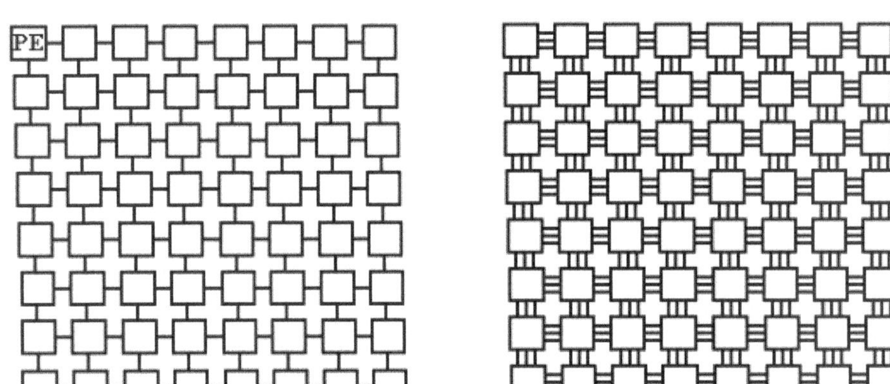

a) MCR "bit-model"   b) MCR "Word-model"

Figure 1: Re-configurable mesh computer model of size 8 x 8

The re-configurable networks that are presented as the processors matrix were improved considerably these last years. Indeed many theoretical and practical works appeared in the literature use this architecture as a computational model [6–8]. More particularly the recent related works propose new re-configurable models [9–14]. These re-configurable networks are based on a dynamic change of the mesh shape. They are qualified as the polymorphic grids of processors. These architectures are provided with an instruction set of reconfiguration in order to get several topological shapes according to the problem to be solved. They are presented typically in the form of a multidimensional network of processing elements connected to a communication bus having a fixed number of wiring of Input/output. When this bus is reduced to only one bit width, we speak about "bit-model" machine, whereas for a mesh of size n x n having a bus of width (log2 n bits), we speak about "Word-model" machine as in [9,15]. Figure 1, shows a 2-D representation of this model. Reconfiguration is locally made by adjusting the bus switches at each PE. The control of these switches offers to the PE's connection autonomy. Indeed, different PE's can simultaneously select various switches to achieve a given configuration. This is based on local decisions made by each PE. Also, it is possible for all the PE's of a selected group to carry out unconditional operations of configuration, where the PE's carry out reconfiguration instructions to activate their switches.

Basic Operations of a PE

Arithmetic Operations

Like any standard processor, the PE's of the RMC have an instruction set relating to the arithmetic and logical operations.

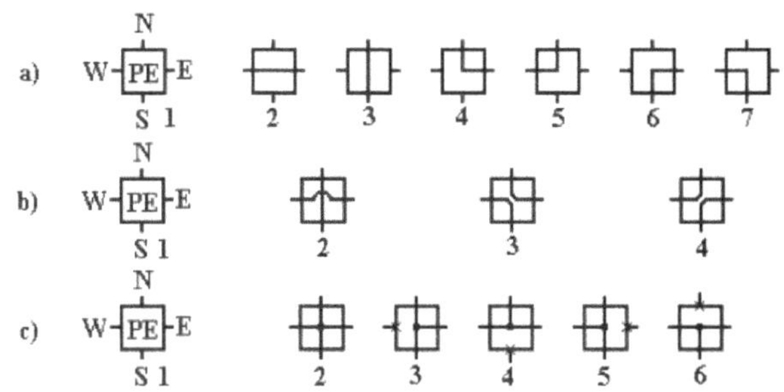

Figure 2: Different bridging configuration of a PE. a) Simple bridge, b) Double bridge, c) Crossed bridge.

The concerned operands can be local data of a PE or the data received on its communication channels after an inter-PE data exchange operation. In the "bitmodel" machine of size n x n, the calculation in the PE's is carried out bit by bit, whereas for the types "Wordmodel" of the same size, calculations are done on words of size at most (k=LogB_{2B} n bits), where k is the width of the communication bus of the PE's

Configuration Operations

In this part, we present the three kinds of bridging operations carried out by the PE's to facilitate the data exchange over the mesh. These configuring operation were largely exploited in several parallel algorithms to enhance the algorithmic complexities [16–18].

Simple Bridge (SB)

A PE of the RMC is considered in SB state when it establishes connections between two of its communication channels. This PE can connect itself to each one of its channel bits, either in transmitting mode, or in receiving mode. It can also isolate itself from some of its bits (i.e. neither transmitter, nor receiver). Various cases of SB figures are realized, they are: {EW, S, N}, {E, W, SN}, {ES, W, N}, {NW, S, E}, {NE, S, W} and {WS, E, N}. E, W, N and S indicate the Port sides of a PE; they are: East, West, North and South respectively. Figure 2(a) shows the different configurations of the SB state.

Double Bridge (DB):

A PE is in a DB state when it carries out the configuration operations creating two independent buses by its communication channels. The different possible configurations that can be obtained are: {EW, NS}, {ES, NW} and {EN, SW}. Figure 2(b) presents the different configurations of the DB state.

Cross Bridge (CB)

A PE puts itself in CB state by connecting all its active communication channels in only one bus. This operation is generally used when we want to transmit information to all the PE's of a connected component at the same time. The CB state is defined by the unique configuration: {NESW }, where only one of the four ports of a PE can be locked, otherwise the CB state becomes an SB state, see Figure 2(c). These various bridges are applicable on the two types of machines "bit-model" and "Word-model". Their establishments require the setting of the associated switching matrix at each PE.

Inter Processors Operations

The inter processor operations are principally classified in the data exchange category. Data exchange may occur between several pairs of PE's each others or between one or more PE's and a group of selected PE's. To illustrate the concept of inter processor operations, we present an example of data exchange procedure named "Direct broadcasting" The "Direct broadcasting" procedure consists of transmitting information from a given PE over a mesh resulted by the CB operation, to all the connected PE's on this mesh. The complexity of this operation is: iteration. The necessary instructions are:

- All the PE's go to the CB state.
- All the PE's couple themselves in receiving mode on the resulted bridge, except for the PE which will transmit data. It must be coupled in transmitting mode.
- The transmitting PE transmits Data on its bridge. Thus all the receiver PE's can read concurrently the same information on their 'communication buses.

More details about the reconfiguration operations in technological point of view and communication cost are discussed in [3], where the polymorphic torus is equipped by the same reconfiguration network as the re-configurable mesh.

OBJECT MODELING OF THE RMC

Presentation

As mentioned in the precedent section, the RMC is a set of processing elements arranged in a squared matrix. Each PE is modeled by an object defined by a state and a behavior. The state of the PE object is represented by the values of its memory registers and its internal linked components, such as, its arithmetic and logical unit (ALU) and its four ports (East, West, North, South). The PE behavior represents the set of operations that it can carry out. The kind of these operations is: arithmetic, logic, bus configuration (e.g. bridge operations) data exchange, marking and unmarking a PE, etc. In addition to these operations, it may be necessary to add other specific operations to delegate to a given PE a task to represent a given group of PE's in the RMC. In this case as in [12,17], the delegated PE is labeled Representative PE (RPE).

Generally, all the basically operations required by a PE belong to its object behavior section. Taking into account the object modeling of all the PE features, it seems that this approach is the appropriate tool to realize our parallel programming emulator. Since the emulator environment is performed on a sequential machine, a parallel to sequential mapping is needed. This means that the realized emulator requires three layouts:

- The sequential layout: It is the kernel of our project. It performs all the operations of the emulating program.
- The parallel layout: It represent the parallel programming RMC environment, where any parallel programmer can write, compile, debug and run its parallel program
- The third layout is the intermediate one between parallel and sequential layouts. It realizes the mapping task, where each parallel instruction is converted into a set of sequential instructions.

Our parallel machine is represented by the instance of the platform class, which represents a mesh. This later is defined by a set of PE's arranged in an n x n matrix. A PE represents an object of processor class. In order to communicate over the mesh, each processor object is linked to four objects of classes: EastPort, WestPort, Northport and Southport. These four classes have the same features; they are grouped in an abstract Port class using the heritage concept. Each of the four ports is linked by one communication bus to its neighboring PE ports. Each PE performs any computation using an arithmetic and logic unit. This unit is modeled by a structure defined in the ALUnit class.

In the realized platform the parallel programmers must edit or open an edited parallel program and compile it before its execution. These later must be written using XML language according to an ad hoc developed XML scheme. The XML language is adopted to elaborate our system because it presents a powerful tool to model the complex components as the processing element. It was used in [23] to describe parallel grid components. To construct a parallel program, some sets of instructions were elaborated with respect to the object programming rules, so that the whole program possesses a unique object representation. This representation translates the following concept scheme:

- A program is a set of instructions
- Each instruction is defined by a name, a set of attributes and can contain other instructions
- Each attribute is defined by a name and a value. The UML class diagram of Figure 3 shows the different classes of our principal model. Also, in this figure, we can see all the relations between the different object models of the real components of the RMC.

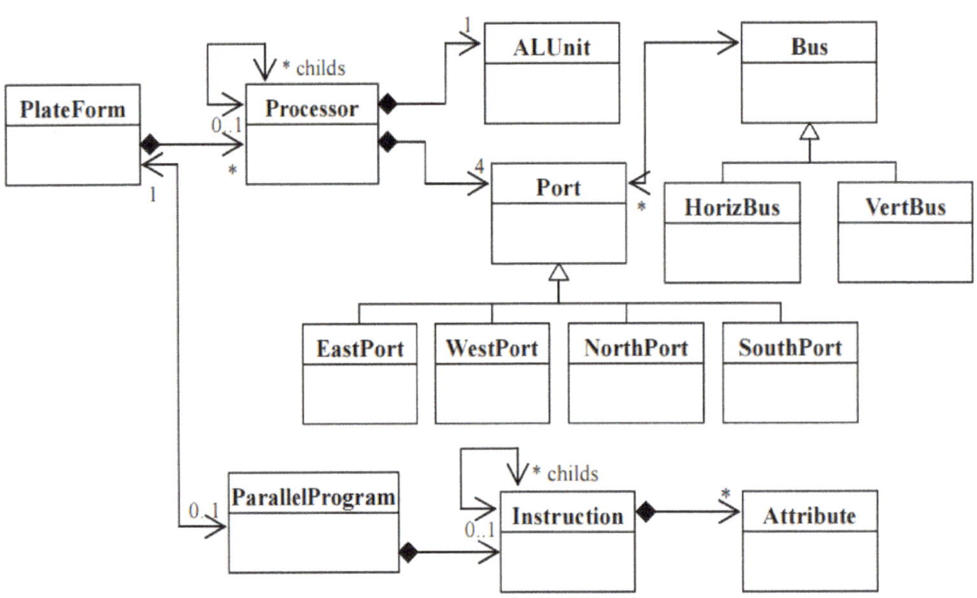

Figure 3: UML diagram of the modeling classes of the parallel platform.

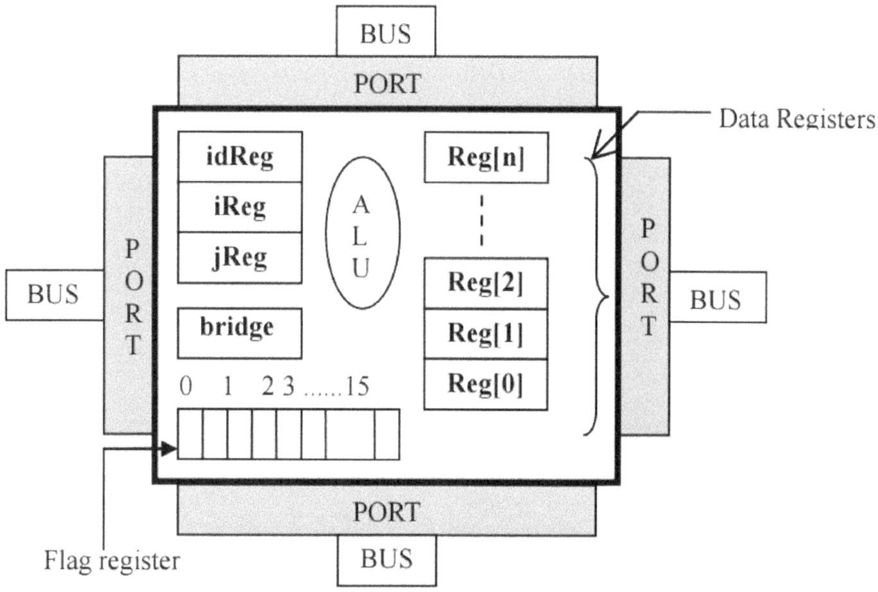

Figure 4: Representation of the components of a processing element model.

Description of the RMC Model Classes

Processor Class

In this part, we have translated all the physical components of a PE as in Figure 4, and its functionalities to the processor model. The defined processor class must take into account all the elementary functions and the set of the elementary physical parts of the PE. Thus, each PE is defined by its state, its behavior and must have an identity.

Processing Element State

The state model of a PE describes all its physical components. They are:

Identifier registers: When a created PE is inserted in the mesh model, its instance variables iReg and jReg which represent its location coordinates in the n x n matrix are set. The identifier register of this PE idReg, will take the value computer in the row major order by: idReg = n*iReg+ jReg.

Internal registers: For any given computation problem, each PE must use some internal registers to save data and the results of any related processing. To do so, we define in the PE model an array of internal data registers named "reg [..]". In this model, we have defined arbitrarily an array of 16 data registers. This array may be extended dynamically to any other size according to the problem in query.

Flags: As any standard processor, we introduce in the PE model a special flag register, where each of its flag bits will indicate the PE state related to any performed instruction. This register is arbitrarily defined by an array of 16 bits, but it can be extended to any large size according to any additional useful instruction.

Communication Ports: In the real RMC machine, all the PE's can exchange data via their communication ports, between each others what ever their locations in the matrix. In order to accomplish this task in the modeled machine, the communication ports of a PE are represented by objects linked to the PE using the reference indicators stored in the defined variables: eastport, westport, northPort and southPort.

ALUnit: To perform advanced logical and arithmetical operations, each PE uses its ALUnit. This later is modeled by an object of the class ALUnit and having a reference stored in the variable named ALUnit.

Other components: Notice that the RMC machine emulator is an open system. It can be dynamically and easily extended in terms of register memories, communication bus width, and special functions according to the problem in query. For example: In the image processing domain and for some specific applications, some hierarchical strategies are often used to enhance the complexity of the corresponding algorithms. (e.g. q-tree based algorithms, component contour based algorithms, labeling etc.). In such cases, of special advanced programming applications, some algorithms require special additional variables or registers. The programmer has the ability to extend easily its computational model.

To illustrate the proposition of this part, we consider an example where a PE can be representative of a group of other PE's. To do so, we define in the processor class a collection of objects of type processor. In this collection we save the represented PE identifiers. Furthermore, a given PE can easily know its representative PE using the representative PE variable which contains the identifier of its representative PE. This representative property was largely used in the literature as in [12,17].

Processing Element Behavior

The behavior of the PE is implemented by methods inside the processor class. These methods are classified in three categories.

Basically operations: The basically operations that can carry out a PE are the same as in any standard processor. Thus in this part we have implemented the methods to model the arithmetic operations (addition, subtraction, multiplication, division, etc.). Also we have implemented two operations to model some complex arithmetic and logic expressions. They are named: executeArithmeticExpression() and executeLogicExpression(). These expressions may respect the format imposed by C++ and java programming language. To do so, we have created a logic and arithmetic expression compiler using a complex process. This process is not presented in this paper because it is not the main idea discussed in this work. Several other methods have been defined in this class to offer to the programmer a large library of useful methods and operations.

Data exchange operations: The previous operations can be viewed as a category belonging to the set of instructions of any sequential programming language. Parallel programming is characterized by other types of instructions. In fact, as mentioned above, the Peps of the RMC must collaborate between each others by exchanging data via their communication buses. Among the implemented methods of this category, we distinguish:

- sendValue (double v): This method allows the PE to send a data value v to its neighboring PE's according to its bridge configuration state.
- receiveData (double data, char port, byte regR): Allows the PE to receive a data value on its port specified by the parameter port and to store the received data in its register regR.
- sendAndReceiveData (char portS, byte regS, char portR, byte regR): allows the PE to send the data value of its register regS on the port specified by the parameter portS, and receive data on the port specified by the parameter portR, the PE stores the received data in its register regR.
- receiveAndSendWithOperation (ProcessPort port, String op): This method is used to receive data, execute some operations on this data and send the result to other PE's according to their bridge states.

Configuration operations: In the parallel programming domain and particularly in the SIMD computational models, the processing element can play several roles depending on its configurations. In the processor class, we have defined a set of methods to change and to know the actual configuration of the PE. During the execution phase of a given parallel program, it is necessary to point at each stage of this phase, the group of active PE's. For these reasons, we define the methods select() and unselect() to select or unselect the Peps that are susceptible to execute or not the instructions. Among the selected PE's, it is possible to assign for some specific instructions the concerned PE's using other methods to mark or unmark them. Thus, we define other methods, mark() and unmark() to distribute a Boolean label to each selected PE. This label can be integrated in the program as a test variable.

To determine the configuration state of a PE at any given stage, some other appropriate operations are introduced. The methods associated to the configuration operations depend usually on the content of the flags register. Figure 5 summarizes the significance and the usefulness of each bit of this register where:

ALUnit Class

In a given parallel program, the PE's must be able to perform the arithmetical and logical expressions defined by any mathematical expression using all the possibilities of a programming language like java. During the compilation procedure, the mathematical expressions must be compiled and stored in temporary files to be used during their execution. The static methods defined in the ALUnit class named, createArithmeticExpression() and createLogicExpression() are used to compile the arithmetic and logic expression. To run the previous compiled expression, we can use the following two methods:

- getLogicExpression(int index,ArrayList params): returns the result of the logical expression of the instruction numbered by the index parameter. If this expression is included in an iterative loop, the iteration values will be stored in the array params.
- executeArithmericOperation(int index, ArrayList params): executes the arithmetic expression of the instruction numbered by index. If this expression is included in an iterative loop, the iteration values will be stored in the array params.

Port Class

As mentioned above, each PE possesses four communication ports. Each port is associated to a communication bus. In our model, we define four types of ports: East, West, North and South. All these four ports have the same characteristics; they are grouped in an abstracted Port class. A port is an object having a state defined by a label (N,E,W,S) and a reference " process" to the processor object to which it belongs.

Bit number	0	1	2	3	4	5	6	7	8	9	10	11	12	13	14	15
State (x =0 or 1)	x	X	x	x	x								x	x	x	X

- Bit 0 : indicates if the PE is marked or not.
- Bit 1 : indicates if the PE is selected or not.
- Bit 2 : indicates if the state of the PE is changed or not.
- Bit 3 : indicates if the PE has loaded data or not.
- Bit 4 : indicates if the PE has a representative PE or not.
- Bit 12 : indicates if the last executed logical operation is valid or not.
- Bit 13 : indicates if the PE has received data or not.
- Bit 14 : indicates if the PE is a representative or not.
- Bit 15 : shows if the parity flag of the PE is true or false.
- Bits 5 to 11 are not used, they are available to define other states in the PE.

Figure 5: The content of the flags register of a modeled PE.

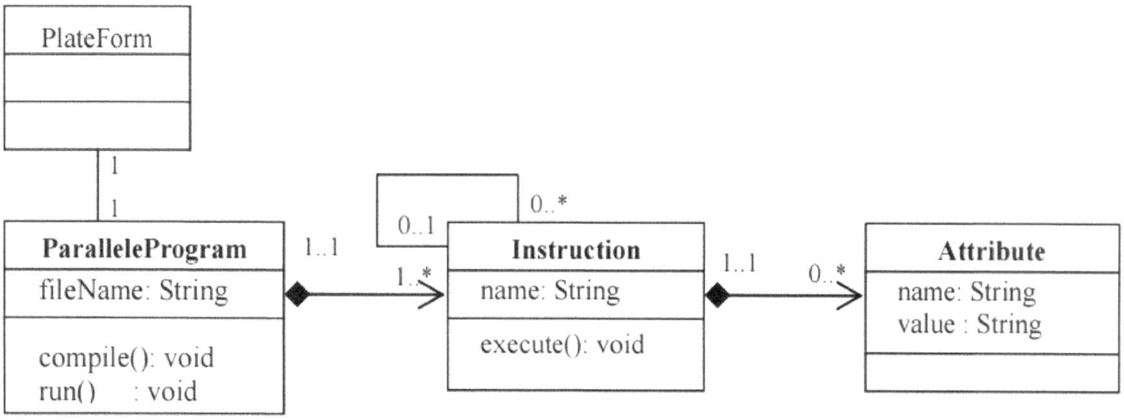

Figure 6: The UML class diagram of a program

A port can be locked by its PE using a Boolean instance variable locked. Since each port is associated to a communication bus, the reference to this bus must be stored in this class. Finally, each port must have one configuration variable to specify how the data can be transferred from the port to its communication bus.

Example: If we consider an 8 bits communication bus, the defaults configuration of a port is defined by the order «01234567». This means that the bit i (i=0 to 7) of the port is linked to the bit i of the bus. In this case the data sent over the port is transmitted without any transformation. While in the configuration «70123456» the bit 0 of the port is connected to bit 1 of the bus and the bit i (i=1 to 6) is linked to bit i+1 of the bus. The bit 7 of the port is linked to bit 0 of the bus. This means that the transmitted data is left rotated over the bus. This kind of commutation operations on ports are often used in several parallel programs [9].

Parallel Program Object Modeling

A parallel program loaded in the plate- form is composed by a set of instruction. Each instruction is defined by zero or several attributes. An instruction contains the child instructions and belongs to a father instruction. The class sheet of Figure 6 shows the class diagram of this model.

Parallel Program Class

A parallel program is defined by the source file name of this program. This source file is created by the programmer with the extension ".par" and must respect the XML norm. The program is defined by the variables: firstInstruction, lastInstruction and currentInstruction that represent the first, the last and the current instruction of the program (respectively). Some other instance variables are defined like: endCompilation to indicate if the compilation of the program is finished. iterationLevel to store the current iteration level in the loop cases.

To run an edited program, we begin by the method compile(). The compiling procedure acts as follows:

- read the program source file
- load it in the memory as a tree of instructions
- The first instruction is stored in the firstInstruction variable.
- The last instruction is stored in the lastInstruction variable.
- Execute the program starting from the first instruction.

Instruction Class

To edit a parallel program in this emulator, we have created a parallel programming language using our specific XML scheme. Each instruction of this language is defined by several attributes and can contain other instructions. Each attribute is an object of the attribute class which is self defined by its name and its value. In the program, each instruction is viewed as a tree structure. It is delimited by a beginning and ending tags. Between these tags, we can find other child instructions having the same structure. Between the tags of the child instruction, we can find other child instructions having the same structure etc. For this reason, an instruction is defined by a dynamic table named childs, to store the references to the other child instruction objects. Furthermore, an instruction can know its father thanks to the variable "parent" which contains its parent reference. Finally, there are other interesting variables used during the execution of the instruction, they are defined in this class, such as, opened and executed variables that indicate if the instruction is opened or executed.

Example

```
<for-eachPE   test="reg[0]>0">
   <mark/>
   <doOperation expression="reg[0]=(reg[1]+reg[2])/2"/>
</for-eachPE>
```

In this example scheme, we show the structure of the parallel instruction «for-eachPE». It is defined by an attribute «test» having the value «reg[0]>0». This instruction contains two instructions: The first is «mark» which is without attribute, the second is the «doOperation» instruction having an attribute of name «expression» and value «reg[0]=(reg[1]+reg[2])/2».

This simple program example selects in the matrix of processors all the PE's having a positive value in their registers reg[0]. The selected PE's are marked (labeled).

Then, all these marked PE's perform the arithmetic operation on their own data registers, reg[1] and reg[2]. Finally the result of each PE is stored in its reg[0] register. Figure 7 presents the object structure of the precedent example after its compilation.

Platform Class

The modeled parallel machine is represented by an object of the Platform class. In this paper, we are interested in the implementation of the mesh as a matrix of n x n PE's. But, we can easily extend the model to other architectures such as: Pipe line, Pyramidal machine etc. The RMC model is characterized by the rows and cols variables that define the size of the matrix. The matrix creation is made by a matrix process[rows][cols] of object processor (PE). The size of the resulted virtual mesh is dynamically configurable and is not limited. It depends only on the available memory space in the used sequential machine supporting the emulator. In addition to the PE's matrix, the platform is associated to an object representing the loaded and compiled parallel program. Some additional Boolean variables are used to complete the Platform state such as:

- Debug , to indicate whether the step by step execution mode is activated
- DrawMode, to indicate the type of the graphic context used in the displaying data zone.
- Compile, to indicate whether the loaded program is compiled or not.

The most important part of this emulator is implemented in the behavior part of the class platform. After loading a program using the method loadProgramme(), we can run the compile() method to construct the instructions tree of the parallelProgram Object. For each of these constructed parallel instructions trees, we realize the parallel to sequential mapping task. Subsequently, this task translates each parallel instruction into a set of iterative sequential instructions. In order to exploit the platform class to run a given parallel program, we classify all its defined methods into the following four categories:

Loading Data on the Mesh

In this category, we use some methods to load data in the mesh which is the matrix of PE's before any processing procedure. As example, we distinguish the following:

- loadImage(): loads data image of any format (bmp, jpg, png, gif) in the matrix of PE's.
- loadMatrix(): loads a data matrix from a text file to the matrix of PE's.
- loadRandomMatrix(): computes and loads a random data matrix in the mesh.

Notice that, all the used data types in any programming language are supported by the modeled PE's (e.g. Byte, int, long, float, double etc.).

Configuration of the Mesh

In the SIMD parallel programming domain, it is necessary to select the PE's that are susceptible to perform some given instructions. For this reasons, we have defined the selection methods basing on different criteria. We will discuss some ones in the instruction set part. After any selection, the method executeConfig(String conf) asks the selected PE's to execute a configuration operation.

Execution of the Program

After loading data and configuring the mesh, we can perform the other instructions of the parallel program related to the loaded data. The principal method used in this part is ExecuteInstruction (Instruction ins). This category of instructions concerns all the data processing and scientific calculus operations.

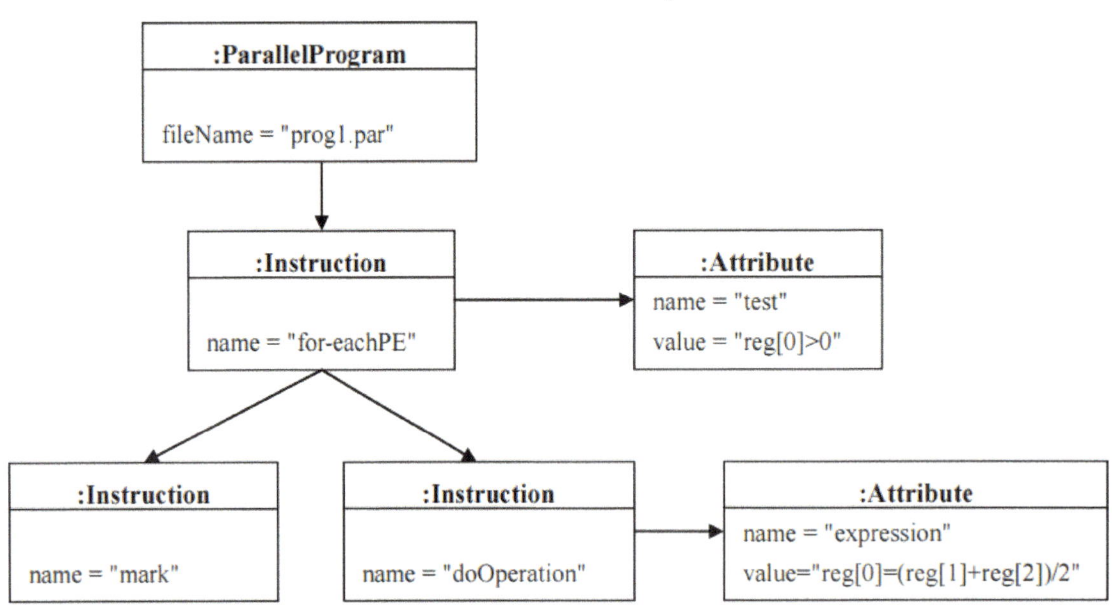

Figure 7: Object representation of an instruction

Displaying Results

During the program execution, we can insert some methods to display the results using several numerical formats. For example, we can use the text format to observe the contents of different registers of the PE's or to display any data results in text format. A graphical context is also available in our platform to display other results in graphical mode such as curves and images.

Instruction Sets

In order to construct our programming language, we have developed an XML scheme which defines the parallel instruction sets to edit parallel programs. A program must begin by the tag and ends by tag. Between the two tags we can edit the instructions. Each instruction begins by the tag indicating the instruction name and ends by the tag indicating the end of the instruction. An instruction can be defined by several attributes, it can encapsulate other instructions. As for the real RMC, the emulating platform has three categories of instruction sets. They are presented as follows:

Instructions for PE Configuration

In the SIMD architectures, the parallel programming is based on a fundamental principle, where it is necessary to select, mark and bridge the PE's concerned by the instruction execution. The configuration instruction set is expressed by the following actions:

Selecting: This action is expressed by the instruction:

<for-eachPE cols= "valCols" rows= "valRows" test= "expression_logic" direction="">
... (Operations to be executed)
</for-eachPE>

The attributes "cols" and "rows" define the concerned columns and rows. When several columns and rows are concerned, they are separated by commas. The attribute direction is defined by a string to indicate the direction of the selected group of PE's starting from the PE of coordinates indicated in "rows" and "cols" attributes. The possible direction attributes are:

- «RE» or «RW»: to define the direction East or West along a Row.
- «CN»or «CS»: to define the direction North or South along a Column.
- «DNE» or «DNW»: for the direction North-Est or North-West along a diagonal.
- «DSE» or «DSW»: for the direction South-Est or South-West along a diagonal.

The attribute test is used to select a set of PE's satisfying the condition defined by a logical expression. For example, in the expression (test=»reg[1]>10») , the selected PE's are those having in their reg[1] the values greater than 10.

Marking: This action uses the following instructions:

<mark type="true| false" />: to mark a PE if its attribute type is true and unmark it, if this attribute is false.
<mark />: to mark a PE without condition.

<unMark />: to Unmark a PE without condition.

Bridging: As mentioned in the physical description of the RMC, a PE can be configured in three kinds of bridges: simple, double or crossed bridge. These bridging states are implemented by the following instruction:

<bridge type= "SB-WE|SB-NS | SB-WN | SB-WS | SB-NE | SB-SE | DB-WN-SE | DB-NE-SW |DB-NS-WE | CB-WNE | CB-NES | CB-ESW | CB-SWN | CB-WNES | NB"/>.

This instruction named bridge is used by a PE by defining its kind in the attribute type.

- Defining the kind by: SB = Simple Bridge, DB= Double Bridge and CB= Crossed Bridge.
- Defining the direction of the bridge E,W,N and S for East, West, North and South (respectively)

The SB configurations are: {SB-NS, SB-WE, SB-WN, SB-WS, SB-NE, SB-SE, SB-WS}. At any mentioned configuration the data is bypassing bi-directionally the PE over its bridges. The DB configurations are: {DB-WN-SE, DB-NESW, DB-NS-WE}. In this case, two communication bridges are constructed by a PE. So, two data can simultaneously bypass bi-directionally the PE. The CB configurations are: {CB-WNE, CB-NES, CBESW, CB-SWN, CB-WNES}.

In this case, the only one obtained communication channel links at least three ports of the PE. Notice that, to return back to the no bridge state from any bridge configuration, we use the instruction bridge with an attribute type {NB} to specify No Bridge.

Arithmetic / Logic Instructions and Control Structures

In the modeled parallel programming language, the arithmetic and logic instructions are expressed using the format defined bellow. In addition to the reconfiguration operations, each PE of the RMC can carry out a set of arithmetic/logic instructions and control structures. These instructions are formatted as defined in the following examples:

Arithmetic / logic instructions

- Arithmetic / logic instructions

<inc reg="numReg"/>: means: *reg [numReg] = reg [numReg]+1*;
<dec reg="numReg"/>: means: *reg [numReg] = reg [numReg]-1*;

<add reg="numReg" value= "val"/>: means : *reg [numReg] = reg [numReg]+Value*;
<sub reg="numReg" value= "val"/>: means : *reg [numReg] = reg [numReg]-Value*;
<mult reg="numReg" value= "val"/>: means : *reg [numReg] = reg [numReg]*Value*;
<div reg="numReg" value= "val"/>: means : *reg [numReg] = reg [numReg]/Value*;

<doOperation expression= "arithmetic_expression" />: This instruction executes the arithmetic expression specified by the expression attribute. We have developped a compiler to execute all the possible arithmetical expressions according to the same syntaxes of the C and Java language.

- Control structures

The control structures defined for our platform are the same as the well known for any language. The following examples give the presentation of some structures.

<if test= "logic_ expression"> ... instructions ... </if>

<for from= "begin_val" to= "end_val">... instructions ...</for>

<while test= "logic_expression">... instructions ...</while>

Data Exchange Instructions

The third instruction set developed for this emulator concerns the specific instructions to exchange data between the PE's of the RMC. This set allows the programmer to manipulate some new concepts introduced in the parallel SIMD algorithms. These instructions use the four Port objects of each PE to send, receive and broadcast data over the mesh. Among the defined instructions we have:

<sendAndReceiveData portS="W|E|N|S" regS="" portR="W|E|N|S" regR=""/>

This instruction allows the PE to send it Data from the specified register regS to the port specified by portS and to receive data from protR and save it in the register regR.

<receiveAndTransmitData portS="W|E|N|S" regR =" " data=" " />

This instruction allows the PE to send it Data from the specified register regS to the port specified by portS and to receive data from protR and save it in the register regR.

<receiveAndTransmitData portS="W|E|N|S" regR =" " data=" " />

This instruction indicates to the PE to receive data specified by data attribute and store it in register regR then send it from the port specified by protS.

Macro Commands and Parallel Functions

As any programming language, the macro commands and functions are generated and inserted in specific libraries to facilitate their use in some advanced procedures. In the same strategy, we have defined some parallel macro commands and some functions to represent some parallel pre-processing procedures which can be inserted easily in any parallel program. The generated library is subject to more extensions and developments. In this section, we present some examples of Macro commands and parallel functions to illustrate their usefulness as the pre-processing procedures.

Macro commands:

- <defineRepresentativePE-forEachRow /> This macro command is used to determine a representative PE of a group of marked PE's for each row of the mesh. This command it based on the Minimum value search procedure at each row of the mesh. The output of this command is the minimal identifier value (idReg) found in at each group of marked PE's in each row of the mesh.
- < defineRepresentativePE-ForEachCol /> It is the same procedure used as in the precedent macro command. But the Minimum value search procedure is applied on columns instead of rows.
- < initialiseRepresentivePE /> This macro command is used to reset all the representative PE's. In this case there is no representative of any group of PE's in the mesh. This means that each PE is self representative.
- < doDistributeParityIndex from="W|E|N|S" /> This macro is used to distribute a special index named "parity index", alternatively to the marked PE's a group. It is an important macro command used as a pre-processing for some high level algorithms. This macro corresponds to a procedure based on bridge and reconfiguration operations where each marked PE receives on its specified port a Boolean label "0" or "1", and then it inverts it before sending it to its neighboring marked PE according to the bridge state in which it is set.

Functions:

- isSelected( ): indicates if the PE is selected or not. It uses the bit 1 of the flags register.
- isChanged( ): indicates if the state of the PE is changed or not. This method is very useful in some graphic refreshment procedures. It uses the bit 2 of the flags register.
- isTestValide( ): indicates if the last executed logical operation is valid or not.
- getParity( ): shows if the parity flag of the PE is true or false. It uses the bit 15 of the flags register.
- isRepresentative( ): indicates if the PE is a representative or not. It uses the bit 14 of the flags register.
- hasReceivedData( ): indicates if the PE has received data or not. It uses the bit 13 of the flags register.
- isMarked( ): indicates if the PE is marked or not. It uses the bit 0 of the flags register.
- hasLoadedData( ): indicates if the PE has loaded data or not. It uses the bit 3 of the flags register.
- hasFinished( ): returns true value if all the PE's are in stand by mode. This function is called in the stopping test of some iterative loops.
- hasRepresentant( ):indicates if the PE has a representative PE or not.
- REGRep[numReg]: indicates the value of the numReg register of its representative.

APPLICATIONS

In this section, we present some parallel algorithm examples where some properties of the RMC are used to examine how they are expressed using some instructions of the instruction sets defined above.

Program 1: Example1.par

```
<prog>
  <for-eachPE cols="0,2,4"   rows="*">
    <mark type="true"/>
    <loadRandomIntValue      minValue="10"      max-
Value="255"/>
      <if test="reg[0]>=100">
          <bridge type="SB-NS"/>
      </if>
  </for-eachPE>
</prog>
```

The result if this program is described as follows:

- It selects all the PE's of the column 0, 2 and 4. Then all the selected PE's are marked "true".
- Each one of these marked PE's must compute and save in its memory register reg[0], a random data having a value between minValue="10" and max Value="255".

All the selected PE's having a data value greater than or equal to 100 must configure themselves in Simple Bridge of direction (North–South) NS. Figure 8 shows the states of all the PE's of the RMC matrix after the program execution. The marked PE's are represented by the hashed squares. The NS bridge is represented by vertical lines linking its North and South ports of the PE is SB state and its neighbors.

Program 2: Example2.par

This example shows the point to point mean computation of two data matrices.

```
<prog>
    <loadMatrix file="matrix1.txt" reg="0"/>
    <loadMatrix file="matrix2.txt" reg="1"/>
    <for-eachPE cols="*" rows="*">
      <mark type="true"/>
      <doOperation
sion="reg[2]=(reg[0]+reg[1])"/>
    </for-eachPE>
</prog>
```

We consider two data matrices saved in the data files «matrix1.txt» and «matrix2.txt» respectively. The results of the different stages of this program example are:

- The first matrix is mapped to the RMC of the same size as this matrix, one element per PE. At each PE the element is stored in its Reg [0] register.
- The second matrix is mapped to the RMC of the same size as this matrix, one element per PE. At each PE the element is stored in its Reg [1] register.
- All the PE's of the RMC are selected and marked.

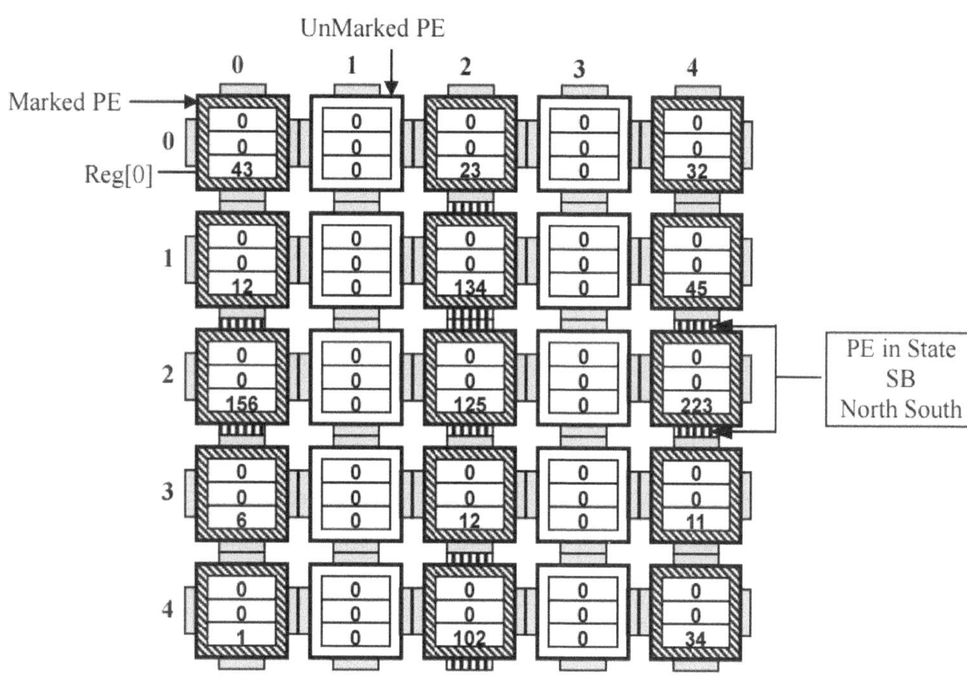

Figure 8: The different PE's states after program execution

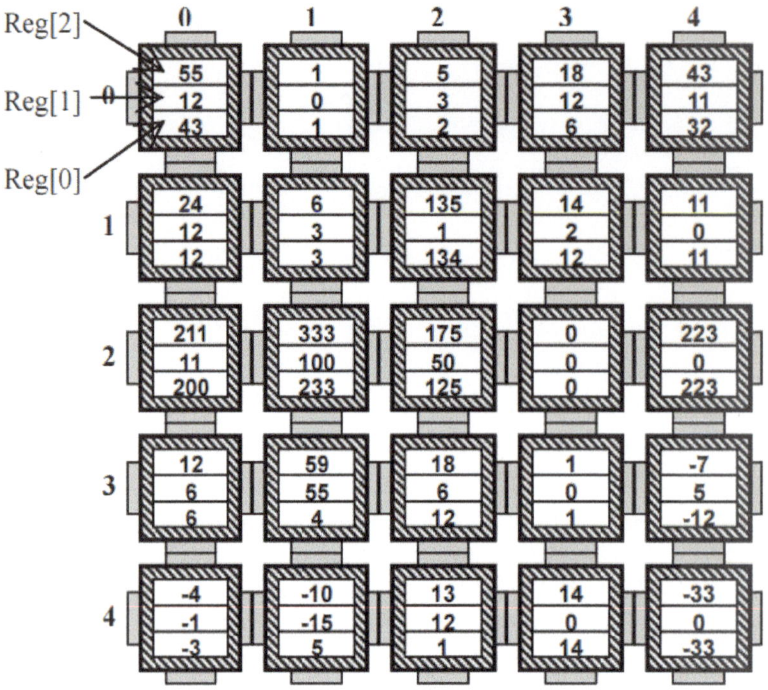

Figure 9: Result of the point to point sum of two matrices on the modeled RMC.

All the marked PE's execute simultaneously the operation (reg[2]=reg[0]+reg[1]). This is the point to point mean computation. At each PE the result is saved in its reg[0] register.(Figure 9)

Program 3: Example 3.par

This example corresponds to an implementation of a component contour detection of a gray leveled image using Sobel operator. The used image is of size 200 x 200 pixels.

```
<prog>
 <for-eachPE rows="*" cols="*">
<mark type="true"/>
<loadImage file="branchng1.jpg" reg="0" coding="8"/>
     <sendAndReceiveData portS="E" regS="0" portR=
'W' regR="1"/>
     <sendAndReceiveData portS="N" regS="1" portR=
'S' regR="2"/>
     <sendAndReceiveData portS="W" regS="0" portR=
'E' regR="3"/>
     <sendAndReceiveData portS="S" regS="3" portR=
'N' regR="4"/>
     <sendAndReceiveData portS="N" regS="0" portR=
'S' regR="5"/>
     <sendAndReceiveData portS="W" regS="5" portR=
'E' regR="6"/>
     <sendAndReceiveData portS="S" regS="0" portR=
'N' regR="7"/>
     <sendAndReceiveData portS="E" regS="7" portR=
'W' regR="8"/>
     <doOperation                          expres-
sion="reg[9]=Math.abs(-reg[8]-2*reg[1]-reg[2]+reg[4]+
2*reg[3]+reg[6])"/>
     <doOperation                          expres-
sion="reg[10]=Math.abs(reg[8]+2*reg[7]-reg[2]+reg[4]-
```

```
2*reg[5]-reg[6])"/>
      <doOperation   expression="reg[1]=reg[9]+reg[10]"/>

</for-eachPE>
</prog>
```

The execution of this program is commented as follows:

- Selecting and marking all the PE's of the (200 x 200) RMC.
- The image is loaded from file="branchng1. jpg" and stored in the RMC one pixel per PE. Each PE saves its own gray level pixel (coding="8") in its register reg[0].

The following eight "sendAndReceiveData" instructions are used by the PE's to exchange data between neighboring PE's, so that each PE will receive its eight neighboring pixel values required by the Sobel operator.

- After the data exchange stage, we compute the absolute values of Gx and Gy of the Sobel operator
- The final result is computed by: expression= "reg[1]=reg[9]+reg[10]"
- The resulted image is located in the RMC, one pixel per PE (i.e. in reg[1] of each PE.), while the input image is still in reg[0].

Figure 10 shows the result of the parallel program of a component contour detection of a gray leveled image using Sobel operator. Each used images is of size 200 x 200 pixels. The images in Figures 10(a), (b) and (c) representing flower, fishes and a tree branch (respectively) are the input images of the program. The resulted output images are shown in Figures 10(d), (e) and (f).

Program 4: Example 4.par

Parallel program of the hierarchical Minimum search algorithm:

```
<prog>
  <for-eachPE   rows="*" cols="*">
     <bridge type="SB-WE"/>
  </for-eachPE>
  <for-eachPE   rows="0,2,3,4" cols="*">
      <mark type="true"/>
   <bridge type="NB"/>
   <loadRandomIntValue      minValue="1"      max-
Value="255"/>
      <push reg="0"/>
     <defineRepresentativeForEachRow/>
     <while test="!hasFinished()">
        < doDistributeParityIndex from="W"/>

        <if
test="(getParity()==true)&&(!isRepresentativePE())">
           <sendData   direction="W"/>
         </if>
      <if test="(getParity()==false)">
           <receiveData   port="E" regR="1"/>
         </if>
      <if
test="(getParity()==true)&&(!isRepresentativePE())">


           <mark type="false"/>
           <bridge type="SB-WE"/>
         </if>
        <if test="hasReceivedData()">
         <doOperation                         expres-
sion="reg[0]=minReg(0,1)"/>
         </if>
      </while>
   <pop reg="1"/>
  </for-eachPE>
  <for-eachRepresentativePE>
   <mark type="false"/>
  </for-eachRepresentativePE>
  <for-eachPE
     test="hasRepresentative()                        and
(reg[1]==REGRep[0])">
     <mark type="true"/>
  </for-eachPE>
  <end/>
  </prog>
```

In this example, we use some sample instructions and control structures defined in the elaborated instruction sets.

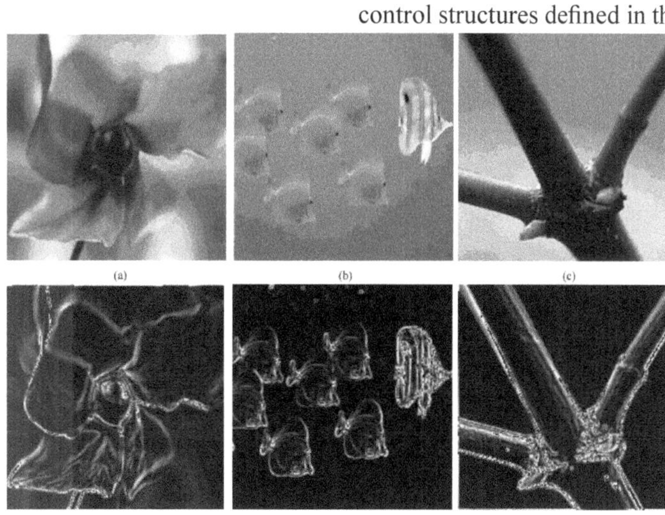

Figure 10: Results of the parallel program of contour detection using Sobel operator. The input images of the program are: (a) flower, (b) fishes and (c) tree branch, figures (d), (e) and (f) are the resulted output images (respectively)

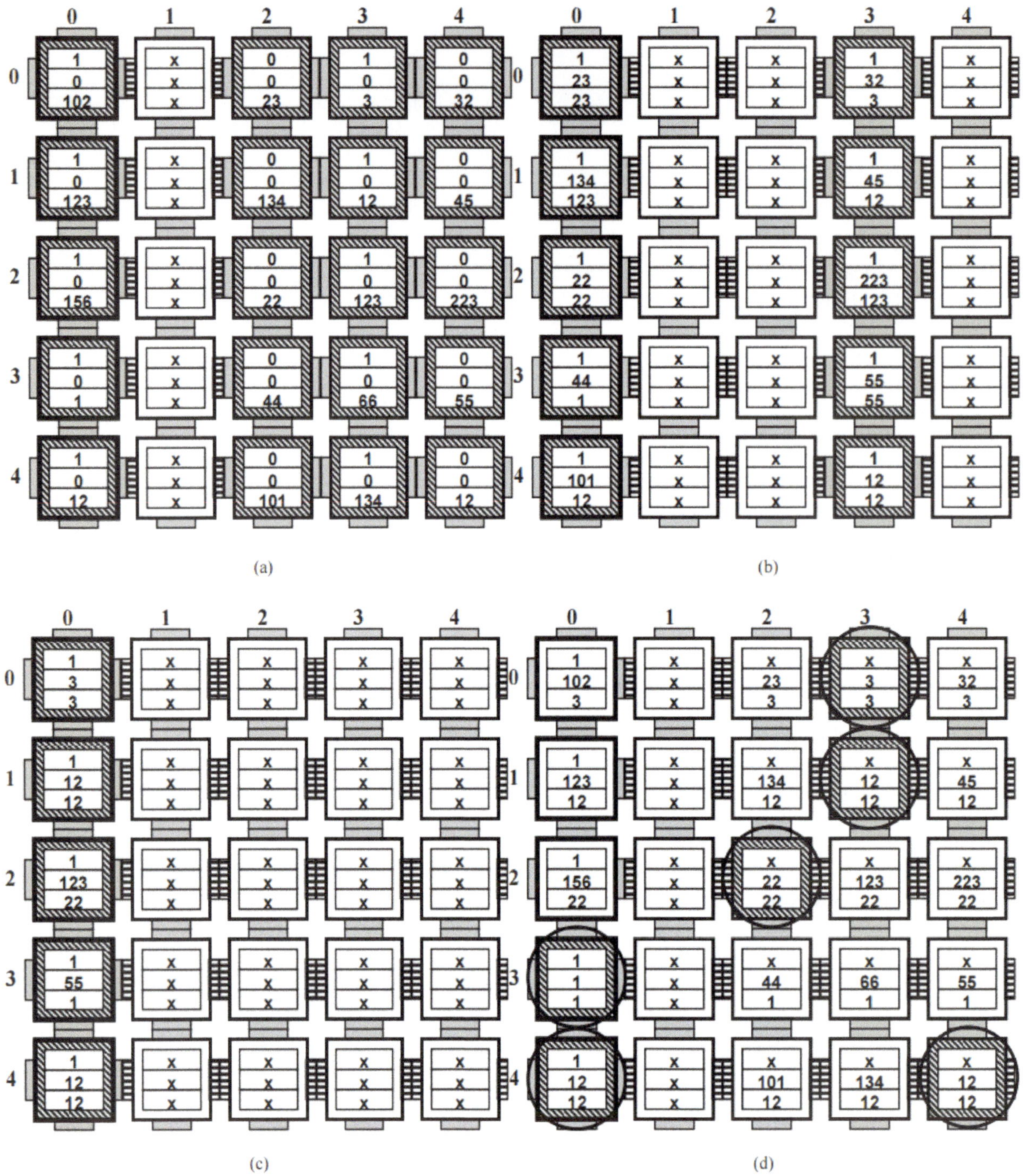

Figure 11: Result of a parallel minimum value search algorithm on all the rows of a matrix

This program contains three stages: In the first stage:

- All the PE's are set in Simple Bridge of direction WE.
- All the PE's of rows 0, 2, 3 and 4 are marked.
- Each marked PE computes a random value and stores it in its register reg[0].
- Finding the representative PE of each row using a macro command< defineRepresentativeForEachRow/> . The second stage is devoted to a «while» loop, where:

1. The marco command «doDistributeParityIndex from ='W'»is used to label the marked PE's alternatively by 0 or 1.
2. In each row, all the PE's of even labels send their data on their West ports. These data will be received on East ports of the corresponding marked PE's having odd labels. Each PE stores the received data in its register reg[1].
3. Each PE having even label and having sent its data, becomes unmarked and turns back to the stand by mode before setting itself in (SB-WE) state (this PE is died).
4. Each PE having received data on its East ports computes the minimum value among its reg [0] and reg[1] contents and stores the result in reg [0].
5. The operations from 1) to 4) constitute the instructions of a loop that is repeated while there exist in any row of the matrix the PE's that are not in stand by mode. This loop is finished when it remains in life just the representative PE at each row.

The remained instruction of this stage corresponds to the back up operations that are used to distribute at each row the minimum value obtained by its representative PE after the last loop. The third stage is used to mark all the PE's having the minimum value in their rows. It is based on the following instruction:

<for-eachPE test="hasRepresentative() and (reg[1]== REGRep[0])">
<mark type="true"/>
</for-eachPE>

This instruction means that each PE is marked if it has a representative PE and its own value in its register reg[1] equals the value of register reg[0] of its representative PE. This stage allows us to display at each row, the PE having the minimum value. See Figure 11 (d). Remark: When two or more PE's have the same minimal value on the same row, they are displayed together and they declare themselves having the minimal value

CONCLUSIONS

In this paper, we have presented an important tool for the parallel programmers to validate their parallel computing algorithms. The developped virtual machine emulates a SIMD structure re-configurable mesh computer. The obtained parallel virtual machine and its programming language compiler can be used as a high performance computing system. It represents in our laboratory a very important tool to validate our algorithms in the parallel image processing domain. Actually, the cost of physical parallel architectures remains very high. Subsequently, their use is very limited over the world. In this context, we start this first part of this project and we continue by developing further related works. They are oriented to model other topological parallel structures, such as: pyramid and hypercube architectures. All the components of this work are subscribed in a strategy of popularizing the parallel computing domain.

REFERENCES

1. R. Miller. et al, "Geometric algorithms for digitized pictures on a mesh connected computer," IEEE Transactions on PAMI, Vol. 7, No. 2, pp. 216–228, 1985.
2. V. K. Prasanna and D. I. Reisis, "Image computation on meshes with multiple broadcast," IEEE Transactions on PAMI, Vol. 11, No. 11, pp. 1194–1201, 1989.
3. H. LI, M. Maresca, "Polymorphic torus network," IEEE Transaction on Computer, Vol. C-38, No. 9, pp. 1345–1351, 1989.
4. T. Hayachi, K. Nakano, and S. Olariu, "An O ((log log n)²) time algorithm to compute the convex hull of sorted points on re-configurable meshes," IEEE Transactions on Parallel and Distributed Systems, Vol. 9, No. 12, 1167– 1179, 1998.
5. R. Miller, V. K. Prasanna-Kummar, D. I. Reisis, and Q. F. Stout, "Parallel computation on re-configurable meshes," IEEE Transactions on Computer, Vol. 42, No. 6, pp. 678–692, 1993.
6. J. P Gray and T. A. Kean, "Configurable hardware: A new paradigm for computation," Proceedings of 10th Cal. Tech. conference on VLSI, pp. 279–295, 1989.
7. H. Li and M. Maresca, "Polymorphic torus architecture for computer vision," IEEE Transactions on PAMI, Vol. 11, No. 3, pp. 233–242, 1989.
8. D. B. Shu, G. Nash, and C. Weems, "Image understanding architecture and applications, in advances in machine vision, J. L. C. SANZ, Ed. Springer-Verlag, NY, pp. 297– 355, 1989.
9. H. M. Alnuweiri et al., "Re-configurable network switchmodels," Technical Report, CICSR, Univ. British Columbia, 1993.
10. J. L. Trahan, R. K. Thiruchelvan, and R. Vaidyanathan, "On the power of segmenting and fusing buses, Proc. Int. Parallel Processing Symposium, pp. 79–83, 1993.
11. R. Miller and Q. F. Stout, "Mesh computer algorithms for computational geometry," IEEE Transactions on computer, Vol. 38, No. 3, pp. 321–340, 1989.
12. J. Elmesbahi, O. Bouattane, and Z. Benabbou, "O(1) time quadtree algorithm and its application for image geometric properties on a Mesh Connected Computer (MCC), IEEE Trans. On Systems, Man, and Cybernetics, Vol. 25, No. 12, pp. 1640–1648, 1995.
13. J. Elmesbahi, O. Bouattane, A. Raihani, M. Elkhaili, A. Rabbaa, "Parallel algorithms representation of points and curvilinear data," International Journal of SAMS, Vol. 33, pp. 479–494, 1998.
14. O. Bouattane, J. Elmesbahi, M. Khaldoun, and A. Rami, "A fast algorithm for k-nearest neighbor problem on a reconfigurable mesh computer," Journal of Intelligent and Robotic Systems, Kluwer academic Publisher, Vol. 32, pp. 347–360, 2001.
15. R. Miller et al, "Meshes with re-configurable Buses," Proceedings of 5th MIT Conference on Advanced Research in VLSI, Cambridge, MA, pp. 163–178, 1988.
16. Ling Tony et al, Efficient parallel processing of image contours," IEEE Transactions on PAMI, Vol. 15, No. 1, pp. 69–81, 1993.
17. O. Bouattane, J. Elmesbahi, and A. Rami, "A fast parallel algorithm for convex hull problem of multi-leveled images," Journal of Intelligent and Robotic Systems, Kluwer academic Publisher, Vol. 33, pp. 285–299, 2002.
18. A. Errami, M. Khaldoun, J. Elmesbahi, and O. Bouattane, "O(1) time algorithm for structural characterization of multi-leveled images and its applications on a re-configurable mesh computer," Journal of Intelligent and Robotic Systems, Springer, Vol. 44, pp. 277–290, 2006.
19. M. Migliardi and V. Sunderam, "Emulating parallel programming environments in the harness meta computing system," Parallel Processing Letters, Vol. 11, No. 2 & 3, pp. 281–295, 2001.
20. D. Kurzyniec, V. Sunderam, and M. Migliardi, "PVM emulation in the harness metacomputing framework -design and performance evaluation," Proc. of the Second IEEE International Symposium on Cluster Computing and the Grid (CCGrid), Berlin, Germany, pp. 282–283, May 2002.
21. M. Migliardi, P. Baglietto, and M. Maresca, "Virtual parallelism allows relaxing the synchronization constraints of SIMD computing paradigm, Proceedings

of HPCN98, Amsterdam (NL), pp. 784–793, April 1998.

22. M. Migliardi and M. Maresca, "Modeling instruction level parallel architectures efficiency in image processing applications," Proceedings of of HPCN97, Lecture Notes in Computer Science, Springer Verlag, Vol. 1225, pp. 738–751, 1997.
23. M. Migliardi and R. Podesta, "Parallel component descriptor language: XML based deployment descriptors for grid application components," Proc. of the 2007 International Conference on Parallel and Distributed Processing Techniques and Applications, Las Vegas, Nevada, USA, pp. 955–961, June 2007.

CHAPTER 4

SEMANTIC ANALYSIS OF NATURAL LANGUAGE QUERIES FOR AN OBJECT ORIENTED DATABASE

Bentamar Hemerelain, Hafida Belbachir

Keywords: Query, Nominal Group, Natural Language, Object Oriented Data Base, Semantic Validation

INTRODUCTION

On the earliest and most widely studied areas of natural language processing is the development of a Natural language interfaces to databases (NLIDB) [1-7]... A NLIDB allows users to input a query in a natural language such rather than in a formal query language and in conceptual terms particular to their understanding of the database application domain. In most works, the underlying database is assumed to be relational. In our work, we are interested in building a NLI for an object-oriented database (OODB). Unfortunately, the relational model and the object model are fundamentally different. Relational database (RDB) systems are based on twodimensional tables in which each item appears as a row. Relationships among the data are expressed by comparing the values stored in theses tables. The object model is based on the tight integration of code and data, flexible data types, hierarchical relationships among data types, and references [8]. This paper is concerned with the semantic validation of natural language query (NLQ) for an OODB. The natural language considered here is French.

A considerable amount of work has been published on the semantics of NLQ. Works, usually carried out by Computer Scientists, can be classified into two categories: 1) work based on established linguistic theories which are modified and/or extended such as [9-12]; 2) new ad hoc but efficient semantics that are not based on established linguistic theories. Examples are quoted by [2]. Some recent works are [13-15]. Our approach falls into category 2) and is designed on the principle of [13] who introduce the idea of semantically tractable (ST) questions. As their database is in the form of RDB, they define the ST questions as questions where the words correspond to relations (tables), attributes and values. The nature of the OODB introduces some new challenges, beyond these addresses for RDB. In this paper, we deal with the concept of class to model complex data, simple attributes, complex (composite) attributes with classes as their domains, and two special kinds of associations between classes: 1) inheritance which is the most powerful concept of object oriented. It is a mechanism of reusability: the news classes, known as sub-classes inherit attributes of the pre-existing classes, which are referred to as super classes; an inheritance relationship is created between the sub-class and the super-class. 2) reference: since a class C may have a complex attribute with domain C', a reference relationship can be established between C and C'.

Our center of interest is the analysis of NLQ consisting of one or two NGs articulating around a verb. At this step of analysis, we consider the NG constituted of one or several keywords and we ignore the DB independent words (article, relative pronoun,...). A keyword can be an application dependent noun or a value. The former matches a class name, a simple attribute name or a composite attribute name in an OODB.

In a NLQ, the verb is created by the DB administrator. It expresses the link which exists between a class and another class or between a class and one of its attributes. The application dependent nouns and the verbs with their semantic features are stored in a lexicon. This last includes inflection forms of nouns and conjugated forms of verbs. It is also augmented with relevant synonyms. This addition makes it possible to the user to write a query in various natural ways. Heritage and reference relationships are added to lexicon allowing the safeguarding of the heritage and reference link of the OODB. These Heritage and reference relationships with the lexicon form the natural language database (NLDB).

Citation: B. Hemerelain and H. Belbachir, "Semantic Analysis of Natural Language Queries for an Object Oriented Database," Journal of Software Engineering and Applications, Vol. 3 No. 11, 2010, pp. 1047-1053. doi: 10.4236/jsea.2010.311123.

The semantic analysis of a query first deals with identification of individual keywords in the NGs. It uses some simple semantic filters to determine their semantic value. If the NG is atomic and the single keyword identified, no further analysis is required. On the contrast, it is necessary to verify if the complex NG respects the conceptual constraints of the domain DB. The conceptual constraints mainly refer to inheritance and reference relationships and are function of the semantic value of the keywords and their combination in the NG. If the NLQ is constituted of a single NG, no supplementary treatment is necessary. If the NLQ covered two valid NGs, it is a subject of studying the semantic coherence of the verb and both NGs which are attached to him.

The paper is organized as follows: The Section 2 describes the lexicon and defines the inheritance and reference relationships in a NLDB. The Section 3 is divided into three parts. In the part 1, semantic filters are defined to identify keywords. With the introduction of the semantic coherence constraints of keywords, the part 2 discusses the process of NG's validation. Part 3 concerns the semantic coherence of the verb with its subject and its object. In Section 4, an example of illustration is treated to simulate the tools developed in preceding section. To understand this example and those that are quoted in the text; we give an extract of the database prototype which is used in our experimentation. The results of the experimentation are reported in Section 5. A conclusion is given in Section 6.

NATURAL LANGUAGE DATABASE

The natural language database (NLDB) is a translation of the object oriented database (OODB). The NLDB contains a lexicon and inheritance and reference relationships.

Lexicon

A natural language query consists of two parts: an interrogative particle and a phrase. A phrase is a succession of nominal and verbal groups. A nominal group (NG) in the natural language query (NLQ) consists of one or several meaningful words. The latter can be an application dependent noun, a verb or a value.

Definitions

Application dependent noun

The former matches a class name, a simple attribute or a composite attribute name in an OODB. Each application dependent noun is represented in the OODB as a variable whose name might be meaningful according to the naming conventions but not necessarily the same word in natural language (NL) (e.g. ENS, X). Thus, we generate, for each variable declared in an OODB, a word in NL (NW) (e.g. NW (ENS) ® enseignant [teacher]; NW(X) ® personne [person]).

Due to this, to each variable declared in the database, corresponds, a word family. It includes all of the inflection forms of the word (masculine singular (ms), masculine plural (mp), feminine singular (fs),...) (e.g. enseignant [teacher] →{enseignant (ms) [teacher], enseignants (mp) [teachers], enseignante (fs) [teacher], enseignantes (fp) [teachers]} and the set of its synonyms. (e.g. enseignant ® {maitre,...} [teacher ® {schoolmaster,...}]).

Verb

The verb of the query expresses the link between two classes or a class and one of its attribute. Then, the verb is transitive. To each created verb, corresponds conjugate forms (3rd person of the singular (s), 3rd person of the plural (p)) (e.g. habiter [to live] ® {habite (s) [lives], habitant (p) [live]} and the set of its synonyms (e.g. (habiter) ® {résider, demeurer,...} [to live ® {to reside, to dwell,...}]).

All the nouns and verbs usually depend heavily on the application. They constitute the lexicon. The initial set of synonyms is created with electronic dictionaries such that Wolf and Crisco and then proposed to expert individual who can modify it to reflect the specific senses of the DB application domain. The sibling relation that exists between the words of the same family permits the database requester to use any of them without affecting the meaning of the query. Thus, a family of words is represented by a single term called the stem which can be the first generated word in natural language.

Value

On the other hand, a value in the query is an instance of a simple attribute. It is identified via a dialogue with the database requester. If an attribute is designated by the DB administrator as key then its value is said to be key and non-key otherwise. A key value can specify a class. For example, in the query "what is the salary of Linda", Linda specifies the class "Employee" then it is a key value. However, in the query "what is the name of the module which has the coefficient 4", the value '4' is not key value because it specifies no class.

Description

Application dependent noun

Depending on the relation of the word to the database being handled, an application dependent noun is described, in the lexicon, by its stem and its semantic value which can be 'C' if it is about a class, 'SA' of a simple attribute or 'CA' of a composite attribute. In the description of a simple attribute, we add the stem of the class containing it and in the case of a composite attribute, the stem of the referenced class by the composite attribute. For example, the composite attribute 'matières' [matters] is described by its stem 'matière' [matter], its semantic value 'AC' and the stem of its referenced class 'module' [module].

Verb

A verb is described by its subject which is the class that contains it and its object which is either a declared attribute in the subject class or a referenced class by a composite attribute of the subject class. It is formally described by its stem, the stem of the subject entity and the stem of the object entity. For example, the verb 'habiter' [to live] is described by its stem 'habiter' [to live], the stem of the subject entity 'personne' [person] and the stem of the object entity 'ville' [town].

Inheritance Relationship

The inheritance relationship in the NLDB is an extension of the traditional inheritance relationship 'HERITE' in an OODB and is given by the relation Herite*. It allows handling the NLQ on a given class using the properties of the class itself or those of its super-classes and subclasses.

The extended inheritance relationship allows moving in both directions up and down the hierarchy of the classes. The direct inheritance relationship 'herite' is defined as follows:

```
Let CLASSE be classes stems of a NLDB.
herite: CLASSExCLASSE → {0,1}
                (x,y) → herite (x,y)
{

   herite (x, y): = 1 if NW⁻¹ (x) HERITE NW⁻¹ (y)/*
 NW(v) = x/'v' is a variable in the OODB and 'x' is the
 word corresponding in natural language */
   herite (x, y):= 0 otherwise;
   }
 The relation Herite* is defined as follows:
    Herite*: CLASSExCLASSE → {0,1}
                     (x,y) → Herite* (x,y)
   {
   Herite*: = 1
        if (x = y) or (x ≠ y and (herite (x, y)
        or herite (y, x))
        or (x ≠ y and ∃ C1, C2,... Cn ∈ CLASSE/
        herite (x, C1)
        and (∀i ∈ [1, n–1] herite (Ci, Ci+1))
        and  herite (Cn, y)
        or (x ≠ y and ∃ C1, C2,... et Cn ∈ CLASSE/
        herite (y, Cn)
        and (∀i ∈ [1, n–1] herite (Ci+1, Ci)
        and herite (C1, x))
   Herite*: = 0 otherwise;
   }
```

Reference Relationship

Let M_1 be a class, M_2 its composite attribute, M_3 the referenced class and $R_{1,2}$ a relation connecting M_1 and M_2. The relation $R_{1,2}$ is also applicable between the class of definition M_1 and the referenced class M3. It represents a direct reference link between these two classes. This relation is called the reference relationship in a NLDB. It is an extension of the traditional reference relationship in an OODB. It allows generating the verbs of the NLDB. We notice that the existence of a reference relationship, does not base itself on a criterion according to these links, but that it is random, thus the solutions in that case relaying on a linguistic analysis which indicates for all the roads of (direct) reference, the existence or the nonexistence of a verb of relation.

They translate direct reference links between the classes. In that case, the existence of the verb can create a indirect reference link (e.g. travailler (chercheur, projet) [to work (searcher, project)] and appartenir (projet, laboratoire) [to belong (project, Laboratory)] Þ travailler (chercheur, laboratoire) [to work (searcher, Laboratory)]). NOTE. - The deducted relations can be calculated by combining the reference links and the links of inheritance (e.g. assurer (enseignant, module) [to ensure (teacher, module)] and Herite* (enseignant, personne) [Herite* (teacher, person)] Þ assurer (personne, module))

Let Ref be an extension of the defined reference relationship previously. This relation is defined as follows:

```
 Let 'ac' be a composite attribute.
  Ref: CLASSExCLASSE → {0,1}
               (x, y) → Ref (x, y)
  {
       Ref (x, y): = 1 if/* exists 'ac'/'x' is the class
 where 'ac' is defined or its sub or super-class and the
 class 'y' is the domain of 'ac' or a indirect reference link
 between the classes 'x' and 'y' */
  Ref (x, y): = 0 else;
  }
```

QUERY SEMANTIC VALIDATION

A NLQ consists of one or two NGs articulating around a verb. We consider a NG constituted by one or several keywords. A keyword is an application dependent noun or a value. So, the process of the validation of the query consists in:

- keyword's identification in the NG; In the case of a NG formed by an identified single keyword, no supplementary treatment is necessary since only one component is used: the NG is valid. If the NG is constituted by more than a keyword and that one of them is not identified, the NG is considered as erroneous. Should the opposite occur, it is necessary to carry out the NG's semantic validation.
- If the query is constituted by a valid NG, no furtheranalysis is required. If the query covered two valid NGs with an identified verb, it is a subject of studying the semantic coherence of the verb with its arguments.

Keyword's Identification

The first step of the analysis is to determine if a word of the query is a keyword. For this, we define a simple semantic filter denoted SF as the set of triplets {(*, *, w)} associated with the semantic value w. The first star in the triplet represents the lexical information while the second designates the syntactic information associated with the word. For an application dependent noun, a semantic filter is defined by:

SF_N<w> = {(*, Noun, w)/w Î {C (class), SA (simple attribute), CA (composite attribute)}} where the star represents the word's stem. For instance, to represent the word 'students' that matches the class 'Student'; we would have the semantic filter SF_N including the triplet (student, Noun, C). Likewise, the semantic filter, for a value, has the same structure except that the category w takes values from the set:

w = {VK (Value_as_Key), VN_K (Value_None_Key)} and the tagging information is the value in the first case, hence SF_V = {(*, value, w)}. For The number '4' in the NG "coefficient 4", we have the triplet (4, value,

VNK). From the query "what is the salary of the teacher Linda", salary Î SF_N<SA>, teacher Î SF_N<C> and Linda Î SF_V<VK> then all words are semantically correct.

The process of identification of a keyword 'mi' consists mainly in determining the corresponding simple semantic filter. It is defined by the following function: Function Ident (m_i): boolean

```
{
ident: = 1 if\exist\ω∈{C, SA, CA, VK, VNK}/
(mi, *, *) ∈ SFN<ω> ∪ SFV<ω>
ident:= 0 otherwise;
}
```

NG's Semantic Validation

In the case of a NG formed by several identified keywords, it is necessary to verify if the complex NG respects the conceptual constraints (semantic coherence constraints) of the domain database which amounts to associate semantic relations between every two consecutive keywords in the NG. These relations mainly refer to inheritance or reference relationships. They are based on the semantic values of the keywords and their combination in the NG. For example, the NG 'salaire de l'enseignant' [salary of the teacher] is valid because the class 'enseignant' uses the attribute 'salaire' of its super class 'employé' [employee]. Thus, at the combination 'simple attributeclass' (SA-C), we must have an inheritance relationship between the class that contains the attribute (i.e. 'employé') and the specified class in the NG (i.e. 'enseignant').

Before giving the coherence constraints, we need to introduce some notations and notions:

- A part of a NG constituted by the succession of two keywords x and y is noted x – y.
- if (m, *, *) Î FSX (w)/w Î {SA, C, CA, VK, VNK} and x Î {N, V}, the keyword 'm' is respectively noted SA', C', CA', VK', VNK'.
- A class can be manipulated through its name, the name of the composite attribute which references it or a key value which is the value of its key attribute (e.g. 'module', 'matter' and 'Compilation' specify the same class 'module'). For that, 'class' will indicate these three information.

In what follows we take:

X_i: = Classe (m_i) if m_i = C'
X_i: = Class-ref (m_i) if m_i = CA'
X_i: = Class (Attrib (m_i)) and Y_i: = Attrib (m_i)
if $m_i \in$ {SA', VK', VNK'}

where Classe is a function which returns, for a class, thestem of this one and for a simple attribute that of the class where it is defined. Attrib gets, for a simple attribute or for a value, the stem of this attribute and Class-ref, for a composite attribute, the stem of its referenced class.

Semantic Coherence Constraints

The combination (COMB) of two keywords according to their semantic value is governed by a set of rules called coherence rules (CR). Based on the patterns of combination, we have formulated coherence constraints (CC) that express the semantic relation between these words.

CR_1: a class can be specified by either its super class or subclass. A class indicated by a key value cannot be specified by a class indicated by another key value. A key value can specify at most one class. The semantic relation is an inheritance relationship.

COMB1: $m_i \in$ {C', CA', VK'} and $m_{i+1} \in$ {C', CA', VK'} /if m_i = VK' then $m_{i+1} \neq$ VK'
CC_1 ($m_i - m_{i+1}$): **Herite* (X_i, X_{i+1})**

CR_2: a simple attribute can be specified by its value. The attribute corresponding to the value must be identical to the specified attribute in the query and their class respective too.

COMB2: $m_i \in$ {SA'} and $m_{i+1} \in$ { VK', VNK'} or $m_i \in$ {VK', VNK'} and $m_{i+1} \in$ {SA'},
CC_2 ($m_i - m_{i+1}$): **$Y_i = Y_{i+1}$; $X_i = X_{i+1}$**

CR_3: a simple attribute of a class can be used by its class, its super-classes or sub-classes. The semantic relation is an inheritance relationship.

COMB3: $m_i \in$ {C', CA', VK'} and $m_{i+1} \in$ {SA'} or $m_i \in$ {SA'} and $m_{i+1} \in$ {C', CA', VK'},
CC_3 ($m_i - m_{i+1}$): **Herite* (X_i, X_{i+1})**

CR_4: a class is associated with another class if there exits a reference link between these classes. The semantic relation is a reference relationship.

COMB4: $m_i \in$ {C', CA', VK'} and $m_{i+1} \in$ {C', CA', VK'},
CC_4 ($m_i - m_{i+1}$): **Ref (X_i, X_{i+1})**

Algorithm of NG Validation

The operation of validation of a NG constituted by several identified keywords m1-m2-...-mn consists in finding a pattern of the combination for every two consecutive words mi and mi+1 for i Î [1, n–1] and verifying the correspondent semantic relation CC_j ($m_i - m_{i+1}$).

The algorithm of validation is defined as follows:

```
{
i: = 1;
if i = n then
/ * NG ≡ 1 keyword */

  if Ident (mi) then 'valid NG' else 'Erroneous NG'
  else
  /* NG ≡ several keywords */
  while (i < n ∧ Ident (mi) ∧ Ident (mi+1) ∧∃ j ∈ [1,4]/
  CCj (mi – mi+1)) do
  i: = i + 1; end;
  if i = n then 'valid NG' else 'Erroneous NG'
  }
```

Semantic Coherence of the Verb with Its Arguments

In the lexicon, a verb is described with its real subject (RS) and its real object (RO). In a query, the subject of a verb is one of keywords of the subject NG which really carries out the action. It is noted (QS). The object is generally the first keyword of object NG which undergoes the action. It is noted (QO).

A verb is compatible with its subject NG (QS) and its complement (QO) if:

- QS is identical to RS or it is its super or sub class because the subject is always a class;
- The object is a class, then QO must be identical to QS or be its super or sub class;
- The object is an attribute (or a value of an attribute) then the attribute QO must be identical to QS.

Example of Query's Validation

To understand the following example and the examples of illustration quoted in the text, we give an extract of a NLDB on the University of Oran, in French and its equivalent in English. The adopted syntax is the following one:

<class> ({<mother class>}, <attribute$_1$>, <attribute$_2$>,... <attribute$_n$> , verb$_1$, verb$_2$,...)
Personne ({}, nom, ville, habiter)
Employé ({Personne}, salaire)
Enseignant ({Employé}, matière: Module)
Chercheur ({Enseignant}, projet: Projet)
Module ({}, nom, coefficient)
Projet ({}, laboratoire: laboratoire)
Laboratoire ({} ...)

Person ({}, name, town, to live)
Employee ({Person}, salary)
Teacher ({Employee}, matter: Module)
Searcher ({Teacher}, project: Project)
Module ({}, name, coefficient)
Project ({}, laboratory: laboratory)
Laboratory({}...)

Example: 'Donner le salaire des enseignants de Compilation qui habitent Oran' [Give the salary of teachers of Compilation who live in

Oran]
Verb = habiter;
$NG1 = m_1 - m_2 - m_3$ = noms – enseignants – Compilation;
$m_1 \in SF_N<SA>$, $m_2 \in SF_N<C>$, $m_3 \in SF_V<VK>$,
$m_1 - m_2 = COMB_3$;
CC_3 = Herite* (Classe (Attrib (nom)), Classe (enseignants)) = Hérite* (employée, enseignant): = true;
$m_2 - m_3 = COMB_4$ = Ref (Classe (enseignants), Classe (Attrib (Compilation))) = Ref (enseignant, module): = true;
NG2 = Oran; $m \in SF_V<VNK>$,
In the lexicon, we have: habiter (personne, ville) and in the query habiter (enseignant, Oran);

Herite* (personne, enseignant): = true, Attrib (Oran) = ville.

The keywords are identified, the CCj between them validated and the verb is coherent with its arguments, and then the query is valid

EXPERIMENTAL RESULTS

To evaluate the performance of the system, we have tested our system on 120 significant queries collected from the students of computer department of university Oran. 7 queries were disregarded because they did not cover the BD application domain. Of the remaining queries, 102 queries were correctly analyzed (i.e. success rate 90, 26%). The errors were mainly due to unregistered keywords in the lexicon. Our lexicon contains nouns, verbs and their various synonyms that typically are used in a particular domain. Their semi-automatic generation involves inevitably false results. A better solution for the interface is the integration of a learning system to enrich the lexicon.

CONCLUSIONS

Our work proposes a method of query's validation for OODB. Define a query key information to be analyzed semantically: its structure from one part and its sense from another part, express the link which connects them and the method of handling them were the strong problems which we tried to solve.

There is not dependency between our system and the DB application domain. When changing one DB to another, the only change occurs at the lexicon. Nevertheless, the study present limits relating to selected requests model (a request includes only one subject, only one complement and only one verb). These limits carried out knowingly, into a qualitative aim, make that, the developed tools remain incomplete but can be wide to more complex queries.

Also note that, the presented information is necessary in NLDB, to treat the second aspect of the semantics which is the translation of the NLQ to formal language query such as OQL [16].

REFERENCES

1. A.Copestake and K. S. Jones, "Natural Language Interfaces to Databases," The Knowledge Engineering Review, Vol. 5, No. 4, 1989, pp. 225-249.
2. I. Androutsopoulos, G. Ritchie and P. Thanisch, "Natural Language Interfaces to Databases – An Introduction," Journal of Language Engineering, Vol. 1, No. 1, 1995, pp. 29-81.
3. J. Chae and S. Lee, "Natural Language Query Processing in Korean Interface for Object-Oriented Databases," Proceedings of First International Workshop on Applications of Natural Language to Databases (NLDB'95), Versailles, 1995, pp.81-94.
4. P. Reis, J. Matias and N. Mamede, "Edite – A Natural Language Interface to Databases: A New Dimension for an Old Approach," Proceedings of the Fourth International Conference on Information and Communication Technology in Tourism (ENTER'97), Edinburgh, 1997.
5. Y. Chandra and R. Mihalcea, "Natural Language Interfaces to Databases," Thesis (M. S.), University of North Texas, Denton, 2006.
6. M. Owda, Z. Bandar and K. Crockett, "Conversation Based Natural Language Interface to Relational Databases," International Conference on Web Intelligence/IAT Workshops, 2007, pp. 363-367.
7. M. Minock, P. Olofsson and A. N. Aslund, "Towards Building Robust Natural Language Interfaces to Databases," Proceedings of the 13th International Conference on Natural Language and Information

Systems, Berlin, 2008, pp 187-198.

8. J. Robie and D. Bartels, "A Comparison between Relational and Object Oriented Databases for Object Oriented Application Development," POET Software Corporation 800-950-8845, 1994.

9. J. Clifford and D. S. Warren, "Formal Semantics for Time in Databases," ACM Transactions on Database Systems, Vol. 8, No. 2, June 1983, pp. 215-254.

10. R. A. Frost and P. Boulos, "An Efficient Compositional Semantics for Natural Language Database Queries with Arbitrarily-Nested Quantification and Negation," Lecture Notes in Computer Science, Vol. 2338, 2002, pp. 252-267.

11. H. D. Lee and J. C. Park, "Interpretation of Natural Language Queries for Relational Database Access with Combinatory Categorial Grammar," International Journal of Computer Processing of Oriental Languages, Vol. 15, No. 3, 2002, pp. 281-304.

12. R. A. Frost and R. J. Fortier, "An Efficient Denotational Semantics for Natural Language Database Queries," Natural Language Processing and Information Systems, Vol. 4592, 2007, pp. 12-24.

13. A. M. Popescu, O. Etzioni and H. Kautz, "Towards a Theory of Natural Language Interfaces to Databases," Proceedings of the 8th International Conference on Intelligent User Interfaces, Miami, 2003, pp. 149-157.

14. J. Little, M. Ga, T. Ozyer and R. Alhajj, "Query Builder: A Natural Language Interface for Structured Databases," Lecture Notes in Computer Science, Vol. 3280, 2004, pp. 470-479.

15. V. Boonjing and C. Hsu, "A New Feasible Natural Language Query Method," International Journal on AI Tools, Vol. 15, No. 2, 2006, pp. 323-330.

16. G. G. R. Cattel, "ODMG-93 Standard des Bases de Données Objet,"Addison-Wesley, Boston, 1995.

CHAPTER 5

INTEGRATING ACAD WITH GIS FOR CIVIL ENGINEERING APPLICATIONS

Asma Thamir Ibraheem, Haidar Alaa Hassan, Mustefa Husam Abd Al-Husain

Keywords: CAD, Civil Engineering, Computer, GIS, Spatial Data

INTRODUCTION

Geographic information system (GIS) integrates hardware, software, and data for capturing, managing, analyzing, and displaying all forms of geographically referenced information.

GIS allows users to view, understand, question, interpret, and visualize data in many ways that reveal relationships, patterns, and trends in the form of maps, globes, reports, and charts. Also GIS helps the user to answer questions and solve problems by looking at data in a way that is quickly understood and easily shared. GIS technology can be integrated into any enterprise information system framework [1].

A GIS is most often associated with a map. A map, however, is only one way that can work with geographic data in a GIS, and only one type of product generated by a GIS. A GIS can provide a great deal more problemsolving capabilities than using a simple mapping program or adding data to an online mapping tool (creating a "mash-up"). A GIS can be viewed in three ways [2]:

- The Database View: A GIS is a unique kind of database of the world—a geographic database (geo-database). It is an "Information System for Geography." Fundamentally, a GIS is based on a structured database that describes the world in geographic terms.
- The Map View: A GIS is a set of intelligent maps and other views that show features and feature relationships on the earth's surface. Maps of the underlying geographic information can be constructed and used as "windows into the database" to support queries, analysis, and editing of the information.
- The Model View: A GIS is a set of information transformation tools that derive new geographic datasets from existing datasets. These geoprocessing functions take information from existing datasets, apply analytic functions, and write results into new derived datasets.

HISTORICAL BACKGROUND

Several developments in the field of computer sciences during the last few decades helped the realization of the GIS concept. The most important one of course, is the invention of the digital computer during the 1940s.

In 1963, the introduction of a software and hardware system gave birth to computer-aided design (CAD), which had much influence on the development of automatic map drafting systems [3].

Next, the influence of database management systems appeared during the 1970s. The rapid developments during recent years, in areas such as distributed processing systems, continue to shape GISs of the next generation.

Since the number of systems increase readily as a result of the development of the computer techniques and equipment, like satellite scanning systems and the increase of images in digital forms.

Nowadays, numbers of systems have been developed in land use fields, map production, general services and in the private establishments. Most of these systems depend on data taken from maps and can processed to get desired local information in geographical or grid coordinates according to the selected projections; like Arc/Info, Kern Maps 200, computer aided data compilation for the analytical plotters, and INFOCAM for geographical information systems [3].

Citation: A. Thamir Ibraheem, H. Alaa Hassan and M. Husam Abd Al-Husain, "Integrating ACAD with GIS for Civil Engineering Applications," Journal of Software Engineering and Applications, Vol. 5 No. 3, 2012, pp. 138-146. doi: 10.4236/jsea.2012.53021.

Upper management should not mandate GIS technology if local support does not exist. Regional coordination can facilitate and assist local managers in evaluating GIS potentials.

Implementation of a major centralized GIS computing facility is not feasible for every region, but some centralized GIS coordination should be implemented either for the region as a whole or within individual programs. Centralized coordination can facilitate documentation and inventory of existing data bases, assist in coordination with other agencies in digital data transfer and interagency data sharing, and provide other specialized GIS services. The centralized coordination will increase enterprise benefits across the Service and will serve as a focal point for GIS activities within the Service.

Decentralized systems can easily handle incremental increases in users and applications as demand for GIS capabilities increases. Decentralized systems have the advantage of being more acceptable in a complex institutional environment where different organizational entities can better justify operating with a distributed processor. Given the geographically scattered locations of Service offices as well as the concept of eco-region management, "Nodes" and "Satellites" should be developed within each eco-region (or other manageable division such as a state).

GIS AND CAD

The ability of GIS to search databases and perform geographic queries has revolutionized many areas of science and business. It can be invaluable during a decisionmaking process. The information can be presented succinctly and clearly in the form of a map and accompanying report, allowing decision makers to focus on the real issues rather than trying to understand the data. Because GIS products can be produced quickly multiple scenarios can be evaluated efficiently and effectively. For this reason, in today's world, the ability to use GIS is increasingly important [2].

The difference between CAD and GIS systems is becoming blurred with the internal attributes and database linkages enhancing CAD's capabilities. At their core, CAD and GIS are complementary technologies that have evolved largely independently but in parallel over the past 30 years. ESRI's longtime best-of-breed approach provides value to engineers by building better linkages between CAD and GIS systems [4].

As it is clearly in **Figure 1**, the main differences between CAD and GIS are:

- GIS is a database program, and CAD is a graphics program.
- With CAD, it's the lines that are important, i.e. the drawing is the information.
- With GIS, the lines are just a representation of the data behind it.
- GIS data model, while similar to CAD approach in that it uses coordinates, is fundamentally different in its simplicity and approach.

Although there are some similarities between CAD and GIS there are many differences. The most fundamental difference is that GIS models the world as it exists, whereas CAD models artifacts yet to be produced. As a result the data manipulated by a GIS is an order of magnitude larger and more complex than CAD systems have to deal with, and the nature of the data, its sources and its uses are quite different.

GIS TECHNOLOGY

GIS technology is increasingly being considered for implementation in many infrastructure planning and management systems, due to its superior spatial data handling capabilities. Textual databases are combined with digitized maps to enable the visual display of various data on a map. GIS technology plays an increasing role in the development of new pavement management applications for all concerned transportation agencies. The sophisticated database in a GIS has the ability to associate and manipulate diverse sets of spatially referenced data that have been geo-coded to a common referencing system. GIS can expand the decision making on repair strategies and project scheduling by incorporating such diverse data as accident histories, and vehicle volumes. A GIS can perform geographic queries in a straightforward, intuitive fashion rather than being limited to textual queries. Thus GIS are now used by [5]:

- Business;
- Tourism;
- Communications;
- Defence and Intelligence;
- Educators;
- Engineering;
- Cellular Network;
- Environmental Management;
- Government;
- Health and Human Services;
- Natural Resources;

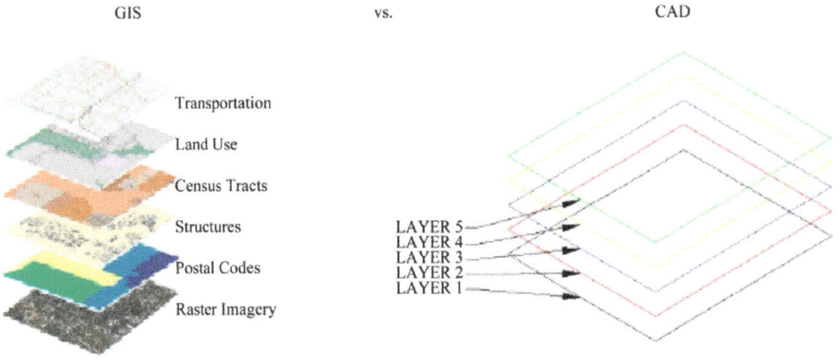

Figure 1: GIS vs. CAD [4].

- Transportation;
- Utilities.

Also GIS are used for the following common reasons [6]:

- GIS is computer based, and has all the advantages (and disadvantages) of a computer tool;
- GIS is established in many workplaces and has proven not to be a passing fad;
- GIS can be an accurate, efficient, effective and scientific tool;
- GIS can be used to improve organizational integration;
- GIS helps to make better decisions;
- GIS makes maps.

BENEFITS OF GIS

The common benefits of GIS are as follows [7]:

- Ensures current, accurate data by Public Safety GIS experts;
- Provides standardized process for timely data delivery for your GIS environment;
- Affords varying levels of service available from one company (advanced to basic);
- Provides data in standardized ESRI formats;
- Increases control of data maintenance;
- Offers seamless service: we are divided into teams for cross-functional project overlap;
- Offers largest public safety GIS staff in the industry;
- Provides cost efficiencies of hiring a contractor.

GIS APPLICATIONS IN CIVIL ENGINEERING

With increasingly complex projects, the interaction of often international multidisciplinary functions requires the introduction of effective and efficient data management and sharing solutions. GIS provides the civil engineer with tools for creating, managing, analyzing and visualizing all types of geographic information. GIS is now being used by Civil Engineers in every application domain and throughout every aspect of the enterprise, be it on the desktop, in the field, or in collaboration with others.

Some of these applications are, as it is concluded in **Figure 2**:

- Centralized Data Management;
- Asset Management;
- Transportation;
- Water Resources;
- Environmental Monitoring.

INTEGRATING ACAD WITH GIS

CAD tools combined with GIS data, is a powerful tool to the land-use suitability analysis problem. Essential components of this combination are the decision maker's preferences, tradeoff evaluations, and assessments of the importance of criteria for any transportation project.

Nowadays geographic information systems (GIS) and CAD are widely used in different applications. Experience shows that the combination of GIS and CAD is an efficient tool for selection best route for distributed linear objects such as railways, roads and pipelines. And selection best location for distributed polygonal objects such as rail station, landfill, park and etc.

Also geographic information systems (GISs) are appropriate for managing and accessing digital library data, and particularly collections of spatial data such as maps or images of the earth. But, they are also appropriate for any collection that can be geographically referenced. Furthermore, advanced GIS tools can link library collections; that is, GIS and coordinate information can be used as a general purpose indexing system to library collections. This would make it possible to access virtually all objects collected by a library that are geographically referenced.

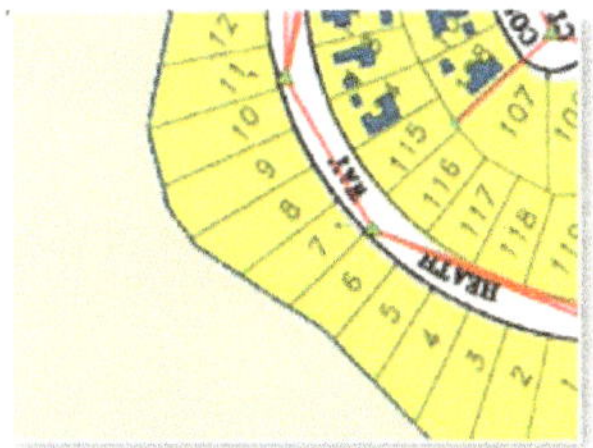

Centralised Data Management
GIS portal technology provides the ideal environment managing and sharing information collected during engineering projects.

AssetManagement
GIS is a powerful framework for monitoring the use and distribution of assets, tracking location, condition and age of capital assets and infrastructure, and measuring asset lifecycles, maintenance costs and depreciation.

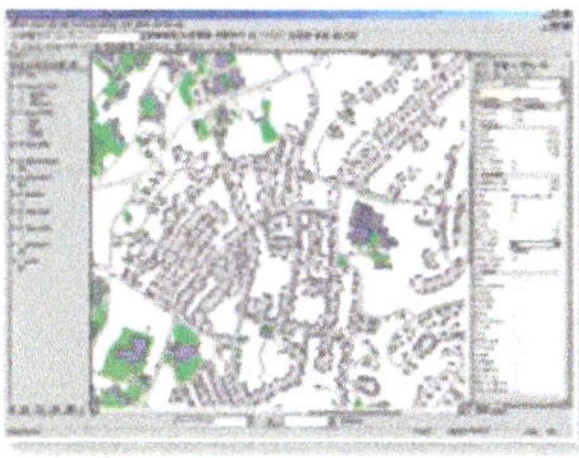

Transportation
Transport projects utilise GIS to bring together data to enhance decision making.

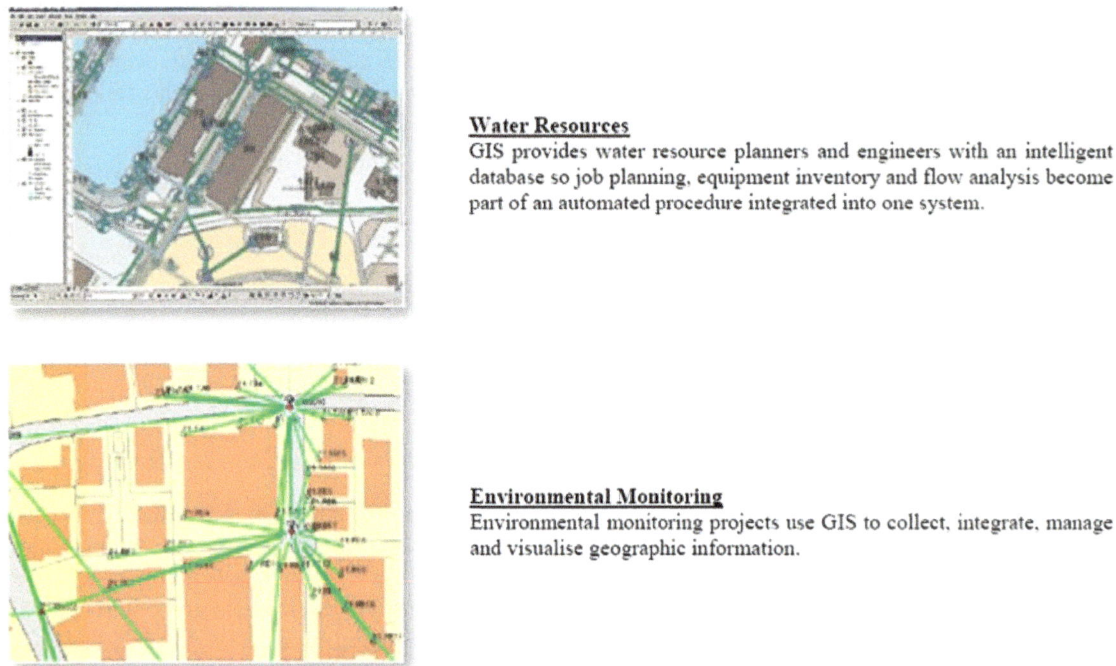

Figure 2: GIS applications in civil engineering [7].

DEVELOPING GIS MAPS BY USING ACAD SOFTWARE

AutoCAD allows the use of nearly 300 tools. Some operators prefer using the word "commands", although command as an alternative to tool is not in common use today. The abbreviations for tools which can be abbreviated are included in brackets after the tool name. Tool names can be entered in upper or lower case [8]. The main tool is how to make the required layers. **Figure 3**shows the Layer Properties Manager.

By this way, nineteen layers were built in this paper for the case study as it is clear in **Figure 4**.

DEVELOPING GIS MAPS BY USING ARCVIEW SOFTWARE

ArcView is a Geographical Information System, GIS, which runs on a wide variety of different computer systems, (often called "platforms"). ArcView behaves in exactly the same way on each of these platforms. There are some tools in ArcView, which cannot operate in certain computing environments; these have been introduced as "Extensions" from ArcView Release 3.3 and will only be met in the more advanced, optional, units of this tutorial.

In ArcView terminology, a View comprises one or more Themes. Each theme is simply a distinct set of information such as roads or rivers or county boundaries etc., rather like the different layers that can be used to build up a map. In addition, each Theme has its own legend, which is a list of the symbology used. Note how the name of the theme with its symbol appears in the View Legend area, together with a little selection box just to the left of the name.

Figure 5 shows the ACAD map showing some of the districts of al Nahrain University, which are developed in the previous section. This map is used as the base of building a new GIS to make an initial data base for the university site.

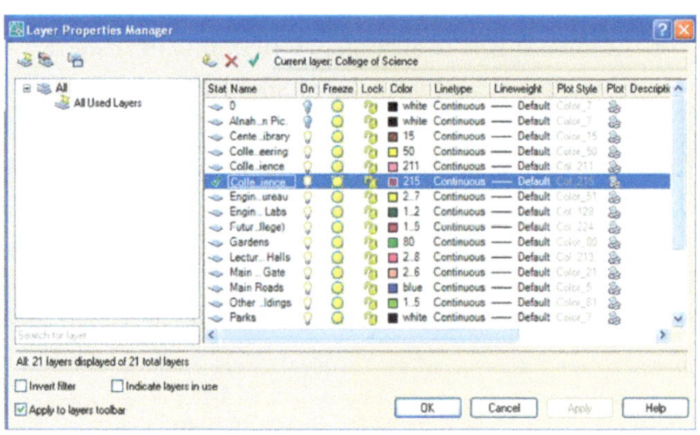

Figure 3: The layer properties manager.

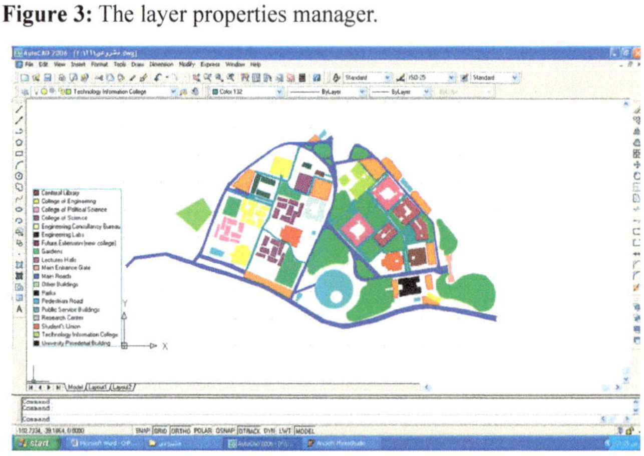

Figure 4: The layers of nahrain university site map.

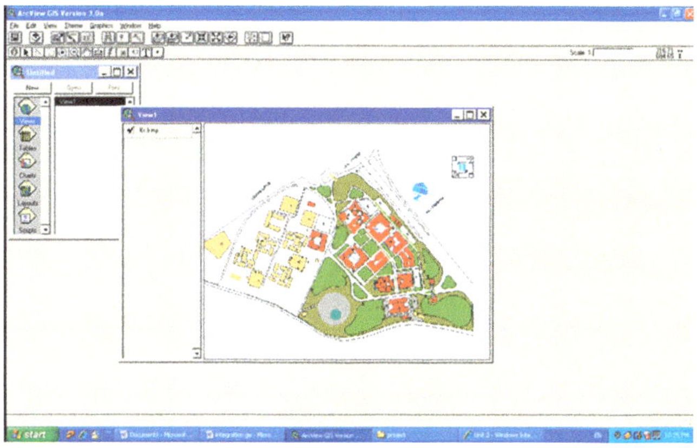

Figure 5: Map selection.

In order to add a new theme to the view, the following steps should be followed:

- Click the Add Theme icon. Alternatively, you can click View on the Menu Bar and then Add Theme from the drop-down menu displayed.
- You should now see the Add Theme dialogue box as shown in Figure 6, which will be listed in the left hand part of the window, although the files and directories listed will, of course, be those, available from the institution.

After saving the new theme we can now to draw a new theme like the circular as shown in **Figure 7**.

By this way we make the following thems:

- Land use theme: in this theme will notice all university buildings content the building that not construct yet as shown in Figure 8.
- Garden theme: this theme contents all the garden of university as shown in Figure 9.
- Park theme: this theme contents all the parks of university as shown in Figure 10.
- Major roads: this theme notices the major roads of the university as shown in Figure 11.

By select all the themes the land use, gardens, parks and major roads the map will be as shown below in **Figure 12**.

Then we can input importance information on any map like name, area and type of any building or road and that can be done by using a TABLE command in this program where a table will appear and we can input all information in it. For Al Nahrain University we input the name of buildings and as it is clear in **Figure 13**.

CONCLUSIONS

On the basis of the project findings, the following conclusions are appropriate:

- GIS has an important application for example in civil engineering projects like involve the management, analysis and integration of large amounts of geographic information to ensure success. This can include a wide range of information such as detailed design drawings originating from CAD solutions, detailed mapping, air photography, geological investigations, population information, traffic flows and environmental models.
- Although there are some similarities between CAD and GIS there are many differences. The most fundamental difference is that GIS models the world as it exists, whereas CAD models artifacts yet to be produced. As a result the data manipulated by a GIS is an order of magnitude larger and more complex than CAD systems have to deal with, and the nature of the data, its sources and its uses are quite different.
- The difference between CAD and GIS systems is becoming blurred with the internal attributes and database linkages enhancing CAD's capabilities.
- GIS is a database program, and CAD is a graphics program. With CAD, it's the lines that are important, i.e. the drawing is the information. With GIS, the lines are just a representation of the data behind it.
- The integration of GIS concepts into civil engineering still faces many challenges. Besides financial and technical problems, the lack of understanding the importance of GIS education by civil engineering educators may be one of the most critical issues that deserve special attention.
- GIS resources on the Internet and GIS on-line activities will benefit education. GIS on-line education should be included in the study domain of spatial information system. This will benefit not only for civil engineers but also other professionals.
- In order to make the linking between CAD and GIS easier and more benefit, the present work shall be re peated by using ArcGIS software.

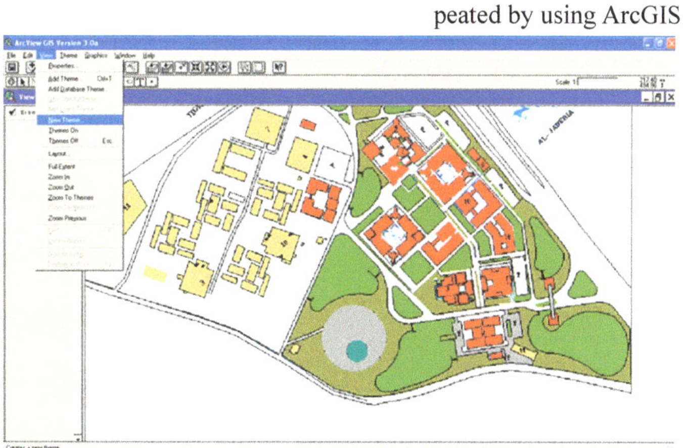

Figure 6: Making theme 1.

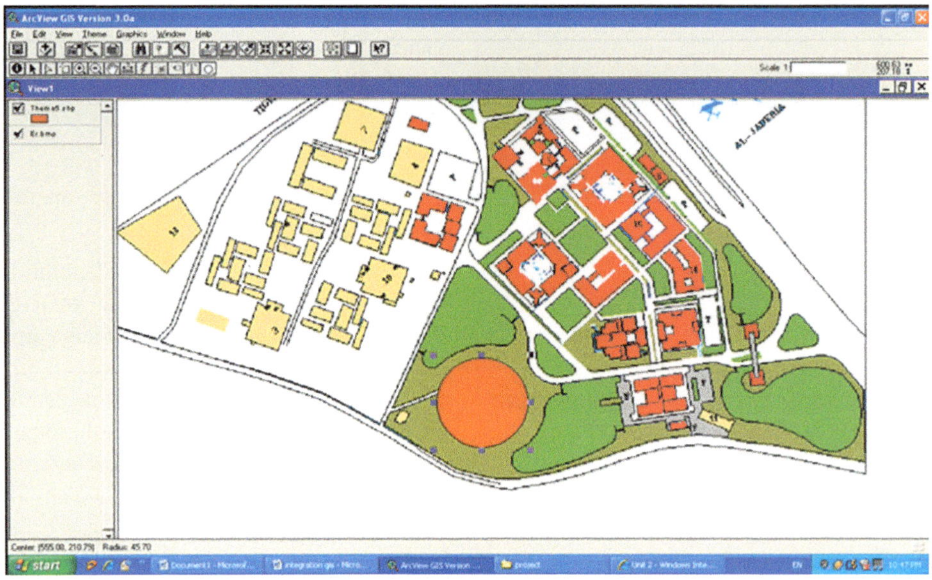

Figure 7: Adding a new theme.

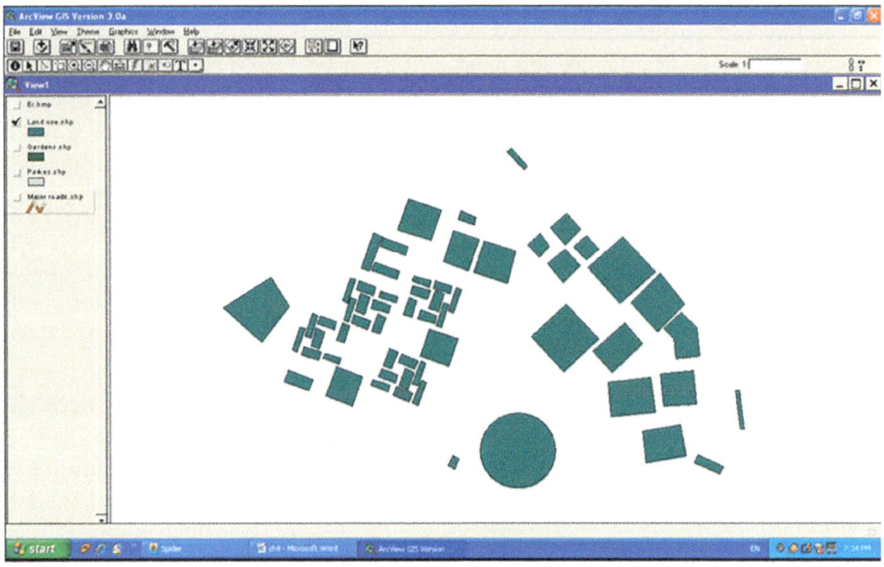

Figure 8: Land use theme.

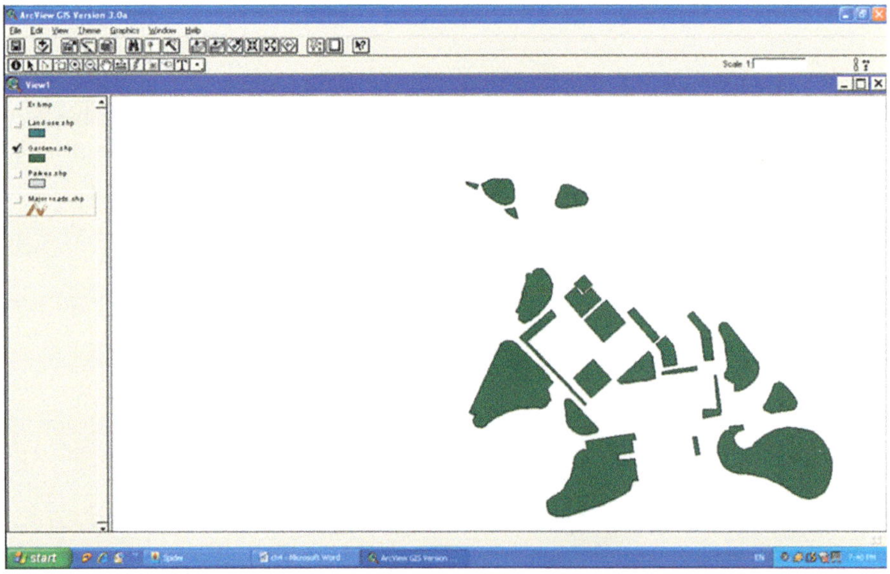

Figure 9: Garden theme.

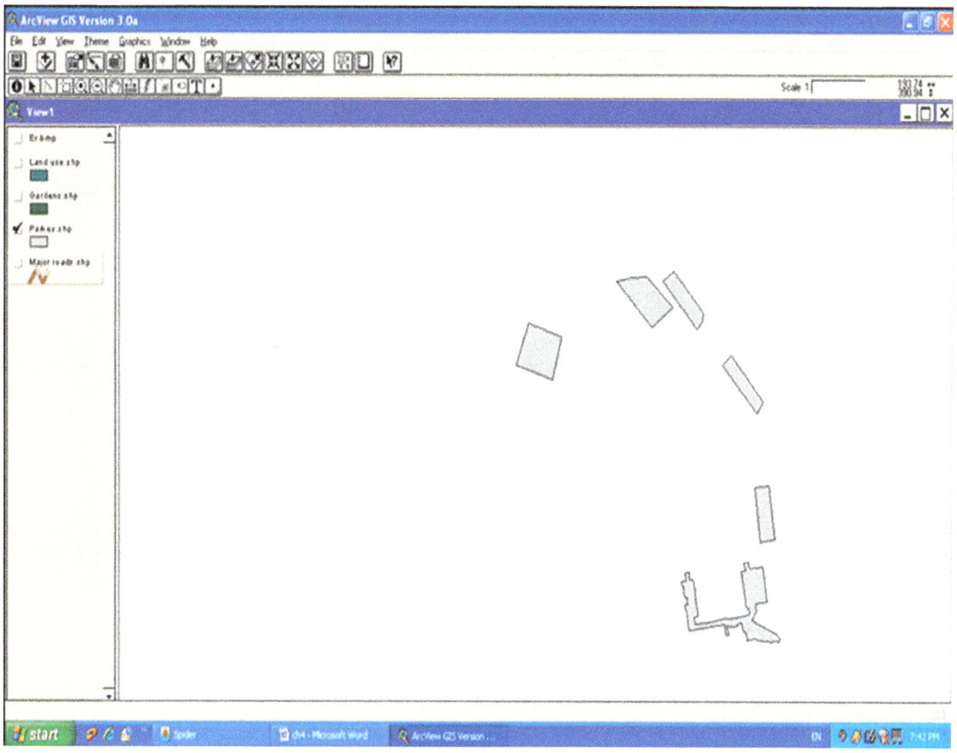

Figure 10: Park theme.

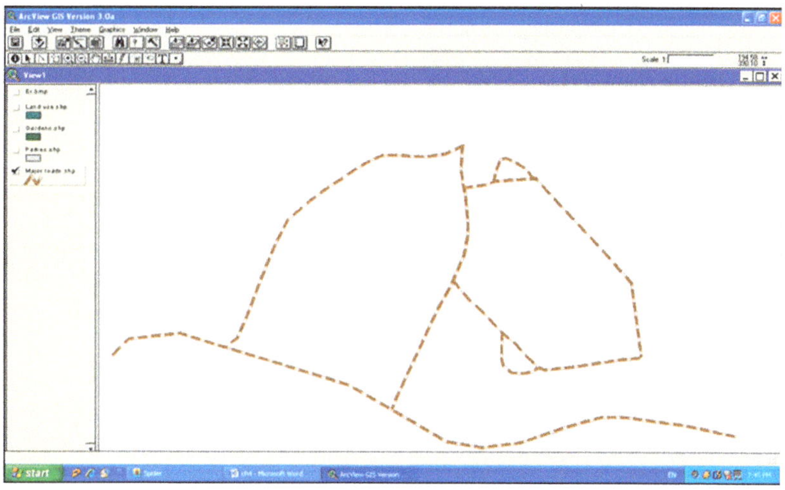

Figure 11: Major road theme.

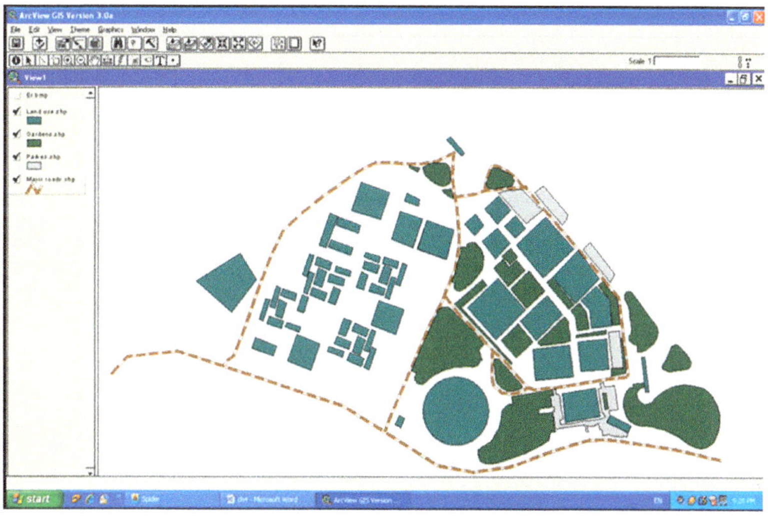

Figure 12: Whole themes.

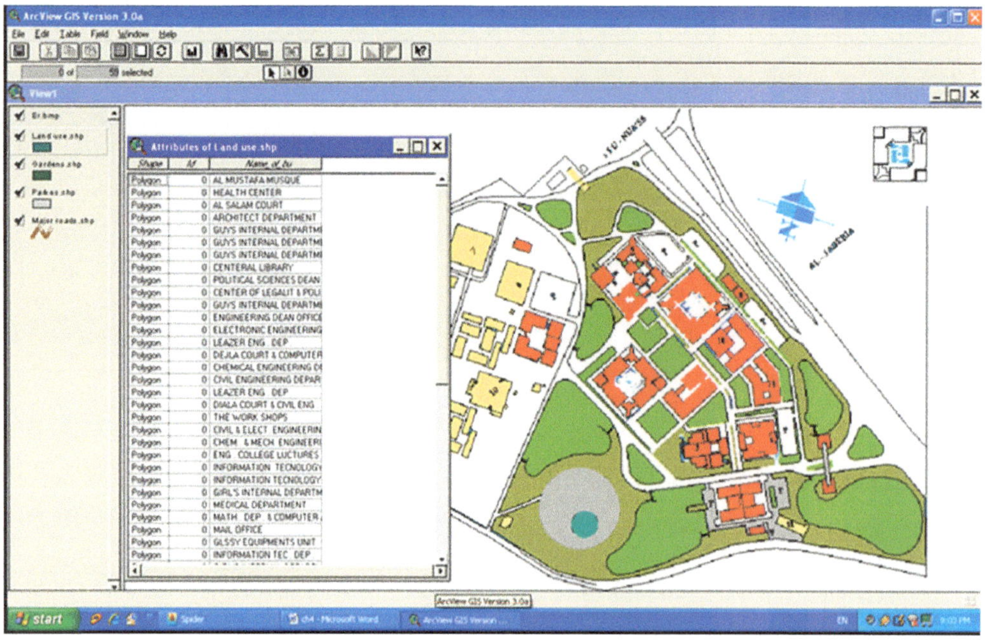

Figure 13: Input data.

REFERENCES

1. J. Dangennond and A. Schutzberg, "Basic of Geographic Information System," Journal of Computing in Civil Engineering, Vol. 12, No. 7, 1998, pp. 121-122. [Paper reference:1]
2. www.GIS.htm, "Geographic Information System," Copyright 2010, Holstead & Redmond Limited, 2010. http://www.gis.com/whatisgis/viewofgis/index.html/ http://www.gis.com/whatisgis/whyusegis.html http://www.gis.com/whatisgis/whatcanyoudowithgis.html http://www.gis.com/implementing_gis/index.html [Paper reference:2]
3. A. Ibraheem, "The Utilization of Local Resources to Develop a GIS in Surveying and Route Design," M.Sc. Thesis, College of Engineering, University of Baghdad, Baghdad, 1997. http://www.scirp.org/journal/paperinformation.aspx?paperid=17099 [Paper reference:2]
4. H. Tim, "CAD versus GIS Which Is Better for Automated Mapping," University of Missouri, Columbia, 2001. [Paper reference:2]
5. T. Bernhardsen, "Geogrphic Information Systems," Wiley Inc., New York, 1999. [Paper reference:1]
6. A. Th Ibraheem and D. A. Falih, "Applying Geographic Information System (GIS) for Maintenance Strategy Selection," Engineering Journal (ENG), Scientific Research Publication, Vol. 4, No. 1, 2012, pp. 44-54. http://www.scirp.org/journal/paperinformation.aspx?paperid=17099 [Paper reference:1]
7. A. Th Ibraheem, "The Application of Geographical Information System in Civil Engineering," Integration Teaching and Research with Community Service, College of Engineering, University of Sharjah, Sharjah, Book No. 87, 2008, pp. 436-455. [Paper reference:2]
8. Y. Alf, "An Introduction to AutoCAD 2006 2D and 3D Design," British Library Cataloguing-in-Publication Data, 2006. [Paper reference:1]

CHAPTER 6

C-LANGUAGE PROGRAMMING FOR DEVELOPMENT OF CONVENTIONAL WATER TREATMENT PLANTS DECISION SUPPORT SYSTEM

Thogare N. Shridhara, Samson O. Ojoawo, Pilli V. Mahaganesha, Mallaura R. Thippeswary, Rahul Anand, Bevinahalli P. Sharath

Keywords: Decision Support System, Treatment Plant, C-Programming, Water Supply

INTRODUCTION

In a simple form, Decision Support System, DSS is any system supporting decision-making, including executive information systems, executive support systems, geographic information systems and software agents [1] . The concept of DSS emerged in the 1970s, as a family of interactive computer-based systems in the field of decision theory and assisting in utilizing data models to solve unstructured problems, especially with great potential in the field of environmental management [2] .

C-programming has emerged as one of the most widely used languages for software development and for DSS. C language supports the powerful low level features like pointer, memory allocation, bit manipulations etc. The features of C language make it possible to see the language for system programming like the development of compiler, interpreter, operating system, system utilities etc.[3] . C language has become the language of choice of two decades among system programmers and application programmers. It is popular because it is powerful and flexible; it is portable; efficient; programmer-oriented; and can be modularized for step-wise refinement [4] .

The overall efficiency of a Water Treatment Plant depends largely on its design and the functionalities of the Unit Processes constituted in it [5] . Most of the design procedures for water treatment plant have been developed using manuals or spreadsheet calculations which are time consuming and costly [6] . Therefore, a DSS is required to speed up the design process and reduce the design cost. The central aim of this study is to develop and employ a DSS tool in the general design of Conventional Water Treatment Plants. A case study of Karkala town, Udupi District, Karnataka State, India has been selected, and the design based on projected population against the year 2043 using C-programming language in Code-Blocks 10.05. Study also focuses on developing an easier, cheaper and user-friendly DSS to assist in selecting appropriate and essential procedures for water treatment process; and to compare the obtained output values of manual design and C-programming. Thus, a general Water Decision Support System named WATER-DSS1 has been developed to reduce the design time and while maximizing the treatment plant efficiency, using Karkala Treatment Plant as a case study.

METHODOLOGY

(A)Study Area

The study area is Karkala Taluk which is located at 13.2°N 74.98°E (Figure 1). It has an average elevation of 81 metres (265 feet) above the Mean Sea Level. It has a population of 25,824 people (according to 2011 census). It has an area of 23.06 sq·km and the annual rainfall is 4372.2 mm. currently the city have 3 MLD of total water supply from the Mundli River. The summer temperature is 38°C and winter temperature is 24°C. Suvarna River has been considered as the source to accomplish the future water demand for Karkala town [4] .

(B)Development of WATER-DSS

The DSS (Decision Support System) in this study is known as WATER-DSS. The development of WATERDSS applies methods of conventional computing practices and programming techniques. WATER-DSS was built by integrating the conceptual design of drinking water treatment through conventional method into a computer program, which has capability as a DSS. The structure design of WATER-DSS [6] is shown in Figure 2.

Citation: Shridhara, T. , Ojoawo, S. , Mahaganesha, P. , Thippeswary, M. , Anand, R. and Sharath, B. (2014) C-Language Programming for Development of Conventional Water Treatment Plants Decision Support System. Computational Water, Energy, and Environmental Engineering, 3, 129-139. doi: 10.4236/cweee.2014.34014.

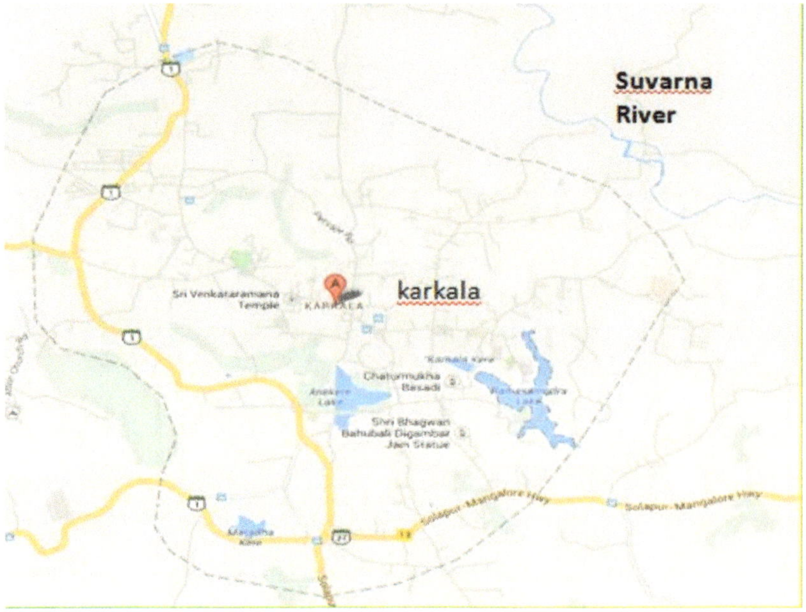

Figure 1. The study area.

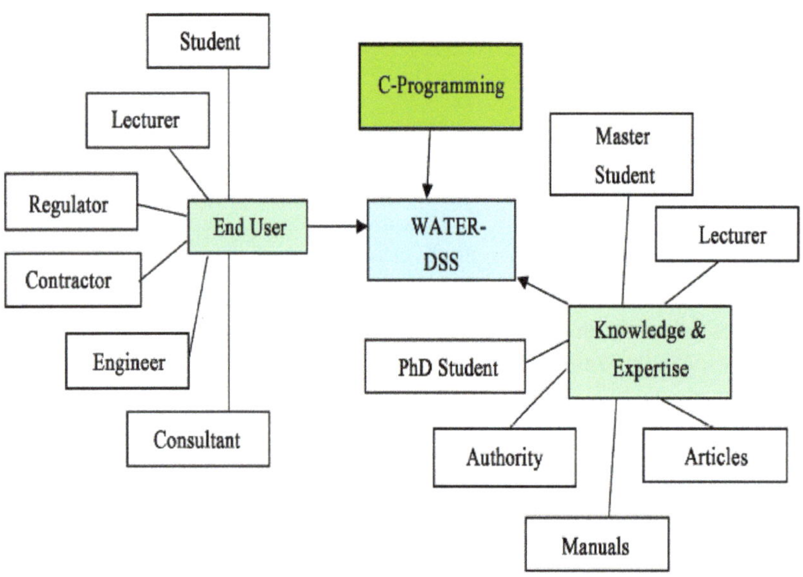

Figure 2: WATER-DSS development structure.

(c) Conventional Water Treatment Plant Units

The units of a typical conventional treatment plant include aeration, plain sedimentation tank, sedimentation aided with coagulation, flocculation, filters, disinfection etc. Figure 3 shows the flowchart of conventional water treatment plant.

(d) Manual design of the Water Treatment Plant ([7] [8])

(i) Forecasting population

The Conventional Water Treatment Plant is being designed for the next 3 decades.

Forecasting population of the study area for 3 decades by the Geometric Increase Method:

If the present is P and the average percentage growth is I_G the population at the end of n decade will be:

$$I_G = P\left[1+\frac{IG}{100}\right]^n$$

So from Table 1, the Expected Population of Karkala by 2043 is 38,396 people.

(ii) Water demand

The water requirement per capita demand of Karkala = 100 LPCD (BIS Code).

Thus, water requirement of Karkala per day = 38,396 ´ 100 = 3,839,600 = 3.84 MLD.

So, the proposed water treatment plant design is of approximately 3.85 MLD in capacity.

(iii) Aeration process

Assuming number of steps = 5 and that tread width, t = 250 mm Diameter of the first step, D_1 = 1 m (including the diameter of pipe)

Diameter of the second step, $D_2 = D_1 + 2t = 1 + 2\times(0.25) = 1.5\ \text{m}$

Diameter of the third step, $D_3 = D_2 + 2t = 1.5 + 2\times(0.25) = 2\ \text{m}$

Diameter of the fourth step, $D_4 = D_3 + 2t = 2 + 2\times(0.25) = 2.5\ \text{m}$

Diameter of the fifth step, $D_5 = D_4 + 2t = 2.5 + 2\times(0.25) = 3\ \text{m}$

Diameter of aeration tank (collector) = $D_5 + 2(1) = 3 + 2 =$ 5 m Further assuming that:

Rise of 1st step = 0.3 m Rise of 2nd step = 0.4 m Rise of 3rd step = 0.5 m Rise of 4th step = 0.6 m Rise of 5th step = 0.7 m Overall Dimension of Aeration tank of diameter 5 m and total height of Cascade is 2.5 m.

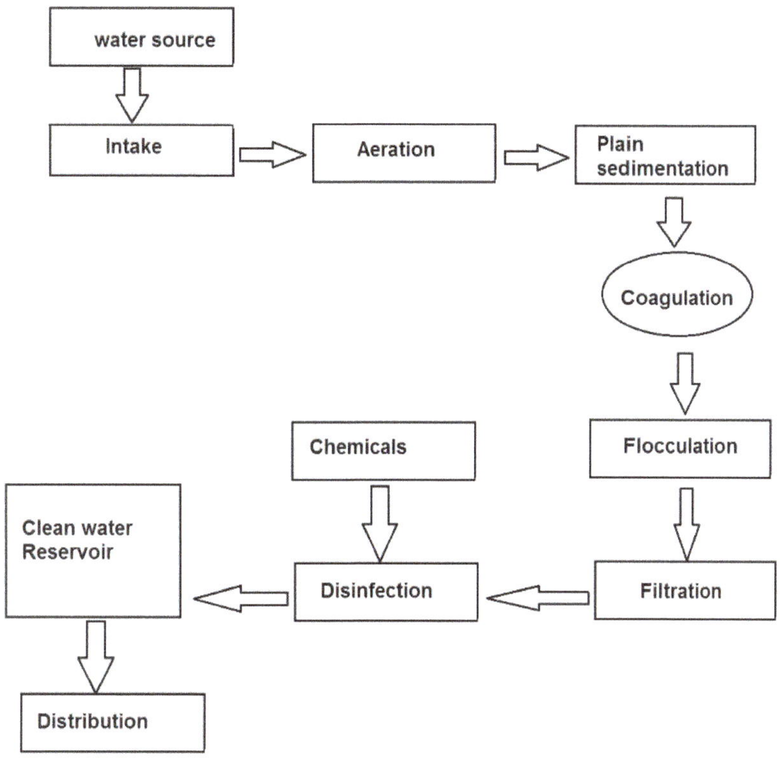

Figure 3: Flowchart of conventional water treatment plant.

Table 1: Forecasting of population for 3 decades

Year	Population	Increase in Population	% Increase in population
1971	18,593	-	
1981	20,713	2120	$\frac{2120}{18,593}\times 100 = 11.402$
1991	24,109	3396	$\frac{3396}{20,713}\times 100 = 16.396$
2001	25,116	1007	$\frac{1007}{24,109}\times 100 = 4.177$
	Total	6523	31.975 %
	Average per decade	2175	10.658 %

Year	Expected Population
2001	$25,116 + \frac{10.658}{100}\times 25,116 = 27,793$
2011	$27,793 + \frac{10.658}{100}\times 27,793 = 30,756$
2021	$30,756 + \frac{10.658}{100}\times 30,756 = 34,007$
2031	$34,007 + \frac{10.658}{100}\times 34,007 = 37,601$
2043	$37,601 + \left(\frac{10.568}{100}\times 37,601\right)\times 0.2 = 38,396$

(iv) Plain sedimentation tank

Quantity of water to be treated in 24 hours = 3.85 ´ 10^6 liters = 3850 m^3.

Quantity of water to be treated by the sedimentation tank during detention period of 6 hours = $\frac{3850}{24} \times 6$ = 962.5 m^3.

Thus the capacity of the sedimentation tank required = 962.5 m^3.

Assume the velocity of flow = 18 cm per min or 0.003 m/s.

Length of the tank required = Velocity of tank (m/s) ´ Detention period (s) = 0.003 ´ (6 ´ 60 ´ 60) = 64.8 m.

Cross section of tank required = $\frac{\text{capacity of tank required (in } m^3)}{\text{Length of tank (in m)}}$ = $\frac{962.5}{64.8}$ = 14.85 m^2.

Assume the depth of water = 4 m which includes allowable allowance for sludge to be made as 80 cm (or 0.8 m).

Required width of tank = $\frac{14.85}{3.2}$ = 4.64 m.

Providing 0.5 m for free board, overall depth of the tank = 4 + 0.5 = 4.5.

Therefore the dimensions of the designed tank are = (64.8 ´ 4.64 ´ 4.5) m.

Note that the length of the tank may be provided in one, two, or three parts depending upon the shape of the area available.

(v) Sedimentation tank aided with coagulants

(1) Chemical feeding

Using alum as coagulant, the optimum quantity of dose will be determined actually by jar test in the laboratory.

Let the optimum dose be 5 - 8 mg/liter.

The average quantity of alum required = $\frac{962.5 \times 10^3 \times 5}{10^6}$ to $\frac{962.5 \times 10^3 \times 8}{10^6}$ = 4.82 to 7.7 kg/day.

The maximum requirement in summer will be 1.5 times more = 7.23 to 11.55 kg/day.

This quantity of alum shall be first mixed with the water to form a solution of 5 strength and then will be added through solution feed device which is given as = 11.55 ´ 20 liters/day = $\frac{11.55 \times 20}{60 \times 24}$ = 0.1604 liters/min.

Minimum dose which will be fed during average demand = $\frac{0.1604}{1.5}$ = 0.1609 liters/min.

Quantity of solution to be fed in 8 hours/day = 0.1604 ´ 60 ´ 8 = 76.99 liters.

Providing solution tank of capacity = 0.07699 m^3 = 0.077 m^3.

Keeping the depth of solution in the tank as 0.35 m and 0.15 m as free board.

The sides of the square tank = $\sqrt{\frac{0.077}{0.35}}$ = 0.4699 m = 0.5 m.

So the designed size of Solution Tank = (0.5 ´ 0.5 ´ 0.5) m.

(2) Approach channel

The flow of channel = $\frac{962.5}{24 \times 60 \times 60}$ = 0.11 m^3/s.

Providing a velocity of 0.4 m/s, the cross sectional area of approach channel = $\frac{0.011}{0.4}$ = 0.0275 m^2.

Provide (0.175 ´ 0.225) m channel with 175 mm water depth and 50 cm free board.

(3) Mixing tank

Mechanical flash mixers will be used for mixing the coagulant solution with the water.

Assuming the detention period of one minute (60 s).

Capacity of flash mixer = 0.11 ´ 60 = 0.66 m^3.

Providing depth of 1m, the sides of the square plan mixing tank = $\sqrt{\frac{0.66}{1}}$ = 0.8 m.

Therefore provide (1 ´ 1 ´ 1) m size of mixing tank with flocculator.

(v) Flocculating Tank

A flocculating tank with mixing slow moving paddles is provided with variable speed electric motors.

Assuming the flocculating time of 30 minutes, the capacity of each flocculating tank = 0.11 ´ 30 = 19.8 m^3.

So, provide a channel of capacity = 19.8 m^3.

Providing 1.6 m depth of water and 10 m of length of channel its width = $\frac{19.8}{1.6 \times 10}$ = 1.2375 m.

Therefore, provide channel of size (10 ´ 1.4 ´ 1.6) m with water depth of water 1.4 m and 0.2 m as free board in continuation on flash mixer.

(vi) Settling Tank

Provide a rectangle sedimentation tank with a square tank with surface loading of 2000 litres/hour/m^2 plan of area.

Surface loading of each tank = $\frac{0.11 \times 60 \times 60 \times 10^3}{2000}$ = 19.8 m^3.

Assume length = 6 m.

Therefore width becomes = $\frac{19.6}{6}$ = 3.3 m.

Therefore weir loading in the settling tank at average flow is given as = $\frac{Q}{\text{Perimeter}}$ = $\frac{962.5}{6 \times 3.3}$ = 48.61 m^3/m/day.

Providing a detention period of 2.5 hours at a time of maximum flow.

Capacity of tank = $\frac{962.5 \times 2.5}{24}$ = 1000.26 m^3.

Now quantity of water to be treated in one hour = $\frac{962.5}{24}$ = 40.104 m^3.

Therefore required depth of tank = $\frac{40.104}{6 \times 3.3}$ = 2.035 m.

Add 0.5 m for storage and 0.5 m for free board, say overall depth = 3 m.

Provide rectangular settling tank (6 ´ 3.3 ´ 3) m. The bottom of the tank is sloped of 1 in 12 pushing the sludge towards the discharging end, with the help of scrappers from where it will be removed by the sludge outlet under hydrostatic pressure of water filled in the tank.

The water will be collected from settling tank over its discharging end along the weir provided all around the water from this channel shall be taken into the rapid gravity filters in covered channels (0.3 ´ 0.3) m.

(vii) Rapid Gravity Filter

Quantity of water to be treated = 3.85 litres/day.

Assume the rate of filtration of rapid gravity filter—2000 litres/m²/hour and also assuming that 30 minutes shall be utilized daily in the back-washing of the filter, the total filter area required = $\frac{3.85\times10^6}{23.5\times2000}$ = 81.92 m².

Provide 4 units of rapid gravity filters with two numbers of stand-by units.

Surface area of each unit = $\frac{81.92}{2}$ = 40.96.

Therefore each unit of size = (6.5 ´ 6.5) m.

(viii) Chlorination Plant

The dose of the chlorine to be added will vary from 0.5 to 1.0 ppm depending on the quantity of water and the chlorine demand tests.

Therefore quantity of chlorine required = $\frac{3.85\times10^3\times0.5}{24\times10\,^\wedge 3}$ = 0.08 kg/hour.

Therefore liquid chlorinator having capacity 0.1 to 5 kg/hour will be installed.

(ix) Underground Reservoir Water

Underground clear water reservoir having capacity of about 8 hours will be provided.

Quantity of water to be stored = 3.85 ´ 10³ m³.

Providing 5 m depth, area of clear water reservoir = $\frac{3.85\times10\,^\wedge 3}{5}$ = 770 m².

So, the dimensions of the designed underground clear water reservoir = (40 ´ 19.25 ´ 5) m.

(x) Design of Pumps (Centrifugal Pumps)

We are adopting two pump stations, one is at source and another is in the middle.

Maximum daily water requirement = 1.5 ´ 3.85 ´ 1000 m³/day = 5.775 ´ 10³ m³/day.

Since Pumping time is 8 hours per day, $Q=\frac{5.775\times10\,^\wedge 3}{8\times60\times60}=0.200\ \text{m}^3/\text{day}$.

Assume: Velocity in pipe, V = 2 m/s.

Now, $V=\frac{Q}{A}=\frac{4Q}{\pi d^2}$,

Therefore $d=\sqrt{\frac{4Q}{\pi d^2}}=\sqrt{\frac{4\times0.200}{\pi\times2}}=0.3568$ m.

Say, therefore d = 0.36 m.

Calculation of total head loss:

Loss of head due to frictionNow,

$$H_f=\frac{flv^2}{2gd}=\frac{0.03\times2000\times2^2}{2\times9.81\times0.36}=33.978.$$

Suction head, H_s = 2.5 m.

Delivery head, H_l = 12.5 m.

Total head, H = 33.978 + 2.5 + 12.5 = 48.978 ≅ 48.98 m.

Therefore the power of pump = $\frac{QwH}{75\mu}=\frac{0.2\times1000\times48.98}{75\times0.8}$ = 163.27.

Pump power ≅ 164 HP.

Provide 41 HP Centrifugal Pumps of six numbers in that two numbers are standby at each pump station.

(e) A portion of Water-DSS1 C-Program for Karkala Treatment Plant Design

The unit processes manually designed above were coded in C-Language and fed into the in Code-Blocks 10.05 software. A portion of the program, for the population forecast, water demand, aeration unit design and underground clear water reservoir, is as shown below:

```
#include
#include
#include
int main()
{
float wr,qty,len,vel,lpcd=100,det,cs,dep,sld,wid,fd,od,dose,alum1,alum2,fd2,dose2,fe,si,de,fl,vi,cs2,wi,den2, ca,dep2,si2,ft,ca2,dep3,wi2,len2;
float sl,sa,len3,wi3,wl,den3,ca3,dep4,qty2,ss,fb,qty3,fa,sa2,s,ae,dep5,s2,stp,tre,dia2,dia3,ris,ris1, count1=0, max, tim,qty4;
float dia4,x,y,total=0,Ig,pn,final_population,result,vel1,dis,hf,th,hp,p1;
int i,popu[125],d,j,n,year[125] ,p;
printf("\nFORECASTING POPULATION OF KARKALA\n");
printf("\nEnter the number of census:\n");
scanf("%d",&n);
for(i=0;i<n;i++)< p=""></n;i++)<>
{
printf("\nEnter the corresponding year:");
scanf("%d",&d);
year[i] =d;
printf("Enter the population in the year %d:",d);
scanf("%d",&popu[i]);
p=popu[i];
```

```
}
for(i=1;i<n;i++)< p=""></n;i++)<>
{
printf("\nIncrease in population in decade %d-%d:",year[i-1], year[i]);
printf("%d\n",popu[i]-popu[i-1]);
x=popu[i]-popu[i-1];
y=x/popu[i-1]*100;
printf("Percentage increase in population of decade %d-%d:",year[i-1],year[i]);
printf("%0.2f percent\n",y);
total=total+y;
}
printf("\nTotal=%0.2f percent\n",total);
Ig=total/(n-1);
printf("Average per Decade=%0.2f percent\n",Ig);
final_population=p*pow((1+(Ig/100)),n);
printf("\nPopulation at the end of %d decades i.e. by the year 2041 is %0.2f",n-1,final_population);
result=final_population*pow(1+(Ig/100),0.2);
printf("\nTherefore Expected population of Karkala by the year 2043 is %0.2f\n",result);
printf("\nThe WATER DEMAND\n");
wr=(result*lpcd)/1000000;
printf("\nWater required of karkala per day=%f Million litres per day\n",wr);
printf("\nDESIGN OF THE AERATION TANK\n");
printf("\nEnter the number of steps\n");
scanf("%f",&stp);
printf("\nEnter the tread width in millimeters\n");
scanf("%f",&tre);
printf("\nEnter the diameter of the first step in meter\n");
scanf("%f",&dia2);
dia3=dia2;
for(i=1; i<=stp-1;i++)
{
printf("\nDiameter of the %d step =%f meters",i,dia3);
dia3=dia3+(2*(tre/1000));
}
printf("\nDiameter of the %d step =%f meters\n",i,dia3);
printf("\nDiameter of the aeration tank collector =%f meters\n",dia3+2*dia2);
printf("\nEnter the rise of the first step in millimeters\n");
scanf("%f",&ris);
ris1=ris/1000;
for(i=1;i<=stp-1;i++)
{
printf("\nRise of the %d step =%f meters",i,ris1);
count1=count1+ris1;
ris1=((ris1+0.100));
}
count1=count1+ris1;
printf("\nRise of the %d step =%f meters\n",i,ris1);
printf("\nThe overall of aeration tank of diameter %f meters and total height of casacade is %f meters",dia3+2*dia2,count1);
printf("\nDESIGN OF UNDERGROUND CLEAR WATER RESERVOIR\n");
printf("\nUnderground clear water reservoir having capacity of about 8 hours will be provided\n");
printf("\nEnter the depth in meters\n");
scanf("%f",&dep5);
ae=(wr*1000)/dep5;
printf("\nArea of the clear water resevoir =%f square meters\n",ae);
printf("\nProviding square clear water resevoir\n ");
s2=sqrt(ae);
printf("\nThe dimension of the clear water resevior is(%f*%f*%f) meters\n",s2,s2,dep5);
return 0;
}
```

RESULTS AND DISCUSSIONS

(a) Results: A portion of the direct output values from the C-program is as presented here:

Population forecasting

Enter the corresponding year: 1971 Enter the population in the year 1971: 18593 Enter the corresponding year: 1981 Enter the population in the year 1981: 20713 Enter the corresponding year: 1991 Enter the population in the year 1991: 24109 Enter the corresponding year: 2001 Enter the population in the year 2001: 25116 Increase in population in decade 1971-1981: 2120 Percentage increase in population of decade 1971-1981: 11.40 percent Increase in population in decade 1981-1991: 3396 Percentage increase in population of decade 1981-1991: 16.40 percent Increase in population in decade 1991-2001: 1007 Percentage increase in population of decade 1991-2001: 4.18 percent Total = 31.97 percent Average per decade = 10.66 percent Population at the end of 3 decades i.e. by the year 2041 is 37660.35 Therefore expected population of Karkala by the year 2043 is 38430.95

Water demand

Water required of Karkala per day=3.843095 million liters per day

Design of the aeration tank

Enter the number of steps 5 Enter the tread width in millimeters 250 Enter the diameter of the first step in meter 1 Diameter of the 1 step = 1.000000 meters Diameter of the 2 step = 1.500000 meters Diameter of the 3 step = 2.000000 meters Diameter of the 4 step = 2.500000 meters Diameter of the 5 step = 3.000000 meters Diameter of the aeration tank collector = 5.000000 meters Enter the rise of the first step in millimeters 300 Rise of the 1 step = 0.300000 meters Rise of the 2 step = 0.400000 meters Rise of the 3 step = 0.500000 meters Rise of the 4 step = 0.600000 meters Rise of the 5 step = 0.700000 meters The overall of aeration tank of diameter 5.000000 meters and total height of casacade is 2.500000 meters

Design of underground clear water reservoir

Underground clear water reservoir having capacity of about 8 hours will be provided Enter the depth in meters 5 Area of the clear water reservoir = 768.618896 square meters Providing square clear water reservoir The dimension of the clear water reservoir is (27.723976 ′ 27.723976 ′ 5.000000) meters Process returned 0 (0 × 0) execution time: 318.415 s Press any key to continue.

(b) Discussions: With the C-programming technique a decision support tool for design and process selection of drinking water treatment plant using conventional method has been developed and named WATER-DSS1. The tool assists in decision making on the process of drinking water treatment plant using conventional treatment methods. The process consists of pre-treatment, coagulation, flocculation, sedimentation, filtration and disinfection. The processes are selected based on the requirement to treat the raw water, chemically, physically and microbiologically. Each parameters of water has its own treatment procedure but often these can be combined.

Table 2: Comparison of the manual and C-program output values.

S/N	Unit operation/Design criteria	Manual design values	C-Programming output values
1	Expected population	38430	38430.95
2	The water demand	3.85 MLD	3.843095 MLD
3	Aeration tank	Diameter of 5 m and total height of cascade 2.5 m	-
4	Plain Sedimentation tank	$64.8 \times 4.64 \times 4.5$ m^3	$64.800003 \times 4.633360 \times 4.5$ m^3
5		Sedimentation aided with coagulants	
	i) Chemical feeding (size of solution tank)	$0.5 \times 0.5 \times 0.5$ m^3	$0.468621 \times 0.468621 \times 0.5$ m^3
	ii) Approach channel	0.175×0.225 m^2	0.166734×0.216734 m^2
	iii) Mixing tank	$1 \times 1 \times 1$ m^3	$0.816826 \times 0.816826 \times 1$ m^3
	iv) Flocculating tank	$10 \times 1.4 \times 1.6$ m^3	$10 \times 1.45100\ 7 \times 1.6$ m^3
	v) Settling tank (rectangular)	$6 \times 3.3 \times 3$ m^3	$6 \times 3.336020 \times 3$ m^3
6	Rapid gravity filter	6.5×6.5 m^2	6.394058×6.394058 m^2
7	Chlorination plant	Liquid chlorinator having capacity of 0.1 to 5 kg/m	-
8	Underground clear water reservoir	$27.75 \times 27.75 \times 5$ m^3	$27.7239 \times 27.7239 \times 5$ m^3
9	Horse power of centrifugal pump	41 HP	41.0889 HP

In validating the developed program, required data was keyed in and run. At the same time, manual computations are done using the conventional method for the designing the different units of the water treatment plant. The output values of the C-program as compared with those of manual design are presented in Table2 Meanwhile, if the user desires to get the design of any particular unit of the water treatment plant, it is possible to access the desired unit's design using the "switch case" statement. This flexibility further confirms the userfriendliness of C-programming Language.

In comparing the C-program output values and the manually designed values only marginal differences were observed, especially in the decimal places. It is so, because in the c-programming "float" data type is used which gives the accurate values up to six decimal points whereas in manual design the values are rounded off to two decimal points.

CONCLUSION

In this paper with the C-programming technique, a decision support tool for design and process selection of drinking water treatment plant using conventional method has been developed and named Water-DSS1. The applied C-program is user friendly, saves time and gives more accurate values. The program is much more efficient and reliable than the manual design and can be used repeatedly for different sets of data. It is universal in its approach and easily adaptable to any similar conventional water treatment plant apart from the Karkala one reported in this paper. Water-DSS1 is therefore recommended for general use in alleviating water supply challenges.

REFERENCES

1. Power, D.J. (1997) What Is DSS? DSstar. The Online Executive Journal for Data-Intensive Decision Support, 2, 15-20. [Paper reference:1]
2. Gorry, G.A. and Scott Morton, M.S. (1971) A Framework for Management Information Systems. Sloan Management Review, 13, 55-70. [Paper reference:1]
3. Kanetkar, Y.P. (2013) Let Us C. 13th Edition, BPB Publications, New Delhi. [Paper reference:1]
4. Mahaganesha, P.V., Thippeswamy, M.R., Anand, R. and Sharath, B.P. (2014) Design of Conventional Water Treatment PLANT for Karkala Town Using

C-Programming. B.E Project Report, Department of Civil Engineering, NMAM Institute of Technology, Nitte. [Paper reference:2]

5. Ojoawo, S.O. (1997) Performance Evaluation of the Ogbomoso Waterworks. B.Tech Project Report Submitted to the Department of Civil Engineering, Ladoke Akintola University of Technology, Ogbomoso, 3. [Paper reference:1]

6. Hung, C.K. (2006) Development of a Decision Support System for Drinking Water Treatment Process Design (WATERDSS). M.E Project Report Submitted to the Faculty of Civil Engineering, Universiti Teknologi Malaysia, 32-35. [Paper reference:1]

7. Garg, S.K. (2004) Water Supply Engineering. 18th Edition, Khanna Publishers, Delhi.

8. Crittenden, J., Trussell, R., Hand, D., Howe, K. and Tchobanoglous, G. (2005) Water Treatment: Principles and Design. John Wiley and Sons, New York.

CHAPTER 7 PGQL: A PROBABILISTIC GRAPHICAL QUERY LANGUAGE FOR GENE EXPRESSION TIME COURSES

Ruben Schilling, Ivan G Costa, Alexander Schliep

BACKGROUND

The analysis of gene expression time courses e.g. from DNA microarrays is crucial in understanding dynamical biological processes such as cell cycle, cell development and cell response to external stimuli. Common data sets consist of 5-30 time points and hundreds or thousands of genes [1, 2]. In the beginning investigators often explore their data by querying for certain qualitative and quantitative behaviors as an informative visual inspection of multivariate time points is indeed difficult. We define *querying* here as the evaluation of a set of conditions on time courses. The result of a query is a score for each time course that can be used to select a subset of time courses exposing behavior specified through the conditions. Among the characteristics of time courses is their variation in speed (cf. Figure 1d), i.e. delay of similar observations inducing uncertainty about exact time periods where measurements are expected to happen and phase shifts (c.f. Figure 1b). Generally, missing values, noise and outliers (cf. Figure 1c) can commonly be expected. In particular, gene expression time courses have only very few, unevenly sampled time points [3], in contrast to temporal data from other domains such as finance or multimedia. Intuitive software tools which support interactive formulation of query parameters by non-experts can foster wider and more flexible usage of time course data analysis tools by scientists and analysts in a range of disciplines. Yet an open research problem is finding a robust method to interactively query short time courses for specific qualitative and quantitative behavior.

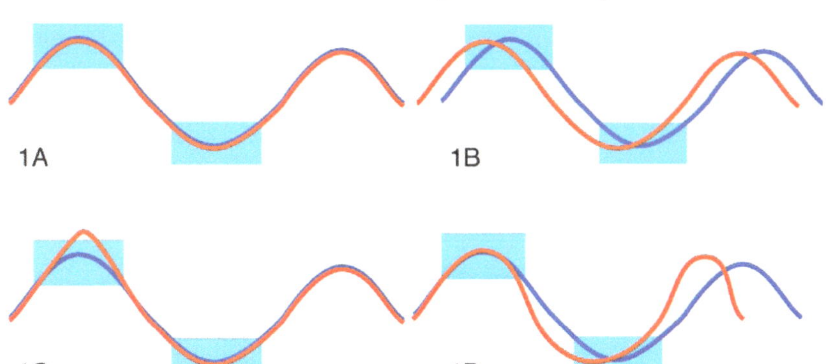

Figure 1: Deterministic queries under the effect of common characteristics of time courses. In (a) both time courses are in the result set of the deterministic query interpretation. For (b), (c) and (d) the red time course is not included in the result set. In (b) a phase shift has moved the red time course out of the query's scope. In (c) an outlier prevents the red time course from being included. In (d) a variation in the speed at which values are taken prevents the red time course from matching the deterministic query interpretation. See the Results section on how deterministic timebox queries are evaluated.

Citation: Schilling, R., Costa, I.G. & Schliep, A. GQL: A probabilistic graphical query language for gene expression time courses, doi:10.1186/1756-0381-4-9.

Previously, timeboxes--specifying minimal and maximal values for a continuous range of time points--were proposed [4] to select time courses of interest. Timeboxes are rectangular, graphical user interface (GUI) widgets, that are embedded in a graphical time course data display. However the method is not robust to noise, temporal or amplitude variations (c.f. Figure 1) common in typical data sets and does not attempt to model them. We previously implemented a method called GQL for analyzing time course data that used graphical sliders to specify parameters of densities used in a HMM [5, 6]. The tool lacked however an intuitive relationship between the query parameters and the data.

We show that timeboxes have a natural interpretation as stochastic, piece-wise linear functions, or linear Hidden Markov Models (HMM) [7]. Their statistical interpretation allows for more flexible and meaningful queries, in particular in the context of analyzing biological data. We refer to our method as Probabilistic Graphical Query Language (pGQL), as HMMs are a specific class of (probabilistic) graphical models [8]. The visual query tool implementing our model allows users to define graphical model parameters; ranking time-courses by likelihood under that model and using a cut-off on the likelihood deter-mines the query result. Note that this is in contrast to the definition of query languages in the field of in-formation science, where graphical query languages are formal languages for querying graphs for graph-theoretical properties and/or attributes of nodes and edges. Although it is not possible to phrase all deterministic queries within pGQL, such as e.g. finding time courses whose values drop by 50% within a time interval or finding time courses for which there exists at least one time period, where they fluctuate by at most some quantity. However it is also not possible to phrase all probabilistic queries in a deterministic query system. The queries you can ask in pGQL are based on expected values and standard deviations. We demonstrate the effectiveness of probabilistic queries on a yeast sporulation data set using our implementation of the probabilistic time-boxes (pGQL). We discuss how our approach contrasts with deterministic timeboxes and identify impact our method has for practitioners.

Results

Algorithm

In the following we will refer to a set time courses as $O = \{o_i\}$, $1 \leq i \leq N$, where each time course $o_i = [o_i^1, \ldots, o_i^t, \ldots, o_i^T]$ takes values $o_i^t \in X$ for times $t \in \{1, \ldots, T\}$.

Timeboxes

Let us start reviewing the definition of [4] for timeboxes and their queries formally:

A timebox b_i is defined by the 4-tuple $b_j = (t_j^-, t_j^+, x_j^-, x_j^+)$, where $t_j^- \leq t_j^+$ and $x_j^- \leq x_j^+$. For a given set of time courses $O = \{o_i\}$, where $1 \leq i \leq N$, $o_i = [o_i^1, \ldots, o_i^t, \ldots, o_i^d]^T$ and d is the number of time points observed, a time courses o_i satisfies a query b_j only if $x_j^- \leq o_i^t \leq x_j^+$ for $t_j^- \leq t \leq t_j^+$.

In Figure 2a, we display all time courses whose values lie in the interval $[x^-, x^+]$ for all time points in the time frame $[t_j^-, t_j^+[$. That is, for a given time-box $b_j = (t_j^-, t_j^+, x_j^-, x_j^+)$ and set of time courses $O = \{o_i\}$, where $o_i = [o_i^1, \ldots, o_i^t, \ldots, o_i^T]$, a query is defined as

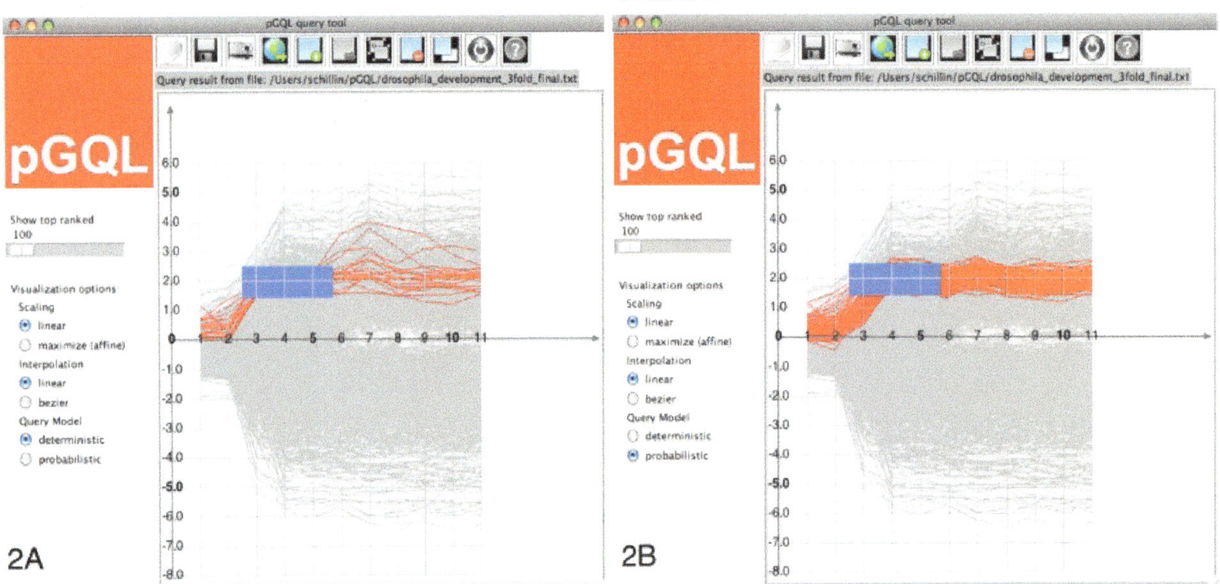

Figure 2: Comparison of deterministic and probabilistic timeboxes. (a) Query evaluation using a deterministic timebox (b) Query evaluation using probabilistic timeboxes The deterministic query in (a) does not contain all time courses showing the trend as defined by the graphical query and even contains time courses that do not follow the trend outside of the specified time interval. The corresponding probabilistic query in (b) however does not have such shortcomings and produces a much more consistent result on this real data set.

$$Q(b_j) = \{o_i \mid o_i^t \in [x_j^-, x_j^+], \forall t \in [t_j^-, t_j^+[, o_i \in O, \}. \qquad (1)$$

Naturally the query operation can be easily extended for multiple timeboxes $\{b_1, ..., b_j, b_{j+1}, ..., b_q\}$ where $t_j^+ < t_{j+1}^-$ holds $\forall j \in [1, q]$. In this case, a time course satisfies the query only if $\forall_{1 \le j \le q} \forall_{t_j^- \le t \le t_j^+} x_j^- \le o_i^t \le x_j^+$, which is the intersection of individual queries: $Q(b_1, ..., b_q) = \cap_j Q(b_j)$.

HMMs and Probabilistic Timeboxes

A HMM can be seen as a probabilistic function of a Markov chain [9] and is fully determined through the specification of its states S, the probability of starting in s_i, the transition probability ϖ_{ij} from state s_i to s_j and the emission densities see [7] for details on Hidden Markov Models.

A particular HMM [2, 9] specialized for time course analysis is the following. The observed states correspond to the user drawn boxes, the hidden states to (graphically) invisible boxes. The latter span any time period not covered by the user defined boxes. The observed states have a normal density, which is parametrized by the mean and variance of the expression values at the time interval defined by the time box (see Figure 3a and 3b). The hidden states have a uniform density. The length of the time boxes are equivalent to the expected duration per state (cf. eq 2). We restrict the topology to contain only successor- and self-transitions (see Figure3B). We require the model to have unique start and end states and normalize the expected durations such, that their sum matches the length of the longest time course in the data set. The HMM has the following free parameters per state: The expected duration and the emission density parameters (see [2] for a detailed description of the model). In the following we detail how we derive these parameters from timeboxes and how queries can be defined using this model.

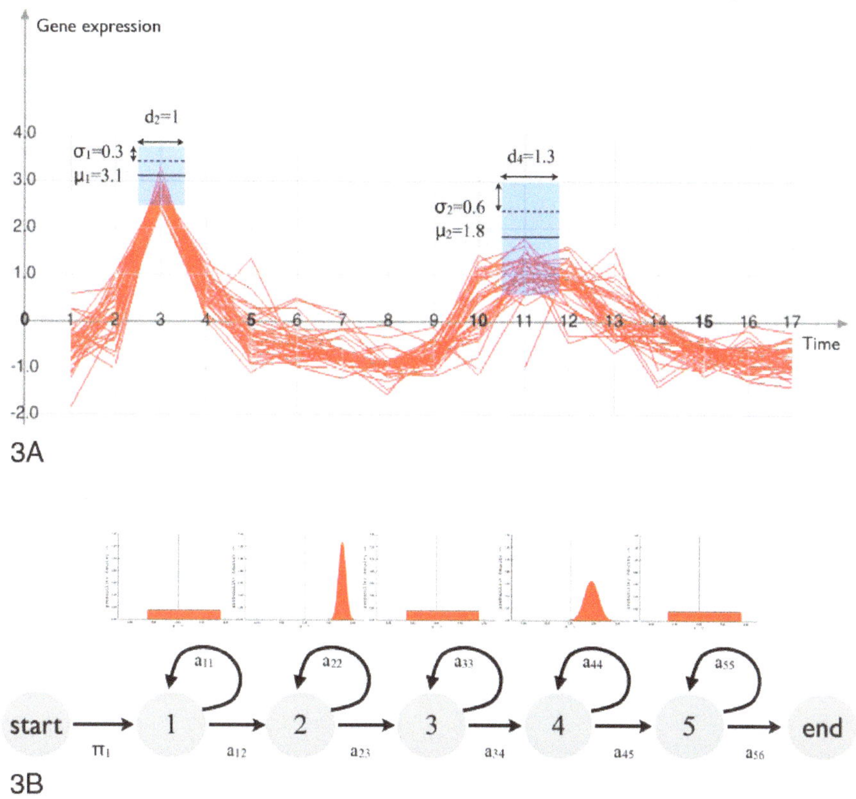

Figure 3: Graphical Query and its interpretation as lHMM. Example of the relation of a probabilistic timebox query (Fig. 3A) to its state model in the corresponding lHMM (Fig. 3B). In Fig. 3A the central black bar within each blue PTB represent the mean value, while a quarter of each PTBs height represents the variance. In Fig. 3B the states 2 and 4 correspond to the blue PTBs in Fig. 3A. When we compare Fig. 3A with Fig. 3B we see, that pGQL inserts automatically hidden states with a uniform distribution in areas where no blue PTB has been placed.

As depicted in Figure 2b, we can allow values out-side of $[x_j^-, x_j^+]$, as long as the overall values of a time course fit the timebox. This can be obtained by modeling the value range covered by a timebox with one uni-variate Normal, where the mean defines the mid point of the value range of the timebox and the standard deviation is proportional to a half of the height of the box.

Additionally, we also want to account for variation along the time axis, in particular time courses with phase-shifts (cf. Figure 1b) and difference in speed (cf. Figure 1d). This can be achieved by modeling the time frame as an expected duration of a timebox. Such probabilistic timeboxes define a state with an uni-variate normal density emission in a lHMM [2]. In this model, we also need to assign states for time frames where no timebox is defined, such as the regions in the left of Figure 2b. Specifying states in such frames substantiates the assumption about *when* we expect the user defined normal models to occur. These hidden boxes can be interpreted as waiting timeboxes, where any observation is equally likely to occur.

More formally, a probabilistic timebox PTB is a state in a lHMM λ with an uni-variate normal density emission (see Figure 3B). This (k th) state is parametrized by the triplet (p_k, μ_k, σ_k), where p_k is the self transition probability or expected duration, and $N(\mu_k, \sigma_k)$ is the state emission density. Given the (graphical) parameters of a timebox (c.f. Figure 3A), the state parameters can be defined as,

$$p_k = 1 - \frac{1}{t_j^+ - t_j^-}, \tag{2}$$

$$\mu_k = \frac{x_j^+ + x_j^-}{2}, \text{ and} \tag{3}$$

$$\sigma_k = \frac{(x_j^+ - \mu_k)}{2}. \tag{4}$$

Note that the current choice of σ_k places approximately 95.5% of the density mass in the interval $[x_j^-, x_j^+]$, and that $(t_j^+ - t_j^-)$ is the expected duration of the timebox. The latter defines p_k, which obeys a geometrical distribution [10]. The relation between transition probability and duration is detailed in [7]. The idea is to consider the probability of staying n times in state s_i, before you make a transition to s_{i+1}.

Hidden states, that have no graphical representation, model time frames between timeboxes. They are defined by a single parameter, their expected length, p_l, and a uniform distribution $U(x_{min}, x_{max})$, where x_{min} (and x_{max}) are the minimum (and maximum) value in O. For two consecutive timeboxes, j and $j + 1$, where $t_j^+ \neq t_{j+1,min}$, we have

$$p_l = 1 - \frac{1}{t_{j+1}^- - t_j^+}. \tag{5}$$

Time ranges before (and after) the first and last timeboxes b_1 and b_q represent special cases. We also include a state emitting a uniform distribution in these ranges when $0 \neq t_1^-$ and $t_q^+ \neq d$.

One additional requirement for querying with PTBs is a parameter m, which defines how many time courses should be returned by the query. Intuitively, the query works by estimating the time course likelihoods ($\mathbf{P}[o_i|\lambda]$) using the Forward-algorithm [7], followed by the selection of the m time courses with highest likelihoods. In particular setting m to the number of time courses will return all time courses as query result and setting m to 1 will return the time course with highest likelihood. More formally, given a full parametrized lHMM λ defined by the timeboxes (b_1, ..., b_q) and m, the probabilistic query is defined as,

$$PQ((b_1, \ldots, b_q), m, \lambda) = \{o_i | \text{rank}(\mathbf{P}[o_i|\lambda]) \leq m, o_i \in O\}. \tag{6}$$

The main computational task behind the query is computing the log-likelihood of the time-courses for a given HMM. This has the computational complexity of $O(N \cdot K \cdot L)$, where N is the number of time-courses, K the number of states (or time-boxes) and L the number of time points. Note that K and L are usually small (< 10) in this application, there-fore the running time only depends linearly on the number of samples N.

TESTING

Case Study - Yeast Sporulation

To show the usefulness of the probabilistic timeboxes in the analysis of gene expression, we perform a case study with the time courses of Yeast during sporulation [11] There, the expression values of approximately 6,200 genes have been measured through the course of seven time points (0 h, 0.5 h, 2 h, 5 h, 7 h, 9 h and 11 h). The biological process is formed by a cascade of transcriptional events, which can be subdivided in three main consecutive events: DNA replication, meiosis and spore maturation. We pre-processed the data, as described in [2], to discard time courses with a large number of missing values or with small temporal expression change, which resulted in a data set with 1,171 genes. In [11], authors hand selected seven groups of genes as prototypes of interesting expression patterns. For example, genes with an increase in expression in early, middle or late time points. The mean expression value of each group was taken, and a nearest neighbor approach based on the correlation coefficient was used to assign other genes to each of the expression patterns.

We show here, how such exploratory analysis of temporal expression patterns, can be interactively performed with the PTBs. In the following we refer to a pattern of over-expression, which is visible in data and can be scored by our model, simply as over-expression. For example, to find all genes with early over-expression patterns, we simply need to draw a timebox in the upper left side of the canvas and set the query stringency to 150 genes (Figure4a). Note that all time courses display high expression at early time points but distinct expression patterns at later time points. A functional analysis of the genes indicates that the query contains genes mostly related to metabolism and meiosis. To refine the query, we can create an additional PTB, now at the upper-right part of the canvas (Figure 4b). This query will return all genes with an over-expression pattern, which is sustained over time. Functional analysis of these genes indicates a relation to meiosis, which is in accordance with the functional analysis performed in [11]. We can then modify the query, by moving the second timebox toward zero expression values, therefore querying genes with a over-expression followed by an expression decrease (Figure 4c). These genes, which are involved in metabolism, are activated as a reflex of the nitrogen starvation caused by the sporulation medium [11]. The user can perform further operations on the timeboxes to find other expression patterns of interest. Deleting the second PTB and moving the first one down returns a query with genes displaying under-expression pattern (Figure 4d). These genes are mostly related to the ribosome, which has been interpreted as effect of the cessation of growth under the nitrogen starvation [11]. This example displays how a user can easily perform an exploratory analysis of temporal expression patterns with PTBs and all main features provided by pGQL.

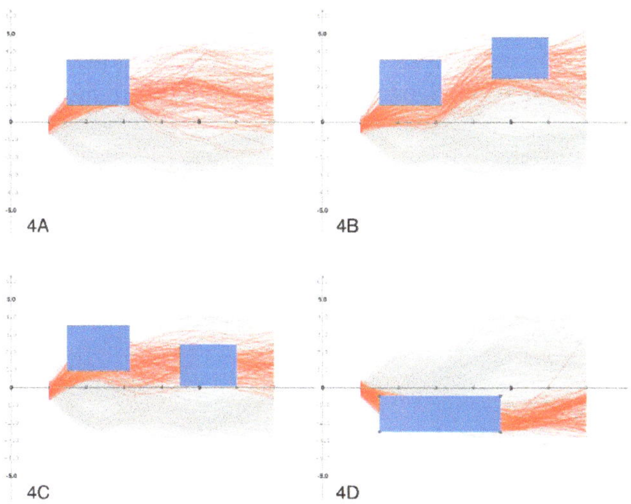

Figure 4: Yeast sporulation case study. We depict query results from a Yeast sporulation data set. In the first query (a), we have 150 genes with early over expression pattern. This query is made more specific by creating a new timebox (b). Now, it returns genes that have a sustained over-expression pattern. By applying a move operation on the second timebox, we query for genes with a over-expression followed by expression decrease (c). We can look for further patterns by deleting the second timebox and move the first timebox down to obtain genes with under-expression patterns(d).

Implementation

The software is implemented in Python and Tkinter using the GHMM library [5] and was tested on Linux and Mac OS X, but works on other modern operating systems including Windows as well. It is licensed under the GPL. The software is available from our web sitehttp://algorithmics.molgen.mpg.de/Software/pGQL/.

The tool automatically inserts (and removes) hidden states into (from) regions, where the user has not (has) defined a PTB for a state corresponding to a normal emission density. These hidden states correspond to uniform emission densities. While drawing and editing PTBs consistency constraints are automatically checked and create a frame for specifying useful models. In particular pGQL checks, that users draw boxes with a minimum of 1.0 expected duration, since we do not assume any interpolation model on the discrete data. Users are also automatically guided to never produce overlapping states or states extending beyond the graph display. When-ever a query is graphically modified pGQL automatically recomputes the query and updates the result. It is possible to display PTBs on top of the time course data for query redefinition or below to inspect query results. pGQL also implements deterministic timebox queries to enable direct comparisons of the methods by switching between query types on the fly.

Functional Analysis

An important method for the biological analysis of a group of genes, as the one returned by a query, is the so called enrichment functional analysis [12]. This method uses databases with functional annotation of genes, such as Gene Ontology [13] to search for functional groups, whose genes are also within the query result. pGQL provides an out-link to the G: Profiler tool [12] to perform an enrichment functional analysis based on the current working query.

DISCUSSION

The PTB based graphical query approach enables users to phrase their hypotheses in a fashion many are already familiar with, i.e. defining normal distributions in the value domain and placing them as expected durations. Uncertainty is naturally incorporated in such models, while the user is not required to bother with the formalisms, but can simply use an interactive tool, that alleviates the usage of these models. The specificity of queries can easily be in-creased by adding more PTBs to a query. It would be interesting to combine pGQL with formal queries known from other field s to benefit from many deterministic queries as well. It is a future research problem how to translate such queries into one common graphical query interface. The only deterministic query pGQL currently provides is of the basic time box query type [4]. Although beyond the scope of the present article, it would be interesting to perform a full usability study of our tool in the future to conduct a user related performance evaluation as well.

The interpretation of query results from pGQL is straightforward: The result set will contain the*m* top ranking time courses, where obviously the highest scores will be assigned to time courses that lie centrally to the query. In contrast deterministic queries do not have a notion of rank as their scoring is binary.

We could in principle approximate the behavior of deterministic boxes by imposing peak like boxes on time periods. From a statistical point of view this is equivalent to overfitting the query model on the time dimension. Since the measurements will be taken in units of time, it generally doesn›t make much sense from a modeling perspective to expect any measurement to last shorter than a a full time unit. Thus pGQL requires at least a unit of time for each timebox. This choice leads to query models, that are robust to time delays, since the self-transition probability in the HMM will not be forced to be infinitesimally small. If a user has a strong belief in values taking place in an exact, predefined time period he might get additional time courses returned from the query model, that exhibit similar behavior delayed in time. The ranking of time courses is one way to re ne the selection of such a result set: Time courses that adhere to the query during the exact time periods of the probabilistic boxes, should always be contained in the results, as they will be ranked highly by the query model.

Deterministic timeboxes could in principle be made approximate by requiring only a certain fraction of measurements to lie within a box. This shifts the problem to determining what this fraction really is. It is unclear how well this concept could capture common time course characteristics we mentioned in the Background section.

An example (again on the yeast sporulation data) demonstrating the robustness of the probabilistic queries is shown in Figure 2b: Despite of outliers on time points four and five the query result shows time courses displaying strongly similar behavior. The ex-act same graphical query in the deterministic setting shown in Figure 2a returns only a subset of the probabilistic query result, which is owed to the sensitivity to outliers. Moreover the result contains a few time courses, that do not seem to fit the overall trend specified by the query well. The latter is an artifact owed to the over fitting in time.

CONCLUSIONS

Probabilistic timeboxes introduced new semantics to timeboxes proposed by [4]. Graphical queries are interactively created and manipulated by enabling users to draw, delete, move and resize any number of PTB's with respect to the incorporated constraints of this approach. This allows for easy and comfortable definition of meaningful, flexible queries even in complex data analysis scenarios. Probabilistic models, in particular in use for gene expression data, are known to be much more appropriate and flexible than their deterministic counter parts [2,14–16]. The ease of the graphical definition encapsulates a sound method for query definition, requiring no in-depth knowledge of the underlying probabilistic methods to use this tool. We have demonstrated the method on a real world data set of yeast sporulation. This case study also revealed typical advantages our method has over deterministic methods. We contrasted the PTBs with the original timeboxes and shown how they cope better with many properties of gene expression time courses. pGQL can be of great help in finding interesting clusters in time course data.

A straight-forward extension to our method would be modeling cyclic data. All that is needed for this is to insert a transition from the end state to the start state and specify the transition probability favoring more or fewer cycles. Then we expect cyclic or periodic data to benefit from queries with probabilistic timeboxes just as well. GHMM supports cyclic queries already.

AUTHORS' CONTRIBUTIONS

RS implemented the graphical tool and drafted the manuscript. IGC and AS implemented the probabilistic models and contributed to the manuscript. AS conceived the study initially. All authors read and approved the final manuscript.

REFERENCES

1. Bar-Joseph Z: Analyzing time series gene expression data. Bioinformatics. 2004, 20 (16): 2493-503. 10.1093/bioinformatics/bth283.
2. .Schliep A, Costa IG, Steinhoff C, Schönhuth AA: Analyzing Gene Expression Time-Courses. IEEE/ACM Transactions on Computational Biology and Bioinformatics. 2005, 2 (3): 179-193. 10.1109/TCBB.2005.31.
3. Ernst J, Bar-Joseph Z: STEM: a tool for the analysis of short time series gene expression data. BMC Bioinformatics. 2006, 7: 191-10.1186/1471-2105-7-191. [http://www.biomedcentral.com/1471-2105/7/191]
4. Hochheiser H, Shneiderman B: Dynamic query tools for time series data sets: Timebox widgets for interactive exploration. Information Visualization. 2004, 3: 1-18. 10.1057/palgrave.ivs.9500061.
5. Costa IG, Schönhuth A, Schliep A: The Graphical Query Language: a tool for analysis of gene expression time-courses. Bioinformatics. 2005, 21 (10): 2544-5. 10.1093/bioinformatics/bti311.
6. The Graphical Query Language (GQL). 2003, Accessed 13.4.2011, [http://ghmm.org/gql]
7. Rabiner LR: A Tutorial on Hidden Markov Models and Selected Applications in Speech Recognition. Proceedings of the IEEE. 1989, 77 (2): 257-285. 10.1109/5.18626.
8. Jordan MI, (Ed): Learning in graphical models. 1999, Cambridge, MA, USA: MIT Press
9. Schliep A, Schonhuth A, Steinhoff C: Using hidden Markov models to analyze gene expression time course data. Bioinformatics. 2003, 19 (suppl_1): i255-263.
10. Durbin R, Eddy S, Krogh A, Mitchison G: Biological Sequence Analysis: probabilistic models of proteins and nucleic acids. 1998, Cambridge Press
11. Chu S, DeRisi J, Eisen M, Mulholland J, Botstein D, Brown PO, Herskowitz I: The Transcriptional Program of Sporulation in Budding Yeast. Science. 1998, 282 (5389): 699-705.
12. Reimand J, Kull M, Peterson H, Hansen J, Vilo J: g: Profiler-a web-based toolset for functional profiling of gene lists from large-scale experiments. Nucleic Acids Res. 2007, W193-W200. 35 Web Server
13. Ashburner M: Gene Ontology: tool for the unification of biology. Nature Genetics. 2000, 25: 25-29. 10.1038/75556.
14. Bar-Joseph Z, Gerber GK, Gifford DK, Jaakkola TS, Simon I: Continuous representations of time-series gene expression data. J Comput Biol. 2003, 10 (3-4): 341-356. 10.1089/10665270360688057.
15. Ramoni MF, Sebastiani P, Kohane IS: Cluster analysis of gene expression dynamics. Proc Natl Acad Sci USA. 2002, 99 (14): 9121-9126. 10.1073/pnas.132656399.
16. Yeung KY, Fraley C, Murua A, Raftery AE, Ruzzo WL: Model-based clustering and data transformations for gene expression data. Bioinformatics. 2001, 17 (10): 977-987. 10.1093/bioinformatics/17.10.977.

CHAPTER 8

BAMQL: A QUERY LANGUAGE FOR EXTRACTING READS FROM BAM FILES

Andre P. Masella, Christopher M. Lalansingh, Pragash Sivasundaram, Michael Fraser, Robert G. Bristow, Paul C. Boutros

Keywords: BAMQL Query language, BAM-format, Electronic supplementary material

BACKGROUND

Binary Alignment/Map (BAM) provides a common format to hold large quantities of genomic read data after alignment to a reference genome. Reads are annotated with supplementary information not present in FASTA or FASTQ files, such as target position and chromosome, and information about the mate pair.

Often, only a subset of reads are needed for further analysis. SAMtools, the standard software for manipulation of BAM files, provides options to perform limited filtering of BAM files and collect matching reads [1]. The interface is neither expressive nor user-friendly: the user must indicate which bit flags they require not using names, but the numeric values of those flags. Further, the selection condition is restricted to a filter that describes which bit flags must match, which must not, a minimum quality score and a list of matching read groups. This limits query expressiveness; for example, selecting reads with poor quality is impossible.

General purpose programming languages can be used with BAM file manipulation libraries to filter a file. Since most subsetting operations are ad hoc, this is cumbersome and requires substantial boilerplate code. More concerning, there is a disparity between the checking done by the language and what is needed by the BAM APIs. For instance, it is possible to read only a subset of a file using an index, but this requires correctly matching chromosome names between the index request and the filtering expression. A mismatch may result in a silent omission of data that is difficult to detect due to the complex, mixed-language query.

To simplify the subsetting process, but retain the ability to have powerful queries, we developed BAM Query Language (BAMQL), a domain-specific language for matching BAM reads.

IMPLEMENTATION

BAMQL queries are specified by predicates and logical connectives. The predicates include ones which match BAM flags, mapping information, auxiliary read information, position and the sequence. For example, to output a BAM file with all reads which are on chromosome 1 and have a mate read, one could do the following: bamql -f input.bam -o output.bam 'chr(1) & paired?'. An outline of all available connectives and predicates can be found in Table 1.

Table 1: Descriptions of BAMQL connectives and predicates

Category	Syntax	Description
Logical Connectives	! expr	Is satisfied if expr is not satisfied.
	expr | expr	Is satisfied if at least one operand is satisfied.

Citation: Andre P. Masella, Christopher M. Lalansingh, Pragash Sivasundaram, Michael Fraser, Robert G. Bristow, Paul C. Boutros-BAMQL: a query language for extracting reads from BAM files, doi:10.1186/s12859-016-1162-y.

	expr ^ expr	Is satisfied if at exactly one operand is satisfied.
	expr & expr	Is satisfied only if both operands are satisfied.
	cond then then_expr else else_ expr	If cond is satisfied, this expression will only be satisfied if then_expr is satisfied. If cond is not satisfied, then this expression will only be satisfied if else_expression is satisfied.
BAM Flags	paired?	The read is paired in sequencing.
	proper_pair?	The read is mapped in a proper pair
	unmapped?	The read is unmapped.
	mate_unmapped?	The mate is unmapped.
	mapped_to_reverse?	The read is mapped to the reverse strand.
	mate_mapped_to_reverse?	The mate is mapped to the reverse strand.
	raw_flag(int)	The read matches the specified SAM flag.
	read1?	The read is the first read in a pair.
	read2?	The read is the second read in a pair.
	secondary?	The alignment is not primary.
	failed_qc?	The read failed platform/vendor quality control checks.
	duplicate?	The read is either a PCR or optical duplicate
	supplementary?	The alignment is supplementary.
Mapping Information	chr(glob)	The read is mapped to the specified chromosome.
	mapping_quality(probability)	Matches the read if the proability of error is less than the specified probability.
	mate_chr(glob)	The mate is mapped to the specified chromosome.
	split_pair?	Matches if both the read and it's mate pair are mapped, but only if to different chromosomes.
Position	after(position)	Matches all reads that cover the specified position or any higher position.
	before(position)	Matches all reads that cover the specified position or any lower position.
	position(start,end)	Matches all sequences that cover the range of position from specified start to end, i.e. N matches any base.
Sequence	nt(position,n)	Matches all reads that are classified as the IUPAC-style nucleotide n at the specified position, i.e. N matches N.
	nt_exact(position,n)	Matches all reads that exactly match the IUPAC-style nucleotide n at the specified position.
Miscellaneous	read_group(glob)	Matches the read group.
	header ~ /regex/	Matches a Perl-compatible regular expression against the read's header.
	random(probability)	The read is chosen based on a uniform pseudo-random variable.
	true	Always satisfied.
	false	Never satisfied.

BAMQL has a library which compiles a query into native code, then checks the reads in the input BAM file, saving the matched reads to a user-specified output BAM file. A recursive descent parser reads the query and the resulting structure is converted into native code using LLVM 3.4.0 or later [2]. A driver program reads the input BAM file, checking each read against the query and tracking the number of accepted and rejected reads, which it then writes to BAM files. All BAM file operations are done using HTSlib 1.3 [1]. The command line interface uses filename specifiers for input and output so, when utilizing pipes in the bash environment, /dev/stdin and /dev/stdout will allow for writing across pipes.

If an indexed BAM is provided, the query automatically determines if only a subset of the file needs to be analysed to improve performance. SAMtools has the same performance gain by specifying regions, but, there is the possibility of mismatching the regions specified and those in filter.

RESULTS

To test the efficacy, we compared several equivalent queries written in BAMQL, SAMtools (v1.3) + GNU AWK (v4.0.1), Sambamba (v0.5.9), Python using pysam (v0.8.2) [3], Perl using Bio-SamTools (v1.41) [4], and C using HTSlib (v1.1). We compared execution times and the quantity of code written. Execution time is an imperfect metric, as it is dependent on various properties of the system at runtime, such as CPU load, disk operations, and the hardware specifications of the system. By keeping these factors equivalent when performing benchmarks, we can see relative differences between the tools. All tests are provided in the additional files and examples of queries and a list of predicates can be found on the github wiki page [see Availability of data and materials]. Six tests were defined:

- **all** – copies the input to establish a baseline I/O cost.
- **paired** – keeps only reads which are paired.
- **chrY** – keeps reads on the Y chromosome, whether it is named "Y" or "24", optionally prefixed with "chr", irrespective of case.
- **mt** – keeps all reads which they or their mate pair are unmapped or mapped to the mitochondrial genome (named "M", "MT" or "25", optionally prefixed with "chr", irrespective of case).
- **nt** – keeps all reads which have base C at position 13353 of the reference genome after alignment.
- **chain** – filters chromosomes 1, 2 and 3 into separate BAM files.

The tests were written as simply as possible. No profiling or intentional optimisations were done as this test code is meant to be a single-use ad hoc query.

Method-comparison

It must be noted that *nt*, *mt* and *chrY* tests could not be written with SAMtools alone and required output to be piped through AWK scripts for the actual filtering process. Similarly, Sambamba required an AWK script to implement filtering for the *nt* test.

The difference in user-friendliness between BAMQL and SAMtools is evident in the relatively simple *chrY* test. The BAMQL query for a *chrY* test (listing ??) is a one-line query since BAMQL recognizes the differing names for the human Y chromosome and checks them automatically.

Listing 1 chrY test in BAMQL

```
bamql -f $1 -o $2 ' chr ( y )
```

The same query implemented using SAMtools (listing ??) however requires the query to be run using an AWK filter in order to manually check for the multiple ways Y chromosome could be labelled in the BAM file.

```
samtools view -h $1 |
awk '/^{@}/ || $3 ~/^(chr)?(y|Y|24)$/
{ print $0 }'
|samtools view -b -S -o $2 -
```

Sambamba was more expressive than SAMtools in this case. However, Sambamba requires chromosomes to be specified using reference ID rather than chromosome name [5]. Sambamba's expressiveness also do not extend to complex queries such as the *chain* test that requires chaining filters. While BAMQL had a dedicated function for handling a chain of filters, each with an optional output file, Sambamba and SAMtools both required separate queries for each of the filters.

A summary of the differences in capabilities of the tools used for testing is shown in Table 2.

Table 2: Comparison of the filtering capabilities of the various tools

Tool	Dedicated filtering	Supports multiple filters	Supports logical connectives	Supports chaining filters	Filters reads by mapping	Filters reads by flags	Filters reads by sequence
BAMQL	✓	✓	✓	✓	✓	✓	✓
C	X	✓	✓	✓	lim	✓	✓
Perl	X	✓	✓	✓	lim	✓	X
Python	X	✓	✓	✓	lim	✓	X
SAMtools	✓	X	X	X	lim	lim	X
Sambamba	✓	✓	lim	X	lim	✓	X

Performance

All tests were run three times on an Intel Core i5 3.4 GHz Ubuntu 14.04 workstation with a 10 GB indexed, sorted BAM file containing male human whole exome sequence as input. The reads from each implementation were compared, and were identical in all cases. The coefficient of variation of user time was < 4 % while that of system and wall times were noisier, up to 15 %.

The *mt* and *nt* tests, shown in Tables 3 and 4 respectively, are more processing-intensive while the *paired* and *chain* tests, shown in Tables 5 and 6 respectively, are less processing-intensive and keeps more sequences, causing it to be more output-intensive. Two notable outliers are Perl and Sambamba. Perl consumes much more CPU time than the other tools; this is evidenced by high user times in the *mt* test. Tests implemented with Sambamba alone, *paired* and *mt*, have a low wall time due to parallel processing capabilities of Sambamba. However, Sambamba+AWK and SAMtools+AWK have high system times, due to the overhead to cope with pipe operations. C, Python and Perl seem to incur a high overhead in the *chain* test due to multiple output files opened for depositing data. Overall, BAMQL, C and Python performed well. In the output-dominated tests, *paired* and *chain*, the differences in real processing become clouded by the cost of writing the output. Notice that the user and wall times show a smaller percentage difference in *paired* compared to *mt*. In the more logic-intensive test, *mt*, the languages separate out more.

Table 3: Comparison of performance for selecting mitochondrial sequences (*mt*)

Tool	System time (s)	User time (s)	Wall time (s)	Code (bytes)
BAMQL	**3.65**	133.86	150.28	**86**
C	3.80	**126.28**	138.16	1315
Perl	4.57	1704.05	1716.72	498
Python	4.06	299.33	313.68	507
SAMtools+AWK	14.56	455.12	240.96	170
Sambamba +AWK	6.53	185.64	**99.56**	112

Best performer is highlighted in bold

Table 4: Comparison of performance for selecting reads with base at a sequence position (*nt*)

Tool	System time (s)	User time (s)	Wall time (s)	Code (bytes)
BAMQL	**3.55**	109.16	115.69	**54**
C	2.89	**107.49**	**114.17**	2590
Perl	3.73	264.84	356.29	1667
Python	4.24	137.06	171.77	1225
SAMtools+AWK	41.42	2591.00	2322.19	831
Sambamba+AWK	56.12	3446.93	3100.96	874

Best performer is highlighted in bold

Table 5: Comparison of performance for selecting paired-end sequences (*paired*)

Tool	System time (s)	User time (s)	Wall time (s)	Code (bytes)
BAMQL	**22.54**	**1271.20**	1364.64	**45**
C	29.31	1277.55	1377.29	706
Perl	28.54	1383.65	1474.48	319
Python	29.48	1314.25	1413.04	262
SAMtools	28.26	1271.97	1382.81	46
Sambamba	35.11	1855.81	**583.02**	53

Best performer is highlighted in bold

Table 6: Comparison of performance for applying chain of filters to separate by chromosomes (*chain*)

Tool	System time (s)	User time (s)	Wall time (s)	Code (bytes)
BAMQL	**4.83**	305.66	345.19	**123**
C	9.31	385.05	422.02	1027
Perl	11.18	2552.69	2585.88	800
Python	11.18	576.44	643.36	907
SAMtools	6.71	**302.15**	329.63	156
Sambamba	8.45	441.58	**145.49**	174

Best performer is highlighted in bold

With the exception of the *nt* test, the BAMQL implementation is the most performant with 24 % to 90 % faster system time than the C implementation. In terms of code volume, BAMQL required much less code; typically half of the SAMtools+AWK and a tenth of the C implementation. An additional csv file shows the compete results for all tests [see Additional file2].

DISCUSSION

Since most BAM filtering operations are ad hoc, the runtime performance of BAMQL is not especially important, although it outperforms most standard approaches. We believe that BAMQL's major impact is the simplicity of the queries and the automatic guards against common mistakes. In particular, BAMQL generates index requests from the BAM and does the filtering using the same query. This guards against accidental mismatches in chromosome names caused by independent index requests and filtering expressions (*e.g.* SAMtools with AWK filter). It also automatically corrects for common chromosomal name irregularities. These features make it easy to write correct queries and, by reducing boilerplate, makes them simple to read and understand.

Since the performance of BAMQL queries is good, it is also possible to use them in other contexts. Queries can be compiled to native machine code, making it trivial to integrate into a larger C or C++ program. There are queries that are outside the domain of BAMQL: BAMQL queries are stateless, while general purpose languages are not. Given the low overhead of integration, it is reasonable to split a stateful query between C or C++ and BAMQL.

CONCLUSIONS

BAMQL is designed to improve the efficacy and user-friendliness of the current tools like SAMtools and Sambamba. It provides a larger collection of predicates than SAMtools or Sambamba. These predicates can be joined together with a wider set of logical connectives, allowing for more expressive queries. By compiling queries into native code using LLVM, BAMQL is also able to perform as well as C but with significantly simpler code. BAMQL provides a powerful yet intuitive approach to ad hoc querying BAM formatted data.

FUNDING

This study was conducted with the support of the Ontario Institute for Cancer Research to PCB through funding provided by the Government of Ontario. This work was supported by Prostate Cancer Canada and is proudly funded by the Movember Foundation – Grant #RS2014-01. PCB was supported by a Terry Fox Research Institute New Investigator Award and a CIHR New Investigator Award. This project was supported by Genome Canada through a Large-Scale Applied Project contract to PCB, Dr. Sohrab Shah and Dr. Ryan Morin.

AUTHORS' CONTRIBUTIONS

APM and CML designed and implemented the software. APM did benchmarking and first draft of the paper. PS wrote the second draft, performed additional benchmarks, and made bug fixing updates to the software. MF, RGB and PCB supervised research. All authors read and approved the final manuscript.

REFERENCES

1. Li H, Handsaker B, Wysoker A, Fennell T, Ruan J, Homer N, Marth G, Abecasis G, Durbin R. The sequence alignment/map format and SAMtools. Bioinformatics. 2009; 25(16):2078–9. doi:10.1093/bioinformatics/btp352.CrossRefPubMedCentral
2. Lattner C, Adve V. LLVM: a compilation framework for lifelong program analysis transformation. In: Proceedings of the International Symposium on Code Generation and Optimization, 2004. Washington: IEEE Computer Society: 2004. p. 75–86. doi:10.1109/CGO.2004.1281665.
3. Heger A, Belgard TG, Finkernagel F, Goodstadt L, Goodson M, Jacobs KB, Lunter G, Martin M, Schiller B. Pysam: Python Interface for the SAM/BAM Sequence Alignment and Mapping Format. via PyPI. https://github.com/pysam-developers/pysam. Accessed 2016-02-01.
4. Stein L. Bio-SamTools. via CPAN. http://search.cpan.org/~lds/Bio-SamTools. Accessed 2016-02-12.
5. Tarasov A, Vilella AJ, Cuppen E, Nijman IJ, Prins P. Sambamba: fast processing of NGS alignment formats. Bioinformatics. 2015; 31(12):2032–4. doi:10.1093/bioinformatics/btv098.

CHAPTER 9

HIGH-LEVEL PORTABLE PROGRAMMING LANGUAGE FOR OPTIMIZED MEMORY USE OF NETWORK PROCESSORS

Yasusi Kanada

Keywords: Network Processors, Portability, High-Level Language, Hardware Independence, Memory Usage, DRAM, SRAM, Network Virtualization

INTRODUCTION

To enable programmability for networking and in-network processing, especially for new network-layer programming for clean-slate virtual-networks [1] , network processors (NPs) have been used [2] and will be more widely used in the near future. NPs, which were developed for software-based high-performance networking solutions, make it possible to quickly develop arbitrary protocol and functions in the case of hardware-based solutions as well.

However, there are three problems that make using NPs for such functions difficult. The first problem is lack of portability. Because low-level languages that are similar to assembly languages must be used for developing NP programs, the programs are not portable. Although extended versions of C can usually be used for developing NP programs, essential libraries depend on vendor-specific proprietary hardware and software, and proprietary rights on NP programs are protected by non-disclosure agreements (NDAs) preventing programs and documents concerning an NP being ported. The second problem is high development cost and that the availability of NP program developers is limited. NP program developments require special skills, and the knowledge they require is not widely available; thus, only a limited number of developers have the ability to develop NP programs. In addition, vendor-specific information is required in NP-program development. Consequently, the learning curve of NP-program development is very gentle, the development takes a very long time, and its cost is very high. The third problem is restriction on publishing developed programs, papers, and documents concerning an NP. This is a serious problem for network researchers.

Citation: Kanada, Y. (2015) High-Level Portable Programming Language for Optimized Memory Use of Network Processors. Communications and Network, 7, 55-69. doi: 10.4236/cn.2015.71006.

The three above-described problems can be solved by successfully designing and implementing a high-level-language, which can translate programs into NP machine code or a vendor-dependent C program. Programs written in this language must be translated into NP-dependent object programs; however, to solve the problems, the language must be hardware- and vendor-independent.

An important common NP feature concerning high-performance packet processing (to avoid packet drops caused by cache misses) is to use static random-access memory (SRAM) and dynamic random-access memory (DRAM) by different methods with explicit awareness by the programmer, making programming difficult and time-consuming. Although memory allocation is not the only issue that causes the above three problems, this is the most important and serious issue because NPs are optimized for wire-rate processing and memory abuse immediately prevents it and severely reduces the performance. In particular, whole packets are stored in DRAM, and only the headers, which must be modified, removed, or added, are cached in SRAM because if data stored in DRAM is accessed by a CPU core, access takes an excessively long time, and wire-rate processing is impossible. The rest of the packets are just forwarded to the next network node without modification in the NP. This is common because it is necessary for NPs to store packets in memory while processing them, but the size of SRAM is limited, so whole packets cannot be stored in short-access-time memory, i.e., SRAM.

When programming a packet-processing program for NPs, programmers must use an assembly language or C with assembly-level features, and must be very careful to get high performance. When using general-purpose CPUs, programmers can use high-level language and do not have to distinguish SRAM (or cache) and DRAM because they are automatically selected when programs load and store data. However, NP programmers must usually know whether the packet to be processed is on SRAM or DRAM (or both) because this knowledge is critical for attaining stable (i.e., mishit-less) wire-rate processing. Two types of NP architectures are available. In one of them, such as Intel IXP, the SRAM and the DRAM are different classes of memory with different addresses. In the other type, such as Cavium Octeon®, the SRAM can be accessed as cache or registers, in a similar manner to general-purpose CPUs, but programmers must still be aware of the SRAM/DRAM distinction because the NP handles them in different ways. These cases are explained in more detail in Section 2.

Although it is a promising approach to design a new open and portable high-level language and to implement a high-performance language processor, i.e., a compiler and run-time routines, it is still very hard to solve the above three problems because of the wide semantic gap between the language and the object program.

However, this paper describes the successful first step toward this goal. Hardware features such as those described above can be abstracted to common high-level language features that do not make programmers conscious of the low-level hardware features. To enable this type of abstraction, a high-level language called "Phonepl" (portable high-level open network processing language) is proposed, and a method for compiling packet- handling programs in Phonepl into high-performance programs that can fully utilize hardware while distinguishing SRAM and DRAM is proposed. Here, "open" means that network processors can be programmed without NDAs. Especially, packet headers are automatically cached, the language processor is aware that the data being handled is stored in either SRAM or DRAM (or both) and manages data transmission between them, and programmers do not have to pay attention to this distinction, so the programming cost can be decreased. Phonepl does not depend on vendor-specific NP hardware and software, and thus the programs in Phonepl can be portable among various NPs.

The rest of this paper is organized as follows. Section 2 describes related work. Section 3 describes Phonepl. Section 4 describes a method for implementing Phonepl for NPs, especially four representations of packet type and a method for handling them. Section 5 describes a prototype implementation of Phonepl for plug-ins for a network-virtualization environment called the VNode Infrastructure, and Section 6 evaluates it by using several applications. Section 7 concludes this paper.

RELATED WORK

This section focuses on previous studies on NPs and languages for packet processing because, although there are many studies on memory-related optimizations concerning high-performance computing, such as Sequoia [3] , they focus on array processing and the requirements for packet-stream processing are quite different from them.

Selection of SRAM/DRAM in NPs

The IXP series of NPs developed by Intel [4] does not have cache, and its SRAM and DRAM have different memory spaces. The developers at Intel reported that cache is not effective in the case of NPs, so this type of memory architecture is good for network processing. However, it is difficult to program IXP processors because programmers, who are not even aware of the difference between SRAM and DRAM, must use them with different methods.

In contrast, the architectures of NPs developed later, for example, Cavium Octeon [5] and Tilera Tile Processors [6] , are more similar to those of general-purpose CPUs with cache. However, because a cache miss may disable wire-rate transmission of packets, there are several devices that can be applied to avoid cache miss. That is, data to be processed at wire rate must be stored in SRAM. However, because an NP cannot usually have sufficient quantity of SRAM to store all the processing packets, it only stores descriptors and headers of packets in SRAM, and the rest or whole packets must be stored in DRAM. Various different types of packet-processing hardware and software behave in a similar way. In addition, to process packets at wire rate, NPs distribute packets to many cores for parallel processing, and they sort the resulting packets by hardware in input order and queue them for output or the next processing.

Selection of SRAM/DRAM with a Packet-Processing Language

In an NP program-development environment called Shangri-La [7] , which was developed by Intel and several universities, a high-level language called Baker [4] was developed for IXP. By assuming that packet bodies are stored in DRAM and descriptors are stored in SRAM, Baker enabled programmers to handle packet data without having to consider whether they are on DRAM or SRAM. The data structure on SRAM, however, must be designed by programmers, so it depends on NP architecture. In addition, programmers must describe data transmission between DRAM and SRAM, so they must explicitly describe caching operations.

Unlike Octeon or Tilera, Baker does not have a mechanism for supporting automatic distinguished use of SRAM and DRAM. It is therefore difficult to process packets at wire rate by using Baker.

Packet-Stream and Data-Stream Languages

Click [8] is software architecture for describing routers modularly. Two-level description is used in Click. The lower level, or component level, is described by C, and the higher level is described by a domain-specific language, which connects modules in several ways. Click programs can be portable, but it is difficult to get high performance from portable Click programs. NP-Click [2] is a specialized implementation of Click for IXP NPs. Modules in NP-Click are written in IXP-specific C language; there-fore, the programs are not portable.

Frenetic [9] is a language for controlling a collection of OpenFlow [10] switches. It is embedded in Python but is based on SQL. It is a declarative language and processes collections (streams) of packets instead of processing individual packets procedurally in the manner of Phonepl. Because Frenetic processes packet streams, it is very similar to CQL (Continuous Query Language) [11] . Unlike Phonepl, Frenetic can only be used to program the control plane; it cannot handle the data plane.

NetCore [12] is a rule-based language for controlling OpenFlow switches. Rules in NetCore are condition- action rules; that is, rules that match incoming packets are activated.

PACKET-PROCESSING LANGUAGE

A high-level language called Phonepl, which solves the three problems described in the introduction, is outlined.

Basic Design of Phonepl

Phonepl is designed for wire-rate (low-level) packet-processing of any format, such as a non-IP and/or non- Ethernet format, as well as designed to be as close as a conventional programming language, i.e., Java, because it should be easy to handle by Java and C++ programmers.

The reason why a new language, which is open, portable, and easy to use, is designed is explained as follows. Although it is close to conventional languages, a new language is required because it is very hard to compile a general-purpose program to high-performance object program for NPs, which very optimized hardware-usage, especially memory usage, is required for. Phonepl may thus be considered as a very restricted and extended version of Java.

Two major design goals of Phonepl are as follows. First, Phonepl must be high-level; that is, it must be designed for the programmer not to be aware of proprietary hardware and software. Second, Phonepl must be able to express high-performance packet-processing programs. Especially, processing at wire-rate, i.e., 10 Gbps or more, without packet drops is required. In an NP, input packets may be partially cached, that is, the header of the packet is stored in SRAM and the rest or whole packet is stored in DRAM, but a DRAM access may disable wire-rate processing and cache miss easily cause packet-drops. However, this goal must be achieved without abandoning the first goal, i.e., high-level programmability.

To achieve these design goals, data structures, especially Packet and String, which are the most important data structures in Phonepl, must be carefully designed and the method for processing them must be developed. Especially, packets are designed to be immutable byte strings in Phonepl and they are distinguished from non-packet strings.

There are five language features concerning this design. The first feature is that packets are byte strings because packets with arbitrary formats should be able to be handled in uniform methods. Packets have variable length, so they can be handled as byte strings (similar to character strings). A packet in Phonepl is not a encapsulated object. This decision makes low-level and cross-layer optimization of packets easier. The protocol-handling method written in Phonepl is thus completely different from that written in Java.

The second feature is that packets are immutable. Packets are handled as immutable (non-rewritable) objects, which are similar to character strings in Java or other languages; that is, packet contents cannot be rewritten. This immutability enables memory areas, especially DRAM areas, to be shared by packets before and after an operation.

The third feature is that types of packets, i.e., Packet, and non-packet strings, i.e., String, are different in Phonepl. They are incompatible for two reasons. First, although they can be logically identical, they must be implemented by using quite different methods and this distinction makes implementation more efficient and easier. Operations such as subpacket and substring described below utilize this difference. Second, programmers can easily distinguish them. Non-packet strings are used for temporary data, e.g., packet fragments, but packets are used for I/O data; that is, packets and packet fragments (non-packets) are different for programmers.

Two assumptions are made in regard to implementation of these data types. The first assumption is that whole String objects are stored in cacheable memory, i.e., in SRAM, but can be stored in DRAM if needed. If they are in cache, purging the cache may have to be inhibited. The second assumption is that only the head of a packet is cached, and the tail is stored only in DRAM. However, a short packet may be wholly cached and may be stored only in SRAM.

The fourth feature is that packet and non-packet byte-substring operations are different in Phonepl because the types of the operation results are different. A new packet can be generated by removing part of another packet using a subpacket operation, and a non-packet byte string can be generated by extracting part of a packet using a substring operation. These operations can have the same name i.e., a substring, but are distinguished.

The fifth feature is that packet- and byte-concatenation operations are specialized. A byte string can be generated by concatenating two or more byte strings by a concat operation, and a packet can be generated by concatenating one or more byte strings and a packet by a packet constructor called "new Packet". Although a packet can logically be generated by concatenating multiple packets, such concatenation seems to be practically less useful and difficult to implement, so no such operation is included (See Section 4.2.3 for more explanations).

Program Example and Packet Operations

To outline Phonepl and to explain several data structures and important packet operations, a program that performs MAC-header addition/removal, which cannot be performed by conventional non-programmable network nodes, is shown in Figure 1. The program in this figure defines class AddRemMAC. It has two functions that handle two bidirectional packet streams, i.e., NetStream1 and NetStream2 (lines 001 - 002), which are bound to physical network interfaces outside this program. One function inputs packets from NetStream1, generates new packets with a new MAC header (i.e., adds a new MAC header at the front) for each packet, and outputs them to NetStream2. The other function inputs packets from NetStream2, removes the MAC header in front, and outputs it to NetStream1. The program is much simplified because it is sufficient to show the functionality and basic implementation of the language; that is, no validation test is performed before the header is added or removed. However, it is easy to add check code to this program.

Packet flows are handled as "streams" in Phonepl. Method of stream handling is described using the constructor of class AddRemMAC here. The parameter declarations of AddRemMAC (lines 006 - 007) specify that input packets to parameter port1 pass to method process1 and input packets to parameter port2 pass to method process2. This type of parameter declaration is Phonepl specific; that is, Java grammar is modified for the sake of stream processing. The parameter values (packet streams) are assigned to instance variables out1 and out2 to make them available in the newly created object. Methods process1 and process2 receive one packet at a time. (One of these methods is executed once on only one core for each packet.) Because Phonepl handles input packets by these methods only, there is no specific method or statement for packet input.

Examples of a substring operation (which is used for accessing packet components), a packet constructor (which is used for packet composition), and a packet-stream output using "put" method can be seen in method process1 (line 011). This method handles a packet that comes from NetStream1, generates a byte string from the first 14 bytes of input packet i (it is assumed that the size of MAC header is 14 bytes) by i.substring(0,14), generates a packet by concatenating this byte string and the original packet by new Packet(· · · ,i), and outputs the resulting packet to NetStream2(out2).

```
001  import NetStream1;
002  import NetStream2;

003  class AddRemMAC {
004     NetStream out1;
005     NetStream out2;

006     public AddRemMAC(NetStream port1 > process1,
007                      NetStream port2 > process2 ){
008       out1 = port1;
009       out2 = port2;
010     }

011     void process1(Packet i) {
                         //Port 1 to 2 (no VLAN -> no VLAN)
012       Packet o = new Packet(i.substring(0,14),i);
            // MAC header of original packet (i: Original packet)
013       out2.put(o);
014     }

015     void process2(Packet i) {
                         // Port 2 to 1 (no VLAN -> no VLAN)
016       Packet o = i.subpacket(14);
           // remove MAC header (no VLAN)
017       out1.put(o);
018     }

019     void main() {
020       new AddRemMAC(new NetStream1(),
021                     new NetStream2());
022     }
023  }
```

Figure 1: Simple MAC-header addition/removal program.

An example of subpacket operation, which generates packets from an existing packet, can be seen in method process2 (line 015). This method handles a packet that comes from NetStream2, generates a packet by removing the first 14 bytes of input packet i by i.subpacket(14), and outputs the resulting packet to NetStream1 (out1).

Finally, an example of stream initialization is seen in function main() (line 019). When class AddRemMAC is initialized, this function is executed. It logically runs only once, but each processor core may execute it once unless there are side-effects. It generates an instance (a singleton) of class AddRemMAC, which runs forever and processes packets repeatedly unless it is externally terminated. Two packet streams are generated and passed as arguments of AddRemMAC. They start to operate (input and/or output packets) when instances are generated.

IMPLEMENTATION METHOD

To implement semantics close to conventional programming languages such as Java, a special method of handling data (object) is required for Phonepl. The key feature of Phonepl implementation is the four representations of packets and operations among them.

Four Representations of Packets

In Phonepl, multiple packet data-representations used in NPs are unified as a single data type called Packet. Four different representations shown in Figure 2(a) (explained below) are therefore used for Packet. These representations are required because of the following two reasons concerning high-performance packet-processing and NP hardware. First, in most packet-processing in network nodes, packet headers are added, removed, or updated, but packet tails, i.e., payloads, are not touched unless very deep packet-inspection is required. So the packet headers must be stored in SRAM (or scratchpad memory) but the packet tails can be stored in DRAM as described in the introduction and in the previous section. It is usually not possible to cache whole packet. Second, NPs are designed to handle input and/or output packets by specialized hardware. The hardware is optimized for the packet-processing requirements described above, but some hardware-specific restrictions apply in addition.

An example of hardware-specific data representation that matches the abstract representation is shown here. In some NPs, there are input-specific and output-specific packet formats using a special descriptor format. Short packets may be fully stored in SRAM but packet heads may be stored in both SRAM and DRAM for longer packets. The four abstract representations are designed to generalize various concrete representations, such as shown in Figure 2(b), used in NPs. Although the descriptor format is specialized, it can be abstracted as shown in Figure 2(a). If vendor-specific C language is used, these representations are handled separately; however, Phonepl, handles them uniformly. Even for cases that the NP has a cache, it is probably useful to distinguish multiple representations because cache miss must be avoided.

The four representations are explained in the following.

- Cached: The whole packet data is stored in SRAM. It is not assumed that a copy of the data is stored in DRAM.
- Mixed: The head of a packet (the number of bytes depends on implementation) is stored in SRAM, and whole packet data is stored in DRAM.
- Gathered: A packet consists of multiple fragments. Each fragment is stored in a memory area (i.e., DRAM or SRAM). A gathered packet can be represented by an array or a linked list of fragments.
- Uncached: The whole packet is stored in DRAM. It is not assumed that a copy of the data is stored in SRAM.

Packets inputted to NPs are usually in cached or mixed representation; that is, short packets may be represented by cached representation but mixed representation is required for long packets. All four representations are used for expressing operation results and may be used for output. However, reasoning of mixed, gathered, and uncached representations are explained more.

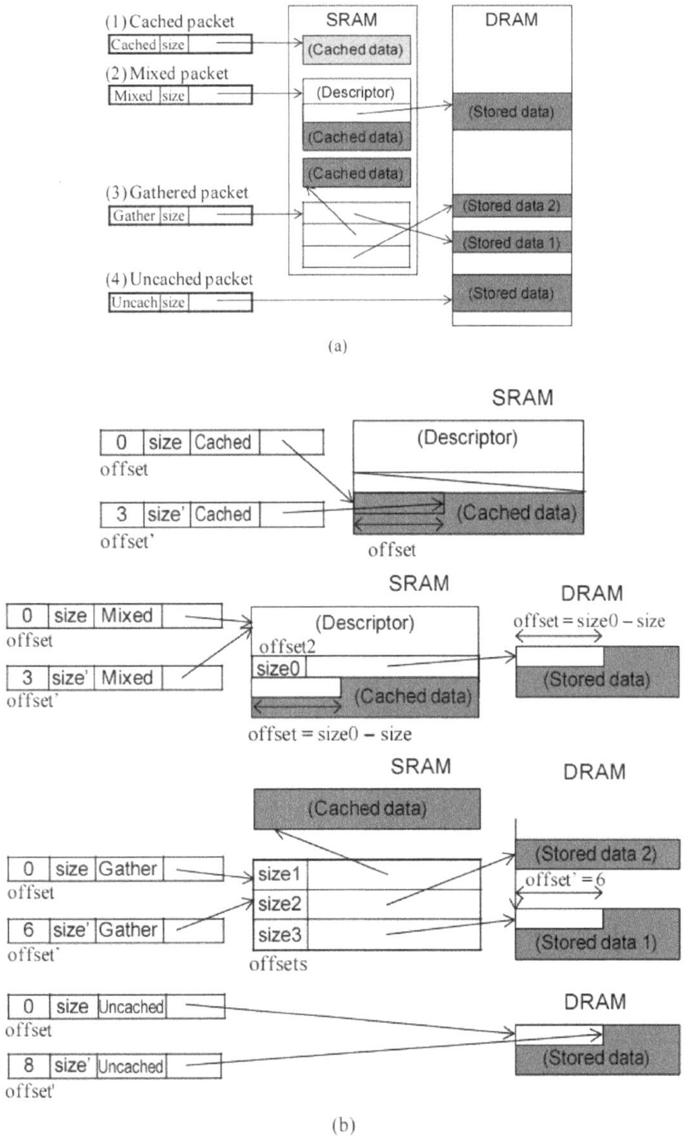

Figure 2: Four representations of packet type. (a) Abstract representations; (b) Examples of more detailed representations.

Mixed representation is required because, in packet processing, only the packet head (containing headers) is usually modified, headers are added or deleted, and the packet tail is kept unchanged. Good performance can therefore be obtained by caching only the head to SRAM and storing the tail only in DRAM. Data accessed by cores must be stored in SRAM because if data stored in DRAM is accessed, it takes excessively long time, and wire-rate processing becomes impossible.

Gathered representation is required when generating a packet from multiple pieces of data stored in DRAM or SRAM. In such a case, if all the pieces are copied to a contiguous area (of DRAM), copy from DRAM to DRAM is required and wire-rate processing becomes impossible. This representation is closely related to the immutability of packets, which enables sharing part of a string.

Uncached representation is required when a packet is generated from a tail of another packet with gathered representation by an operation such as a header deletion.

Because the four representations may have to be distinguished at run time, a tag must be supplied. The tags should be in packet-data pointers. However, because packet data are handled by hardware in NPs, the data representation and handling methods in the case of a high-level language must be very carefully designed and implemented. If the address space is sufficiently large, a part of the address can be used for a tag. This representation is close to widely used methods for dynamically-typed languages, such as Python or Lisp.

Packet Operations and Four Representations

Because there are four packet-data representations and each packet data has a tag, packet operations must be implemented for all these representations, and sometimes run-time tag check is required.

Run-Time Tag Check

Because there are multiple representations in Packet type, they must be distinguished dynamically (by the run-time routines in the NP) or statically (by the Phonepl compiler). In terms of efficiency, it is better for the representation to be statically distinguished. However, it is impossible to distinguish every representation of a packet statically, so run-time tag-check is, at least sometimes, necessary. Especially, if a non-optimizing compiler is used, tag check is always necessary at run time. Such a run-time check causes overhead, but it does not usually prevent wire-rate processing because the tags are in cached pointers and a tag can be added and removed with very small cost.

Packet I/O

Some NP hardware creates a descriptor when receiving a packet. The descriptor is in SRAM, and whole packet data may be stored in DRAM. The input packet format, thus, is close to mixed representation (or cached representation in the case of a short packet); however, a tag must be added when run-time tag-check is required. The run-time routine should thus decide which representation is to be used and insert the tag value. This means that the language processor must fill the gap (i.e., convert) between data representations in the hardware and in Phonepl. If the gap is wide, significant CPU time is required to fill it, and performance may decrease. An appropriate representation design is therefore important.

An output packet format must be prepared for some NPs when sending a packet. One of the four representations should be close to the output format; however, the tag must be removed before passing the data to the packet output hardware. For example, the output format may be close to gathered representation, but the tag value "gathered" must be cleared. The hardware concatenates the fragments pointed to by the gathered representation and outputs the result.

Subpacket

Each representation requires different implementations of an operation to achieve a subpacket operation. In all the cases described below, the operations are executed using data stored in SRAM, and DRAM is not accessed.

If the packet has a cached representation, a subpacket of the packet is in a cached format. The original packet can be stored in the allocated SRAM area. The resulting subpacket may share the original packet data or may be a copy of the original data. In this case, because both the original and copied data are stored in SRAM, this copy operation probably does not prevent wire-rate processing.

If the packet has a mixed representation, a subpacket of the packet may be in a mixed or uncached format. That is, there are two cases. Firstly, if the resulting packet contains both head data stored in SRAM and tail data stored in DRAM, the result is mixed format. Secondly, if the resulting packet only contains tail data, the result is uncached format. In general, the resulting representation is not known at compile time because the range specified in subpacket operation might not be known at compile time. In both cases, a new descriptor is generated in SRAM by using the original descriptor, but no packet data stored in DRAM is accessed.

If the packet has a gathered representation, a substring of the packet is usually in a gathered format. The original and resulting packets may share the array of fragments (i.e., only a packet-type pointer is generated) or the resulting pointer may point to a new array copied from the original array. An array copy probably does not prevent wire-rate processing because both arrays are stored in SRAM.

If the packet has an uncached representation, a substring of the packet is in an uncached format. Both the original and resulting packet data are stored in DRAM and shared. The address and the length of the resulting packet are stored in a packet-type pointer. No packet data stored in DRAM are accessed.

Concatenation

When a packet is generated by concatenating one or more byte strings (such as new headers and a packet content), a constructor, "new Packet()", is used. In the current implementation method, this constructor generates a gathered-format packet. That means, the parameter values of the constructors are the elements of the array in the gathered format. However, a more optimized method, which uses other representations, may be developed.

The last element of the constructor may be a packet of any representation. If this element has a mixed format, the DRAM part (which represents the whole packet) becomes an element of the array. If this element has a gathered format, each input array element becomes an element of the array of the output gathered format.

Generating Packet without Using Input Packet

A packet can be created without using a pre-existing packet by using a packet constructor. The generated packet is in cached or gathered format. If the constructor has only one argument that contains a byte string, the resulting packet is in cached format, and if it has two or more arguments, the resulting packet is in gathered format.

Several Miscellaneous Issues

Two issues related to the proposed packet-handling method are explained in the following. The first issue is memory deallocation. Sharing part of packets and strings makes memory deallocation difficult. Garbage collection or reference counting can solve this problem completely, but the overhead is large. In the current implementation, strings that are (potentially) assigned to global (instance) variables are not deallocated. However, the current deallocation policy may cause memory leak. A more precise method should be devised in future work.

The second issue is adaptation to hardware-based memory allocation. Some NPs allocate and deallocate packet memory automatically to avoid software-memory-management overhead. When a packet arrives, the SRAM and DRAM required for the packet is allocated. However, it is difficult for NP hardware to decide when the packet memory can be deallocated. A Phonepl compiler must therefore generate code for deallocate it.

PROTOTYPING

The above-described implementation method has been applied to a programming environment called +Net, which contains a Phonepl processor called +Net Phonepl. +Net Phonepl is used for programming physical nodes with a network-virtualization function and NPs.

Platform

The prototype compiles a Phonepl program and runs it on a "virtualization node" (VNode) [1] [13] . A virtualization platform called VNode Infrastructure, which supports multiple slices (i.e., virtual networks) using a single network infrastructure, and a high-performance fully functional virtualization testbed were developed. The components of a VNode contain NPs. The prototype is a replacement of one or more NPs in this environment. The program has packet I/O streams as described in Section 3.

A source program is compiled according to the following procedure. First, an intermediate language program (ILP) is generated by using a Phonepl syntax/token analyzer. The syntax analyzer was generated using "Yet Another Perl Parser" (YAPP) compiler, which has similar functions as those of YACC (Yet Another Compiler Compiler) or Bison parser-generators but is written in and generates Perl code. The ILP is translated by using a Phonepl translator into a specialized C program. A GNU C compiler for Octeon compiles this C program and generates object code for an Octeon board called WANic-56512 developed by General Electric Company. A run-time library is linked to the object program. The main components of this library are an initializer, packet processors, and a packet-output routine.

Compiled Code of +Net-Phonepl Compiler

To outline the object-code structure and the compilation (or program transformation), an example of compiled code is explained here. The C program generated by the Phonepl compiler from the MAC-header addition/removal program (in Figure 1) is shown in Figure 3.

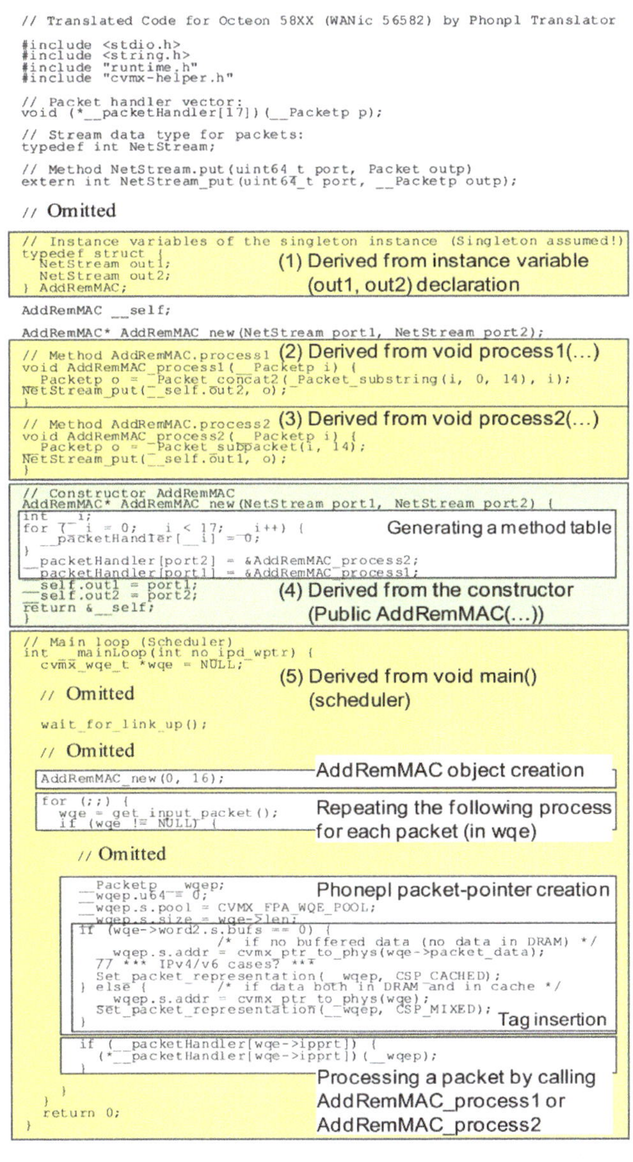

Figure 3: Compiled code of MAC-header insertion/deletion program.

This program is explained instead of describing detailed compilation process because the process is too much complicated and the program structure can probably be used for other types of NPs. A compilation technique specialized for a singleton (i.e., single-instance class) is applied to this program. Cores in an Octeon processor execute this program in parallel; that is, each core processes a packet. The program consists of five parts: part 1 derived from instance-variable declaration, parts 2 and 3 derived from methods process1 and process2, part 4 derived from the constructor, and part 5 derived from the main program.

In part 1, AddRemMAC type, which corresponds to instance of class AddRemMAC in Phonepl, is declared. Because a compiled object of class AddRemMAC has two objects of NetStream type, the corresponding structure components are declared. In parts 2 and 3, i.e., method definitions, the element names in the source program are replaced by the element names in the run-time library. The run-time routines may be expanded in-line; however, they are not expanded in this example program. In part 4, i.e., the constructor of class AddRemMAC, methods process1 and process2 are initialized. Assignment statements that correspond to the assignment statements in the source program are included in this part. In part 5, i.e., the main program, the above constructor is called, and every time it receives a packet, one of the above two methods are called. Because NetStream type is an abstraction of a packet stream, the stream elements are handled one by one, and the scheduler for this process occupies the main part of part 5. When the function get_input_packet() is called, a packet is received, and the data representation of this packet is converted to that of +Net Phonepl by adding a tag, i.e., cached (CSP_CACHED) or mixed (CSP_MIXED).

EVALUATION

Both the programmability, especially ease of language use, and the performance of the implementation should be evaluated; however, because Phonepl is being improved, performance is focused in this evaluation. Two Phonepl programs for network-layer packet handling were written. Prototypes with these object programs were used for extending VNode, and the traffic was measured.

MAC-Header Addition/Deletion Program

The first program performs MAC-header addition/removal. It is a modified version of the program shown in Figure 1, and similar programs are used for extending virtualization-node (VNode) functions by using the node plug-in architecture [14] -[16] . Instead of duplicating the MAC header, the Phonepl program inserts a constant MAC header that contains fixed source and destination MAC addresses and a TEB type value (i.e., transparent Ethernet bridge, x6558).

As shown in Figure 4, the above program was used in an extended VNode, which is a gateway between slices and external networks and is called NACE or NC [17] . This network consists of the VNode and two personal computers, PC1 and PC2. PC1 simulates a terminal or a virtual node in a slice. PC2 is in an external physical network. The VNode connects the slice and the external network, and it must convert the packet format, i.e., convert from the internal to external protocols, and vice versa, but the base component of the VNode does not have this conversion function. The VNode is experimentally extended by the node plug-in architecture with the

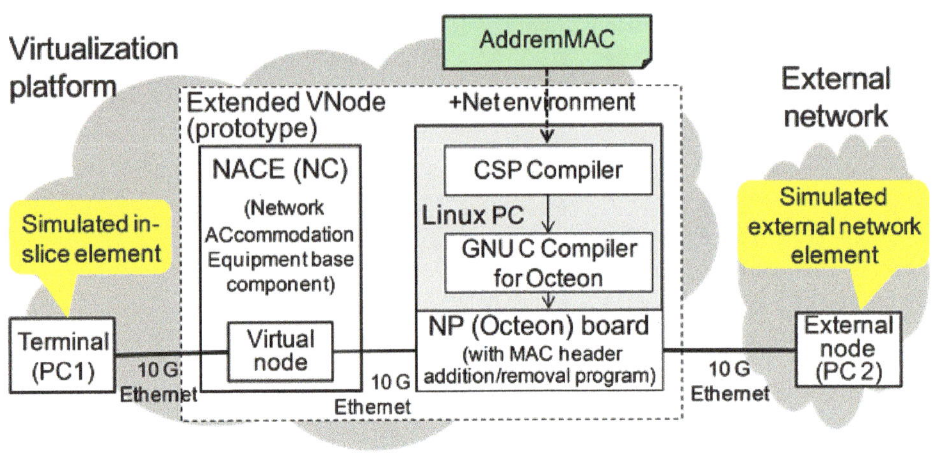

Figure 4: Extended VNode environment for experiments.

+Net environment, which consists of a PC with a Phonepl compiler, run-time routines, a GNU C compiler for Octeon, and WANic-56512 with twelve-core 750-MHz Octeon. By using conversion programs written in Phonepl, the VNode can adapt to various types of external networks.

Maximum performance of the test program was measured by using a network-measurement-tool suite called IXIA. Both operations, i.e., MAC-header addition and deletion, were measured, and compared with a pass- through program, which is also written in Phonepl. The measurement results are shown in Figure 5. In this experiment, the input packet representation is mixed or cached, and the output packet representation is mixed or cached for header deletion and it is gathered for header addition. Uncached format is not used here because not whole cached data is removed by the header deletion. The maximum throughput (input rate) that can be passed with almost no packet drop is over 7.5 Gbps when the packet size is 256 bytes or larger. This throughput is close to the wire rate. The throughputs of two programs are mostly the same, indicating that the major overhead lies in the hardware or the initialization/finalization code, namely, not in the compiled code or the packet/string run- time routines.

Table 1 compares the performance of the Phonepl program on the Octeon and a sequential C program on eight-core 3-GHz Intel Xeon processors. Although the performance of the former is much higher, it is mainly caused by the number of used cores. If all the cores are used, the throughput of Xeon may be better; however, it is very hard to use multiple cores and to preserve the order of packets in Xeon. As shown in Table 1, the Phonepl program is much shorter even when compared with the C program.

Moreover, Table 1 suggests an important difference between the two implementations; that is, the packet loss ratio is slowly increasing in the Xeon implementation because cache miss is slowly increasing, but packets are almost never lost if the input ratio is 9.2 Gbps or less in the Phonepl implementation because the memory usage is completely controlled.

Timestamp Handler for Network Virtualization Platform

The second program, which is described in detail in another paper [18] , is a program for measuring communication delay between two points in the virtualization network. In this evaluation, NPs and the program was used only in VNodes, and a slow-path program was used in the gateways.

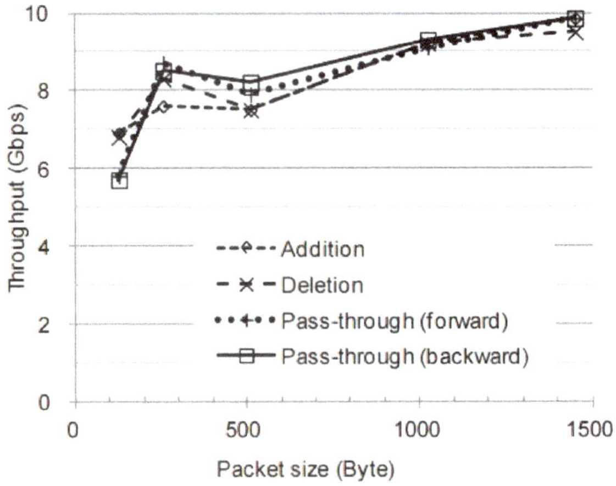

Figure 5: Performance of MAC-header addition/deletion.

Table 1: Results of MAC header addition/deletion

Implementation	Throughput (Gbps)*		Program lines
	Header addition	Header deletion	
Phonepl program	9.2†	9.2†	26‡
C program (Xeon, single core)**	2.3† (4.0††)	1.7† (4.0††)	161‡

*Packet size: 1024 B; **Promiscuous mode is used; †No packet loss (ratio < 10^{-6}); ††Packet loss ratio = 10^{-3}; ‡Comment-only lines are not counted.

A VNode platform can support delay measurement function without adding programs and data (i.e., packet format) for measurement to programs in virtual nodes. This function is useful when slice developers want to measure delay of a high-bandwidth application with certain intelligent functions in relaying nodes. A special type of virtual links between nodes, which is called measurable VLAN virtual link (MVL) type and developed by using the VNode plug-in architecture, is used to implement this function. MVLs are implemented by using timestamp insertion/deletion programs in the nodes. A VNode removes the platform header, which includes a GRE/IP or VLAN header and the timestamp, from an incoming packet and adds one to an outgoing packet, so programs that handles packets on a slice never see the platform header.

The virtualization-network structure used for this experiment is drawn in Figure 6. Two terminals communicate using a slice. The physical network contains two VNodes. Each VNode contains a virtual node, which are connected by an MVL. In the platform, each packet has a platform header with a timestamp.

The communication and measurement methods used for this experiment is as follows. The timestamp is inserted at the entrance gateway. Each VNode generates a packet for the virtual node by removing the platform header from an incoming packet and restores the timestamp to outgoing packets that comes from the virtual node and are identified with a stored incoming packet. The timestamp is tested and deleted at the exit gateway, which calculates the delay between the entrance and exit gateways. In the network described in Figure 6, the two VNodes and one PC is used for the two gateways (and terminals) to avoid the difficult synchronization problem. Terminal PCs communicate each other by using Ethernet packets, which are switched by the MAC addresses in the virtual nodes. A WANic-56512 that contains the program handles both incoming and outgoing packets. An Ethernet switch program, which is a slow-path program, works on a virtual node in a VNode.

The NP also swaps the external and internal MAC addresses in the platform header [1] . To swap addresses, the program contains a conversion table for these MAC addresses, which is implemented using a string array, and accepts virtual-link-creation and deletion requests. A creation request adds an entry to the conversion table.

The results show the gateway-to-gateway delay is 178 μS (σ = 24 μS). Table 2 compares the performance of the 750 MHz Octeon and the 3-GHz Xeon. The performance is very close to wire rate. The C program is relatively short because this program does not contain conversion-table configuration code but the Phonepl program contains it. However, the former is still much longer.

CONCLUDING REMARKS

An open, portal, and high-level language, called Phonepl, is proposed. By using Phonepl, a programmer can develop a program that uses SRAM and DRAM appropriately without having to be aware of a distinction between SRAM and DRAM. To handle packets appropriately in this environment, four packet data-representations and packet-operation methods are proposed. A prototype using Octeon NP was developed and evaluated. The throughput of the prototype system is close to the wire rate, i.e., 10 Gbps, when the packet size is 256 bytes or larger, in several packet-conversion applications.

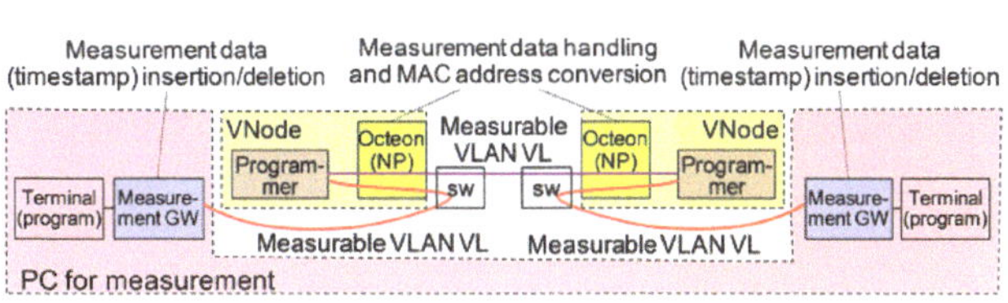

Figure 6: Virtualization-network structure for time-stamp handling.

Table 2: Results of timestamp handling and conversion

Implementation	Throughput (Gbps)*		Program lines
	Header addition	Header deletion	
Phonepl program	10.0†	9.5†	99‡
C program (Xeon, single core)**	2.3† (4.0††)	2.2† (4.0††)	190‡

*Packet size: 1024 B; **Promiscuous mode is used; †No packet loss (ratio < 10^{-6}); ††Packet loss ratio = 10^{-3}; ‡Comment-only lines are not counted.

*Packet size: 1024 B; **Promiscuous mode is used; †No packet loss (ratio < 10^{-6}); †Packet loss ratio = 10^{-3}; ‡Comment-only lines are not counted.

Although this is a preliminary result, it proves the proposed method is promising in achieving our objectives, i.e., popularity among developers, reduced cost in programmability, and portability.

Future work includes evaluation of Phonepl language and processor by human programmers and improvement of the language design and implementation according to the evaluation result. Although Phonepl and the language processor inevitably have limitations, they should be acceptable and, if possible, natural to programmers. Future work also includes implementation of Phonepl for other types of NPs to prove the portability. Moreover, the memory allocation and deallocation mechanism must be improved to reduce memory leak caused by global variable assignments and the performance of the Phonepl language processor should be improved.

ACKNOWLEDGEMENTS

Yasusi Kanada (NICT).

REFERENCES

1. Kanada, Y., Shiraishi, K. and Nakao, A. (2012) Network-Virtualization Nodes That Support Mutually Independent Development and Evolution of Components. IEEE International Conference on Communication Systems (ICCS 2012).http://dx.doi.org/10.1109/iccs.2012.6406171
2. Shah, N., Plishker, W., Ravindran, K. and Keutzer, K. (2004) NP-Click: A Productive Software Development Approach for Network Processors. IEEE Micro, 24, 45-54.http://dx.doi.org/10.1109/mm.2004.53
3. Fatahalian, K., Knight, T.J., Houston, M., Erez, M., Horn, D.R., Leem, L., Park, J.Y., Ren, M., Aiken, A., Dally, W. J. and Hanrahan, P. (2006) Sequoia: Programming the Memory Hierarchy. 2006 ACM/IEEE Conference on Supercomputing.http://dx.doi.org/10.1109/sc.2006.55
4. Goglin, S.D., Hooper, D., Kumar, A. and Yavatkar, R. (2003) Advanced Software Framework, Tools, and Languages for the IXP Family. Intel Technology Journal, 7, 64-76.
5. Cavium Networks (2010) OCTEON Programmer's Guide. The Fundamentals.http://university.caviumnetworks.com/downloads/Mini_version_of_Prog_Guide_EDU_July_2010.pdf
6. Bell, S., Edwards, B., Amann, J., Conlin, R., Joyce, K., Leung, V., MacKay, J., Reif, M., Bao, L.W., Brown, J., Mattina, M., Miao, C.-C., Ramey, C., Wentzlaff, D., Anderson, W., Berger, E., Fairbanks, N., Khan, D., Montenegro, F., Stickney, J. and Zook, J. (2008) TILE64-Processor: A 64-Core SoC with Mesh Interconnect. IEEE International Solid- State Circuits Conference (ISSCC 2008), San Francisco, 3-7 February 2008, 88-598.http://dx.doi.org/10.1109/isscc.2008.4523070
7. Chen, M.K., Li, X.F., Lian, R., Lin, J.H., Liu, L.X., Liu, T. and Ju, R. (2005) Shangri-La: Achieving High Performance from Compiled Network Applications While Enabling Ease of Programming. 2005 ACM SIGPLAN Conference on Programming Language Design and Implementation (PLDI'05), 224-236. http://dx.doi.org/10.1145/1064978.1065038
8. Kohler, E., Morris, R., Chen, B.J., Jannotti, J. and Frans Kaashoek, M. (2000) The Click Modular Router. ACM Transactions on Computer Systems, 18, 263-297.http://dx.doi.org/10.1145/354871.354874
9. Foster, N., Harrison, R., Freedman, M.J., Monsanto, C., Rexford, J., Story, A. and Walker, D. (2011) Frenetic: A Network Programming Language. 16th ACM SIGPLAN International Conference on Functional Programming (ICFP'11).http://dx.doi.org/10.1145/2034773.2034812
10. McKeown, N., Anderson, T., Balakrishnan, H., Parulkar, G., Peterson, L., Rexford, J., Shenker, S. and Turner, J. (2008) Open Flow: Enabling Innovation in Campus Networks. ACM SIGCOMM Computer Communication Review, 38, 69-74.http://dx.doi.org/10.1145/1355734.1355746
11. Arasu, A., Babu, S. and Widom, J. (2006) The CQL Continuous Query Language: Semantic Foundations and Query Execution. The VLDB Journal, 15, 121-142. http://dx.doi.org/10.1007/s00778-004-0147-z
12. Monsanto, C., Foster, N., Harrison, R. and Walker, D. (2012) A Compiler and Run-Time System for Network Programming Languages. Proceedings of the 39th ACM SIGPLAN-SIGACT Symposium on Principles of Programming Languages, Philadelphia, 25-27 January 2012, 217-230. http://dx.doi.org/10.1145/2103656.2103685
13. Nakao, A. (2012) VNode: A Deeply Programmable Network Testbed through Network Virtualization. Proceedings of the 3rd IEICE Technical Committee on Network Virtualization, Tokyo, 2 March 2012. http://www.ieice.org/~nv/05-nv20120302-nakao.pdf
14. Kanada, Y. (2013) A Node Plug-In Architecture for Evolving Network Virtualization Nodes. 2013 Software Defined Networks for Future Networks

and Services (SDN4FNS).http://dx.doi.org/10.1109/sdn4fns.2013.6702531

15. Kanada, Y. (2014) A Method for Evolving Networks by Introducing New Virtual Node/Link Types Using Node Plug- Ins. Proceedings of the IEEE Network Operations and Management Symposium (NOMS), Krakow, 5-9 May 2014, 1-8.http://dx.doi.org/10.1109/noms.2014.6838417
16. Kanada, Y. (2014) Controlling Network Processors by Using Packet-Processing Cores. Proceedings of the 28th International Conference on Advanced Information Networking and Applications Workshops (WAINA), Victoria, 13-16 May 2014, 690-695.http://dx.doi.org/10.1109/waina.2014.112
17. Kanada, Y., Shiraishi, K. and Nakao, A. (2012) High-Performance Network Accommodation into Slices and In-Slice Switching Using a Type of Virtualization Node. 2nd International Conference on Advanced Communications and Computation (Infocomp 2012), IARIA.
18. Kanada, Y. (2014) Extending Network-Virtualization Platforms Using a Specialized Packet-Header and Node Plug-Ins. Proceedings of the 22nd International Conference on Telecommunications and Computer Networks, Split, 17-19 September 2014.

CHAPTER 10 A COMPARISON OF COMMON PROGRAMMING LANGUAGES USED IN BIOINFORMATICS

Mathieu Fourment, Michael R Gillings

BACKGROUND

Bioinformatic analyses involve a range of tasks and processes. Diverse programs have been written for various bioinformatics applications using every available language. Because of the size of bioinformatics datasets, computation time is not trivial, and efficiencies in computational speed are desirable. Comparisons of the algorithm accuracy of different programs that undertake similar tasks have been published [1–7] allowing assessment of the best algorithms to use for specific tasks. However, it is possible that the same program, written in different languages, or running under different operating systems, may exhibit significant differences in speed and efficiency. There is, at present, little direct data on the underlying speed and efficiency of equivalent algorithms written in different languages. While languages themselves have been benchmarked, such comparisons have not been done using algorithms that are relevant to bioinformatics [8].

A typical bioinformatics program reads FASTA files, holds the DNA sequences in memory, performs different computing tasks on the sequences, and finally writes the results to a file. Another common task in bioinformatics is text mining or text parsing. Large amounts of data can be generated in different formats. Because file formats can be different, linking programs in a pipeline is difficult, hence scripts are written to act as interfaces between programs performing the sequential parts of an analysis. Scripts are also used to extract information from large data files, thus enhancing the presentation of results. These quick scripts are usually implemented in Perl or Python. Consequently, any bioinformatics procedure has a number of areas where programming might be improved, these being: the space required to temporarily store data, the speed of computation, linkage between programs, and presentation of analyses.

In this paper we examined three commonly used tasks in biology, the Sellers algorithm [9] the Neighbor-Joining NJ algorithm [10] and a program parsing the output of BLAST [11]. In each case we tested the programs using different languages. This benchmark was conducted on both Linux and Windows, since the computer used had a dual boot. There were several reasons for this benchmarking exercise. We specifically wanted to determine if C would be faster than Java for performing recombination detection, which is an inherently difficult computational exercise. We also wanted to examine the memory requirements of each program/language combination, since although memory capacity increases constantly and hardware gets cheaper, the large datasets in bioinformatics analyses can be a problem for desktop computers. We also wanted to compare a script language, such as Perl, with the compiled languages Java and C. To complete the comparison, "rival" languages were also included. These included C++, C# and Python. The languages selected for this study were chosen on the basis that they are the most popular and frequently used for biological applications.

Python and Perl are often called script languages and when executed, are compiled in an intermediate representation without creating an intermediate file (syntax tree in Perl and byte code in Python) and then interpreted. Both languages use automatic memory management and have large free libraries. They are suitable for web scripting (e.g. CGI), parsing and pipeline implementation such as InterProScan [12].

C and C++ are fully compiled languages, suitable for system-intensive tasks.

Java and C# are semi-compiled languages using automatic memory management. A Java program is compiled in an intermediate-level code or bytecode then it is run by either an

Citation: Fourment, M. & Gillings, A comparison of common programming languages used in bioinformatics, doi:10.1186/1471-2105-9-82.

interpreter or compiler at runtime, in this case, the Java Virtual Machine (JVM). In C# the intermediate-level code is called Microsoft Intermediate Language and is run on the .NET Common Language Runtime engine.

Volunteer projects have produced libraries or modules for biologists. The most popular open source projects, which are incorporated in the Open Bioinformatics Foundation, are BioPerl, BioPython and BioJava [13].

RESULTS

The languages we investigated can be divided into 3 groups: The script group of Perl and Python; the semi-compiled group of Java and C#; and the compiled group of C and C++.

Firstly we compared languages within groups, then we compared the groups to each other (Fig.1, 2, 3, 4), and finally we compared speed performance between Windows and Linux. In this paper we will refer to ease of coding as the number of coding lines needed to write a program, taking into account the availability of libraries, which is a factor in the number of coding lines needed for compiling a program.

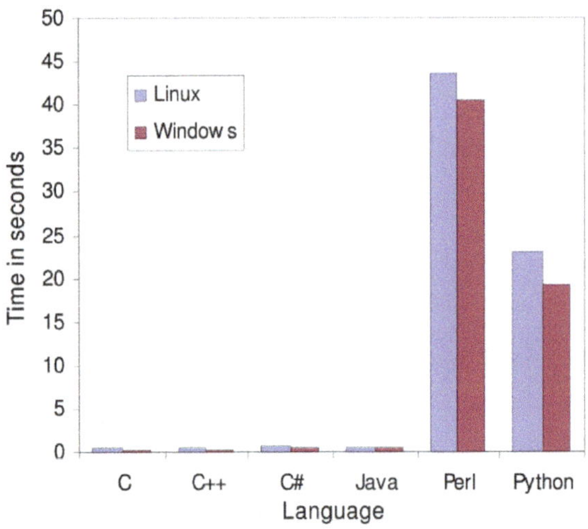

Figure 1: Speed comparison of the global alignment program. Speed comparison of the global alignment algorithm using a gap penalty of 10 implemented in C, C++, C#, Java, Perl and Python. The programs were run on Linux and Windows platforms. Two DNA sequences of 3216 bp and 3217 bp were used.

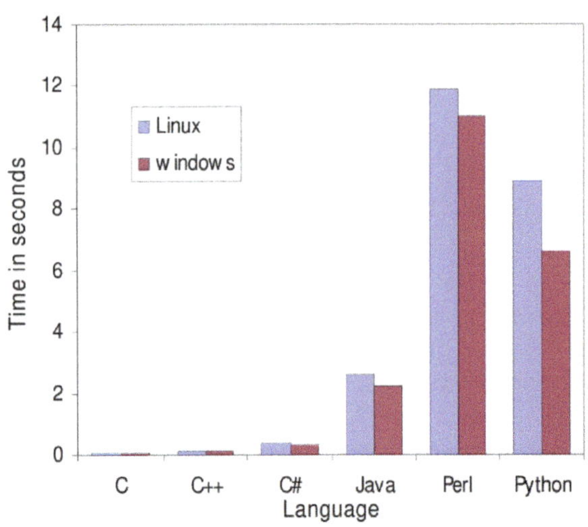

Figure 2: Speed comparison of the Neighbor-Joining program. Speed comparison of the Neighbor-Joining algorithm using the Jukes-Cantor evolutionary model implemented in C, C++, C#, Java, Perl and Python. The programs were run on Linux and Windows platforms. The input file was an alignment of 76 DNA sequences.

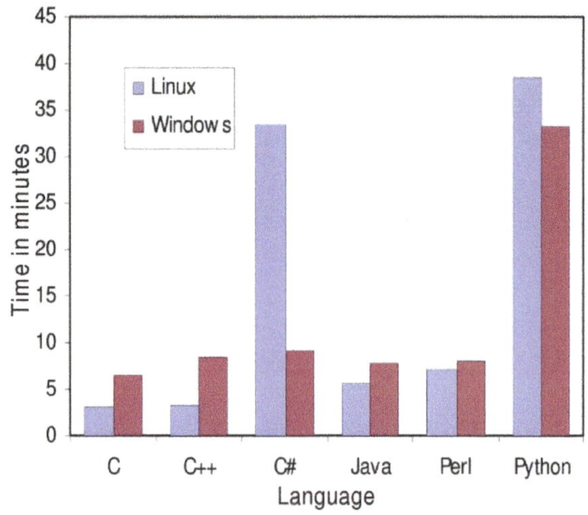

Figure 3: Speed comparison of the BLAST parsing program. Speed comparison of the BLAST parsing program implemented in C, C++, C#, Java, Perl and Python. The programs were run on Linux and Windows platforms. The input file was a 9.8 Gb file from a BLASTP run.

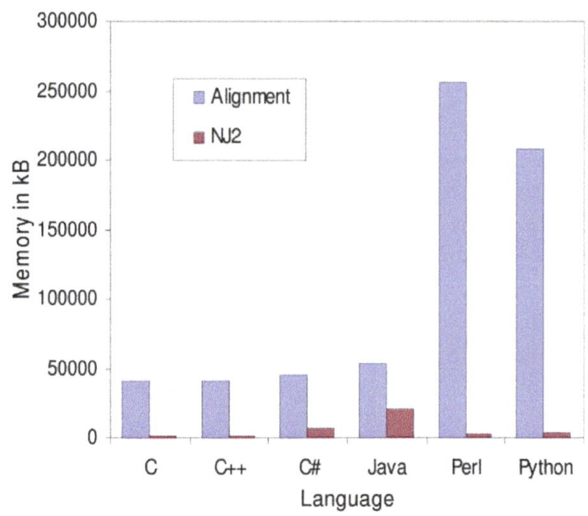

Figure 4: Memory usage comparison of the Neighbor-Joining and global alignment programs. Memory usage comparison for the Neighbor-Joining and global alignment programs implemented in C, C++, C#, Java, Perl and Python. The programs were run on a Linux platform.

Perl versus Python

Perl clearly outperformed Python for I/O operations. Perl was three times as fast as Python when reading a FASTA file and needed half of the space to store the sequences in memory (Fig4). From the results of the global alignment and NJ programs Python appeared to have better character string manipulation capabilities than Perl. Even though the NJ program required reading a file, where Python did not perform well compared to Perl (Fig 2), the computation of the dissimilarity matrix was actually the most discriminating task, since more than 90% of processing time was taken up by this step for every language except C, where it took up 75% of processing time.

Python was the worst performer for parsing a BLAST file (Fig 3), taking more than 38 minutes to process the file compared to Perl, which took only 7.28 minutes. This difference did not arise from any inability of Python to handle large files, since it took only 3.2 minutes to read the file without processing the lines. Perl accomplished the same task in only 1.4 minutes.

Perl emphasizes support for common application-oriented tasks, by having built-in regular expressions, file scanning and report generating features. Python emphasizes support for common programming methodologies such as data structure design and object-oriented programming.

Java versus C#

C# appeared to require less memory than Java for holding strings in memory, as demonstrated when reading DNA sequences from a file (Fig 4). C# also needed less time to read this type of file. Interestingly, Java was slightly faster in the global alignment program (Fig 1) but much slower in the NJ program (Fig 2). Java regular expression implementation appeared to outperform C# (Fig 3). This difference did not arise through any inability of C# to handle large files, since it read these files faster than Java did. Java needed 3.2 minutes whereas C# took only 2.8 minutes to read the same file.

C versus C++

The performance of C and C++ was very similar (Fig 1, 2, 3, 4). This is perhaps not surprising since C++ is an extension of C. When a C program was compiled with the C++ compiler we obtained near-identical results, but when C++ standard libraries (ie. character strings) were used, the performances tended to slightly deteriorate. It is important to note that tokenization was twice as fast as regular expressions for parsing the same BLAST file, but it took more time to write the program using tokens.

Group versus group

The global alignment example demonstrated that the semi-compiled languages (Java and C#) were nearly as fast as the compiled group (C and C++), whereas the interpreted languages (Perl and Python) were sixty-fold slower (Fig 1). In the NJ program, the performance of C# was similar to C and C++, while Java took significantly more time (Fig 2).

The biggest drawback for semi-compiled languages is their memory usage, since they required about 20 times more memory than C and 3 times more memory than Perl (Fig 4).

Java and C# appeared to be a compromise between the speed of C/C++ and the ease of coding of Perl/Python.

Surprisingly, Java performed better than Perl during the regular expression benchmark.

In Java it is possible to embed C code to enhance the efficiency of a program using Java Native Interface (JNI) extensions. The equivalent in Perl would be the e Xternal Subroutine (XS) extension. For example, the core of the NJ program was written in Perl, but when the subroutine calculating a pairwise comparison was written in C, it sped up the program from 11.8 seconds to 0.29 seconds. JNI improved this speed to a lesser extent, from 2.58 seconds to 0.71 seconds. Any loss of portability was compensated for by the gain in performance, since there was no need to rewrite the entire program.

Windows versus Linux

The relative performance of the tested languages did not change on Windows but the overall performance changed depending on the program compared. Only C# and Python appeared consistently faster in every program on Windows. In the global alignment program all the implementations performed better in the Windows environment (Fig 1). In the NJ (Fig 2) and the BLAST parser (Fig 3), C and C++ were both slower on Windows whereas on Windows, Java and Perl were faster in the NJ example (Fig 2) but slower in the BLAST parser example.

The comparison of Linux and Windows has to be carefully interpreted, since the compiler implementations are different, as well as the operating system running them. In the end, speed and memory usage are the critical factors, since the user is looking for performance in the programs, not more generally in the OS or compilers.

Case study: BLAST server

A fast and memory efficient program can make a significant difference when running on a public server such as BLAST, which is queried millions of time a day. The obvious choice for such a computer intensive program was to use C with Perl CGI for the web interface. If we consider that Perl was nearly 60 times slower than C in the global alignment benchmark and that a query sequence of 3500 nucleotides against the non-redundant database took roughly 10 seconds (including the transfer over the web), then if the query is submitted a million times during the day, the total computation time would have increased 60 fold, taking considerably more server time. The same observation would apply for the memory usage. After choosing the appropriate programming language, it is also important to keep improving the base algorithm. New algorithms for analyzing phylogenetic relationships have reduced computing time from weeks to days, or even hours [14].

DISCUSSION

All the programs examined here were written by the same programmer with different levels of experience in Java, Perl and C++. The other languages were implemented while learning them. Even though the semantics of these languages is similar, since C influenced C++, C#, Java, Perl and Python directly or indirectly, the philosophy of some of the languages is different and programs should be implemented according to the language paradigm. For example, Perl programmers favor hash tables to arrays, coupled with a loop which is more widely used in C. It is also important to keep in mind that the hash function can be costly when adding a new value and the memory allocated would be larger than an array containing the same number of elements. The advantage of a hash table is the speed in retrieving some data, but when the programmer needs to examine sequentially all the values in the hash table, then a hash table should be avoided because of the extra cost occurring when adding the key-value pair. In the Perl NJ algorithm an implementation using an array to store the sequences appeared to be faster and more memory efficient than a program using a hash table. Hence no hashtable was used in this benchmark. There is an important tradeoff between performance and convenience. Perl and Python allow reading and loading a file in memory in one statement. While this approach is convenient compared to reading and processing a file line by line, the operating system could start swapping memory out, thus slowing everything down.

Object creation, garbage collection and memory recycling are costly in terms of CPU and memory usage, hence some precautions should be taken when creating objects and the number of objects should be reduced as much as possible. To prevent memory leaks or heavy applications, objects should also be reused when possible and immutable objects such as the String object in Java should be avoided especially when temporary objects are created in frequently used routines. C# and Java have a higher memory-size penalty for objects than other object oriented languages such as C++ due to their ability to use reflection. Reflection is a powerful tool that contributes to the flexibility of these two languages. However this feature should only be used when needed, since reflection method calls have a substantial performance overhead, make the code harder to understand and errors are found at runtime instead of compile-time.

The way objects are accessed and stored in memory influences the performance of each language. C++, C# and Java store objects as a block of data and access them via constant offsets, whereas objects in Python are implemented as hash tables. There are several ways to create objects in Perl. Different data structures can be used, but most programmers use hashes, even though arrays are faster, prevent attribute collisions and take less memory.

It is worth noting that the Perl implementation of the NJ algorithm was substantially improved by converting each sequence to an array instead of using the substr function on the string of characters for computing the similarity matrix. Although the program was 10% faster, the memory footprint showed a ten-fold increase.

Expressiveness

The number of lines in a program varies from one programmer to another, and also on their willingness to shorten the code to the detriment of readability. It is important to emphasize that it is hardly possible to find a correlation between expressiveness and performance.

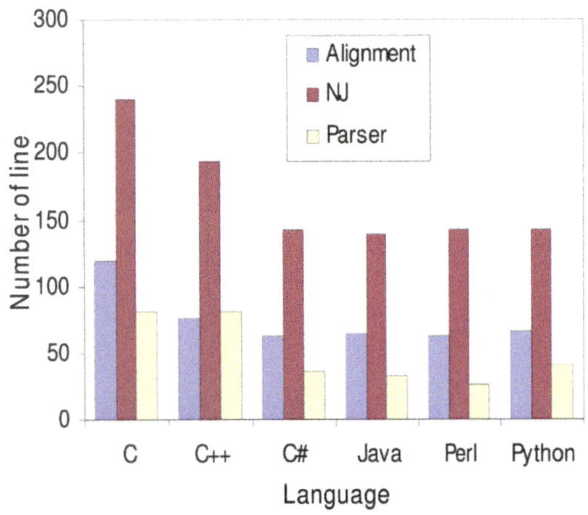

Figure 5: Number of lines for each program. Number of lines for the global alignment, BLAST parser and Neighbor-Joining programs implemented in C, C++, C#, Java, Perl and Python.

Nevertheless, a noticeable difference was observed (Fig. 5), especially with regular expressions. In Perl, a unique statement can be used to detect a pattern and the captured pattern is retrieved with the special variable $1, whereas in Java the programmer has to instantiate a Pattern object which is a compiled representation of the regular expression, then create a Matcher object which performs match operations on a character sequence by interpreting the pattern object. The following examples illustrate the retrieval of a GI number from a FASTA file:

Perl:

```
print $1 if($string =~/^>gi\ |(\ d{3,})/);
```

Java:

```
Pattern p = Pattern.compile("^>gi\ |(\ d{3,})");

Matcher m = p.matcher(string);

if(m.find()) System.out.print(m.group(1));
```

Language philosophies often explain differences in the relative expressiveness and readability of languages. For example, the philosophy of Python is to take the clearest, simplest and most straightforward approach to writing a program, and to accept the resulting performance penalty. Whereas Perl gives more freedom to the programmer resulting, in some cases, in programs that are unreadable for non Perl programmers.

Factors such as performance and memory usage are important, but need not be the sole determinant when choosing a language. Since time management is also an important factor, a language can be chosen for its library, future scalability, active community and interface to other languages.

While it is hard to define a learning curve for each language, advantages and disadvantages of each language can be found. Memory management such as memory allocation makes tasks easier for Java, C#, Perl, Python and Perl programmers, even though memory usage should always be under scrutiny. The use of pointers in C and C++ can be overwhelming for a learner, and it may take some time to master their use. Python is designed to be a highly readable language, frequently using English keywords, whereas the five other languages use punctuation.

Platform independence can be a factor for choosing a language and can also facilitate its learning. Java uses a virtual machine to run on different operating systems and since Perl and Python are stored in a text file and not in a binary file these scripts can be run on any computer having the appropriate interpreter.

The standard library diversity and size of Java, Python and C# are a major advantage compared to the other languages,. including sets of classes to create graphical interfaces, data structures (vectors, hash tables, stacks, queues), regular expression, database access and networking.

Although the Perl standard library appears smaller compared to Java, Python and C#'s, it benefits from a large community of programmers creating modules gathered by the CPAN network [15].

C has a very limited standard library supporting input and output streams, memory allocation, mathematics, character strings, and time values. The C++ library contains the C library as well as a class to manipulate string of characters and the Standard Template Library containing containers or data structures such as algorithms, an improved String library and input/output stream libraries.

As shown previously in the global alignment example, Java and Perl can communicate with a program written in C, speeding up the program using JNI and XS respectively. For example, if a computer intensive command based program written in C needs a graphical interface, an easy solution would be to use the Swing library and the JNI framework instead of rewriting the whole program in Java. The possibility of a language to language interface is useful when some code is already written in one of them.

As well as C, the JNI framework allows Java to interact with C++ and Fortran. The downside of this approach is the loss of portability. Java can also interact with Python using Jython, which is an implementation of Python in Java.

Some bioinformatics tasks, such as loading a FASTA file or parsing a BLAST file, are so frequently used that it makes sense to reuse bits of code by creating libraries or modules. Many programmers produce modules for the bioinformatics community and make them available through their websites. The most widely used libraries are BioPerl, BioPython and BioJava. These Open Source projects belong to the Open Bioinformatics Foundation and they provide toolkits with multiple functionality that make it easier to create customized pipelines or analysis.

Unfortunately libraries with this level of organization and diversity are not available for C, C++ and C# even though some small libraries are available independently [16, 17]

In this paper we focused on the performance of languages, not on the performance of the algorithm implementations. For example the speed of the alignment program could be improved by using a one-dimension array of size $n \times m$ instead of a 2-dimensional matrix of size $n \times m$. This approach would speed up the memory allocation, but this was not the goal of this benchmark.

In this paper, to find the fastest implementations we used profiling tools included in libraries or using compilation/execution options. Profiling provides important information about applications, such as memory usage and the fraction of time spent in each function. By using profiling and a trial-and-error approach programs were significantly improved. We used the Devel::DProf library in Perl, the Xprof option in Java, the cProfile module in Python, the default profiler in C# using -profile = default and the -pg compiler option coupled with the gprof program in C and C++.

CONCLUSION

As expected, C was the best performer in this benchmark, in terms of both speed and memory usage. But to achieve such performances generally requires more code because of the reduced standard library. This benchmark is only a preliminary test involving a limited number of analysis types. Comparisons using different programs may change the relative performance of the languages. Graphic interfaces are very important in biology, hence it would be interesting to compare the libraries available.

The best choice of language for a task would be according to the original philosophy, keeping in mind that Java is portable web oriented language, Perl is a powerful script language, Python is an easily coded language and C and C++ are efficient languages used in operating systems and drivers.

Performances can also vary depending on the compiler and version used. Sun is constantly improving the Java compiler and interpreter and other JVM implementations are also available such as Kaffe [18] and IBM's.

The primary motivation for this benchmark was to compare a recombination detection program in Java and C. The recombination program written in Java ran in 11 minutes and the new version in C ran in 9 minutes with the same dataset and the same parameters. This test involved some hundreds of sequences and a single gene target. Given the rapid improvements in high throughput sequencing technologies, it is likely that tests involving orders of magnitude more sequences will be conducted in the future. Savings in computing time will be essential for such analyses to be efficient.

METHODS

Benchmark design

During the benchmarking process, unnecessary services were disabled. Each program was run three times and the minimum time and memory usage were recorded.

C and C++ programs were optimized with the flag -O3. No multi-threading was used explicitly to write the programs. Compilers or interpreters are described in Table 1.

Table 1: Language list with respective compiler or interpreter name and version

	Linux		**Windows**	
Language	Compiler/interpreter	version	Compiler/interpreter	version
C	GNU gcc	4.1.1	gcc	3.4.2
C++	GNU g++	4.1.1	g++	3.4.2
C#	gmcs/mono	1.1.17.1	.NET csc	2.0.50727
Java	Sun JDK javac/java	1.5.0_09	Sun JDK javac/java	1.5.0_12
Perl	Perl	5.8.8	Active state perl	5.8.8
Python	Python	2.4.4	python	2.5.1

The speed of processing was timed using the GNU program 'time' which is present in most of the Linux distributions. In this paper we present only the user time from the output. Profiling was also used to inspect the time repartition and memory allocation. On Windows, a simple Perl script launching the programs with the option -Dprof was used to time all processes. The memory usage was measured on Linux using the command "grep Vm/proc/pid/status", only for the NJ and global alignment programs since parsing does not use much memory.

All the programs were run on the following machine with a dual boot Linux/Windows:

Linux: Fedora core 7, kernel 2.6.21-1.3228

Windows: Windows XP professional, Version 2002, service pack 2

Intel(R) Core(TM)2 CPU 6400 @ 2.13 GHz

4 GB DDR2 memory

250 GB hard drive

ALGORITHMS

Sellers Algorithm [9]

The Sellers algorithm is a simple global sequence alignment method using a dynamic programming approach with a gap penalty. Scores for aligned characters are computed (see equation 1) and stored in a similarity matrix F with a linear gap penalty d, and where s(i, j) is the substitution score for character i and j.

$$F(i,j) = \max\begin{cases} F(i-1,j)+d \\ F(i-1,j-1)+s(i,j) \\ F(i,j-1)+d \end{cases} \quad (1)$$

In this example a two-dimensional matrix is used to store the highest scores with the top left corner representing the beginning of the sequences and the bottom right corner representing the end of the sequences, which is the starting point of the alignment. For sequences of sizes n and m, the running time of the algorithm is O(nm) and the amount of memory used is in O(nm). This program requires reading sequences from FASTA files, initializing a two-dimensional matrix, character comparison and character string concatenation. A sub-sequence of 3216 nucleotides from the L segment of a *Hantavirus* genome [GeneBank:AJ005637] was used and then deletions, insertions and SNPs were introduced manually along the sequence at random to generate a second sequence of 3217 nucleotides. The sequences were not read from a file but were hard coded to avoid input streams, and thus focus entirely on memory allocation and character string manipulations.

Neighbor-Joining method [10]

NJ is a distance-based algorithm for constructing phylogenetic trees and is probably the most widely used distance based method. The method uses the minimum evolutionary criterion and starts by assuming a bush-like tree that has no internal branches. Then it combines node i and node j that minimizes equation 2 where r is the current number of nodes and d(i, j) is the distance between i and j. At each stage in the process two terminal nodes are replaced by one new node. This process is repeated until two nodes are separated by one branch.

$$Q(i,j) = (r-2)d(i,j) - \sum_{k=1}^{r} d(i,k) - \sum_{k=1}^{r} d(j,k) \quad (2)$$

The running time of the algorithm is $O(n^3)$ and the amount of memory used is in $O(n^2)$.

This program requires reading sequences from FASTA files, initializing a two-dimensional dissimilarity matrix from a pairwise comparison of the DNA sequences, and finally performing the clustering algorithm. Memory allocation, input and output streams, character string manipulation and tree building are the main components of this program. The nodes of the tree were implemented as structures in C and C++, as objects in C#, Java and Python and anonymous hash tables in Perl.

The most computer intensive component of this program is the pairwise comparison used to compute the dissimilarity matrix. In the test example 76 *Hantavirus* segment L sequences were used with an overall alignment length of 6580 nucleotides.

Basic Local Alignment Search Tool parsing BLAST [11]

BLAST is a tool calculating sequence similarities between a query sequence and sequences lodged in a specially formatted database. It uses a lookup table to match words and a local alignment method to extend them. In the output one can find the query aligned to a similar sequence and statistics about the significance of the alignment.

BLAST results can be as large as several gigabytes and a program is usually needed to parse the interesting parts or to feed another program. For example, numerous Gene Ontology [19] programs use BLAST outputs to assign GO terms to unknown sequences.

Tokenization can be used to parse BLAST result files but this can be tedious and requires a good knowledge of the structure of the input. Regular expressions make this kind of task easier, with the only inconvenience being potential loss in speed. The program parses and prints in a one line comma separated file, the name of the sequence, containing the gene identifier, bit score, identity percentage, e-value and positive matches. In the example we tested, the output was redirect to/ dev/null on Linux and NUL on Windows.

The test program made use of input streams and regular expressions. A program using tokenization was written in C as a control to benchmark regular expressions.

A 9.8 Gb file from a BLASTP search with a *Caenorhabditis elegans* sequence (accession number [GeneBank:ABD75716] was used in this program. Our program did not aim to compare the regular expression performances of each language but the overall speed of such a task. Since the regular expressions used are quite simple and are applied to relatively short strings of characters (a line in a BLAST file is usually not longer than 80 characters) the program will spend more time reading the file than actually parsing it.

To read such a large file and overcome the 2 GB file size limitation the flags «-D LARGEFILE_SOURCE -D_FILE_ OFFSET_BITS = 64» were used when compiling the C and C++ source code.

The Perl Compatible Regular Expression [20] library was used for C and C++ since their standard library does not implement built-in regular expressions.

ACKNOWLEDGEMENTS

The work in this paper was supported by Macquarie University through an IMURS PhD scholarship granted to MF.

AUTHORS' CONTRIBUTIONS

MF participated in the design of the study and in the implementation of the programs. MRG participated in the design and coordination of the study and helped to draft the manuscript. All authors read and approved the final manuscript.

REFERENCES

1. Raghava GPS, Searle SMJ, Audley PC, Barber JD, Barton GJ: OXBench: A benchmark for evaluation of protein multiple sequence alignment accuracy. *BMC Bioinformatics* 2003, 4: 47. 10.1186/1471-2105-4-47
2. Posada D: Evaluation for detecting recombination from DNA sequences: Empirical data.*Mol Bio Evol* 2002, 19(5):708–717.
3. McGuffin LJ: Benchmarking consensus model quality assessment for protein fold recognition. *BMC Bioinformatics* 2007, 8: 345. 10.1186/1471-2105-8-345
4. Irizarry RA, Wu Z, Jaffee HA: Comparison of Affymetrix GeneChip expression measures.*Bioinformatics* 2006, 22: 789–794. 10.1093/bioinformatics/btk046
5. Kuhner MK, Felsenstein J: A simulation comparison of phylogeny algorithms under equal and unequal evolutionary rates. *Mol Biol Evol* 1994, 11: 459–468.
6. Clegg AB, Shepherd AJ: Benchmarking natural-language parsers for biological applications using dependency graphs. *BMC Bioinformatics* 2007, 8: 24. 10.1186/1471-2105-8-24
7. Tompa M, Li N, Bailey TL, Church GM, De Moor B, Eskin E, Favorov AV, Frith MC, Fu Y, Kent WJ, Makeev VJ, Mironov AA, Noble WS, Pavesi G, Pesole G, Regnier M, Simonis N, Sinha S, Thijs G, van Helden J, Vandenbogaert M, Weng Z, Workman C, Ye C, Zhu Z: Assessing computational tools for the discovery of transcription factor binding sites. *Nat Biotechnol* 23: 137–144. 10.1038/nbt1053
8. Prechelt L: An empirical comparison of C, C++, Java, Perl, Python, Rexx and Tcl. *IEEE Computer* 2000, 33: 23–29.
9. Sellers PH: On the theory and computation of evolutionary distances. *SIAM J Appl Math*26: 787–793. 10.1137/0126070
10. Saitou N, Nei M: The neighbor joining method: A new method for constructing phylogenetic trees. *Mol Biol Evol* 1987, 4: 406–42.
11. Altschul SF, Gish W, Miller W, Myers EW, Lipman DJ: Basic Local Alignment Search Tool.*J Mol Biol* 1990, 215: 403–410.
12. Zdobnov EM, Apweiler R: InterProScan – an integration platform for the signature-recognition methods in InterPro. *Bioinformatics* 2001, 17: 847–848. 10.1093/bioinformatics/17.9.847
13. Mangalam H: The Bio* toolkits – a brief overview. *Brief Bioinform* 2002, 3: 296–302. 10.1093/bib/3.3.296
14. Guindon S, Gascuel O: PhyML – A simple, fast, and accurate algorithm to estimate large phylogenies by maximum likelihood. *Systematic Biology* 2003, 52: 696–704. 10.1080/10635150390235520
15. Comprehensive Perl Archive Network (CPAN)[http://www.cpan.org]
16. Butt D, Roger AJ, Blouin C: libcov: A C++ bioinformatic library to manipulate protein structures, sequence alignments and phylogeny. *BMC Bioinformatics* 2005, 6: 138. 10.1186/1471-2105-6-138
17. BioC++[http://biocpp.sourceforge.net]
18. Kaffe[http://www.kaffe.org]
19. Conesa A, Götz S, García-Gómez JM, Terol J, Talón M, Robles M: Blast2GO: A universal tool for annotation, visualization and analysis in functional genomics research.*Bioinformatics* 2005, 21: 3674–3676. 10.1093/bioinformatics/bti610
20. Perl Compatible Regular Expression[http://www.pcre.org]

CHAPTER 11

AN INTRODUCTION TO SCRIPTING IN RUBY FOR BIOLOGISTS

Jan Aerts, Andy Law

BACKGROUND

The past twenty years have seen an explosion in the quantity of data available to life scientists. Advances in DNA sequencing technology have resulted in ever cheaper and faster ways to sequence genomes, genotype individuals, essay gene and protein expression and otherwise generate raw data from biological samples. All fields of biology have been affected and the challenge facing the biologist now is how to most effectively analyze the vast amount of data available. Manual inspection has become impossible and scientists must use programmatic methods to filter raw data in order to interpret it or to provide the information required to generate or test new hypotheses.

Scripting has been defined as "... a way to automate repetitive tasks and handle large amounts of data" [1]. We believe that scripting will become an essential basic skill for any life-scientist, even for those who would consider themselves to be entirely wet lab-based.

There are many scripting languages available (including Perl, Python, Ruby and shell scripting languages), each of which has strengths and weaknesses as well as fanatical devotees and denigrators in almost equal measure. However, it should be noted that there is no single scripting language perfect for all use-cases. In addition, the interaction between the language syntax and constructs and the programmer's internal thought process is significant, such that what appears a perfectly logical choice and representation in one language to one programmer can appear obfuscated to another.

With all this in mind, in this short article we will introduce Ruby as a highly suitable scripting language for biologists to learn and use. We believe that Ruby is an excellent first step for people new to scripting. Its shallow learning curve combined with the consistency within the language make it easy to get started. At the same time, several properties of the language (e.g. the fact that built-in classes can be easily extended to fit different needs) make advanced scripting simple. Thus we also hope to provide exponents of other scripting/programming languages such as Perl, Python or Java some insights as to the capabilities of the Ruby language and encourage them to add an extra tool to their toolbox.

Features of Ruby.

Ruby is a programming (scripting) language devised by Yukihiro 'Matz' Matsumoto initially released for general use in 1995. It aims to achieve ease-of-use and, as Matsumoto claims in the foreword to the Programming Ruby book [2], "It allows you to concentrate on the creative side of programming, with less stress". It provides a lot of functionality on which the programmer can build without having to worry about the underlying mechanics. Like many other programming languages, it borrows heavily from pre-existing languages (*i.c.* Perl, Smalltalk and Lisp).

Interpreted language

In order for a computer to execute a set of instructions, those instructions need to be converted into a form that the machine processor can understand. The process of conversion from high-level, human-readable code into machine-executable instructions can be done either on the fly as and when needed, or as an explicit step during development. The distinction between these two approaches separates languages into 'compiled' (i.e. convert to machine executable as a separate step) and 'interpreted' (i.e. convert as required) subsets. Compiled languages offer advantages in terms of speed of execution of the finished program whereas interpreted languages often have

Citation: Aerts, J. & Law, An introduction to scripting in Ruby for biologists, doi:10.1186/1471-2105-10-221.

the edge when it comes to overall speed of development. The latter is partly due to elimination of compilation time, but also to the fact that scripting languages typically work at a more abstract or higher level than compiled languages, which means that a single statement on average does more work [3], leading to shorter programs.

Object-orientation

One of the primary features of Ruby is that it is a strict Object-Oriented (OO) language. Everything in Ruby is an object with defined attributes that can be manipulated using associated methods. Objects are instances of classes, which describe the object concept. For example an object "Tom" can be an instance of the Person class. In this respect it is similar to Smalltalk and Python and less so to Perl which, although Perl can be used as an OO language, is more often to be found utilized as procedural code. This is an important point as it allows the Ruby language to provide a lot of built-in functionality in an extensible way.

To illustrate the difference Listings 1 and 2 contain some equivalent code fragments in Perl and in Ruby which read a series of lines from a file (e.g. called 'my file.txt') and print them out with each line reversed. Both code fragments will produce identical output given the same input file.

In the Perl version (Listing 1), the script opens the file, then pulls lines from it one by one. For each line, it removes trailing line-feed characters (chomp()), splits it into individual characters, reverses the order of those characters and then re-assembles the string which it prints out. In Perl, a string is simply a concatenation of characters. Therefore, the programmer has to explicitly write code split each string into an array of characters, reverse that array and then join the characters back up into a new string.

Listing 1 A Perl script to reverse a series of lines from a file

```
open INFILE, «my_file.txt»;
while (defined ($line = <INFILE>)) {
  chomp($line);
  @letters = split(//, $line);
  @reverse_letters = reverse(@letters);
  $reverse_string = join(«», @reverse_letters);
  print $reverse_string, «\n»;
}
```

In the Ruby version (Listing 2), the script creates a file object using a built-in routine (File.open(«my_file.txt»)). Because files are objects in Ruby, they ‹know› how to do certain things like return a list of all the lines that the file contains (each). This list can be passed to a block (do ... end) that loops over the list putting each line in turn into a variable placeholder called line. Since each line is a string object rather than just a concatenation of characters, it comes packed with added functionality: it can be told to remove trailing line-feed characters from itself (line.chomp) and then to reverse itself as well.

Listing 2 A Ruby script to reverse a series of lines from a file

```
File.open(«my_file.txt»).each do |line|
  puts line.chomp.reverse
end
```

Even though the distinction between these two approaches might not be entirely obvious to the uninitiated, it is profound. A program written in a procedural way (such as the Perl example) provides a list of tasks that have to be performed by the computer. An object-oriented program, however, can be seen as a collection of objects that interact with each other by sending messages. Each object is an instance of a general class that describes a concept (for example the String class) and carries its own operators (e.g. chomp and reverse). In the Perl version, it is the script that has to handle the file, read lines (strings) from that file one by one and then perform explicit actions on those strings. The programmer needs to know that each line can be converted into an array of characters and that the array can be reversed and then converted back into a string. In the Ruby version, however, the script acts at a higher level. It creates objects representing the file and the lines and then tells those objects to produce the desired effect. It is the objects that are responsible for the mechanics of implementation of that behaviour. The script does not care about the specifics of the implementation; it is only concerned with the end result.

The example in Perl code can be made shorter or implemented in an object-oriented way by loading additional Perl libraries. However, we believe that people new to programming are more likely to start working with unmodified (so-called «vanilla») installations of a programming language.

Class definition

Listing 3 shows a simple Ruby script illustrating some of the basic concepts. The line numbering is added here for explanatory purposes and is not part of the program (and should therefore not be in the script file). Anything preceded with a hash symbol (#) is a comment inserted purely for better human comprehension of the code and will be skipped by the interpreter.

Listing 3 A simple Ruby object to demonstrate some basic principles

```
1 # Let›s start with a class definition
2 class Person
3   attr_accessor :name
4   def identify
5     puts «hello - my name is « + @name
6   end
7 end
8
9 # and then use that class to do something
10 person_one = Person.new
11 person_one = ‹Tom›
12 person_two = Person.new
13 person_two.name = ‹Nathalie›
14 person_one.identify
15 person_two.identify
```

This short program generates a Person class, representing the concept of a person. Note that class names must be capitalised. We first describe the class and what it should do, defining a Person as being an object with a (settable and retrievable) name that can report its name when asked to identify itself. The attr_accessor :name code on line 3 makes it possible to access the name property of a person as on lines 11 and 13.

Line 10 creates an instance (or object) of the class Person and puts it in a variable calledperson_one (variable names begin with lowercase letters). Line 11 sets the name of this particular Person (person_one) to be ‹Tom›. Lines 12 and 13 do the same for a second instance of Person (person_two, called ‹Nathalie›). Lines 14 and 15 tell each Person instance in turn to report their name. Because the Person›s @name attribute is a so-called ‹instance› variable, each instance of Person has its own name. All person objects are independent of each other but share the same behaviour.

This is admittedly a trivial example, but imagine a more complex example where each Person has @father and @ mother attributes. With a single object class definition, it becomes possible to implement and explore an entire family tree.

Classes that describe concepts within a well-defined domain can be functionally grouped into so-called modules. A relevant example here is the Bio module provided by the BioRuby project [4]. BioRuby is an effort by a global group of bioinformaticians (led from Japan) to create such module in the domain of biological research. This module describes the concepts of a DNA or protein sequence with their different representations (e.g. EMBL, GenBank, Fasta), an alignment, the results from a similarity search, pathways, references and other biological/bioinformatics concepts. For example, the Bio::Sequence class holds all functionality associated with a biological sequence. Any object of that class can generate the reverse complement of itself (e.g. puts Bio::Sequence. new(‹AATGCC›).complement). This module does not yet provide all functionality that is available in the sister-project BioPerl for the Perl language, but can already be of much value for writing biology-related scripts. See the BioRuby website for more details of the functionality of the classes that this module provides.

Blocks

One powerful feature of Ruby is its use of blocks. Blocks are nameless functions that can be passed to other functions easily and do not have to be defined before being used. Take for example a collection of people. The approach to traverse this collection often used in scripting languages is a for-loop as shown in section A of Listing 4. In contrast, Ruby scripts typically use the each iterator as exemplified in section B. As the name implies, iterators are methods that iterate over a collection and perform a task on each element of that collection.

The each method takes a block as its argument (either delineated by "do..end" or by curly braces) and substitutes the variable person within the block with each consecutive value in the people collection. Although each is a method defined in the Array class, iterators can be defined on other classes as well. A simple example is shown in Listing 4 section C. This code will print "Hello world" five times. The times method is defined in the Integer class.

Another common task to be performed on collections is to select those elements that comply to a given criterion. To create a list containing only those people younger than 20 years, for example, one could write the code in section D of Listing 4. Blocks however make it possible to make an abstraction of this looping. The select method as shown in section E of Listing 4 has a single block argument which defines the criteria for selection.

Finally, the strength of blocks can be illustrated with the sort_by method which takes a block that defines the rules for sorting. Section F of Listing 4 shows a very simple example where the people are sorted only by age, but more complicated sorting algorithms can easily be implemented by changing the code within the block.

Although it is possible and even common to create custom loop abstractions (e.g. a function that would traverse a tree depth-first) and create methods that take a block as argument, this functionality is typically not used by people new to programming and therefore exceeds the scope of this article.

Listing 4 Using blocks in Ruby

```
# A. Using a for-loop
for person in people
  puts person.name
end

# B. Using the each iterator
people.each do |person|
  puts person.name
end

# C. Doing something 5 times
5.times do
  puts «Hello world»
end

# D. Making a subselection for a collection
young_people = Array.new
for person in people
  if person.age < 20
    young_people.push(person)
  end
end

# E. Making a subselection for a collection using a block
young_people = people.select{|person| person.age < 20}

# F. Sorting people
people_sorted_by_age = people.sort_by{|person| person.
age}
```

Reflection

Ruby classes and objects have the ability to reflect on their own states and functionality. For example, every object implements a methods function that looks inside the object's own definition and returns a list of methods that the object implements. Consequently, because everything is an object and every object can be queried for its methods it is very simple to determine how to accomplish tasks. For example, asking a String object for its list of methods results in a list of 145 functions, including reverse, capitalize, chomp (as used in the example above), swapcase and length.

Meta-programming

Because Ruby classes and objects can reflect on themselves, meta-programming is easy in Ruby. Meta-programming refers to either writing code that writes code, or to changing code at runtime, i.e. while the program is running. A good example of this is demonstrated in Listing 3. The attr_accessor :name code on line 3 is actually translated automatically into methods that allow any code using a Person object to access (get or set) the object's name field. If we had wanted only to allow getting or setting of the name field, we could have used the alternativesattr_reader or attr_writer instead.

Meta-programming often starts with providing a method_missing method in a class. This acts as a catch-all for methods that do not exist for that class. Listing 5 provides a trivial example. Using this addition to the standard Integer class, it is possible to use methods such asmultiply_3 or add_9, even though they are never explicitly defined. When calling5. multiply_3, for example, ruby will notice that that method does not exist and diverts it tomethod_missing. This approach is the basis for much of the ActiveRecord module (see below) that provides a find_by_ method for any column in a database table without having to explicitly define each.

Listing 5 A simple meta-programming example

```
1 class Integer
2  def method_missing(method_name)
3    command, number = method_name.to_s.split(/_/)
4    if command == ‹multiply›
5      return self * number.to_i
6    elsif command == ‹add›
7      return self + number.to_i
9  end
10 end
```

Results

To demonstrate the way Ruby can be used in bioinformatics, we will briefly present three simple examples.

Wrapping repetitive commands to run in batch

The authors recently worked on a project in which they needed to run an analysis program (spidey, [5]) that takes two inputs – the first a file containing a number of transcript sequences and the second a file with a single genomic sequence. The general format of the command to be run was: spidey -m transcript_sequences.fa -i genomic_sequence.fa >> output.txt

where transcript_sequences.fa is a FASTA-formatted file containing one or more transcript sequences; genomic_sequence.fa is a FASTA file with a single genomic DNA sequence. The results of the analysis are appended to a file called output.txt.

Unfortunately, the genome in question was not completely assembled beyond the scaffold stage and was therefore represented by thousands of separate sequence files. Running the command manually against each of those genomic fragments in turn was not a practical proposition. Instead, we used Ruby to deal with the repetition for us.

In Listing 2 we used a Ruby built-in class called File to open a file on disk and return each line that it contained. Here we used a similar built-in class called Dir to return a list of all the filenames within a directory (Listing 6). We were then able to use the Ruby system command to run the spidey program, inserting each filename in turn into the relevant position.

Listing 6 Wrapping repetitive commands in Ruby

```
Dir.foreach(«.») do |filename|
 system(«spidey -m transcript_sequences.fa -i « + filename + « >> output.txt»)
end
```

Extracting information from a text file

Researchers are often presented with the challenge of selecting a subset of lines or columns from a datafile, i.e. filtering data. This can be done with Microsoft Excel or standard linux shell commands, but a script becomes necessary for more complicated problems.

Here we will use a list of features described in a GFF file (General Feature Format, [6]) that resembles Table 1 and identify those features that overlap with a given region. An example file containing a small quantity of GFF-formatted data is provided as Additional File 1. To find out which of the features (i.e. genes) are contained within a target range of 300,000 to 450,000 basepairs, we can use the script in Listing 7.

Table 1: Example data in GFF format

chr1	**Ensembl**	**gene**	**40344**	**40376**	**.**	**+**	**.**	**Accession "ENSG00000177757"**
chr1	Ensembl	gene	134390	134439	.	+	.	Accession "ENSG00000177750"
chr1	Ensembl	gene	394524	394570	.	+	.	Accession "ENSG00000177741"
chr1	Ensembl	gene	412258	412298	.	+	.	Accession "ENSG00000187583"
chr1	Ensembl	gene	552024	552064	.	+	.	Accession "ENSG00000187642"

Listing 7 Finding features in a range

```
1 class Range
2   def contained_by?(other_range)
3     if self.begin > other_range.begin and self.end < other_range.end
4       return true
5     else
6       return false
7     end
8   end
9 end
10
11 class GffRecord
12   attr_accessor :seq_id, :source, :type, :start, :stop, :score, :strand, :phase, :attributes
13   def initialize(gff_line)
14     @seq_id, @source, @type, @start, @stop, @score, @strand, @phase, @attributes = gff_line.split(/\t/)
15   end
16
17   def range
18     return Range.new(@start.to_i, @stop.to_i)
19   end
20 end
21
22 target_range = Range.new(300000,450000)
23 File.open(‹additional_file_1.txt›).each do |line|
24   line.chomp!
25   gff_record = GffRecord.new(line)
26   if gff_record.range.contained_by?(target_range)
27     puts gff_record.attributes
28   end
29 end
```

In lines 23 to 29 of the script, each line from the datafile is read and the feature it describes is reported if it falls completely within the target range we set at line 22.

In more detail, line 23 reads the file and passes each line one by one to the block defined between lines 24 and 29. Line 24 removes the newline at the end of the input line and the line is passed as the argument to create a new GffRecord object. Next, the range contained in that GFF record is tested to lie within a target range. If so, the 'attributes' part of the GFF record is printed to the screen.

This example shows how, typically, the part of the script containing the business logic is quite short (i.e. from line 22 to 29). It is the class definitions that precede it that make this possible. In line 1 to 9 a new method is added to the built-in Range class (which is then used on line 26). This class is used to represent intervals, i.e. sets of values with a start and an end (e.g. ‹1 to 5›). Lines 11 to 20 define our new GffRecord class. The initialize method handles the creation of a new object, which should be given a single line of a GFF file (see line 25). This line is then split on tabs and each component is put in its particular instance variable (line 14). In addition to the initialize method, we also define a range method (lines 17 to 19). This method returns a Range object using the object start and stop positions as boundaries. Because we return a Range object, and because we have already extended the Range class (and hence allRange objects regardless of their origin), we can use the contained_by? method to determine if this is a record in which we are interested.

The above example demonstrates a further useful property of the language: class definitions are open. This means that it is possible to alter existing and even built-in class definitions at runtime to add or change behaviour. The standard Range class does not have acontained_by? method. Here we just added this functionality on the fly by defining it between lines 1 and 9, retaining the full existing functionality of the Range class but extending it for our needs.

Typically, people writing scripts will start to reuse the same class definitions (e.g. for aGffRecord) which then can be put together in a central library. As a result, many scripts will end up containing only the business logic (i.e. lines 22 to 29 above) and the custom class definitions as presented here can be omitted.

Accessing Data in a Database

Most bioinformaticians will agree that a database is often the best tool for storing data. It is therefore an important consideration when choosing a scripting language that it provide an easy way of interacting with databases. Database interaction in Ruby is typically performed via the ActiveRecord module.

ActiveRecord is a Ruby module that allows easy interfacing with the tables in a database. Using meta-programming as described above, it connects database tables to Ruby classes, linking each record in a table to a single object (i.e. instance) of the corresponding class. This provides the scripter with a double layer of abstraction – not only hiding away the specific database engine implementation details (c.f. the Perl DBI or Java JDBC interfaces) but also completely removing the need to write SQL (Structured Query Language) if the database owner agrees to follow a few simple naming conventions. This is a theme that recurs throughout Ruby, particularly in the ActiveRecord framework: convention over configuration. It is possible to configure Ruby to handle scenarios which don't map to the convention but to do so is much harder than to just 'go with the flow' of convention. This of course leaves the bioinformatician with the choice: either follow strict rules on how to organize your data, or add a lot of configurations in your scripts. It is our opinion that if possible general conventions should be used to simplify Ruby scripts.

If a database schema follows the documented conventions, ActiveRecord can access the data automatically through a process called Object/Relationship Mapping (ORM). The conventions that are relevant here are: (1) table names have to be plural, (2) the primary key must be called id, and (3) foreign keys to other tables should consist of the singular form of that table name followed by _id.

Listing 8 provides an example of how to interact with an existing database. Suppose the data from the GFF file in the previous example was stored in a MySQL database with three tables, called genes, mappings and transcripts. Additional File 2 contains the SQL commands to create a minimal mySQL relational database with the same data as in Additional File 1. The genes table contains the columns id, name and accession; the mappings table contains the columns id, gene id (foreign key to the genes table), chromosome, start and stop; the transcripts table has the columns id, gene id (foreign key to the genes table) and accession. A simple SQL script suitable for loading example data that can be used with the code in Listing 8 is provided as an additional file. The script illustrates the use of ActiveRecord (and again reuses our Range class extension from the previous example).

Output of the script using the data in Additional File 2 will be:

Q96BN7_HUMAN is in the range 300,000 – 450,000

PLEKHN1 is in the range 300,000 – 450,000

Transcript for ENSG00000187583: ENST00000379409

Transcript for ENSG00000187583: ENST00000379410

Transcript for ENSG00000187583: ENST00000379407

Many things are happening automatically. First of all, any class that inherits from ActiveRecord::Base (< ActiveRecord::Base) is automatically linked to the table that has the lowercase plural version of the class name. Secondly, using has_many, has_one andbelongs_to creates methods for every gene to get its mapping and all its transcripts. To get the mapping for a gene (my_gene), you call my_gene. mapping; to get the transcripts for a gene, you call my_gene. transcripts. The latter returns a list of transcript objects. In many cases, this list will only contain one element, but sometimes (e.g. for PLEKHN1) multiple transcripts will be returned. Similar to line.chomp.reverse in Listing 2, line 38 shows how different methods can be concatenated: g.mapping. start calls the start method ong.mapping, which itself is a call of the mapping method on the object g. Tables can be queried by any column, by appending the column name to find_by_, as exemplified inGene.find_by_accession (task B in the script).

Listing 8 Extracting data from database

```
1 require ‹activerecord›
2
3 class Range
4   def contained_by?(other_range)
5     if self.begin > other_range.begin and self.end < other_range.end
6       return true
7     else
8       return false
9     end
10  end
11 end
12
13 # Establish the connection to the database
14 # and create the classes.
15 ActiveRecord::Base.establish_connection(
16  :adapter => ‹mysql›,
17  :database => ‹my_database›
18 )
19
20 class Gene < ActiveRecord::Base
21  has_one :mapping
22  has_many :transcripts
23 end
24
25 class Mapping < ActiveRecord::Base
26  belongs_to :gene
27 end
28
29 class Transcript < ActiveRecord::Base
30  belongs_to :gene
31 end
32
33 # And then use the classes to do some tasks:
34 # A. Find all genes in a certain region
35 target_range = Range.new(300000,450000)
36 all_genes = Gene.find(:all)
37 all_genes.each do |g|
38  gene_range = Range.new(g.mapping.start,g.mapping.stop)
39  if gene_range.contained_by?(target_range)
40    puts g.name + « is in the range 300,000 – 450,000»
41 end
42 end
43
44 # B. Find the transcripts for ENSG00000187583
45 my_gene = Gene.find_by_accession(‹ENSG00000187583›)
46 my_gene.transcripts.each do |t|
47  puts «Transcript for ENSG00000187583: « + t.accession
48 end
```

CONCLUSION

We hope that this gentle introduction to the Ruby programming language provides a framework for biologists to start investigating scripting in general. Given the large amounts of data that are often generated in research, such as sequences and expression data, scripting might become a basic tool for researchers in general and not only bioinformaticians.

We believe the Ruby language is a good stepping stone for people not familiar with programming due to its shallow learning curve, its conciseness, the way iterations are handled and the well-established modules for handling data such as ActiveRecord.

FURTHER INFORMATION

There is a plethora of information sources available to assist the reader first in learning Ruby and subsequently in using it in (biological) research. Many websites provide documentation, tutorials and advice for Ruby programmers of all levels from novice to expert. These include the official Ruby website [7], the 'poignant guide to Ruby' [8], and a website that allows the user to try out Ruby from within a browser [9]. In addition, a large number of books are available describing the language, including Programming Ruby: The Pragmatic Programmers' Guide [2], the Ruby Cookbook [10] and Learning Ruby [11].

ACKNOWLEDGEMENTS

The authors thank colleagues and reviewers for helpful comments and BiomedCentral for waiving part of the publication cost.

AUTHORS' CONTRIBUTIONS

JA provided the original idea and the impetus to write the paper. JA and AL contributed equally to the writing of the document. Both authors read and approved the final manuscript.

REFERENCES

1. Mount DW: *Bioinformatics: Sequence and Genome Analysis*. 2nd edition. Woodbury, New York: Cold Spring Harbor Laboratory Press; 2004.
2. Thomas D: *Programming Ruby. The Pragmatic Programmers' Guide*. 2nd edition. The Pragmatic Programmers LLC; 2004.
3. Ousterhout J: Scripting: Higher-Level Programming for the 21st Century. *COMPUTER*1998, 31(3):23–30. 10.1109/2.660187CrossRef
4. BioRuby[http://bioruby.open-bio.org/]
5. Wheelan SJ, Church DM, Ostell JM: Spidey: a tool for mRNA-to-genomic alignments.*Genome Research* 2001, 11: 1952–1957.PubMedCentralPubMed
6. GFF[http://www.sanger.ac.uk/Software/formats/GFF/]
7. Ruby Programming Language[http://www.ruby-lang.org/]
8. why›s (poignant) guide to ruby[http://qa.poignantguide.net/]
9. try ruby! (in your browser)[http://tryruby.hobix.com/]
10. Carlson L, Richardson L: *Ruby Cookbook*. O'Reilly Media, Inc; 2006.
11. Fitzgerald M: *Learning Ruby*. O'Reilly Media, Inc; 2007.

CHAPTER 12 S3QL: A DISTRIBUTED DOMAIN SPECIFIC LANGUAGE FOR CONTROLLED SEMANTIC INTEGRATION OF LIFE SCIENCES DATA

Helena F Deus, Miriã C Correa, Romesh Stanislaus, Maria Miragaia, Wolfgang Maass, Hermínia de Lencastre, Ronan Fox and Jonas S Almeida

BACKGROUND

Knowledge engineering in the Life Sciences is challenged by the combination of high specificity and high heterogeneity of the data needed to represent and understand Biology's systemic puzzles. Despite the deluge of data that has invaded life sciences in the past decade [1], data-driven discovery in Biology is hindered by a lack of enough interlinked information to allow statistical algorithms to find the patterns that inform hypothesis-driven research [2, 3]. Life Sciences research relies heavily on bioinformatics integration tools like Ensembl [4], the UCSC genome browser [5], Entrez Gene [6] or the gene ontology [7] because these offer researchers portals to a wealth of interlinked biological annotations within the context of their experimentally derived results, thus playing a lead role in advancing scientific discovery. The amount of time and effort required to develop and maintain such tools has prompted Linked Data approaches for data integration to become increasingly relevant in Health Care and Life Sciences (HCLS) domains [8–10]. Briefly stated, Linked Data can be described as a bottom-up solution for data integration: its focus is on creating a global Web of Data where typed links between data sources provide rich context and expressive reusable queries over aggregated and distributed heterogeneous datasets [8, 11–13]. The architecture of that Web is expected by its original architects [14] to require a representation of usage contexts that can be applied in the collaboration and controlled sharing of data. When this functionality is supported, as that report anticipates, "social machines" will be able to manage the simultaneous and conflicting views of data that fuel scientific debate. The S3DB knowledge organization system was designed to provide baseline support for that bottom-up process by addressing a recurrent need for controlled sharing of HCLS datasets [15, 16]. This report describes a convention, the S3QL language, to query and manipulate it. It will also be demonstrated that S3QL provides a convenient mechanism to engage Linked Data in general.

Linked Data Best Practices

Linked data best practices set the stage for an interlingua of relational data and logic in the web [17] by the definition of core principles that can be summarized as: 1) information resources should be identified with HTTP universal resource identifiers (URIs); 2) information should be served against a URI in a standard semantic web format such as the Resource Description Framework (RDF) and 3) links should be established to information resources elsewhere [10]. For large datasets, it is also convenient that a web service supporting SPARQL, the protocol and RDF query language, is also deployed [18]. Aggregation of data sources is available either by accessing metadata about the datasets as RDF [19, 20], or through direct aggregation of RDF assertions in a single knowledgebase [21, 22]. To ensure contextual consistency and reusability across datasets, data elements and descriptors are mapped using standard vocabularies, namespaces and ontologies [23–25].

Challenges involved in Publishing Primary Experimental Life Sciences Datasets as Linked Data

The value of linked data for life scientists lies primarily in the possibility to quickly discover information about proteins or genes of interest derived, for example, from a microarray or protein array experiment [26]. Life scientists involved in primary research still face significant challenges in harnessing

Citation: Helena F Deus, Miriã C Correa, Romesh Stanislaus, Maria Miragaia, Wolfgang Maass, Hermínia de Lencastre, Ronan Fox, Jonas S Almeida, S3QL: A distributed domain specific language for controlled semantic integration of life sciences data, DOI: 10.1186/1471-2105-12-285.

the power of Linked Data to improve biological discovery. Part of the difficulty lies in the lack of adequate and user-friendly mechanisms to publish biological results as Linked Data prior to publication in scientific articles. Efforts in linking life sciences data typically focus on datasets which are already available in structured and annotated formats, i.e. after the researchers have analysed, correlated and manually annotated their results by browsing the literature or submitting their data to multiple web-based interfaces [27, 28]. Current research [29, 30] and our own experience in developing content management systems for health care and life sciences [26, 31, 32], has identified the need to go beyond those data sets by creating mechanisms for contextualizing linked life sciences data with attribution and version before it can be shared with a stable annotation. Advances have been made in that direction by other research efforts such as the recent publication of VoiD as a W3C note [33].

The technological advancements that will make primary Life Sciences experimental results an integral part of the Web of Data are also thwarted by challenges which go beyond infrastructure and standards [30]. In particular, HCLS datasets often include data elements, such as those that could be used to identify individual patients, with stringent requirements for privacy and protection [34]. The typical approach to privatizing data has been to make it the responsibility of the data providers. Although this may provide a temporary solution for a small number of self-contained datasets, it quickly becomes unmanageable when datasets aggregate both public and sensitive data from multiple sources, each with its own requirements for privacy and access control [35].

One final common concern in Life Sciences is the need to enable data experts to edit and augment the data representation models; failure to support this flexibility has lead in the past to misinterpretation of primary experimental data due to absence of critical contextual information [36, 37].

Knowledge organization systems for Linked Data

In order to address the information management needs of Life Scientists, the practice of Linked Data standards must be coupled with the implementation of Knowledge Organization Systems (KOSs), a view also espoused by the W3C, where the Simple Knowledge Organization System (SKOS) has been recently proposed as a standard [38, 39]. In previous work we proposed the design principles of a KOS, the Simple Sloppy Semantic Database (S3DB) [15, 16, 40]. The S3DB core model is, much like SKOS, task-independent and light-weight. Implementation of the S3DB Core Model and operators resulted in a prototype that has been validated and tested by Life Scientists to address pressing data management needs or, in particular, as a controlled Read-Write Linked Data system [31, 41–43]. S3DB was shown to include the minimum set of features required to support the management of experimental and analytic results by Life Sciences experts while making use of Linked Data best practices such as HTTP URI, subject-predicate-object triples represented using RDF Schema, links to widely used ontologies suggested by NCBO ontology widgets [44] or new OWL classes created by the users and a SPARQL endpoint [41]. Although complying with these practices is enough to cover the immediate query or "read" requirements of a Linked Data KOS, we found that efficient data management or "write" operations, such as inserting, updating and deprecating data instances within a KOS could be more efficiently addressed with the identification of the S3DB Query Language (S3QL), a Domain Specific Language (DSL) devised to abstract most of the details involved in managing interlinked, contextualized, RDF statements.

S3QL is not meant as an alternative to SPARQL but rather as a complement: data management operations enabled by S3QL can also be formalized in SPARQL. However, the availability of a data management DSL that can be serialized to SPARQL provides an abstraction layer that can be intuitively used by domain experts. As such, DSLs can provide a solution for bridging the gap between the formalisms required by Linked Data best practices such as SPARQL and RDFS, and the basic controlled read/write management requirements of HCLS experts [12, 45, 46]. DSLs optimize beyond general purpose languages in the identification of the domain in which a task belongs, drastically reducing the development time [47]. The task of adding a graph to a triple store is supported by most graph stores by means of the SPARQL 1.1. Update language [48]. To enable controlled "write" operations targeting the dataset, it would be useful to annotate, for example, the creator of a named graph, under which circumstances it was created and who has permission to modify it. Similarly, upon changes to the dataset, annotation of the modifier and a comment describing the change would be in the interest of the communities using the data. Many triple stores are in fact quad stores to enable partial support of that requirement for contextual representation. The most common approach is to use a named graph, a set of triples identified by a URI [49] that indicates the source of a graph. The S3DB Query Language (S3QL) presented in this report was devised with the intent of automating Linked Data management by creating those contextual descriptors in a single S3QL transaction, including author, creation date and description of the data.

By making use of those contextual descriptors, we propose a method for fine grained permission control in S3QL that relies on *s3db:operators*[50], a class of functions, with states, that may be used as the predicate of an RDF triple between a user and a dataset with privacy requirements. These operators, described in [40] and made available for experimentation at [51], operate on the adjacency matrix defined by the nodes and edges of an RDF graph. They can be applied in a variety of scenarios such as optimizing queries or, as is the case with S3QL, to propagate permission assignments. In the latter case, an adjacency matrix includes both the edges between instances of S3DB entities and the transitions of permission on S3DB entities such as, e.g. the assertion that a User's permission on a Project propagates to its entities. Accordingly, by defining user permissions as states of *s3db:operators*, the core model's adjacency matrix is used to propagate the ability to control, view and modify S3DB entities.

We have found the target audience for S3QL to be both life sciences application developers, who use it through a RESTful application programming interface (API), and life sciences researchers who use it through user interfaces for weaving the ontologies that best represent the critical contextual information in their experimental results. The applicability of S3QL to other linked data KOSs such as the Simple Knowledge Organization System (SKOS) [39] is explored with an example and the advantages of the solution proposed are discussed in three biomedical datasets with very different requirements for controlled operations: gastrointestinal clinical trials [42], cancer genomic characterization [41] and molecular epidemiology [52].

METHODS

This section overviews the core model for S3DB, including the set of operators that enable fine grained permission control and the distributed infrastructure supporting S3QL. The principles defined here are implemented as a prototypical application available at http://s3db.org.

The S3DB Knowledge Organization Model

S3QL is a DSL to programmatically manipulate data as instances of entities defined in a KOS. One of the key features of the KOS defined using the S3DB core model [16] is the use of typed named graphs to separate the identification of the domain, the metadata describing the data, from its observational instantiation - the data itself. We have previously shown that this approach to representing RDF greatly facilitates the assembly of SPARQL and lowers the entry barrier for biomedical researchers interested in using Semantic Web Technologies to address their data management needs [41]. That separation is achieved by using the representation of domain as triples that are themselves the predicates of the statements that instantiate that domain (as detailed by Fig. two in [40]). For example, the triple *[Person hasAge Age]*, identified as *:R12* through a named graph of type *s3db:rule*, describes the domain while the triple *[John: R12 26]*, identified by a named graph of type *s3db:statement*, instantiates that domain. Through the logic encoded in the RDF Schema definition of domain (rdfs:domain) and range (rdfs:range), the assertion that "John" is of type "Person" and that "26" is an "Age" is enabled in the S3DB KOS. S3DB's use of named graphs to describe the domain enables updates to the domain without affecting the consistency of its instantiation - in the example above, modifying "hasAge" with "hasAgeInYears" will not affect queries that have already been assembled using that property.

In the S3DB core [40], a meta-model for this data is also created with the specific objective of enabling propagation of operations, such as permission assignments, between the domain description and the data itself, described in the following section (see Figures 1, 2 and 3). In the example above, the two triples are respectively assigned to entities of type *s3db:rule* and*s3db:statement* where indexes "Person" is identified by a named graph of type *s3db:collection*and "John" is identified by a named graph of type *s3db:item*. The S3DB Core specifies three other entities which are specifically devised to enable knowledge organization and operator propagation: *s3db:project* entails a list of *s3db:rule* and *s3db:collection* and are typically applied in domain contextualization; *s3db:deployment* corresponds to the physical location of an S3DB system (its URL) and *s3db:user* is the subject of permission assignment operations. It is worth noting that, by making use of S3DB entities, blank nodes are avoided by assigning a unique alphanumeric identifier to every instance of an S3DB entity. The S3DB entities can also be identified using the first letter of their names, D, P, R, C, I, S or U, which will be used in subsequent examples to indicate, respectively, *s3db:deployment, s3db:project, s3db:rule, s3db:collection, s3db:item, s3db:statement* or *s3db:user*.

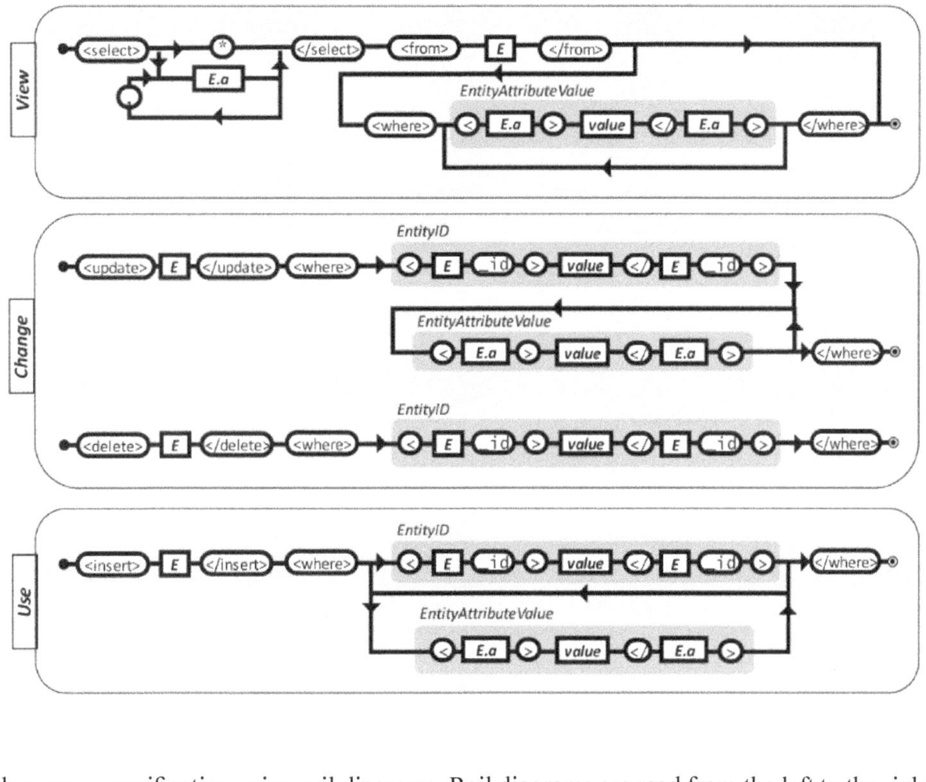

Figure 1: S3QL language specification using rail diagrams. Rail diagrams are read from the left to the right - any string that can be composed following these diagrams is a valid S3QL query. Valid forms of *E* and *E.a* will vary according to the Core Model used in the KOS. For example, if the S3DB Core model is used, any entity in figure 2 can be used in place of *E*; upon choice of *E, E.a* is any attribute that can be attained by following a line from *E*.

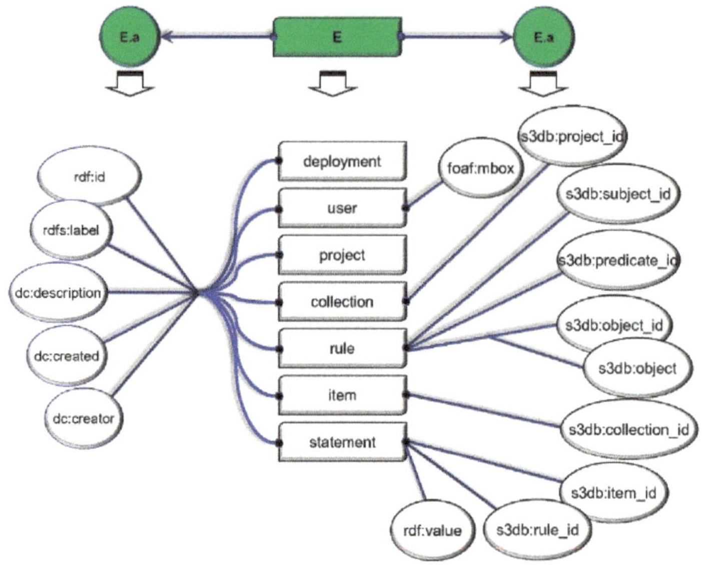

Figure 2: Entities in the S3DB Core Model and its attributes. A minimal set of common attributes was defined (left) for each of the S3DB entities using RDF Schema (rdfs) and Dublin core (dc) terminology - these are *rdf:id, rdfs:label, dc:description, dc:created* and*dc:creator*. Other attributes, which are specific to each of the S3DB entities (right), such as *foaf:mbox* for the entity *User* or *s3db:project_id* for the entity *Collection* reflect the*s3db:relationships* described above and formalized in the S3DB conceptual model (figure 3).

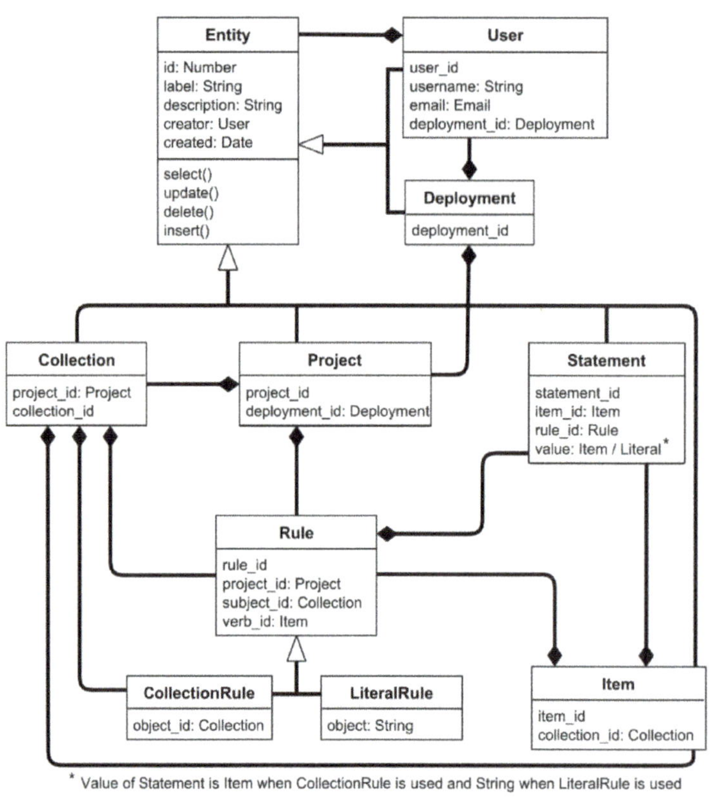

Figure 3: The S3DB conceptual model. Five attributes (id, label, description, creator and created) and four methods (select, update, insert and delete) are common to all S3DB entities. In the current S3QL implementation, the label and description attributes are defined by the submitter of the data, whereas the id, created and creator attributes are automatically assigned by the system. Other dependencies were devised to comply with the definition of *s3db:relationships*.

Operators for Permission Control

The second key feature that makes S3DB appropriate for controlled management operations is support for permission control embedded in its core model. As described above and in [40], the hierarchy of permissions to view/edit entities in S3DB is modelled by an adjacency matrix, which is used as a transition matrix in the propagation of permission states. For a walkthrough of the propagation mechanism, see additional file 1. The *s3db:operator* states applied to the S3DB transition matrix modulate propagation by three core functions - merge, migrate and percolate. This behaviour for propagation of permission is described in detail in equation 5 of [40] and is reproduced here in Equation 1. The S3DB transition matrix (T) is defined by 12*s3db:relationships* describing dependencies and inference rules between entities of the S3DB core model. The operator state vector (f) is used as the predicate of a triple established between an *s3db:user* and an entity of the S3DB core model. The JavaScript application at [51] can also be used to attempt this set of propagation behaviours for *s3db:operators* both on the S3DB transition matrix or with alternative adjacency matrixes.

$$
\begin{aligned}
&f_{object,k+1} = merge([f_{object,k}, migrate(T \times f_{subject,k})]) \\
&l = length(f) \\
&l = 1 \rightarrow migrate(f) = f = f[1] \\
&l > 1 \rightarrow migrate(f) = f[2, \ldots, l]
\end{aligned} \tag{1}
$$

The *s3db:operators*[40] have a scope and applicability in linked data beyond permission management. In S3QL we define three operator types for controlled management operations: for each of the rights to view, change/edit or use instances of S3DB entities. The format used to assign permission was defined as a three character string, where each operator occupies respectively the first, second or third positions and may assume value N, S or Y according to the level of permission intended: no permission (N), permission limited to the creator of the resource (S) or full permission (Y). For example, the permission assignment "YSN" specifies complete permission to view (Y) the subject entity, partial permission to change it (S) and no permission to use it (N). States may be defined as dominant, by use of uppercase (Y, N or S) or recessive, by use of lowercase characters (y, n or s). Dominant and recessive permissions are used to decide on the outcome of multiple permissions converging on the same entity (as detailed in [40]). Missing permission states, indicated by the dash character '-' (which has no lower or upper case) are also allowed, as well as a mechanism to succinctly specify transitions with variable memory length (l in equation 1). The propagation of permissions in the S3DB Core Model ensures that for every entity and every user, two types of permission are defined: the assigned permission, or the permission state assigned directly to a user in an entity, and the effective permission, which is the result of the propagation of *s3db:operators*.

Components of a Distributed System

One of the requirements for RDF-based knowledge management ecosystems is the availability of queries spanning across multiple SPARQL endpoints. Automation of distributed queries in systems supporting permission control, such as S3DB, is challenged by user authentication. In S3QL, we propose addressing this through delegation to authentication authorities. As a result, a user (or usage), can be identified by a URI that is independent of the authorities that validate it. Whenever possible, it is recommended that authentication credentials be protected by use of OAuth [53].

Use of URIs and Internationalized Resource Identifiers (IRIs) to identify data elements is one of the core principles of Linked Data. However, many programming environments cannot easily handle URIs as element identifiers. Problems range from decreased processing speed to a need for encoding the URIs in web service exchanges. As an anticipation for that class of problems, the URIs for entities in S3DB are interchangeable with alphanumeric identifiers formulated as the concatenation of one of D, U, P, C, R, I or S (referring to S3DB entities described in The S3DB Knowledge Organizational Model) identifying the entity and a unique number. As an example, for a deployment located at URL http://q.s3db.org/demo, the alphanumeric P126 is resolvable to an entity of type Project with URI http://q.s3db.org/s3dbdemo/P126. To facilitate exchange of URI in distinct deployments, the URI above could also be specified as D282:P126, where "D282" is the alphanumeric identifier of the S3DB deployment located at URL http://q.s3db.org/demo. Every *s3db:deployment* is identified by a named graph in the form D[number]; for completeness, metadata pertaining to each *s3db:deployment*, such as the corresponding URL, is described using the vocabulary of interlinked datasets (VoiD) [19] and shared through a root location.

Availability and Documentation

The specification of the S3QL language has been made available at http://link.s3db.org/specsand one example of the output RDF is available at http://link.s3db.org/example. S3QL has been implemented through a REST application programming interface (API) for the S3DB prototype, which is publicly available at http://s3db.org. Both the prototype and its API were developed in PHP with MySQL or PostgreSQL for data storage. Documentation about the S3DB implementation of S3QL as an API can be found at http://link.s3db.org/docs. S3QL queries may be tested at the demo implementation at http://link.s3db.org/s3qldemo and a translator for the compact notation is available at http://link.s3db.org/translate.

RESULTS

S3QL Syntax

S3QL is a domain specific language devised for facilitating management operations such as "insert", "update" or "delete" using entities of a Linked Data KOS such as the S3DB core model described above. Its syntax, however, is loosely tied to the S3DB Core Model, and can easily be applied to a set of KOS' core models in which S3DB is included. The complete syntax of S3QL in its XML (eXtended Markup Language) flavour is represented in the railroad diagram of Figure1. The S3QL syntax includes three elements: the description of the operation, the target entity and the input parameters. Four basic operation descriptions were deemed necessary to fully support read/write operations: select, insert, update and delete. The action of these operations mimic those of the structured query language (SQL) and target instances of entities (*E*) defined in the core model. Input parameters include the set of attributes defined for each of the entities either in the alphanumeric form associated with entity instances (*EntityId*) or in the form of*EntityAttributeValue (E.a)*. The values for *E.a* are determined upon choice of E - for an example using S3DB entities and attributes see Figure 2: E may be replaced with any of the entities defined in the S3DB Core Model (*Deployment, User, Project, Collection, Rule, Item* or*Statement*); upon choice of *E*, valid forms of *E.a* include any of the attributes defined for *E* (e.g. rdf:id, rdfs:label, rdfs:comment). A table summarizing all available operations, targets and input parameters is made available at http://link.s3db.org/specs. The formal S3QL syntax is completed by enclosing the outcome of one of the diagrams on Figure 1 with the <S3QL> tag. For example, the following XML structure is a valid S3QL query for an operation of type insert where the target is the S3DB entity Project and the input parameter, formulated as EntityAtributeValue is "label = Test":

```
<S3QL>
  <insert>project</insert>
  <where>
   <label>Test</label>
  </where>
</S3QL>
```

The set of 12 *s3db:relationships* (see Table one of [40]) in the S3DB Model determine the organizational dependencies of S3DB entities. For example *s3db:PC* is the *s3db:relationship* that specifies a dependency between an instance of a *Collection* (C) and an instance of a *Project*(P) (Figure 3). The S3QL syntax fulfils this constraint by assigning *project_id* (the identifier of an S3DB *Project*) as an attribute of a *Collection*. In this description of attributes associated with the S3DB core model we make use of the assumption, as in other KOSs and in the Linked Data in general, that there is no restriction to adding relationships beyond those described here. S3QL was identified as the minimal representation to interoperate with the S3DB core model and therefore only those relationships are explored in this report.

The syntax diagram in Figure 1 generates XML, a standard widely used in web service implementations. That alternative often results in verbose queries that could easily be assembled from more compact notations. One example to consider is the form: *action (E | E.a = value)*. Here the symbol '|' should be interpreted, as in Bayesian inference, as a condition and be read "given that". The letter "*E*" corresponds to the first letter of any S3DB entity (D, P, R, C, I, S or U) and *E.a* is any of its attributes as described in Figure 2. In this example, the query*insert(P | label = test)* is equivalent to the example query above. That particular variant is also accepted by the S3DB prototype and a converter for this syntax into complete S3QL/XML syntax was made available at http://link.s3db.org/translate. For further compactness of this alternative formulation, entity identifiers used as parameters may be replaced with its corresponding alphanumeric identifiers - for example *project_id = 156* may be replaced with*P156*. This alternative notation will be used in the subsequent examples.

S3QL Permission Control

Permission states are assigned using an S3QL query such as *insert(U| U1,P157,permission_level = ysn)*, which includes the action insert, the target entity User and three input parameters: identifier of the User (U1), identifier of the entity (P157) and permission assignment (ysn). Effectively, this will result in the creation of the triple *[:U1: ysn: P157]*, where the subject is of type *s3db:user*, the predicate is of type *s3db:operator* and the object is of type *s3db:project*. The inclusion of this triple in a dataset will modulate the type of management operation that a user may perform. As described in the Methods section, each position in the permission assignment operator (ysn) encodes, respectively, for permission to "view", "change" or "use" the object entity. Values y, s and n indicate, respectively, that the user has full permission to view it (y), permission to change its metadata only if he was the creator of the entity (s) and no permission to insert (n) child entities. Each S3QL operation is therefore tightly woven to each of the three operators: select is controlled by "view"; update and delete are controlled by "change" and insert is controlled by "use" (shaded areas in Figure 1). The 'use' operator encodes for the ability of a user to create new relationships with the target entity, which is defined separately from the right to "change" it. For example, in the case of a user (U1) being granted "y" as the effective permission to "change" an *s3db:rule*, then the metadata describing it may be altered. If, however, that same user is granted permission "n" to 'use' that same Rule, she is prevented from creating Statements using that Rule. Although "use" may be interpreted as being equivalent to "insert" or "append" in other systems, we have chosen to separate the terms describing the operator "use" from the S3QL action "insert". The permission assigned at the dataset level will then propagate in the S3DB transition matrix following the behaviour formalized in equation 1, therefore avoiding the need to assign permission to every user on every entity. It is worth noting that the DSL presented here is extensible beyond the 4 management actions (select, insert, update, delete) described. The *s3db:operators* that control permission on these actions are also extensible beyond "view", "change" and "use" and different implementations may support alternative states.

The permission control behaviour for S3QL operations can be illustrated through the use of the Quadratus, an application available at http://q.s3db.org/quadratus that can be pointed at any S3DB deployment to assign permission states on S3DB entities to different users (Figure 4). Other use case scenarios are also explored in the S3QL specification athttp://link.s3db.org/specs.

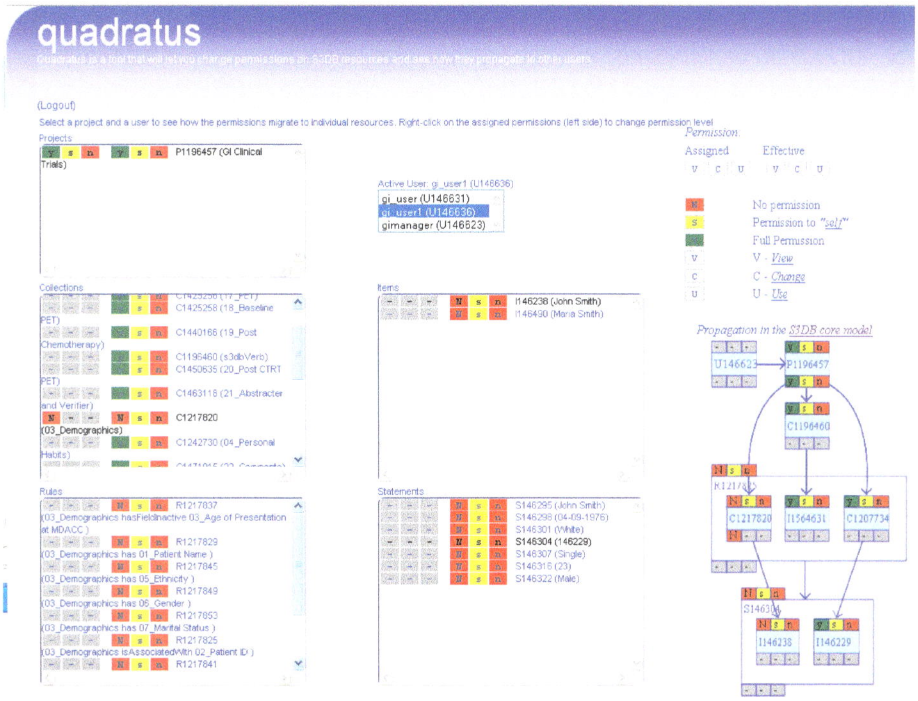

Figure 4: Quadratus, an interface to illustrate S3QL's permission control mechanism and its effect on S3QL queries. *Projects, Collections, Rules, Items* and *Statements*associated with GI Clinical Trials *Project* are displayed with effective and assigned permissions. *Collections* and *Rules* retrieved using S3QL queries *select(**C**|P1196457)* and*select(**R**| P1196457)* inherit the permission *assignment* in the *Project* "ysn"; *assigned*permission "N--" in *Collection* "Demographics" results in the *effective* permission of "Nsn" inherited by all *Rules* and *Items* that have a relationship with that *Collection*, effectively preventing gi_user1 from accessing its data. The directed labelled graph of the propagation resolution is displayed on the right side of the application illustrating the propagation mechanism.

Global Dereferencing for Distributed Queries

A simple dereferencing system was devised for S3DB identifiers that relies on the identification of root deployments, i.e. S3DB systems where alphanumeric identifiers for S3DB deployments can be dereferenced to URL. This simple mechanism enables complex transactions of controlled data. For an example of this behaviour see Figure 5, where the S3DB UID *D327:R172930*, identifying an entity of type Rule (R172930) available in deployment D327 is being request by a user registered in deployment D309. In order to retrieve the requested data, the URL of deployment D327 must first be resolved at a root deployment such as, for example,http://root.s3db.org.

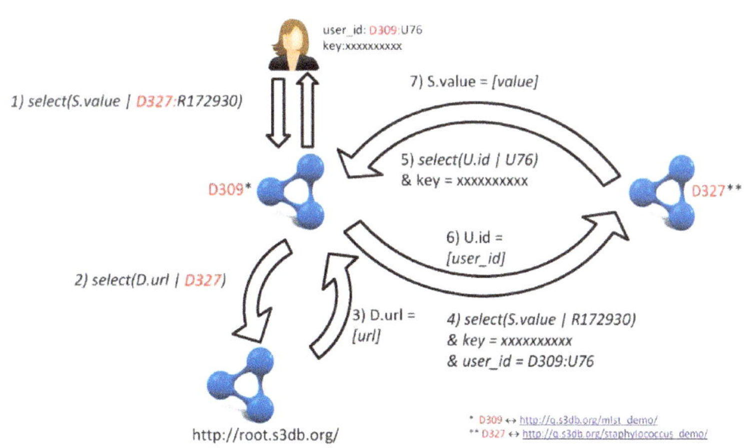

Figure 5: The global S3QL dereferencing system. User *U78* of deployment *D309* issues a command to request all entities of type *Statement* where the attribute *Rule _id*corresponds to the value *D327:R172930* through S3QL operation*select(S. value|D327:R172930)* (1). If the URL corresponding to *deployment D327* is not cached locally or has not been validated in the past 24 h, a query is issued and executed at the root deployment to retrieve the corresponding URL *select(D.*

url|D327) (2,3). Once the URL is returned, query (1) is re-issued as *select(S.value| R172930)* and executed at the URL for *D327* (4). To validate the user, deployment *D327* issues the command*select(U.id|U76)* at *D309* using the key provided (5,6) and returns the data only if *U.id*matches the value for *user_id* (7).

The dereferencing mechanism is also applicable in more complex cases where the root of two deployments sharing data is not the same. Prepending the deployment identifier of the root to the UIDs such as, for example, *D1016666:D327:R172930*, where D1016666 identifies the root deployment, would result in recursive URL resolution steps such as *select(D.url| D1016666)*prior to step 4 in Figure 5. This mechanism avoids broken links when S3DB deployments are moved to different URLs by enabling deployment metadata to be updated securely at the root using a public/private key encryption system.

Implementation and Benchmarking

In the current prototype implementation, S3QL is submitted to S3DB deployments using either a GET or POST request and may include an optional authentication token (key). The REST specification [54] suggest separate HTTP methods according to the intention of the operation: often, "GET" is used to retrieve data, "PUT" is used to submit data, "POST" is used to update data and "DELETE" is used to remove data. There are, however, many programming environments that implement only the REST "GET" method, including many popular computational statistics programming frameworks such as R and Matlab. Therefore, in order to fully explore the integrative potential of this read/write semantic web service, and to support operations beyond the 4 implemented, the S3DB prototype implementation of S3QL supports the "GET" method for all S3QL operations, with the parameters of the S3QL call appended to the URL. One drawback of relying on GET is the limits imposed by the browser on URL length. To address this potential problem, the S3DB prototype also supports the use of "POST" for S3QL calls.

Two further challenges needed to be addressed in the prototypical implementation of S3QL: 1) the need for a centralized root location to support dereferencing of deployment URI when the condensed version is used (e.g. D282) and 2) distributed queries on REST systems required users to authenticate in multiple KOSs. The first challenge was addressed by configuring an S3DB deployment as the root location, available at http://root.s3db.org. Deployment metadata is submitted to this root deployment at configuration time using S3QL; data pertaining to each deployment can therefore be dereferenced to a URL usinghttp://root.s3db.org/D[numeric]. The option to refer to another root deployment than the default is possible during installation. To avoid overloading these root deployments with too many requests, a local 24 hour cache of all accessed deployments is kept in each S3DB deployment using the same strategy; if the URL is cached, it will not be requested from the root deployment. To address the second challenge, each *s3db:deployment* can store any number of authentication services supporting HTTP, FTP or LDAP protocols. Once the user is authenticated, temporary surrogate tokens are issued with each query. When coupled with the user identifier in the format of a URI, these tokens effectively identify the user performing the query regardless of the S3DB deployment where the query is requested.

Screencasts illustrating processing time of data manipulation using S3QL are available athttp://www.youtube.com/watch?v=2KZC6kI609s and http://www.youtube.com/watch?v=FJSYLCwBaPI.

DISCUSSION

One of the major concerns in making use of Linked Data to improve health care and life sciences research is the need to ensure both the availability of contextual information about experimental datasets and the ability to protect the privacy of certain data elements which may identify an individual patient. Domain specific languages (DSL) can ease the task of managing the contextual descriptors that would be necessary to implement permission control in RDF and, by doing so, could greatly accelerate the rate of adoption of Linked Data formalisms in the life sciences communities to improve scientific discovery. We have described S3QL, a DSL to perform read/write operations on entities of the S3DB Core Model. S3QL attempts to address the requirements in linking Life Sciences datasets including both publishable and un-publishable data elements by 1) including contextual descriptors for every submitted data element and 2) making use of those descriptors to ensure permission control managed by the data experts themselves. This avoids the need to break a consolidated dataset into its public and private parts when the results are acceptable for publication.

Applying S3QL to the S3DB Core Model in a prototypical application benefited from the definition of loosely defined boundaries for RDF data that enabled propagation of permission while avoiding the need to document a relationship for each data instance, individually, and for each user. The assembly of SPARQL queries is also facilitated by the identification of domain triples using named graphs, from the data itself [41] and can be illustrated in the application at [55], where a subset of S3QL can be readily converted into the W3C standard SPARQL. Although the prototypical implementation of S3QL fits the definition of an API for S3DB systems, it is immediately apparent that the same notation could be easily and intuitively extended to other KOS' core models. For example, pointing the tool athttp://q.s3db.org/translate to a JavaScript Object Notation (JSON) representation of the SKOS core model (skos.js) instead of the default S3DB core model (s3db.js) results in a valid S3QL syntax that could easily be applied as an API for SKOS based systems, as illustrated by applying the example query "*select(C|prefLabel = animal)*" usinghttp://link.s3db.org/translate?core=skos.js&query=select(C|prefLabel=animal) to retrieve SKOS concepts labelled "animal". The progress of adoption for life sciences application developers can be further smoothed by complete reliance on the REST protocol for data exchange and the availability of widely used formats such as JSON, XML or RDF/turtle.

The applicability of S3QL to life sciences domains is illustrated here with three case studies: 1) in the domain of clinical trials, a project [42] that requires collaboration between departments with different interests; 2) in the domain of the cancer genome atlas (TCGA) project, a multi-institutional effort that requires multiple authentication mechanism and sharing of data among multiple institutions [41] and 3) in the domain of molecular epidemiology, a project where non-public data stored in an S3DB deployment needs to be statistically integrated with data from a public repository. All described use cases shared one considerable requirement - the ability to include, in the same dataset, both published and unpublished results. As such, they required both the annotation of contextual descriptors of the data, enabled by S3QL, and the availability of controlled permission propagation, enabled by the S3DB model transition matrix. Future work in this effort may include the application of S3QL in a Knowledge Organization System based on SKOS terminology and the definition of a transition matrix for SKOS to enable controlled permission propagation.

Gastro-intestinal Clinical Trials Use Case

As part of collaboration with the Department of Gastrointestinal Medical Oncology at The University of Texas M.D. Anderson Cancer Center, an S3DB deployment was configured to host data from gastro-intestinal (GI) clinical trials. A schema was developed using S3DB Collections and Rules and S3QL insert queries were used to submit data elements as Items and Statements (see Figure 6). Two permission propagation examples are illustrated, one of a restrictive nature and the other permissive, which can also be explored at http://q.s3db.org/quadratus (Figure4). In this example, the simple mechanisms of propagation defined for S3QL support the complex social interaction that requires a fraction of the dataset to be shared with certain users but not with others. Contextual usage is therefore a function of the attributes of the data itself (e.g. its creator) and the user identification token that is submitted with every read/write operation.

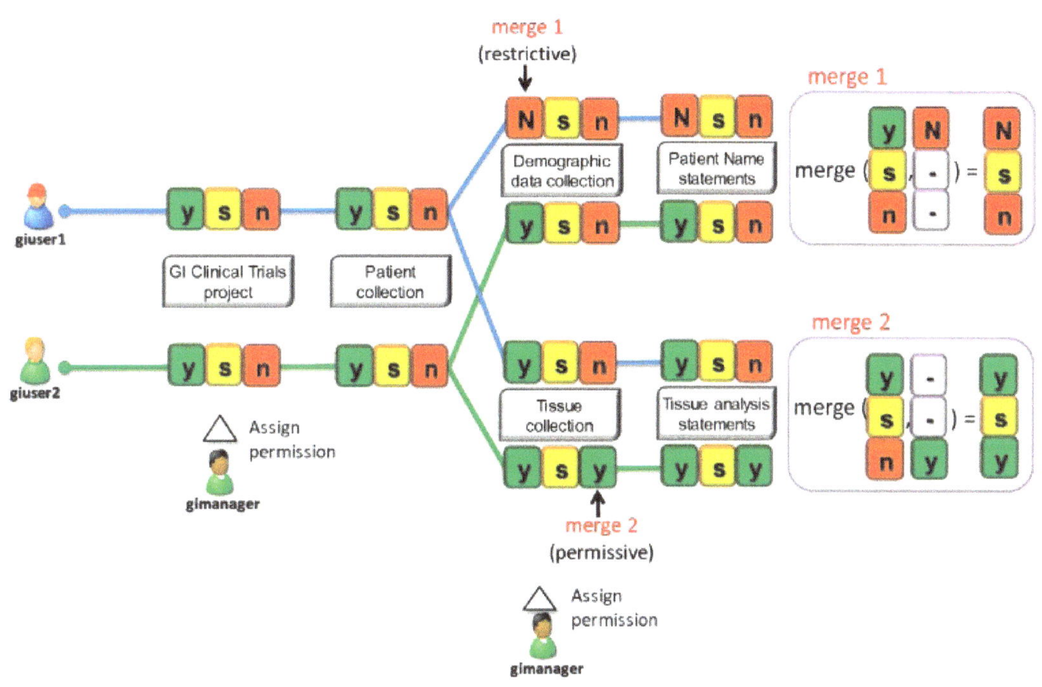

Figure 6: Two use cases of permission propagation. Two users are granted full permission to*view* GI Clinical Trials *Project* ("y"), however none of them can add new data ("n") nor edit existing data unless they were its original creator ("s"). One of the users (giuser1) is prevented from accessing any data with demographic elements such as, for example, the names of the Patients. In this case, an uppercase "N" is assigned in the right to *view* the*Collection* DemographicData, which will be merged with the inherited "y" to produce an effective permission level of "N" for the right to *view* (merge 1). For the second user (giuser2), permission is granted to *use* the *Collection* TissueData, indicating that the user can create new instances in that *Collection* (merge 2).

The Cancer Genome Atlas Use Case

The cancer genome atlas (TCGA) is a pilot project to characterize several types of cancer by sequencing and genetically characterizing tumours for over 500 patients throughout multiple institutions. S3QL was used in this case study to produce an infrastructure that exposes the public portion of the TCGA datasets as a SPARQL endpoint [41]. This was possible because SPARQL is entailed by S3QL but not the opposite. Specifically, SPARQL queries can be serialized to S3QL but the opposite is not always possible, particularly as regards write and access control operations. The structure of the S3DB Core Model which explicitly distinguishes domain from instantiation enables SPARQL query patterns, such as *?Patient: R390 ?cancerType* to be readily serialized into its S3QL equivalent *select(S|R390)*. Although this will not be further explored in this discussion, it is worth noting that the availability of this serialization allows for an intuitive syntax of SPARQL queries by patterning them on the description of the user-defined domain Rule, such as, *"Patient hasCancerType cancerType"*.

A Molecular Epidemiology Use Case

In this example, SPARQL was serialized to S3QL to support a computational statistics application. As a first step, an S3DB data store was deployed using S3QL to manage molecular epidemiology data related to strains of *Staphylococcus aureus* bacteria collected at the Instituto de Tecnologia Química e Biológica (ITQB), in Portugal. Specifically, the ITQB *Staphylococcus*reference database was devised with a purpose of managing Multilocus Sequence Typing (MLST) data, a typing method used to track the molecular epidemiology of infectious bacteria [54–57]. As a second step, we downloaded the public *Staphylococcus aureus* MLST profiles database at http://www.mlst.net and made it available through a SPARQL endpoint athttp://q.s3db.org/mlst_sparql/endpoint.php. The process of integration of MLST profiles from the ITQB Staphylococcus database with the publicly available MLST profiles is illustrated in Figure 7. In this example, a federated SPARQL query is assembled to access both MLST sources; data stored in the S3DB deployment is retrieved by serializing the SPARQL query into S3QL and providing an authentication token to identify the user, as described in Figure 3. The assembled graph resulting from the federated SPARQL query (see additional file 2), can be imported into a statistical computing environment such as Matlab (Mathworks Inc). Using this methodology, it was possible to cluster strains from two different data sources with very different authentication requirements. The observation that some Portuguese strains (PT1, PT2, PT15 and PT21) that are not publicly shared cluster together with a group of public UK strains (UK17, UK16, UK11, UK14, UK15, UK13, UK12) and therefore may share a common ancestor is an observation enabled by the data integrated through S3QL.

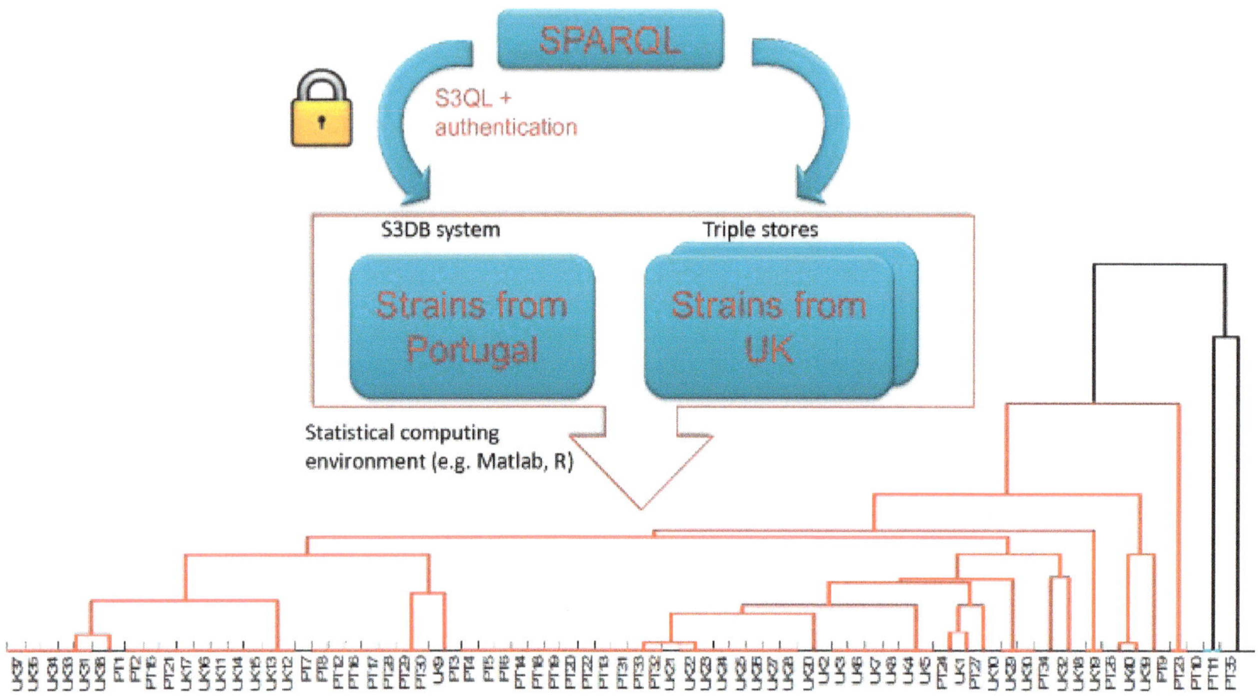

Figure 7: Workflow for the creation of a hierarchical cluster of MLST profiles from strains collected in Portugal and in the UK. Two sources are chosen to perform the MLST profile assembly - an S3DB *deployment*, which holds the ITQB *Staphylococcus*database, and the SPARQL endpoint configured to host the *Staphylococcus aureus* MLST database. Although data in the MLST SPARQL endpoint is publicly available, to access data in S3DB, the user needs to provide an authentication token and a *user_id* as well as assemble the S3QL queries to retrieve the data [*select(S|R172930)* and*select(S|R167271)*], which may also be formulated as SPARQL. A data structure is assembled that can finally be analysed using hierarchical clustering methods such as the ones made available by Matlab. The complete MLST dataset used to obtain the graph is provided in additional file 2.

CONCLUSIONS

Life sciences applications are set to greatly benefit from coupling Semantic Web Linked Data standards and KOSs. In the current report we illustrate data models from life sciences domains weaved using the S3DB knowledge organization system. In line with the requirements for the emergence of evolvable "social machines", different perspectives on the data are made possible by a permission propagation mechanism controlled by contextual attributes of data elements such as its creator. The operation of the S3DB KOS is mediated by the S3QL protocol described in this report, which exposes its Application Programming Interface for viewing, inserting, updating and removing data elements. Because S3QL is implemented with a distributed architecture where URIs can be dereferenced into multiple S3DB deployments, domain experts can share data on their own deployments with users of other systems, without the need for local accounts. Therefore, S3QL's fine grained permission control defined as instances of*s3db:operators* enables domain experts to clearly specify the degree of permission that a user should have on a resource and how that permission should propagate in a distributed infrastructure. This is in contrast to the conventional approach of delegating permission management to the point of access. In the current SPARQL specification extension various data sources can be queried simultaneously or sequentially. There is still no accepted convention for tying a query pattern to an authenticated user, probably because SPARQL engines would have no use for that information as most have been created in a context of Linked Open Data efforts. The critical limitation in applying this solution for Health Care and Life Sciences is the ability to make use of contextual information to determine both the level of trust on the data and to enable controlled access to elements in a dataset without breaking it and storing it in multiple systems. To address this requirement, S3QL was fitted with distributed control operational features that follow design criteria found desirable for biomedical applications. S3QL is not unique in its class, for example the linked data API, which is being used by data.gov.uk is an alternative DSL to manage linked data [58]. However, we believe that S3QL is closer to the technologies currently used by application developers and therefore may provide a more suitable middle layer between linked data formalisms and application development. It is argued that these features may assist, and anticipate, future extensions of semantic web provenance control formalisms.

ACKNOWLEDGEMENTS AND FUNDING

This work was supported in part by the Center for Clinical and Translational Sciences of the University of Alabama at Birmingham under contract no. 5UL1 RR025777-03 from NIH National Center for Research Resources, by the National Cancer Institute grant 1U24CA143883-01, by the European Union FP7 PNEUMOPATH project award and by the Portuguese Science and Technology foundation under contracts PTDC/EIA-EIA/105245/2008 and PTDC/EEA-ACR/69530/2006. HFD also thankfully acknowledges PhD fellowship from the same foundation, award SFRH/BD/45963/2008 and the Science Foundation Ireland project Lion under Grant No. SFI/02/CE1/I131. The authors would also like to thank three anonymous reviewers whose comments and advice were extremely valuable for improving the manuscript.

COMPETING INTERESTS

The authors declare that they have no competing interests.

AUTHORS' CONTRIBUTIONS

HFD developed the S3QL domain specific language, implemented it in the S3DB prototype, validated it with examples and wrote the manuscript. MCC, RS, MM, HL, RF, WM and JSA tested and validated the language with examples and made suggestions which lead to its improvement. All authors read and approved the final manuscript.

REFERENCES

1. Bell G, Hey T, Szalay A: Computer science. Beyond the data deluge. Science (New York, NY) 2009, 323: 1297–8. 10.1126/science.1170411
2. Chiang AP, Butte AJ: Data-driven methods to discover molecular determinants of serious adverse drug events. Clinical pharmacology and therapeutics 2009, 85: 259–68. 10.1038/clpt.2008.274
3. The end of theory: the data deluge makes the scientific method obsolete[http://www.wired.com/science/discoveries/magazine/16–07/pb_theory]
4. Hubbard T: The Ensembl genome database project. Nucleic Acids Research 2002, 30: 38–41. 10.1093/nar/30.1.38
5. Karolchik D: The UCSC Genome Browser Database. Nucleic Acids Research 2003, 31: 51–54. 10.1093/nar/gkg129
6. Maglott D, Ostell J, Pruitt KD, Tatusova T: Entrez Gene: gene-centered information at NCBI. Nucleic acids research 2005, 33: D54–8. 10.1093/nar/gni052
7. Ashburner M, Ball CA, Blake JA, et al.: Gene ontology: tool for the unification of biology. The Gene Ontology Consortium. Nature genetics 2000, 25: 25–9. 10.1038/75556
8. Bizer C, Heath T, Berners-Lee T: Linked Data - The Story So Far. International Journal on Semantic Web and Information Systems (IJSWIS) 2009.
9. Linked Data Linked Data - Connect Distributed Data across the Web[http://linkeddata.org/]
10. Linked data - Design issues[http://www.w3.org/DesignIssues/LinkedData.html]
11. Vandervalk BP, McCarthy EL, Wilkinson MD: Moby and Moby 2: creatures of the deep (web). Briefings in bioinformatics 2009, 10: 114–28. 10.1093/bib/bbn051
12. Where the semantic web stumbled, linked data will succeed - O'Reilly Radar[http://radar.oreilly.com/2010/11/semantic-web-linked-data.html]
13. Berners-Lee T, Weitzner DJ, Hall W, et al.: A Framework for Web Science. Foundations and Trends® in Web Science 2006, 1: 1–130. 10.1561/1800000001
14. Hendler J, Berners-Lee T: From the Semantic Web to social machines: A research challenge for AI on the World Wide Web. Artificial Intelligence 2010, 174: 156–161. 10.1016/j.artint.2009.11.010
15. Almeida JS, Chen C, Gorlitsky R, et al.: Data integration gets "Sloppy". Nature biotechnology 2006, 24: 1070–1. 10.1038/nbt0906-1070
16. Deus HF, Stanislaus R, Veiga DF, et al.: A Semantic Web management model for integrative biomedical informatics. PloS one 2008, 3: e2946. 10.1371/journal.pone.0002946
17. Putting the Web back in Semantic Web[http://www.w3.org/2005/Talks/1110-iswc-tbl/#(1)]
18. SPARQL Query Language for RDF[http://www.w3.org/TR/rdf-sparql-query]
19. Alexander K, Cyganiak R, Hausenblas M, Zhao J: Describing Linked Datasets On the Design and Usage of voiD, the " Vocabulary Of Interlinked Datasets". Linked Data on the Web Workshop (LDOW 09), in conjunction with 18th International World Wide Web Conference (WWW 09) 2009.
20. Cheung KH, Frost HR, Marshall MS, et al.: A journey to Semantic Web query federation in the life sciences. BMC bioinformatics 2009, 10(Suppl 1):S10. 10.1186/1471-2105-10-S1-S10
21. A Prototype Knowledge Base for the Life Sciences[http://www.w3.org/TR/hcls-kb/]
22. Belleau F, Nolin M-A, Tourigny N, Rigault P, Morissette J: Bio2RDF: towards a mashup to build bioinformatics knowledge systems. Journal of biomedical informatics 2008, 41: 706–16. 10.1016/j.jbi.2008.03.004
23. Smith B, Ashburner M, Rosse C, et al.: The OBO Foundry: coordinated evolution of ontologies to support

biomedical data integration. Nature biotechnology 2007, 25: 1251–5. 10.1038/nbt1346

24. Taylor CF, Field D, Sansone SA, et al.: Promoting coherent minimum reporting guidelines for biological and biomedical investigations: the MIBBI project. Nature biotechnology 2008, 26: 889–96. 10.1038/nbt.1411
25. Noy NF, Shah NH, Whetzel PL, et al.: BioPortal: ontologies and integrated data resources at the click of a mouse. Nucleic acids research 2009, 37: W170–3. 10.1093/nar/gkp440
26. Deus HF, Prud E, Zhao J, Marshall MS, Samwald M: Provenance of Microarray Experiments for a Better Understanding of Experiment Results. ISWC 2010 SWPM 2010.
27. Stein LD: Integrating biological databases. Nature reviews Genetics 2003, 4: 337–45.
28. Goble C, Stevens R: State of the nation in data integration for bioinformatics. Journal of Biomedical Informatics 2008, 41: 687–693. 10.1016/j.jbi.2008.01.008
29. Ludäscher B, Altintas I, Bowers S, et al.: Scientific Process Automation and Workflow Management. In Scientific Data Management. Edited by: Shoshani A, Rotem D. Chapman & Hall; 2009.
30. Nelson B: Data sharing: Empty archives. Nature 2009, 461: 160–3. 10.1038/461160a
31. Stanislaus R, Chen C, Franklin J, Arthur J, Almeida JS: AGML Central: web based gel proteomic infrastructure. Bioinformatics (Oxford, England) 2005, 21: 1754–7. 10.1093/bioinformatics/bti246
32. Silva S, Gouveia-Oliveira R, Maretzek A, et al.: EURISWEB--Web-based epidemiological surveillance of antibiotic-resistant pneumococci in day care centers. BMC medical informatics and decision making 2003, 3: 9. 10.1186/1472-6947-3-9
33. Describing Linked Datasets with the VoiD Vocabulary[http://www.w3.org/TR/2011/NOTE-void-20110303/]
34. HIPAA Administrative Simplification Statute and Rules[http://www.hhs.gov/ocr/privacy/hipaa/administrative/index.html]
35. Socially Aware Cloud Storage[http://www.w3.org/DesignIssues/CloudStorage.html]
36. Koslow SH: Opinion: Sharing primary data: a threat or asset to discovery? Nature reviews Neuroscience 2002, 3: 311–3.
37. Baggerly KA, Coombes KR: Deriving chemosensitivity from cell lines: Forensic bioinformatics and reproducible research in high-throughput biology. The Annals of Applied Statistics 2009, 3: 1309–1334.
38. Hodge G: Systems of Knowledge Organization for Digital Libraries: Beyond Traditional Authority Files. 2000.
39. SKOS Simple Knowledge Organization System Reference[http://www.w3.org/TR/skos-reference/]
40. Almeida JS, Deus HF, Maass W: S3DB core: a framework for RDF generation and management in bioinformatics infrastructures. BMC bioinformatics 2010, 11: 387. 10.1186/1471-2105-11-387
41. Deus HF, Veiga DF, Freire PR, et al.: Exposing The Cancer Genome Atlas as a SPARQL endpoint. Journal of Biomedical Informatics 2010, 43: 998–1008. 10.1016/j.jbi.2010.09.004
42. Correa MC, Deus HF, Vasconcelos AT, et al.: AGUIA: autonomous graphical user interface assembly for clinical trials semantic data services. BMC medical informatics and decision making 2010., 10:
43. Freire P, Vilela M, Deus H, et al.: Exploratory analysis of the copy number alterations in glioblastoma multiforme. PloS one 2008, 3: e4076. 10.1371/journal.pone.0004076
44. NCBO Ontology Widgets[http://www.bioontology.org/wiki/index.php/NCBO_Widgets]
45. Bussler C: Is Semantic Web Technology Taking the Wrong Turn? Ieee Internet Computing 2008, 12: 75–79.
46. What people find hard about linked data[http://dynamicorange.com/2010/11/15/what-people-find-hard-about-linked-data/]
47. Raja A, Lakshmanan D: Domain Specific Languages. International Journal of Computer Applications 2010, 1: 99–105.
48. SPARQL Update[http://www.w3.org/TR/sparql11-update/]
49. Carroll JJ, Bizer C, Hayes P, Stickler P: Named graphs, provenance and trust. Proceedings of the 14th international conference on World Wide Web WWW 05 2005, 14: 613.
50. S3DB operator function states[http://code.google.com/p/s3db-operator/]
51. S3DB Operators[http://s3db-operator.googlecode.com/hg/propagation.html]
52. Deus HF, Sousa MA de, Carrico JA, Lencastre H de, Almeida JS: Adapting experimental ontologies for molecular epidemiology. AMIA Annual Symposium proceedings 2007, 935.
53. The OAuth 1.0 Protocol[http://tools.ietf.org/html/rfc5849]
54. Francisco AP, Bugalho M, Ramirez M, Carriço JA: Global optimal eBURST analysis of multilocus typing data using a graphic matroid approach. BMC bioinformatics 2009, 10: 152. 10.1186/1471-2105-10-152
55. S3QL serialization engine[http://js.s3db.googlecode.com/hg/translate/quickTranslate.html]
56. Ippolito G, Leone S, Lauria FN, Nicastri E, Wenzel RP: Methicillin-resistant Staphylococcus aureus: the superbug. International journal of infectious diseases 2010, 14: S7-S11.
57. Harris SR, Feil EJ, Holden MTG, et al.: Evolution of MRSA during hospital transmission and intercontinental spread. Science (New York, NY) 2010, 327: 469–74. 10.1126/science.1182395
58. Linked Data API[http://code.google.com/p/linked-data-api/]

CHAPTER 13 RGG: A GENERAL GUI FRAMEWORK FOR R SCRIPTS

Ilhami Visne, Erkan Dilaveroglu, Klemens Vierlinger, Martin Lauss, Ahmet Yildiz, Andreas Weinhaeusel, Christa Noehammer, Friedrich Leisch, Albert Kriegner

BACKGROUND

R is an environment in which statistical techniques can be implemented [1]. R is an open source project, licensed under the General Public License, and is used by a growing number of researchers in the field of bioinformatics/biostatistics. Many new statistical procedures are published with corresponding R scripts or packages. Over 1,600 packages can be obtained from the Comprehensive R Archive Network [2] and further 300 bioinformatics packages can be obtained from the website of the Bioconductor project [3]. Notably, microarray analysis has been greatly improved by several packages like limma [4], affy [5], siggenes/samr [6], pamr [7], limmaGUI [8] and by software applications like BRB-ArrayTools [9] or by web applications like CARMAweb [10], MIDAW [11], and RACE [12] (all of these are using R and Bioconductor). R is based on an effective programming language that includes conditionals, loops, user-defined recursive functions as well as input and output facilities. The user frequently needs to change R code like the one for setting the working directory, reading an input file and changing parameters to new values, which usually requires profound knowledge of the R scripting language. For many applications, large parts of the code remain unchanged.

There are different approaches for the GUI-based usage of R: an option is the use of GUI toolkits such as Tcl/Tk [13], Gtk2 [14], Java Swing [15] and wxWidgets [16] employing the R packages tcltk [17], RGtk2 [18], rJava [19] and RwxWidgets [20]. Every toolkit has special characteristics that require the programming of its own custom GUI. gWidgets [21] serve as an abstraction of the named R packages and offers a standard gateway. A GUI that is written using gWidgets is easily compatible with these toolkits and can thus be executed. All these packages including gWidgets use R to describe GUIs and require R to generate the GUI. Such GUIs depend on R and are less flexibly integrated in other softwares.

Stand-alone frontends present another approach for the GUI-based usage of R. Rcmdr [22] and Rkward [23] runs on Linux and has a similar usability to Rcmdr yet with a richer interface. The user interface of Rkward was developed using the Qt Toolkit [24] in C++ [25]. Like in RGG, GUIs are described with XML making it easier for the end-user to expand Rkward with further GUI functions. Rpad [26] is a web-based analysis program which integrates R to an Apache web server on the backend. The R code embedded in the HTML is sent back to the server for statistical evaluation. Extending these tools to new functions requires programming skills in HTML, JavaScript [27] and/or PHP [28].

In this context, this project's aim is to develop a general GUI Framework for R. This should be independent from the GUI toolkits and integrating software and make R based statistical computing available to a wider audience less familiar with R programming.

Implementation

The R GUI Generator (RGG) framework allows the R user to generate Graphical User Interfaces (GUIs) for R scripts. RGG uses a component-based approach and consists of two parts: an XML [29] (Extensible Markup Language)-based GUI definition language to use the existing components (GUI elements) and a GUI engine that is implemented in Java.

RGG – GUI Engine

Within the RGG framework, the GUI engine is the interpreter of an RGG file which generates the GUI in runtime. GUI

Citation: Ilhami Visne, Erkan Dilaveroglu, Klemens Vierlinger, Martin Lauss, Ahmet Yildiz, Andreas Weinhaeusel, Christa Noehammer, Friedrich Leisch, Albert Kriegner, RGG: A general GUI Framework for R scripts, doi:10.1186/1471-2105-10-74.

engines are language-specific and contain the implementation of GUI elements. The current engine was implemented in Java using the Java Swing Library.

However, new engines using other programming languages including R based on the same RGG GUI definition language specification may further be implemented. Thus the RGG GUI definition language is independent from the GUI toolkit.

Java based RGG GUI Engine

Figure 1 shows the software architecture of the RGG GUI engine. It consists of four parts: the GUI elements, the RGGModel, the RGGPanelModel, and the RGGPanelBuilder. The GUI engine creates the GUI elements for each XML tag in the *rgg* file. These GUI elements are added to the RGGModel from which the new R script is generated. The RGGPanelModel is created from the RGGModel and contains the GUI model. It has a two-dimensional structure for laying out the GUI widgets in rows and columns. The RGGPanelBuilder generates the GUI using the RGGPanelModel. The GUI element consists of three subcomponents, an RElement, a VisualComponent, and an RElementFactory. The RElementFactory receives XML tags including their attributes from the RGG file and initializes the RElements and their visual components. The VisualComponent draws the GUI elements on the screen and the RElement converts the user inputs into the corresponding R code.

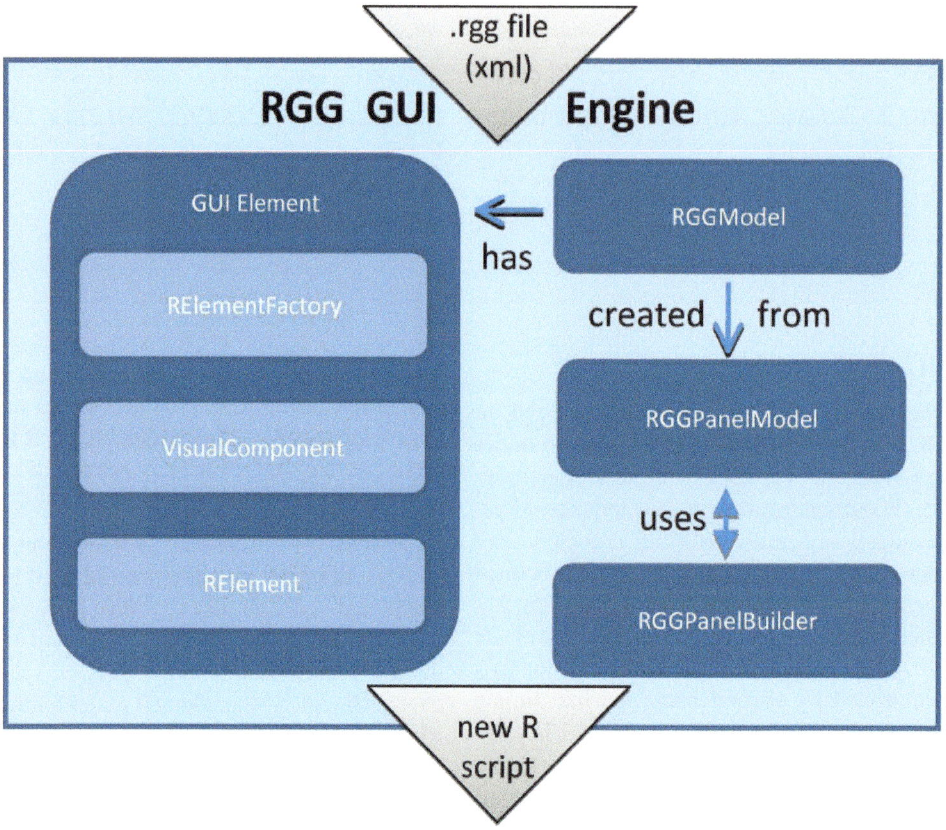

Figure 1: Software Architecture of Java based RGG GUI Engine. The GUI has four main parts: GUI elements, RGGModel, RGGPanelModel, and RGGPanelBuilder. The engine creates GUI elements for each XML tag. These GUI elements are added to the RGGModel from which the new R script is then generated. The RGGPanelModel is created from the RGGModel. RGGPanelBuilder generates the GUI using RGGPanelModel. The GUI element has three subparts: RElement, VisualComponent, and RElementFactory. RElementFactory initializes the RElement and its visual parts, the VisualComponent. VisualComponent draws the GUI elements on the screen and RElement converts the user inputs into the corresponding R code.

RGG – GUI Definition Language

The RGG GUI definition language is based on XML and contains all basic GUI elements. RGG files are thus XML files. Rules applying to an XML file also apply to RGG files. To distinguish RGG files from other XML files, the root tag must be set to <rgg>. In between the two tags <rgg> and </rgg> the user can combine GUI elements and R code. There are common GUI elements such as <filechooser>, <slider>, <checkbox> or more complex and specific elements like a dataframe/matrix editor <matrix> or an importer of microarray data, the <maimporter>. Each GUI element consists of a given number of GUI widgets. Frequently, the basic elements like <textfield> (a label and a text field), <filechooser> (a label, a text field, and a button), consist of two or three GUI widgets. However, there are no limitations to the complexity of GUI elements. A file containing both R code and GUI elements is saved with the suffix .rgg. Such RGG files serve as templates for the GUI engine. The GUI engine loads the RGG file and dynamically creates and arranges GUI elements from the XML tags. Each GUI element converts the user settings (e.g. text in a <textfield>) into the corresponding R code; i.e., the XML tags in the RGG file are replaced by the corresponding R codes. In this way a new R script is generated which is then executed in R. Several XML tags leave the R script unchanged, but improve the GUI layout. These tags include the container elements <vbox> and <hbox>. The GUI components and elements can be arranged both horizontally and vertically, i.e. spread across several columns and rows of the GUI. By default, GUI components and elements are arranged vertically. To ensure horizontal arrangement of child elements, the container element <hbox> can be used, whereas the vertical arrangement can be restored using <vbox>. The <separator> tag introduces a horizontal line to separate groups of independent GUI elements, and the <gaprow> tag modifies the spatial separation of single GUI elements. Each GUI element has its attributes, which aids its fine-tuning. Some attributes are common in many GUI elements such as "var" and "label". The var attribute's value corresponds to the R variable name that the returned user input is assigned to. The label attribute defines the label of the element in the GUI. Each of the more than fifteen GUI elements and their definition by XML tags are described in detail on the project webpage http://rgg.r-forge.r-project.org and an HTML page (provided as Additional file 1) gives an overview of the GUI elements and their attributes. New GUI elements are continuously uploaded and documented on the website. The development of RGG was inspired by XUL, several components such as the <hbox> and <vbox> concept were directly adapted from the XUL. The reason why we could not use XUL directly is related to the choice of the programming language JAVA which should make it easier to integrate RGG in other JAVA based softwares (e.g. Taverna) [30].

JGR Plug-in & RGGRunner

The current version of RGG is available as a stand-alone software (RGGRunner) and as a plug-in for JGR (Figure 2), which is a Java frontend for R [31]. RGG generates an R script that is executed locally by RGGRunner or JGR-Plug-in. However, new execution environments can be developed, which provide a server-client architecture e.g. via Rserve. RGG does not have a server-client architecture yet, and runs R scripts locally (by JGR-Plug-in and RGGRunner). RGG files can be developed in any text editor; however, using the RGG plug-in for JGR, the developer can control both the R prompt and the nascent GUI. The RGG framework can be integrated into any software supporting R and Java. Users with limited R programming skills can operate RGG using the stand-alone application RGGRunner (provided as Additional File 2and 3), where any given GUI can be imported and executed. Further, the source code of an RGG file and the generated R code can be viewed directly within RGGRunner. The RGGRunner is available for all major operating systems, such as Linux, Windows and Mac OS X.

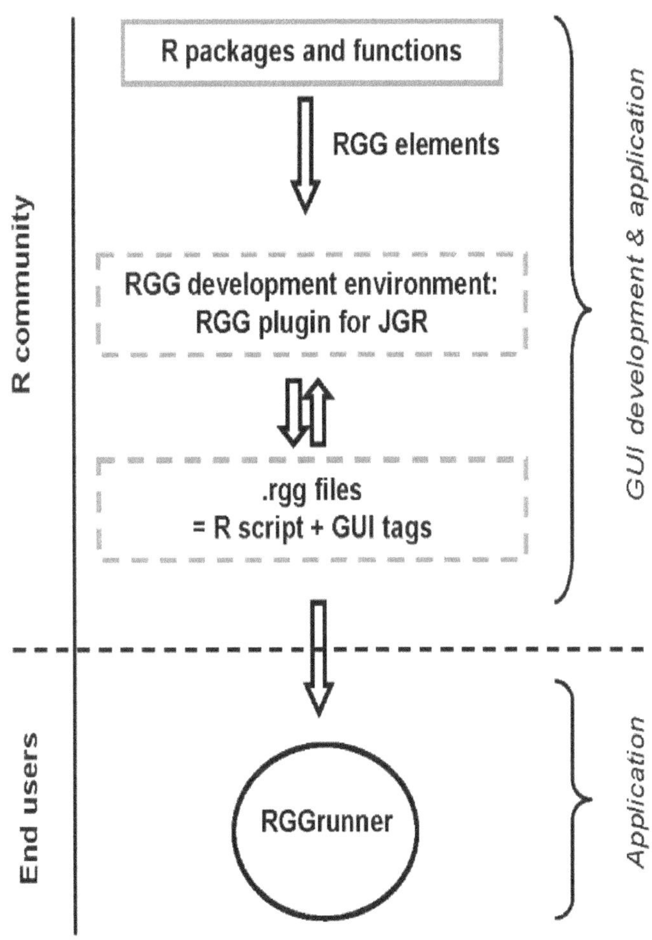

Figure 2: Concept of R GUI Generator (RGG). For the development of R Graphical User Interfaces (GUIs) we recommend the RGG plug-in for JGR, however, any text editor can be used. Combining an R script with predefined GUI definition tags (RGG elements) results in an *rgg* file. The stand-alone software RGGRunner interprets the *rgg* file and generates the GUI for the end-user with no R skills.

Outlook

The RGG project is going to provide a well-organized and documented web-repository for RGG files. In addition, the RGG framework will be integrated into the Taverna environment which enables the composition of bioinformatic workflows [32]. RGG is an open source project under the Lesser General Public License. The source code of these elements and of the GUI engine is freely available via a public subversion repository (see project web-site). Downloads and installation instructions are available at the project homepage http://rgg.r-forge.r-project.org.

SIMPLE EXAMPLE

It may be desirable that a successful R script evolves into a GUI based function. Figure 3A gives an example of a self-explaining R-script for a Fisher's exact test on a 2 × 2 contingency table, a test frequently used in biomedical research. To run the Fisher test in R with different count data, the numeric values have to be changed in this R script. The user has to change the R script accordingly, which requires knowledge of R scripting. An RGG-GUI was created for the Fisher's exact test using a text editor or, alternatively, the RGG plug-in for JGR. This GUI includes the RGG GUI elements matrix editor <matrix>, dropdown menu <combobox> and a header text <h3 text> (Figure 3B). In the matrix editor, the numeric values can be typed in manually, or a data file can be imported by clicking on the ‹Browse› button. Furthermore, rows and columns can be added or deleted from the matrix. In the additional drop down menu the test may be chosen to be ‹two-sided› (Figure 3C). The resulting R code (Figure 3D), that is returned from the user-GUI input, is finally executed in R by clicking the ‹Run› button. The GUI element ‹matrix editor› can be restricted to two rows/columns. Alternatively, larger matrices can be allowed when the according function parameters are also supported by appropriate GUI elements in the RGG file. For a generic RGG for the Fisher›s exact test, see Additional File 4. To obtain a user-friendly GUI for more sophisticated RGG files, the arrangement of the GUI elements and its components should be carefully planned in advance. The following procedure for the development of an RGG file is recommended: first, the GUI elements have to be selected. Second, the GUI elements are arranged horizontally and vertically on a virtual grid (using the <hbox> and <vbox> elements), keeping the component composition of each element in mind. Third, the selected GUI elements have to be put in their correct positions in the R script. More sample RGG files are available at the project homepage.

A (a simple R script)

```
data <- matrix(c(1,2,3,4), ncol=2)
fisher.test(data,alternative="greater")
```

B (the GUI definition file)

```
<rgg>
 < h3 text="Fisher`s Exact Test for Count Data"/>
   <matrix var="data"/>
   <group>
   <combobox var="x" label="Alternative Hypothesis"
        items="two.sided,greater,less"/>
    </group>
   fisher.test(data,alternative=x)
</rgg>
```

C (GUI with user settings)

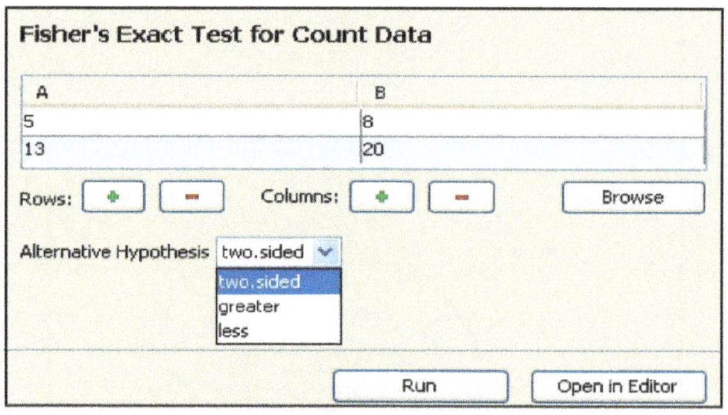

D (the resulting R script)

```
data <- matrix(c(5,8,13,20), ncol=2)
x <- "two.sided"
fisher.test(data,alternative=x)
```

Figure 3: Development of a short sample GUI using the RGG plug-in for JGR. A) Native R script, B) *rgg* file (R script + GUI definition), C) the generated GUI, D) R commands resulting from GUI-user interaction. R code is highlighted in bold.

RESULTS AND DISCUSSION

We have developed a general GUI framework for R scripts for a broad range of R users: Developers with skills in XML and R can provide GUIs, whereas users of bioinformatics software (without programming skills) can run those GUIs with the software RGGRunner.

RGG consists of an XML based GUI definition language and a GUI engine that interprets the GUI language and generates a new R code. Describing GUIs with XML decouples RGG from any concrete GUI toolkit. Unlike R based toolkits such as gWidgets [21], XML simplifies the integration of RGG in software not developed in R. The current version of RGG is available as stand-alone software RGGRunner and as a plug-in for JGR.

RGG-GUI Application

To execute RGG files, they are loaded into the RGGRunner software (for requirements and installation instructions see the project homepage). The current version of RGGRunner doesn't include a graphic device yet. Therefore the plots are automatically saved in the working directory. Figure 3 illustrates a simple example. However, following this concept, any statistical function, including more complex scripts and packages, can be made available for the RGG framework. Routine analysis of complex data, like data obtained from microarray analysis, is an important bioinformatical application field of R. As a starting point for analysis, microarray raw data files, have to be imported using the corresponding R package for the microarray platform. Then the data are pre-processed and the quality of the microarray data is assessed. In Figure 4we demonstrate an RGG-GUI for the R package ‹arrayQualityMetrics›, suitable for the assessment of microarray quality by experimentators with limited R programming skills. The RGGRunner interprets an RGG file that contains the GUI element micorarray importer <maimporter>, and downstream GUI elements for the function parameters of the ‹arrayQualityMetrics› package (Additional File 5). These downstream elements include two checkboxes for normalization and mapping of reporters, respectively, which enable further GUI elements when checked by the GUI user. Finally there are two checkboxes for report production options and a file-chooser to set the output directory for the results.

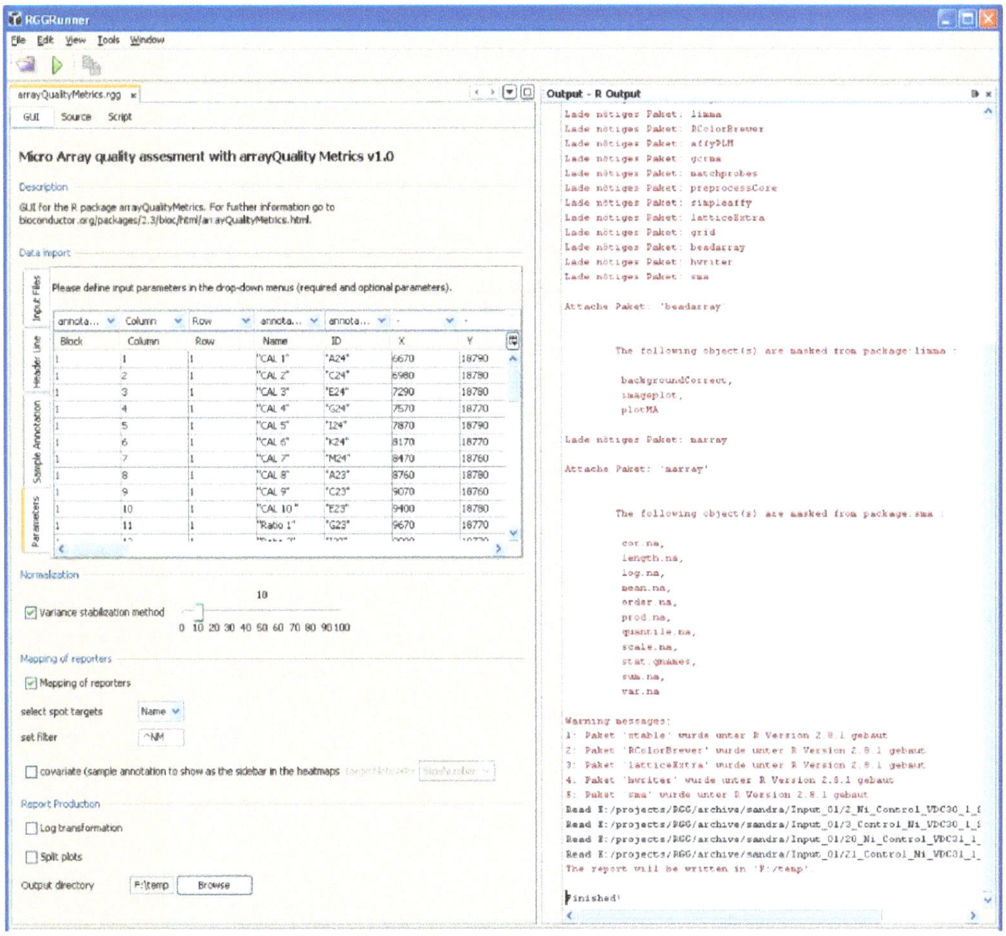

Figure 4: An*rgg*file for the package 'arrayQualityMetrics' executed with the stand-alone software RGGRunner. The GUI consists of several GUI elements: a microarray importer, a checkbox and a slider for 'vsn normalization', a checkbox and further elements for 'mapping of reporters', two checkboxes for report production parameters and a filechooser. The output log from the R console resulting from the GUI-user interaction is returned to the window on the right. An output folder is created containing the results/plots recorded by the 'arrayQualityMetrics' package.

The GUI element 'microarray importer' generalizes the import of microarray files by using a wizard system. The importer reads the raw data files and/or the experiment descriptor file and then automatically detects the microarray platform: If the raw data files are Affymetrix ('CEL') files, then the 'readAffy' function from the 'affy' package [5] is used and an 'AffyBatch'-object is generated. In the case of Agilent, GenePix, or other custom array data files, an 'RGlist' object is generated by the 'read.maimages' function of the 'limma' package [4]. The user-interaction for the downstream GUI elements (an optional 'vsn' normalization procedure from the 'arrayQualityMetrics' package, an optional mapping of reporters, and the setting of parameters of the main function) is further interpreted. The resulting R commands can be checked in the log on the right window of the RGGRunner. All output from the quality control package 'arrayQualityMetrics' is saved to the selected project folder. This GUI can be extended by customized downstream analysis steps for the entire analysis of micorarray data, including subsequent pathway [33] and gene-ontology [34] analysis.

PERSPECTIVES

One of the biggest advantages of R is its large and active user community, providing a vast number of scripts, functions and packages. Through a common GUI definition language for R, the generation of R GUIs could evolve into a community effort. Each standard statistical function such as built-in functions (e.g. t-test, ANOVA) and packages (Bioconductor, CRAN, etc.) could be provided with standard GUIs. A unified concept of GUI generation would also facilitate the teaching of introductory as well as of advanced statistics lectures. In the course of the rapid methodological progress in life sciences, novel (bio)statistical approaches are permanently required. When provided on a GUI base, novel statistical procedures can be shared directly with other GUI-dependent users. The R package 'Sweave' documents R analysis by integrating R commands and output text, figures and tables into a pdf/LaTeX report [35] and thus could contribute to the transparency of research findings [36]. If used together with RGG, pdf/LaTeX files could be produced much faster.

RGG is based on an intuitive GUI definition language which enables the description of GUIs declaratively, without extensive programming, directly by R users. RGG provides a GUI framework that is designed to be integrated with different R frontends and other softwares supporting R. Currently the RGG project is at the stage of a general framework but does not provide a collection of GUIs. At the moment, our focus is on writing RGG files for the standard functions of R and to extend the range of available GUI elements. However, RGG files for complex and specific statistical procedures can only be efficiently developed by the R community. Therefore, the community is invited to take advantage of the RGG framework and to submit biostatistical solutions not only as R packages/scripts but also with concomitant RGG files. Clearly, the addition of such RGG libraries, would significantly contribute to RGG's utility in many scientific studies.

CONCLUSION

We introduce a generic concept that allows R users to extend their statistical and bioinformatical procedures, which are relying on commands in the R prompt, with standard graphical user interfaces. The R script developer can use the RGG framework to make biostatistical and bioinformatical solutions directly available for routine applications. The current project will further include the development of a web repository for RGG files and integration to a workflow environment, enabling the combination of GUIs and connection to web services and databases. Such community driven collections of RGG-GUIs and analytical pipelines could help to bridge the gap between the R developer community and GUI-dependent users with limited R scripting skills.

ACKNOWLEDGEMENTS

The project is funded by the Austrian Research Centers GmbH-ARC.

The authors declare that no conflicts of interest exist.

AUTHORS' CONTRIBUTIONS

AK and FL conceived of the project, designed the software/framework and supervised software implementation. IV programmed the RGG GUI engine and the project's web-site. AY implemented the microarray importer GUI element. ED implemented the RGGRunner. KV and AW implemented sample RGG GUIs and provided R test scripts. CN was responsible for software testing and defined conceptual requirements. ML wrote the manuscript and was additionally involved in software development. All authors read and approved the manuscript.

REFERENCES

1. R Development Core Team: *R: A Language and Environment for Statistical Computing*. Vienna, Austria: R Foundation for Statistical Computing; 2005.
2. The Comprehensive R Archive Network[http://cran.r-project.org/]
3. Gentleman RC, Carey VJ, Bates DM, Bolstad B, Dettling M, Dudoit S, Ellis B, Gautier L, Ge Y, Gentry J, Hornik K, Hothorn T, Huber W, Iacus S, Irizarry R, Leisch F, Li C, Maechler M, Rossini AJ, Sawitzki G, Smith C, Smyth G, Tierney L, Yang JY, Zhang J: Bioconductor: open software development for computational biology and bioinformatics. *Genome Biol*2004, 5: R80. 10.1186/gb-2004-5-10-r80
4. Smyth GK: Linear models and empirical bayes methods for assessing differential expression in microarray experiments. *Stat Appl Genet Mol Biol* 2004., 3:
5. Gautier L, Cope L, Bolstad BM, Irizarry RA: affy – analysis of Affymetrix GeneChip data at the probe level. *Bioinformatics* 2004, 20: 307–315. 10.1093/bioinformatics/btg405
6. Tusher VG, Tibshirani R, Chu G: Significance analysis of microarrays applied to the ionizing radiation response. *Proc Natl Acad Sci USA* 2001, 98: 5116–5121. 10.1073/pnas.091062498
7. Tibshirani R, Hastie T, Narasimhan B, Chu G: Diagnosis of multiple cancer types by shrunken centroids of gene expression. *Proc Natl Acad Sci USA* 2002, 99: 6567–6572. 10.1073/pnas.082099299

8. Wettenhall JM, Smyth GK: limmaGUI: a graphical user interface for linear modeling of microarray data. *Bioinformatics* 2004, 20: 3705–3706. 10.1093/bioinformatics/bth449
9. Xu X, Zhao Y, Simon R: Gene Set Expression Comparison kit for BRB-ArrayTools.*Bioinformatics* 2008, 24: 137–139. 10.1093/bioinformatics/btm541
10. Rainer J, Sanchez-Cabo F, Stocker G, Sturn A, Trajanoski Z: CARMAweb: comprehensive R- and bioconductor-based web service for microarray data analysis. *Nucleic Acids Res*2006, 34: W498-W503. 10.1093/nar/gkl038
11. Romualdi C, Vitulo N, Del FM, Lanfranchi G: MIDAW: a web tool for statistical analysis of microarray data. *Nucleic Acids Res* 2005, 33: W644-W649. 10.1093/nar/gki497
12. Psarros M, Heber S, Sick M, Thoppae G, Harshman K, Sick B: RACE: Remote Analysis Computation for gene Expression data. *Nucleic Acids Res* 2005, 33: W638-W643. 10.1093/nar/gki490
13. Tcl/Tk[http://www.tcl.tk]
14. GTK2[http://www.gtk.org]
15. Java Swing[http://java.sun.com/docs/books/tutorial/uiswing]
16. wxWidgets[http://wxwidgets.org]
17. Dalgaard P: The R-Tcl/Tk Interface. In *Proceedings of the 2nd International Workshop on Distributed Statistical Computing: March 15–17 2001; Vienna* Edited by: Hornik K, Leisch F.
18. RGtk2[http://www.ggobi.org/rgtk2]
19. rJava[http://www.rforge.net/rJava]
20. RwxWidgets[http://www.omegahat.org/RwxWidgets]
21. gWidgets[http://wiener.math.csi.cuny.edu/pmg/gWidgets]
22. Fox J: Rcmdr: The R Commander: A Basic-Statistics Graphical User Interface to R.*Journalof Statistical Software* 2005, 14: 1–42.
23. Rkward[http://rkward.sourceforge.net/]
24. Qt Toolkit[http://trolltech.com/products]
25. C++[http://en.wikipedia.org/wiki/C%2B%2B]
26. Rpad[http://www.rpad.org/Rpad/]
27. JavaScript[http://www.mozilla.org/rhino/]
28. PHP[http://www.php.net/]
29. Extensible Markup Language[http://www.w3.org/XML/]
30. XML User Interface Language[http://www.mozilla.org/projects/xul/]
31. Helbig M, Theus M, Urbanek S: JGR: Java GUI for R. *Statistical Computing and Graphics Newsletter* 2005, 16: 9–12.
32. Oinn T, Addis M, Ferris J, Marvin D, Senger M, Greenwood M, Carver T, Glover K, Pocock MR, Wipat A, Li P: Taverna: a tool for the composition and enactment of bioinformatics workflows. *Bioinformatics* 2004, 20: 3045–3054. 10.1093/bioinformatics/bth361
33. Kanehisa M, Goto S, Hattori M, Aoki-Kinoshita KF, Itoh M, Kawashima S, Katayama T, Araki M, Hirakawa M: From genomics to chemical genomics: new developments in KEGG.*Nucleic Acids Res* 2006, 34: D354-D357. 10.1093/nar/gkj102
34. Ashburner M, Ball CA, Blake JA, Botstein D, Butler H, Cherry JM, Davis AP, Dolinski K, Dwight SS, Eppig JT, Harris MA, Hill DP, Issel-Tarver L, Kasarskis A, Lewis S, Matese JC, Richardson JE, Ringwald M, Rubin GM, Sherlock G: Gene ontology: tool for the unification of biology. The Gene Ontology Consortium. *Nat Genet* 2000, 25: 25–29. 10.1038/75556
35. Leisch F: Sweave: dynamic generation of statistical reports using literate data analysis. In*Proceedings in Computational Statistics*. Edited by: Härdle W, Rönz B. Physica Verlag; 2002:575–580.
36. Ioannidis JP, Polyzos NP, Trikalinos TA: Selective discussion and transparency in microarray research findings for cancer outcomes. *Eur J Cancer* 2007, 43: 1999–2010. 10.1016/j.ejca.2007.05.019

CHAPTER 14

IMPROVING TYPE ERROR MESSAGES FOR GENERIC JAVA

Nabil el Boustani and Jurriaan Hage

Keywords: Compilers, Type checking, Error diagnosis, Java generics

INTRODUCTION

Since the introduction of generics in Java, the programmers who seek to actually use this powerful feature may have discovered that production strength compilers such as Eclipse's EJC and Sun's JAVAC, do not always carefully explain why a given generic method invocation fails to type check.

```
import java.util.*;

class Listing1{
    <T> void foo(Map<T,T> a){
        Map<Number, Integer> m1 = null;
        foo(m1);
    }
}
```

```
listings/Listing1.java:6: <T>foo(java.util.Map<T,T>) in Listing1 cannot be
applied to (java.util.Map<java.lang.Number,java.lang.Integer>)
        foo(m1);
        ^
```

JAVAC

```
1. ERROR in listings/Listing1.java (at line 6)
    foo(m1);
    ^^^
The method foo(Map<T,T>) in the type Listing1 is not applicable for the
arguments (Map<Number,Integer>)
```

EJC

```
listings/Listing1.java:6
Method <T>foo(Map<T, T>) of type Listing1 is not applicable for the argument of
type (Map<Number, Integer>), because:
  [*] The type variable T is invariant, but the types:
  - Integer in Map<Number, Integer> on 5:9(5:21)
  - Number in Map<Number, Integer> on 5:9(5:13)
  are not the same type.
```

ours

Figure 1. A Java code fragment harbouring a type equality conflict, and the type error messages for JAVAC, EJC and our implementation respectively.

Citation: Nabil el Boustani and Jurriaan Hage. Improving type error messages for generic Java, Higher-Order and Symbolic Computation, June 2011; Volume 24, Issue 1, pp 3–39. DOI: 10.1007/s10990-011-9070-3.

Consider the code and the corresponding error messages in Fig. 1. Both EJC and JAVAC merely claim that there is no method declared with the signature foo(Map<Number, Integer>). However, they do not explain why the foo method that is declared does not match the invocation. Our message, on the other hand, does make such an attempt.

In this paper, we describe how to rearchictect the Java type checking process in order to obtain more informative error messages. We have implemented our solution into the JastAdd Extensible Java Compiler and provide many examples of programs that benefit from our approach. Our modifications also pave the way for the implementation of special heuristics that can go beyond explaining what the problem is, by showing how the problem can be fixed. These heuristics are, however, considered in another paper [2].

Having some experience in improving type error messages for functional languages [9, 13], it turns out that in the current study we faced a number of additional problems. The first problem is that the Java Language Specification (JLS) [7] is large, complicated and full of all kinds of restrictions and limitations that the programmer needs to know about. The fact that not even EJC and JAVAC always agree on the type correctness of a program suggests that also the implementers of Java have problems coming to grips with it. Furthermore, Smith and Cartwright have shown that type inference in Generic Java is neither sound nor complete [27]. It is worthwhile to note here that type inference is not the same as type checking: type inference, in the case of Java, refers to the process that tries to come up with suitable instantiations for type variables that occur in the program. In the case of Java this process can come up with instantiations that will later be found to be inconsistent. In that sense, type inference can be considered to be unsound, but it does not mean that the specification allows type incorrect programs. A further illustration of the complexity of Generic Java is the sizable FAQ maintained by Angelika Langer [16].

The second problem is that the combination of generics with subtyping, i.e., the fact that you can bind an object of type T to an identifier of type S if T is a subtype of S, yields a type system that is inherently complex. This is further complicated by other demands on the language, such as backwards compatibility and the recent addition of various other features such as variable arity methods and autoboxing and unboxing.

Given the size of the language, we restrict ourselves to type error diagnosis for *generic method invocations*. In our solution we adhere to three general principles: we do not change, but only add to the original type checking process, in that our extension only comes into play after an inconsistency has been detected. Second, in order to provide more elaborate error messages, we retain the constraints generated for an inconsistent invocation in order to better explain what went wrong, and to be able to execute heuristics that work directly on the constraints. The final principle is to avoid acting on those parts of the program that are more likely to contain mistakes. Since we believe that the generic arguments of the generic types are likely to be the source of a mistake when an inconsistency arises, this implies we should ignore these arguments as long as we can.

To better substantiate and position our contribution, we consider the properties proposed by Yang and others [34] that a good type error message should have: *correctness*, *accuracy*, *intuitiveness*, *succinctness* and *source-basedness*. Although these properties tend to be hard to establish formally, we believe the examples in this paper show that compared to the error messages provided by EJC and JAVAC our messages are more intuitive and source-based. We also believe that we strike a better balance in being more informative, although at the price of being less concise. Finally, we believe our implementation is not less correct than that of the compiler into which our research has been implemented (but proving that would be very hard). In general, we think that we have improved the situation with respect to JAVAC and EJC in particular by striking a better balance between verbosity and terseness, and that our messages are less tied the internal type inference process.

AN OVERVIEW OF JAVA GENERICS

For completeness we run through the essentials of the generics of Java. We assume the reader is familiar with the non-generic part of Java. For more details, the reader can consult the Java standard [7] and the Java Generics FAQ [16].

Arguably, the main reason for introducing generics into Java was to counter the large number of casts needed to deal with collection classes, e.g., sets and vectors. Before generics, all collection classes were defined so that any Object could be stored in them. However, this makes all collections potentially heterogeneous and makes it necessary to explicitly downcast objects obtained from such a collection. This is both cumbersome and potentially unsafe.

With generics, the programmer can specify upper bounds, besides Object, for the objects that can be stored in a collection. For example, a List<Number> can store Numbers and objects of any type that is a subclass of Number, such as Integer. If an object is retrieved from such a list, then it can be stored as a Number without any type cast, and if the need arises it can be further downcast to, say, Integer.

An important and maybe subtle point is that although Integer is a subclass of Number, List<Integer> is not a subclass of List<Number>. Indeed, this holds for all collection classes: they are all invariant type constructors. All things considered, this is not so strange: a List<Integer> is not supposed to store Numbers, but if we assign it to a variable of type List<Number> we cannot safely guarantee this. However, a value of type HashMap<Integer,String> may be passed safely to a parameter of type Map<Integer,String>, because HashMap extends Map.

A consequence of the invariance restriction is that there is no type that denotes a list of any kind of element. We still need such a type, for example to write a length method for lists. This is why the wildcard was introduced: List<?> denotes a list for which nothing is known of the element type. We can store a List<T> for any type T in a variable of such a type. The price to be paid is that we cannot store anything into the list, and we can only read Objects from it.

The wildcard introduces a problem by itself. If we would like to write a method that computes the reverse of a list, we can easily do so for non-wild card types, and only for wild-card types if we do not mind losing the knowledge that the input list and the output list have the same element type. In Java this can, in some cases, be solved by *wildcard capture conversion* [30], in which case the compiler can determine that although it may not know the concrete type at compile-time, it is still known to be safe at run-time.

In many cases, we can be more precise in our estimation of the possible types that a certain type variable or a wildcard may have. For that reasons *bounds* were introduced. For example T extends Number expresses that the type inferred for T should be a subtype of Number. Similarly, T super Number expresses the inverse relation. The same applies to wildcards. For example, the declaration

```
void foo (Map<? extends Number, ? super Integer> mp)
```

expresses that the key type of an actual parameter should be a subtype of Number and that the value type should be a supertype of Integer. Note however, that the fact that a wildcard ? refers to both key and value type does *not* imply that the types are the same, or even related. For example, we can pass a value of type Map<Double, Integer>, Map<Number, Number> or even Map<Integer, Object> to foo.

In Generic Java, the *raw type*, e.g., a type constructor such as List without its type arguments, is assignment compatible with all instantiations of the generic type. So, if you write List as a type somewhere, the inferencer can decide to interpret it as List<T> for whatever T it finds suitable at that point. This mixing of type constructor and type is used in dealing with legacy code.

The JLS imposes a number of seemingly arbitrary restrictions. To give a few examples: Wildcard capture conversion only works when wildcards are at top-level, and not for a type like List<List<?>>. Wildcards may only occur as arguments to a generic type constructor, i. e, you cannot write ? x = ... to describe an identifier of unknown type. Primitive types may not occur as parameters of a generic type constructor, e.g., Vector<int> is not allowed, but Vector<Integer> is. There are also some restrictions on how type variables may be bounded: we may write T extends Number, but not T super Number [7, §4.4]. This restriction does not apply to wildcards: both ? extends Number and ? super Number are allowed [7, §4.5.1].

Notation and Terminology

We shortly introduce some notation used throughout the paper, linking these to the pertinent paragraphs of the JLS [7], to which we refer for more details.

Since we deal exclusively with method invocations in this paper, and focus on generic classes and interfaces, the basic operation is that of method invocation conversion (§5.3). It specifies when actual arguments are compatible with formal parameters. In our case, the main conversion operation is widening reference conversion (§5.1.5), which basically specifies that compatibility is governed by the subtype relation (§4.10): T <: S if T is a subtype of S; we also write S :> T for T <: S. The relation :> is defined as the reflexive and transitive closure of the direct supertype relation >1, which contains the *extends* relationship between classes and interfaces: if A extends B then B >1 A. As §4.10.2 of the JLS makes clear, the subtyping relation among (generic) classes and interfaces is quite complicated. For the purposes of the examples in this paper, we need not to consider these definitions in full detail. Instead, we prefer to give a restricted version of the definition:

```
C<S1,...,Sn> <: D<T1,...,Tn>
```

if and only if C <: D and for all $1 \leq i \leq n$: Si ≤: Ti (pronounced Si *contains* Ti) where

- T ≤: T,
- T ≤: ? extends T,
- T ≤: ? super T,
- ? extends T ≤: ? extends S, if T <: S,
- ? super T ≤: ? super S, if S <: T.

Intersection types are written T_1 & ... & T_n, $n > 0$, , where the Ti are type expressions (Sect. 4.9). At most one of these types may specify a class type, since Java does not support multiple inheritance.

The *least upper bound* (*lub*) of a collection of classes and interfaces S is the most specific type that is a supertype of each S ∈ S. For example, *lub*({Integer, Double}) = Number. Often, the *lub* is not simply a class name, but also specifies a number of interfaces. For example, *lub*({Integer, String}) equals

```
Object & Serializable &
      Comparable<? extends Object & Serializable &
      Comparable<?>>.
```

Dually, the greatest lower bound (*glb*) of S is the most general type in the hierarchy that extends each S ∈ S. Note that the *glb* is sometimes undefined, e.g., *glb*({String, Number}).

EXAMPLES

To illustrate what can be gained from the developments in this paper, we compare the messages generated by our implementation with those generated by the standard compilers for Java, EJC (0.883_R34x, 3.4.1 release, in mode 1.5, MacOSX) and JAVAC (version 1.5.0_22, MacOSX). We have taken the liberty to insert some newlines in order to make the output fit the width of a page. The examples we show tend to be contrived in the sense that they show a particular phenomenon with as little code as possible. We shall however start with a somewhat more realistic and intuitive longer example. The number of examples is relatively small, but Appendix describes where to obtain programs to generate many more examples of the messages we can provide, as part of the test set for our implementation.

Consider the code in Fig. 2 which describes a class for doing static operations on HashMaps. Four methods are provided: copy adds the pairs in from to those in to, and project restricts the domain of the map to the list of elements in the second argument. The method printRange can be used to show that the operations work as expected. The final operation is selfcompose which composes a map with itself: the result contains a pair (x, y) if there is some u such that (x, u) and (u, y) are pairs in the argument HashMap. A critical requirement is that in the argument to selfcompose, the map may not have an arbitrary range and domain, but that these should coincide. We believe the code to be sufficiently standard to need no further explanation. If the type-incorrect invocation hm1 = MapOps.selfcompose(hm1); is deleted, then the output of the program is [twenty]. If the classes in Fig. 2 are compiled, then we obtain the type error messages given in Fig. 3. We note that JAVAC and EJC are not very informative, and only say that no matching method could be found. Our message explains the inconsistency between the defined selfcompose and the invocation: the method expects a map from a type to the same type, but this is not the case for hm1 which maps numbers to strings.

It is quite easy to change MapOps.java to show the behaviour of our system for other kinds of errors. Consider that the line marked as incorrectly typed is omitted. We shall now describe three modifications of the signature of project. In each case, EJC and JAVAC continue to generate messages similar to those in Fig. 3, which we omit. The first modification is to change extends into super in the signature of project. If we compile the MapOps.java after this first modification, then the error message reads:

```
listings/MapOps.java:49
Method <T, S>project(HashMap<T, S>, ArrayList<? super T>)
of type MapOps is not applicable for the arguments
of type (HashMap<Number, String>, ArrayList<Integer>), because:
  [*] The type Integer in ArrayList<Integer> on 46:8(46:18)
      is not a supertype of the inferred type for T: Number.
```

If we write `? extends S` instead of `? extends T`, then we obtain the message

```
listings/MapOps.java:49
Method <T, S>project(HashMap<T, S>, ArrayList<? extends S>)
of type MapOps is not applicable for the arguments
of type (HashMap<Number, String>, ArrayList<Integer>), because:
  [*] The type Integer in ArrayList<Integer> on 46:8(46:18)
      is not a subtype of the inferred type for S: String.
```

Finally, if we replace ? extends T with T, then the message becomes:

```
listings/MapOps.java:49
Method <T, S>project(HashMap<T, S>, ArrayList<T>)
of type MapOps is not applicable for the arguments
of type (HashMap<Number, String>, ArrayList<Integer>), because:
  [*] The type variable T is invariant, but the types:
  - Integer in ArrayList<Integer> on 46:8(46:18)
  - Number in HashMap<Number, String> on 42:8(42:16)
  are not the same type.
```

```
import java.util.*;

class MapOps {
    MapOps() {
    }

    static <T,S> void copy(HashMap<T,S> from, HashMap<T,S> to) {
      for (T key : from.keySet()) {
        to.put(key, from.get(key));
      }
    }

    static <T,S> HashMap<T,S> project(HashMap<T,S> cmap,
                                      ArrayList<? extends T> dom) {
        HashMap<T,S> retmap = new HashMap<T,S>();
        copy(cmap,retmap);
        Set<T> keyset = retmap.keySet();
        keyset.retainAll(dom);
        return retmap;
    }

    static <T,S> void printRange(HashMap<T,S> cmap) {
        System.out.println(cmap.values().toString());
    }

    static <T> HashMap<T,T> selfcompose(HashMap<T,T> map) {
        HashMap<T,T> twm = new HashMap<T,T>();
        Set<T> domain = map.keySet();

        for (T key : domain) {
          T img = map.get(key);
          if (domain.contains(img)) {
            twm.put(key, map.get(img));
          }
        }
        return twm;
    }
}

class Main {
    public static void main(String[] parameters)
    {
       HashMap<Number, String> hm1 = new HashMap<Number,String>();
       hm1.put(10,"ten");
       hm1.put(20,"twenty");
       hm1.put(21.5,"twenty-one-and-a-half");
       ArrayList<Integer> l1 = new ArrayList<Integer>();
       l1.add(20);
       l1.add(30);
       hm1 = MapOps.project(hm1,l1);
       hm1 = MapOps.selfcompose(hm1); // Type-incorrect
       MapOps.printRange(hm1);
    }

}
```

Figure 2. A class defining operations on HashMaps that is used type incorrectly.

```
listings/MapOps.java:50: <T>selfcompose(java.util.HashMap<T,T>) in MapOps cannot
be applied to (java.util.HashMap<java.lang.Number,java.lang.String>)
        hm1 = MapOps.selfcompose(hm1);
                    ^
```
JAVAC

```
1. ERROR in listings/MapOps.java (at line 50)
    hm1 = MapOps.selfcompose(hm1);
                 ^^^^^^^^^^^^
The method selfcompose(HashMap<T,T>) in the type MapOps is not applicable for
the arguments (HashMap<Number,String>)
```
EJC

```
listings/MapOps.java:50
Method <T>selfcompose(HashMap<T, T>) of type MapOps is not applicable for the
argument of type (HashMap<Number, String>), because:
  [*] The type variable T is invariant, but the types:
  - String in HashMap<Number, String> on 42:8(42:24)
  - Number in HashMap<Number, String> on 42:8(42:16)
  are not the same type.
```
ours

Figure 3. The three error messages for the inconsistency caused by the wrong invocation to self-Compose.

We now continue with the smaller, more contrived examples in order to show the kind of situations we can handle. We already saw an example of a type equality conflict, but we shall list a few more to illustrate some further differences between our compiler and EJC and JAVAC. The first example can be found in Fig. 4. Note that our message explains that there are in fact two independent errors (indicated by [*]), and that it also explains why the invocation does not match the given definition. Again, neither EJC nor JAVAC explains what the problem is, only that the invocation does not match.

In Fig. 5, the conflicts are not independent, because all inconsistencies involve the same type variable, and our message reflects this. We have omitted the messages of EJC and JAVAC since they follow the same pattern as in Fig. 4.

As a final type equality conflict consider the fragment in Fig. 6. In this case, both calls are inconsistent, and although the return type of the inner foo does not depend on the types of its inputs, all three compilers only mention the inconsistency arising from the inner invocation: the inconsistency will only show up after fixing the innermost one.

We now continue with an example of a subtyping conflict. Consider the code fragment and associated messages in Fig. 7. Such a conflict arises when an equality constraint determines the type of a particular type variable; in this case T becomes equal to Integer, which then leads to an inconsistency in the second parameter, because Number is not a subtype of Integer. Neither EJC nor JAVAC explain why the invocation does not match the declared type of bar; our message does provide such an explanation.

```
import java.util.*;

class Listingindep{
    <T,S> void foo(Map<T,T> a, Map<S,S> b){
        Map<Number,String> m1 = null;
        Map<Integer,String> m2 = null;
        foo(m1,m2);
    }
}
```

```
listings/Listingindep.java:7: <T,S>foo(java.util.Map<T,T>,java.util.Map<S,S>)
in Listingindep cannot be applied to (java.util.Map<java.lang.Number,
java.lang.String>,java.util.Map<java.lang.Integer,java.lang.String>)
        foo(m1,m2);
        ^
```
JAVAC

```
1. ERROR in listings/Listingindep.java (at line 7)
    foo(m1,m2);
    ^^^
The method foo(Map<T,T>, Map<S,S>) in the type Listingindep is not applicable
for the arguments (Map<Number,String>, Map<Integer,String>)
```
EJC

```
listings/Listingindep.java:7
Method <T, S>foo(Map<T, T>, Map<S, S>) of type Listingindep is not applicable
for the arguments of type (Map<Number, String>, Map<Integer, String>), because:
  [*] The type variable T is invariant, but the types:
  - String in Map<Number, String> on 5:9(5:20)
  - Number in Map<Number, String> on 5:9(5:13)
  are not the same type.
  [*] The type variable S is invariant, but the types:
  - String in Map<Integer, String> on 6:9(6:21)
  - Integer in Map<Integer, String> on 6:9(6:13)
  are not the same type.
```
ours

Figure 4. A code fragment with two independent equality type conflicts (one in each argument), and the type error messages for JAVAC, EJC and our implementation respectively.

It is quite easy, but not very interesting, to come up with a similar mistake to that in Fig. 7, but which involves super rather than extends. A more interesting source of mistakes, that is typical for supertype constraints, is due to the inability to find a single type that extends two different types. In the case of the code fragment in Fig. 8, the return type of foo is void so the assignment context cannot be used to find a proper instance for T. Following the JLS, the type T is then computed by taking the largest type that extends both Number and String. However, such a type does not exist, as our error message explains. As usual, both EJC and JAVAC simply complain that the invocation does not match the method.

```
import java.util.*;

class Listingref{
    <T> void foo(Map<T,Map<T,T>> a){
        Map<Number, Map<Integer,String>> m1 = null;
        foo(m1);
    }
}
```

```
listings/Listingref.java:6
Method <T>foo(Map<T, Map<T, T>>) of type Listingref is not applicable for the
argument of type (Map<Number, Map<Integer, String>>), because:
  [*] The type variable T is invariant, but the types:
  - Integer in Map<Number, Map<Integer, String>> on 5:9(5:25)
  - String in Map<Number, Map<Integer, String>> on 5:9(5:33)
  - Number in Map<Number, Map<Integer, String>> on 5:9(5:13)
  are not the same type.
ours
```

Figure 5. A code fragment with multiple conflicts arising from the variable m1, and the error message we provide.

```
import java.util.*;

class Listingnested{
    <T> Map<Number,Integer> foo(Map<T,T> a){
        Map<Number,String> m1 = null;
        foo(foo(m1));
    }
}
```

```
listings/Listingnested.java:6: <T>foo(java.util.Map<T,T>) in Listingnested
cannot be applied to (java.util.Map<java.lang.Number,java.lang.String>)
        foo(foo(m1));
           ^
JAVAC
```

```
1. ERROR in listings/Listingnested.java (at line 6)
    foo(foo(m1));
        ^^^
The method foo(Map<T,T>) in the type Listingnested is not applicable for
the arguments (Map<Number,String>)
EJC
```

```
listings/Listingnested.java:6
Method <T>foo(Map<T, T>) of type Listingnested is not applicable for the
argument of type (Map<Number, String>), because:
  [*] The type variable T is invariant, but the types:
  - String in Map<Number, String> on 5:9(5:20)
  - Number in Map<Number, String> on 5:9(5:13)
  are not the same type.
ours
```

Figure 6. Although our error message provides more explanation, for all three compilers the type inconsistency in the inner invocation of foo eclipses the inconsistency in the outer invocation.

```
import java.util.*;

class Listing2{
    static <T> void bar(Map<T, ? extends T> a){
        Map<Integer, Number> m2 = null;
        bar(m2);
    }
}
```

```
listings/Listing2.java:6: <T>bar(java.util.Map<T,? extends T>) in Listing2
cannot be applied to (java.util.Map<java.lang.Integer,java.lang.Number>)
        bar(m2);
        ^
```
JAVAC

```
1. ERROR in listings/Listing2.java (at line 6)
    bar(m2);
    ^^^
The method bar(Map<T,? extends T>) in the type Listing2 is not applicable for
the arguments (Map<Integer,Number>)
```
EJC

```
listings/Listing2.java:6
Method <T>bar(Map<T, ? extends T>) of type Listing2 is not applicable for the
argument of type (Map<Integer, Number>), because:
  [*] The type Number in Map<Integer, Number> on 5:9(5:22) is not a subtype of
      the inferred type for T: Integer.
```
ours

Figure 7. A code fragment with a subtyping conflict and the three corresponding type error messages.

```
import java.util.*;

class Listing6{
    <T extends Number> void foo(Map<? super T, ? super T> a){
        Map<Number, String> m = null;
        foo(m);
    }
}
```

```
listings/Listing6.java:7: <T>foo(java.util.Map<? super T,? super T>) in Listing6
cannot be applied to (java.util.Map<java.lang.Number,java.lang.String>)
        foo(m);
        ^
```
JAVAC

```
1. ERROR in listings/Listing6.java (at line 6)
    foo(m);
    ^^^
The method foo(Map<? super T,? super T>) in the type Listing6 is not applicable
for the arguments (Map<Number,String>)
```
EJC

```
listings/Listing6.java:7
Method <T extends Number>foo(Map<? super T, ? super T>) of type Listing6 is not
applicable for the argument of type (Map<Number, String>), because:
  [*] The types Number in Map<Number, String> on 5:9(5:13) and String in
      Map<Number, String> on 5:9(5:21) do not share a common subtype.
```
ours

Figure 8. A code fragment without assignment context, so that in absence of equality and subtype constraints the supertype constraints determine the type.

A similar kind of situation occurs in Fig. 9, but here the cause of the problem is a subtype conflict: because of the second argument type for Map and the invariance of collection class type constructors, T will be instantiated to Number. However, this choice clashes with the fact that Number is not a subtype of Integer.

We continue with some examples that involve a bound conflict, starting with Fig. 10. Surprisingly, JAVAC gives exactly the same error messages as in Fig. 1, although the reason why this particular invocation fails is completely different: it is illegal, because the type that the type variable T should be instantiated with must be a subtype of Number. Since the type Comparable<Integer> of the actual parameter is not a subtype of Number, the invocation is incorrect.

A second example of a bound error can be found in Fig. 11. In this case the error message of EJC is quite reasonable, although our message does not resort to mentioning an intersection type, which is an artifact constructed by the type inference phase. Surprisingly, some versions of JAVAC crash for this particular program due to an infinite number of calls to the least upper bound function, while some other version of JAVAC generate an internal error.

```
import java.util.*;

class Listing8{
   <T> void foo(Map<? super T, T> a) {
      Map<Integer, Number> m = null;
      foo(m);
   }
}
```

```
listings/Listing8.java:6: <T>foo(java.util.Map<? super T,T>) in Listing8 cannot
be applied to (java.util.Map<java.lang.Integer,java.lang.Number>)
        foo(m);
        ^
```

JAVAC

```
1. ERROR in listings/Listing8.java (at line 6)
     foo(m);
     ^^^
The method foo(Map<? super T,T>) in the type Listing8 is not applicable for the
arguments (Map<Integer,Number>)
```

EJC

```
listings/Listing8.java:6
Method <T>foo(Map<? super T, T>) of type Listing8 is not applicable for the
argument of type (Map<Integer, Number>), because:
   [*] The type Integer in Map<Integer, Number> on 5:7(5:11) is not a supertype
       of the inferred type for T: Number.
```

ours

Figure 9. A conflict due to the fact that Integer is not a supertype of Number, a constraint that follows from the second argument to Map.

```
import java.util.*;

class Listing3{
    <T extends Number> void baz(List<T> a){
        List<Comparable<Integer>> x = null;
        baz(x);
    }
}
```

```
listings/Listing3.java:6: <T>baz(java.util.List<T>) in Listing3 cannot be
applied to (java.util.List<java.lang.Comparable<java.lang.Integer>>)
          baz(x);
          ^
```

JAVAC

```
1. ERROR in listings/Listing3.java (at line 6)
     baz(x);
     ^^^
Bound mismatch: The generic method baz(List<T>) of type Listing3 is not
applicable for the arguments (List<Comparable<Integer>>). The inferred type
Comparable<Integer> is not a valid substitute for the bounded parameter
<T extends Number>
```

EJC

```
listings/Listing3.java:6
Method <T extends Number>baz(List<T>) of type Listing3 is not applicable for the
argument of type (List<Comparable<Integer>>), because:
   [*] The type Comparable<Integer> in List<Comparable<Integer>> on 5:9(5:9) is
       not a subtype of T's upper bound Number in 'T extends Number'.
```

ours

Figure 10. A code fragment with a bound conflict followed by the three corresponding type error messages.

```
class JavacError1 {
  <T extends Number> void foo(T a, T b){
    foo(1, false);
  }
}
```

```
listings/JavacError1.java:3: internal error; cannot instantiate <T>foo(T,T) at
JavacError1 to (int,boolean)
    foo(1, false);
       ^
```
JAVAC

```
1. ERROR in listings/JavacError1.java (at line 3)
    foo(1, false);
    ^^^
Bound mismatch: The generic method foo(T, T) of type JavacError1 is not
applicable for the arguments (Integer, Boolean). The inferred type
Object&Comparable<?>&Serializable is not a valid substitute for the bounded
parameter <T extends Number>
```
EJC

```
listings/JavacError1.java:3
Method <T extends Number>foo(T, T) of type JavacError1 is not applicable for the
arguments of type (int, boolean), because:
  [*] The type boolean of the expression 'false' on 3:12 is not a subtype of T's
      upper bound Number in 'T extends Number'.
```
ours

Figure 11. The value false cannot be considered an element of any type that extends Number; everything is okay for the first argument 1.

An example of a type error involving wildcards can be found in Fig. 12. The code fragment shows what might be a typical mistake on the part of a novice programmer: assuming that the type ? extends Number equals ? extends Number which, if provable, would make the invocation correct. However, these types are not equivalent. Our message follows the tenets of the manifesto of Yang [33] in that an error message should never reveal anything internal to compiler. However, the error messages provided by EJC and JAVAC explicitly refer to a captured wildcard.

```
import java.util.*;

class Listing4{
    <T> void bar(Map<T, T> a){
        Map<? extends Number, ? extends Number> m = null;
        bar(m);
    }
}
```

```
listings/Listing4.java:6: <T>bar(java.util.Map<T,T>) in Listing4 cannot be
applied to (java.util.Map<capture of ? extends java.lang.Number,
capture of ? extends java.lang.Number>)
        bar(m);
        ^
```
JAVAC

```
1. ERROR in listings/Listing4.java (at line 6)
    bar(m);
    ^^^
The method bar(Map<T,T>) in the type Listing4 is not applicable for the arguments
(Map<capture#1-of ? extends Number,capture#2-of ? extends Number>)
```
EJC

```
listings/Listing4.java:6
Method <T>bar(Map<T, T>) of type Listing4 is not applicable for the argument of
type (Map<? extends Number, ? extends Number>), because:
  [*] The type variable T is invariant, but the type '? extends Number' is not.
```
ours

Figure 12. Two wildcards (even with the same bounds) are never provably the same, which is a likely reason for the inconsistency. Both JAVAC and EJC make explicit reference to captured variables, while our message does not.

Strange Behaviour

In some cases we have observed that the compilers may behave strangely, or simply not according to the JLS.

Sometimes the type inferencer computes the largest subtype of a pair of types, and recall from the preliminaries that such a type may not always exist. This is the case for the program given in Fig. 13, in which T should be instantiated to the largest subtype of Number and String, which is not a valid type. Surprisingly, JAVAC accepts the program, due to the fact that it ignores the bound constraint when inferring a type for T.

A second example of a program that is erroneously accepted by JAVAC can be found in Fig. 14. In fact, none of the method invocations in this program should be allowed according to the JLS. Both EJC and our own compiler generate the type error messages as provided.

So why are these invocations type incorrect? The type of a generic type variable T for which no constraints of the form T = ... or ... <: T are generated, is determined by the type to which the result of the call to bar is assigned (if present). This, in the case of bar(m1) results in T being instantiated to Integer due to the type given for l. For the second call, T is instantiated to Integer. However, in both cases, and the third one as well, the constraint derived from the invocation itself T <: List<String> then cannot be satisfied.

```
import java.util.*;

class JavacError2 {
  <T extends Number> void foo(List<? super T> a){
    List<String> x = null;
    foo(x);
  }
}
```

```
1. ERROR in listings/JavacError2.java (at line 6)
     foo(x);
     ^^^
Bound mismatch: The generic method foo(List<? super T>) of type JavacError2 is
not applicable for the arguments (List<String>). The inferred type String is not
a valid substitute for the bounded parameter <T extends Number>
```

EJC

```
listings/JavacError2.java:6
Method <T extends Number>foo(List<? super T>) of type JavacError2 is not
applicable for the argument of type (List<String>), because:
  [*] The types String in List<String> on 5:5(5:10) and Number do not share a
      common subtype. (...)
```

ours

Figure 13. The argument type implies that T is String, which is clearly not a subtype of Number. Still, the program is accepted by JAVAC.

```
import java.util.*;

class JavacError3{
    <T extends Number> List<T> bar(Map<? super T, ? super T> a){
        Map<List<String>, List<String>> m1 = null;
        Map<Double, Number> m2 = null;
        List<Integer> l = bar(m1);
        List<Integer> s = bar(m2);
        s = bar(m1);
        return null;
    }
}
```

```
1. ERROR in listings/JavacError3.java (at line 7)
    List<Integer> l = bar(m1);
                      ^^^
The method bar(Map<? super T,? super T>) in the type JavacError3 is not
applicable for the arguments (Map<List<String>,List<String>>)
----------
2. ERROR in listings/JavacError3.java (at line 8)
    List<Integer> s = bar(m2);
                      ^^^
The method bar(Map<? super T,? super T>) in the type JavacError3 is not
applicable for the arguments (Map<Double,Number>)
----------
3. ERROR in listings/JavacError3.java (at line 9)
    s = bar(m1);
        ^^^
The method bar(Map<? super T,? super T>) in the type JavacError3 is not
applicable for the arguments (Map<List<String>,List<String>>)
```
EJC

```
listings/JavacError3.java:7
Method <T extends Number>bar(Map<? super T, ? super T>) of type JavacError3
is not applicable for the argument of type (Map<List<String>, List<String>>),
because:
  [*] The type List<String> in Map<List<String>, List<String>> on 5:9(5:9) is
      not a supertype of the inferred type for T: Integer.

listings/JavacError3.java:8
Method <T extends Number>bar(Map<? super T, ? super T>) of type JavacError3
is not applicable for the argument of type (Map<Double, Number>), because:
  [*] The type Double in Map<Double, Number> on 6:9(6:13) is not a supertype of
      the inferred type for T: Integer.

listings/JavacError3.java:9
Method <T extends Number>bar(Map<? super T, ? super T>) of type JavacError3
is not applicable for the argument of type (Map<List<String>, List<String>>),
because:
  [*] The type List<String> in Map<List<String>, List<String>> on 5:9(5:9) is
      not a supertype of the inferred type for T: Integer.
```
ours

Figure 14. Another code fragment erroneously accepted by JAVAC.

```
import java.util.Map;

class Listing51{
    <T extends Number> void foo(Map<? super T, ? super T> a){
        Map<String, Number> m = null;
        foo(m);
    }
}
```

```
listings/Listing5-1.java:6: <T>foo(java.util.Map<? super T,? super T>) in
Listing51 cannot be applied to
(java.util.Map<java.lang.String,java.lang.Number>)
        foo(m);
        ^
```
JAVAC

```
1. ERROR in listings/Listing5-1.java (at line 6)
    foo(m);
    ^^^
Bound mismatch: The generic method foo(Map<? super T,? super T>) of type
Listing51 is not applicable for the arguments (Map<String,Number>). The inferred
type String is not a valid substitute for the bounded parameter
<T extends Number>
```
EJC

```
listings/Listing5-1.java:6
Method <T extends Number>foo(Map<? super T, ? super T>) of type Listing51 is not
applicable for the argument of type (Map<String, Number>), because:
  [*] The types String in Map<String, Number> on 5:9(5:13) and Number in
      Map<String, Number> on 5:9(5:21) do not share a common subtype. (...)
```
ours

Figure 15. An inconsistency that for EJC reveals some of the underlying type checking machinery: the diagnosis given by EJC for the erroneous invocation should be the same as that for Fig. 16, but this is not the case.

The EJC compiler also sometimes exhibits strange behaviour. Consider the code fragments in Figs. 15 and 16. The only difference between the two is in the order of the type arguments of the value passed to the method. The constraints generated for both method calls are the same according to the JLS:

{T <: Number, T <: String}

One would expect, therefore, the error messages for the two programs to be identical, as they are for our implementation. However, the type error diagnosis for these programs by EJC is quite different. This is due to how EJC resolves subtype constraints. Note that although the error messages generated by JAVAC are the same, neither is very informative.

Obtaining different type error messages for very similar, in some sense isomorphic, programs is an often observed but not so pleasant phenomenon. It is typically due to the fact that the implementation of the type checking process leaks through to the type error messages. Since programmers typically do not have any knowledge of the implementation, they are at a disadvantage when trying to interpret the messages. We saw two examples of this earlier: the captured wildcards (Fig. 12) and the intersection types (Fig. 11) computed by the inference process.

THE TYPE CHECKING PROCESS

To be able to describe our modifications to the Java type checking process, we first discuss the original process. The modifications are then described in the next section.

```
import java.util.Map;

class Listing52{
    <T extends Number> void foo(Map<? super T, ? super T> a){
        Map<Number, String> m = null;
        foo(m);
    }
}
```

```
listings/Listing5-2.java:6: <T>foo(java.util.Map<? super T,? super T>) in
Listing52 cannot be applied to (java.util.Map<java.lang.Number,
java.lang.String>)
        foo(m);
        ^
```

JAVAC

```
1. ERROR in listings/Listing5-2.java (at line 6)
    foo(m);
    ^^^
The method foo(Map<? super T,? super T>) in the type Listing52 is not applicable
for the arguments (Map<Number,String>)
```

EJC

```
listings/Listing5-2.java:6
Method <T extends Number>foo(Map<? super T, ? super T>) of type Listing52 is not
applicable for the argument of type (Map<Number, String>), because:
  [*] The types Number in Map<Number, String> on 5:9(5:13) and String in
      Map<Number, String> on 5:9(5:21) do not share a common subtype. (...)
```

ours

Figure 16. The inconsistency is very similar to that in Fig. 15, but nonetheless diagnosed differently by EJC.

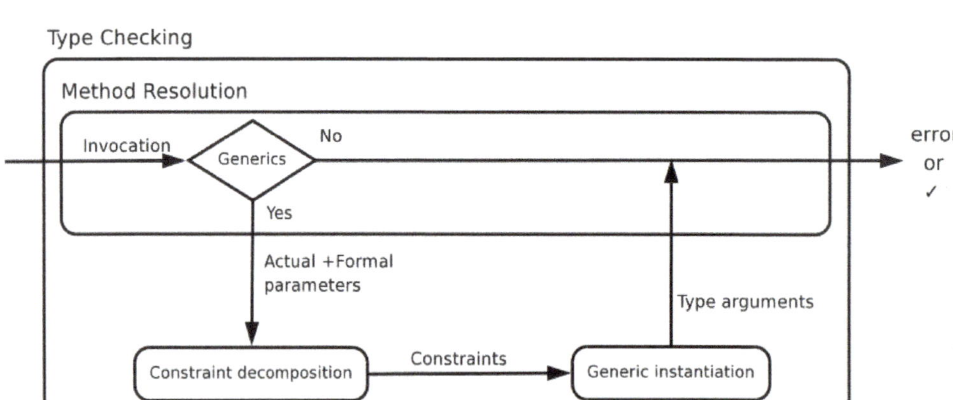

Figure 17. The type checking process.

To avoid any misunderstanding, we first explain our terminology. In this paper, *type checking process* refers to the complete process of determining the type correctness of a particular program fragment. In our particular case these program fragments are always *method invocations*.

The type checking process is depicted in Fig. 17. It starts off by performing *method resolution*, which determines, for a given invocation, a set of methods that the programmer may be invoking. We describe the complex process of method resolution in some detail below.

The set of methods obtained by method resolution may contain a number of generic methods. Pairing the concrete parameter types to the formal parameter types of a generic method:

```
<T, S> List<S> foo (Map<T, T> a,
                    List <? super S> b);
...
Map<Integer, Number> m = ...;
List<String> l = ...;
List<Integer> ret = foo(m, l);
```

results in a set of constraints

$\{\texttt{Map<Integer, Number>} <: \texttt{Map<T, T>}, \texttt{List<String>} <: \texttt{List<? super S>}\}$.

that should hold if this invocation is to typecheck.

The set of constraints is subsequently decomposed into atomic constraints between type variables on the one hand and types on the other. Although there are quite a few cases to be covered, this part of the process is conceptually quite easy and is described in detail in §15.12.2.7 of [7]. Here, we give only the result of decomposition for our example:

$$\{\texttt{T} = \texttt{Integer}, \texttt{T} = \texttt{Number}, \texttt{String} :> \texttt{S}\}.$$

The type checking process then proceeds with *generic instantiation* to infer the types of the generic variables, essentially a process of finding a concrete type for each type variable. Although its name might imply otherwise, the inference process has a surprising property: if multiple, conflicting instantiations for a type variable are possible, then the inference process simply selects one, leaving it up to the later type checking phase to find that the instantiation is incorrect. The JLS states that if a conflict exists, then it will indeed not show up until in the type checking phase at the end of the type checking process. In the above example, a possible outcome of the inference phase is:

T = Integer.

In the presence of multiple supertype constraints, say

{Integer <: T, Double <: T},

this results in the instantiation of T to the *least upper bound* (*lub*) of the two, Number. However, things are not always so simple: for {Integer <: T, String <: T}, the lub is

```
Object & Serializable &Comparable<? extends Object &
        Serializable & Comparable<?>>,
```

because both Integer and String implement these interfaces. Note that in many compilers, not only are these types computed by the inference process, they are sometimes also used in the type error message displayed to the programmer. This contradicts one of the crucial properties that we, and others [33], believe a type checking process should have: it should only refer to types or expressions that are part of the original source program. Without any information on how the lub was computed, it can be very difficult for programmers to reconstruct what has happened and why.

The dual of the least upper bound is the *greatest lower bound* (*glb*), which is used to capture the most general type that extends both argument types (which may include classes *and* interfaces). However, if all constraints in which a type variable is involved are of this kind and the invocation occurs in an assignment context, then the JLS specifies that the type of the variable to which the result is assigned should, if possible, be used to determine to

what type a type variable should be instantiated. This happens to be the case in our example for S. Therefore, the constraint List<S> <: List<Integer> is added to the constraint set. It decomposes into S = Integer. Together, the decomposed constraints are

$\{\texttt{T} = \texttt{Integer}, \texttt{T} = \texttt{Number}, \texttt{S} = \texttt{Integer}, \texttt{String} :> \texttt{S}\}$.

The inference process then instantiates S to Integer on the basis of the third constraint above; note that T was already instantiated to Integer.

One may wonder what happens if a declared type variable is not constrained in any way. The JLS specifies that the variable should then be instantiated to Object; this helps the JLS deal with legacy code.

In the final step, it is determined whether the remaining constraints, which are by now all equivalence and subtype relations between concrete types, are consistent. This part of the type checking process we call the type checking *phase*.

It is important to realize that in the type checking phase each invocation is considered *in isolation*. This even holds for nested invocations foo(bar(x),y), where first the bar invocation will be considered in isolation from its context. It can therefore well be that the bar invocation type checks, but that types chosen by the inference phase turn out to be inconsistent with the enclosing call to foo. Or, it may be that the call to bar is not valid due to a case of ambiguous method invocation, but that on the basis of the type of foo, this ambiguity could have been resolved. By contrast, in the polymorphic lambda-calculus type information from the encapsulating call would be used to determine the proper instantiations for bar. This lack of propagation in Java has its advantages, as types are instantiated based on local information only and not through a long and complicated sequence of unifications. But this may also surprise the programmer, particularly in the case of an ambiguous method invocation.

Method resolution

The goal of method resolution, for a given invocation, is to come up with a single method in the program that the programmer intends to call. This decision has to be made statically, and cannot depend on run-time type information.

The process of method resolution is rather complex, due to such features as overloading (multiple methods having the same name), overriding (methods can be overridden by subclasses), variable arity methods, and visibility. Visibility depends not only on lexical scope, but also on, e.g., the access modifiers of the method. This includes the fact that you may not call a private method from certain contexts, but also that you cannot access (non-static) instance fields from a static method.

Method resolution consists of three main steps. For a given method invocation,

- Determine the name of the method to be invoked, say mthd, and the class or interface that receives the invocation. Java has five different forms of method invocation. Examples respectively are a.byteValue(), this.Foo(), super.intVal(), Baz.super.intVal() and Collections<X>.emptySet(). In the case of the invocation a.byteValue(), byteValue() is the name of the method, and the receiver is the innermost class or interface that encloses the method declaration (if indeed, byteValue is visible from the invocation site). Note that for this case alone there are two additional variants: a. may be omitted, and a type name may be used instead of a. For more details see the JLS.
- Consider every method of the receiver in turn to find all possible accessible and applicable method members. A method potential in the receiver is a candidate if and only if
- the names potential and mthd are the same,
- potential is accessible from the invocation site,
- if potential is a variable arity method of arity, say n, then the number of arguments passed to mthd must be greater than or equal to $n - 1$,
- if potential is a fixed arity method of arity n, then the number of arguments passed to mthd must be equal to n,
- if the method invocation includes explicit type parameters, and potential is a generic method, then the number of actual type parameters must equal the number of formal type parameters.

Then the compiler tries to weed out potential methods by comparing actual to formal parameters. Due to the presence of subtyping, auto-boxing, and variable arity methods, this is quite a complicated process, consisting of three alternative decision procedures. A decision procedure is only applied if all the preceding decision procedures eliminated *all* candidates. Below, we assume the method invocation is mthd(A_1,..., A_n).

- Identify methods mthd(F_1,..., F_n), and in which only "weakening by subtyping" is allowed to match actual argument types to formal argument types. In other words, for all $1 \leq i \leq n$:

  $A_i <: F_i$, or

  A_i is a raw type that can be parametrized into a type C_i so that $C_i <: F_i$.

  If the method is generic, then all type variables in the F_i are bound to a concrete type provided by the method invocation. If such type information is unavailable then type inference, as described earlier, is used to find concrete types. The potential method is then only applicable if all instantiated type variables are within their stated bounds.
- Similar to the previous case, but now in combination with (un)boxing.
- Similar to the previous case, but now allowing also variable arity methods. Details can be found in the JLS.

If all the sets of candidates delivered by the three previous cases are empty, then no matching method exists, and an error message is produced. Otherwise, we take the first non-empty one, say S, and proceed to try to eliminate candidates until only one is left. For example, we remove from S those methods for which a more specific signature in S exists, e.g., if both mthd(List<T>) and mthd (List<Integer>) are in S, then the former is deleted. A similar but more complicated rule can be formulated for variable arity methods.

If for any pair of methods it cannot be decided which is the most specific, the compiler has a few rules to deal with this, largely by preferring non-abstract over abstract methods. In the absence of the former, an arbitrary abstract method with the most specific return type is chosen.

If that still does not work, then an ambiguous method invocation error message is generated.

In the third and final step, the method chosen in the previous step is screened for appropriateness. For example, an instance method cannot be invoked from a static context.

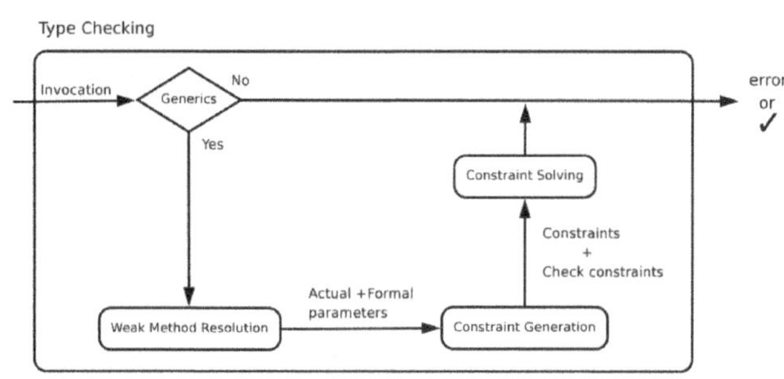

Figure 18. The modified type checking process.

As the reader can see, method resolution is indeed a complicated, stepwise process. In our extension of the type checking process, which we describe in the following section, we relax the constraints somewhat to try and figure out which method the programmer might have been trying to call, and to use that information in our type error message.

THE MODIFIED TYPE CHECKING PROCESS

Figure 18 shows the overall architecture of our modified type checking process. The structure of the process is not much different, only the contents of the phases themselves change. It is important to realize that this modified process is only invoked after the original process has found a particular invocation to be type incorrect.

Weakened Method Resolution

First, we define a weaker form of method resolution that allows more candidate methods to be targeted by the method invocation. We are not interested in identifying a single method that is being called, but want to consider multiple candidate methods and provide a diagnosis for each method that is reasonably close to what the programmer intended to call.

A major decision we have to make is how exactly we weaken method resolution. Our choice here is to erase *generic* information from the invocation and the candidate method. In other words, when we are looking for a suitable method in the second step (ii) of method resolution we base our comparison between the signatures on the raw types, instead of the generic types. Conversion to raw types involves replacing type variables (and possible bounds) with Object and changing generic types like List<Number> to the raw type List.

The original process of method resolution aims to come up with a single method to be called (or it may fail to find one at all). Because we drop information that might be used during the original method resolution phase, the set of candidates might now be larger. This is not a problem. Remember that we already know that in the end none of these methods will be acceptable. But since we have more candidates to pass on to the part of the process that is still to come, that part of the process may then be able to tell us more precisely *why* each of the candidates fails to qualify. In our particular case, for example, we have defined and implemented a number of heuristics [2] that work directly on the constraints derived from a particular method invocation and method definition, but these heuristics will only be applied to method definitions that pass (weakened) method resolution.

The (heuristic) assumption we make is that when it comes to the types of arguments, the generic parts of Java are more likely to contain mistakes than the raw types. This assumption derives from the fact that the generic part of Java is pretty complicated and therefore more easily misunderstood. Moreover, it is a fairly recent addition to the language, and a refinement of the raw types.

Another way to view our assumption, is that we prefer not to commit too early to certain choices because that immediately biases the type checking process, in that it becomes less likely that we shall ever blame that which we commit upon first. This indicates that, as a rule, it pays to commit first to facts in which your confidence is the highest. Since our assumption is that we should have less confidence in the generic parts of the types, it makes sense to ignore them in the early phases of the process.

Another instance of this idea can be found in work on removing the bias from Algorithm W [3]: in a standard implementation, constraints are solved (i.e., unifications are performed) while traversing the abstract syntax tree of the program (from left to right), thereby building a type substitution on the fly. So if we have multiple, inconsistent constraints for a particular type variable, the leftmost constraint is seen first and will determine the type we find for the type variable, even in cases where we find that all other constraints for that type variable say differently. In [9] it was shown how the bias can be removed by a constraint solving approach in which sets of constraints are considered simultaneously, and heuristics that work on these sets of constraints, either select the constraint(s) that are most likely to be the cause of the inconsistency, or eliminate constraints for which the opposite is the case.

The specification of weakened method resolution in the form of pseudocode can be found in Figs. 19, 20 and 21. The function methodResolution takes a method invocation as an argument and returns a set of most specific method declarations. The procedure starts by searching for potentially applicable methods, by considering all methods that are members of the receiver of the invocation. These are methods with the same name as the method that is invoked, and have an arity equal the number of arguments in the invocation (if the method is of fixed arity), or an arity less than the number of arguments in the invocation (if the method is of variable arity). This part is performed by the procedure potentiallyApplicable in Fig. 19. As explained before, three attempts will be made to come to a non-empty set of methods: first we are only allowed to match up to subtyping, then we allow method conversion (methodConvertible, that considers candidate methods modulo boxing, unboxing and various forms of widening, §5.3 of [7]), and finally we also allow methods of variable arity to be considered.

```
[Method] methodResolution(invocation)
  potentialMethods = [m in invocation.receiver
                      | potentiallyApplicable(m,invocation)]
  specificMethods = [m in potentialMethods
                     | m of fixed arity and
                       applicableBySubtyping(m,invocation)]
  mostSpecificMethods = mostSpecificMethodFixed(specificMethods)
  if empty mostSpecificMethods then
    methodConvertedMethods = [m in potentialMethods
                              | m of fixed arity and
                                applicableByMethodConversion(m,invocation)]
    mostSpecificMethods = mostSpecificMethodFixed(methodConvertedMethods)
    if empty mostSpecificMethods then
      methodVarArity = [m in potentialMethods
                        | m of variable arity and
                          applicableByMethodConversion(m,invocation)]
      mostSpecificMethods = mostSpecificMethodVariable(methodConvertedMethods)
  return [m in mostSpecificMethods | m appropriate]
```

```
boolean potentiallyApplicable(method, invocation)
  return
     method.name == invocation.name and
     method accessible from invocation.location and
     (method.arity == length(invocation.arguments) or
      (method of variable arity and
       length(invocation.arguments) >= method.arity-1))

boolean applicableBySubtyping(method, invocation)
  foreach (parameter,argument) in (method.arguments,invocation.arguments) do
    erasedParameter = wideErasure(parameter)
    if (argument <: erasedParameter) then
      continue
    else
      return false
  return true


boolean applicableByMethodConversion(method, invocation)
  (* Works both for variable and fixed arity methods *)
  k = method.arity-1
  for i = 1 to k
    erasedParameter = wideErasure(method.arguments[i])
    argument  = invocation.arguments[i]
    if methodConvertible(argument, erasedParameter) then
      continue
    else
      return false
  (* The "variable" part *)
  erasedParameter = wideErasure(method.arguments[k+1]
  for i = k+1 to n
    argument   = invocation.arguments[i]
    if methodConvertible(argument, erasedParameter) then
      continue
    else
      return false
  return true
```

Figure 19. Pseudocode for weakened method resolution (part 1).

```
Type wideErasure(tp)
  if tp is a type variable then
     return Object
  else
     if tp is generic then
        return raw form of tp
     else
        return tp

[Method] mostSpecificMethodFixed(methods)
  foreach m1 in methods
    foreach m2 in methods
      if moreSpecificFixed(m1,m2) then
        methods.delete(m2)

[Method] mostSpecificMethodVariable(methods)
  foreach m1 in methods
    foreach m2 in methods
      if moreSpecificVariable(m1,m2) then
        methods.delete(m2)
```

Figure 20. Pseudocode for weakened method resolution (part 2).

In each case, methods will be eliminated if they are less specific than at least one other in the list. This check is implemented for the fixed arity and variable arity case in mostSpecificMethodFixed and mostSpecificMethodVariable, as given in Fig. 20. The methods behave exactly as in the original type checking process, except that they ignore any kind of generic information. The specification of the auxiliary function moreSpecificVariable in Fig. 21 is rather lengthy, because we have to deal with the fact that the number of parameters can be unequal in two ways, but that the subtype relation is independent of the respective lengths. Note that we could have abstracted away from the particular type comparison operator in order to save code, but for reasons of clarity and correspondence with the JLS (§15.12.2.5) we preferred to write it out.

After having constructed a set of most specific methods, methodResolution will remove any method declaration that is not appropriate from the set (e.g. not accessible from the call site), and returns the set of remaining methods.

We illustrate the process by means of an example. Consider the code in Fig. 22 where we define a many-times overloaded method foo (we designate foo on line x by foox). Consider first the invocation on line 20. The method foo_2 does not qualify as a candidate because it has the wrong number of parameters. All the other declarations have the right number of parameters, so they are marked as candidates in step (i). Their signatures are converted into their raw form, and we obtain

foo_4(Map, Collection), foo_7(Map, List), foo_{10}(HashMap, List), foo_{13}(HashMap, LinkedList), foo_{16}(HashMap, Set).

In the absence of primitive types and variable arity methods, the applicable methods can be determined using subtyping only, i.e., we only need to look at case (a) of step (ii) in the method resolution phase. The second parameter LinkedList in the invocation is not a subtype of the generic interface type Set. Therefore, foo_{16} is disqualified as a candidate. Next, our weak method resolution reduces the set of applicable methods

$$\{foo_4, foo_7, foo_{10}, foo_{13}\}$$

to a set of most specific methods. Comparing foo_4 with foo_7 results in the removal of foo_4, because List <: Collection. Similarly, foo_7 and foo_{10} are removed in favour of foo_{13}. For the second and third invocation in Fig. 22 the same set of candidates is obtained.

```
boolean moreSpecificFixed(m1,m2)
  (* In case both methods are of fixed arity *)
  foreach (paramm1,paramm2) in (m1.arguments, m2.arguments) do
    paramm1 = wideErasure(paramm1)
    paramm2 = wideErasure(paramm2)
    if (paramm1 <: paramm2) then
      continue
    else
      return false
  return true

boolean moreSpecificVariable(m1,m2)
  (* In case both methods are of variable arity *)
  if m1.arity >= m2.arity then
    k = m2.arity - 1
    m = m1.arity
    for i = 1 to k
      paramm1 = wideErasure(m1.arguments[i])
      paramm2 = wideErasure(m2.arguments[i])
      if (paramm1 <: paramm2) then
        continue
      else
        return false
    paramm2 = wideErasure(m2.arguments[k+1])

    for i = k+1 to n
      paramm1 = wideErasure(m1.arguments[i])
      if (paramm1 <: paramm2) then
        continue
      else
        return false
    return true
```

```
else
  k = m1.arity - 1
  m = m2.arity
  for i = 1 to k
    paramm1 = wideErasure(m1.arguments[i])
    paramm2 = wideErasure(m2.arguments[i])
    if (paramm1 <: paramm2) then
      continue
    else
      return false
  paramm1 = wideErasure(m1.arguments[k+1])

  for i = k+1 to n
    paramm2 = wideErasure(m2.arguments[i])
    if (paramm1 <: paramm2) then
      continue
    else
      return false
  return true
```

Figure 21. Pseudocode for weakened method resolution (part 3).

In all cases, we ended up with a singleton set, but our resolution method does not demand this, contrary to the original resolution method. For example, for the code fragment of Fig. 28, which we shall discuss in more detail later, both declarations of bar pass method resolution.

```
class FooLib{
   <T> void foo(Map<T, ? extends T> a){}

   <T> void foo(Map<T, ? extends T> a,
                  Collection<? super T> b){}

   <T> void foo(Map<T, ? extends T> a,
                  List<? super T> b){}

   <T> void foo(HashMap<T, ? extends T> a,
                  List<? super T> b){}

   <T> void foo(HashMap<T, ? extends T> a,
                  LinkedList<? super T> b){}

   <T> void foo(HashMap<T, ? extends T> a,
                  Set<? super T> b){}
}
...
UtilLib.foo(new HashMap<Integer, Integer>(),
               new LinkedList<Number>());
UtilLib.foo(new HashMap<Double, Number>(),
               new LinkedList<Integer>());
LinkedList<? extends Number> wl = ...;
UtilLib.foo(new HashMap<Number, Double>(), wl);
```

Figure 22. A utility class for illustrating weakened method resolution.

```
<T> void foo(List<T> a, List<? super T> b){
...
List<Number> l1 = ...;
List<? extends Number> l2 = ...;
foo(l1, l2);
```

Figure 23. Inference succeeds to find instantiations for all variables, but then checking fails.

Constraint Generation

Constraint generation is our version of the phase of constraint decomposition. Recall that the original type inference phase does not check for inconsistencies. Inconsistencies are discovered later during the type checking phase. This choice leads to type error messages that cannot explain very well what the problem is, because information has been lost between the type inferencing and type checking phase.

Consider the code fragment in Fig. 23. Here, the type parameter T is instantiated to Number, because l1 is passed as the first argument. But unfortunately, List<? extends Number> is not a subtype of List<? super Number>. In this situation, an implementation based on the JLS will typically say that foo cannot be applied to the variables l1 and l2, but it cannot for example explain to the programmer why the error occurred or how to fix it: it does not have enough knowledge to do so.

In our extension, we provide the constraint solver, introduced in detail below, with more constraints that will ensure that a type is inferred only if all type constraints are satisfied and no type-checking error will occur. To that purpose, the original constraint decomposition algorithm is extended to keep track of constraints that were left alone during decomposition, because they did not match any of the cases of the constraint decomposition procedures. In fact, the new procedures can be obtained from the old ones (based on §15.12.2.7 of [7]), simply by adding cases that store the non-atomic constraints for which no case is defined, into a special set of constraints. In the following we therefore keep track of two sets of constraints X and Y by writing $X \Cap Y$. Here, the left operand X contains the decomposed constraints, and Y contains those constraints that could not be decomposed.

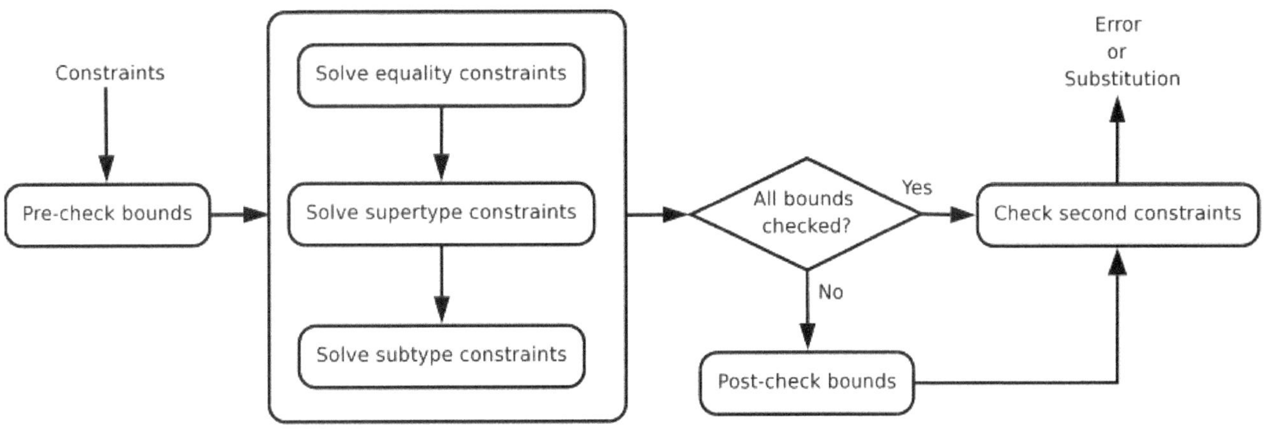

Figure 24. The constraint solving phase.

For the example in Fig. 23, the new constraint generation algorithm will collect the following constraints:

$$\{\texttt{T} = \texttt{Number}\} \Cup \{\texttt{List<? extends Number>} <: \texttt{List<? super T>}\}$$

Coming back to the example of Fig. 22, we generate constraints for the invocation of foo at line 20 to type check. The only remaining candidate method is foo$_{13}$, in which case we obtain

$$\{\texttt{T} = \texttt{Integer}, \texttt{Integer} <: \texttt{T}, \texttt{T} <: \texttt{Number}\} \Cup \emptyset$$

For the second invocation we obtain

$$\{\texttt{T} = \texttt{Double}, \texttt{Number} <: \texttt{T}, \texttt{T} <: \texttt{Integer}\} \Cup \emptyset$$

and for the third

$$\{\texttt{T} = \texttt{Number}, \texttt{Double} <: \texttt{T}\} \Cup \{\texttt{LinkedList<? extends Number>} <: \texttt{LinkedList<? super T>}\}$$

The Constraint Solving Phase

In Fig. 24 we summarize the constraint solving phase. In the pre-check for bounds, we check that all types in the atomic constraints of a type parameter T satisfy the bounds of T. If not, a type error message is generated for each failed check. Then it infers the instantiations for every type variable, based on the decomposed constraints (the left operand of $\Cup$). This either results in a substitution or, in case of failure, a list of type error messages. If there are still bounds for T left unchecked, e.g., they involve also other type variables, then these bounds checks are performed next. Finally, we verify that the non-atomic constraints (the right operand of ⊎) are satisfied.

```
<T, S extends T> void foo(Map<S, S> a, T a){
...
Map<Integer, String> m = ...;
foo(m, 1);
```

Figure 25. The order of inference for type variable matters.

The reason for doing the pre-check is best illustrated by an example. Consider the following set of constraints

{String <: T, Integer <: T, T <: Number}.

The original algorithm instantiates T to Object, the lub of String and Integer. Later, during type checking it finds that Object is not a subtype of Number. Since the type checker does not have information available about how T got its type, it cannot really say what went wrong. If on the other hand, the bound had been checked immediately (or alternatively, information about the inference of T had been retained), we would have found that String <: T is not consistent with T <: Number; and choosing any type that is a supertype of String is not going to help. In other words, for constraints of the given form, it can be determined at an early stage that an inconsistency will result, and a type error message can be generated immediately.

The second modification we made is to tune the order in which type inference instantiates the type variables. It is well known that for the polymorphic lambda-calculus the different implementations of the type system solve constraints in different orders and that the order influences the error message the implementations provide [12, 18]. In our inference algorithm, type variables are considered separately, but because we involve the bounds constraints at an early stage, the inferred type for a particular type variable may impact that of another.

To illustrate, consider the code fragment in Fig. 25. If we first infer the type of S, then we cannot exploit the information that the bound S extends T might give us. On the other hand, if we first infer T (to be Integer, obviously), then we obtain an additional pre-check bound for S: S <: Integer. During the pre-check we can then establish that the constraint S = Integer is consistent with the bound and S = String is not.

It should not be a surprise, therefore, that we have chosen the *degree heuristic* for deter- mining the order of inference [26]. This heuristic selects first the type variables that determines the largest number of other variables. Consider the following generic parameter:

```
<T, S extends T, R, U extends Map<R, S> &
  T, V extends Map<U, T>>
```

From this generic parameter we can construct the graph in Fig. 26 as follows: the type variables form the vertices of the graph, and we have a solid edge from S to T if T occurs in a bound for S. The dashed edges in the graph are edges that additionally result from taking the transitive closure of the direct dependencies. The degree heuristic now specifies that we should first instantiate the type variable that has the highest number of incoming edges, whether solid or dashed. The reasoning is that an instance for such a type variable provides the most information, i.e., the largest number of type variables can potentially profit from the additional information. Hence, in the example type inference should start by inferring T.

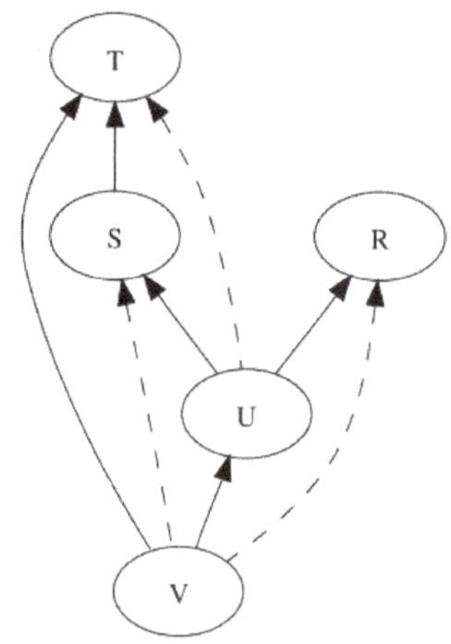

Figure 26. A type variable dependency graph, with *solid edges* denoting a direct dependency, and *dashed edges* for indirect ones.

```
if empty E then
  if empty P then
    if empty B then
      set T = Object
    else
      set C = constraints from the context
      if T inferred on the basis of union(B,C)
        set T = inferred type
      else
        generate error message
  else
    set A = { alpha | alpha <: T in P }
    set T = lub(A)
    if B are satisfied then
      okay
    else
      generate error message
else
  if all constraints in E of the form T = X then
    set T = X
    if union(P, B) are satisfied then
      okay
    else
      generate error message
  else
    generate error message
```

Figure 27. A pseudocode algorithm for type inference.

The Inferencer

The large rounded rectangle in Fig. 24 is the core of the constraint solving phase, where inference takes place. The algorithm processes the type variables one at the time, in the order obtained using the dependency graph, as described in Sect. 5.3.

Suppose we now deal with type variable T, and E, P and B contain the type equality, supertype and subtype constraints involving T, respectively. Then Fig. 27 gives the pseudocode to describe the inference process.

We conclude this section by revisiting the running example of Fig. 22.

For the first invocation we find

$$\{\texttt{T} = \texttt{Integer}, \texttt{Integer} <: \texttt{T}, \texttt{T} <: \texttt{Number}\} \uplus \emptyset.$$

In this case, there is a single equality constraint for T, so we infer T to be Integer and proceed to verify the remaining constraints: the supertype and subtype constraints turn out to be satisfied as well. Because the set of non-atomic constraints is empty, and therefore trivially satisfied, the invocation on line 20 invokes the method on line 13 correctly and unambiguously.

For the second invocation we obtained

$$\{\texttt{T} = \texttt{Double}, \texttt{Number} <: \texttt{T}, \texttt{T} <: \texttt{Integer}\} \uplus \emptyset.$$

The type variable T is inferred to be Double, but in this case both subtype and supertype constraints fail to be satisfied. Hence an error message is generated.

Finally, for the third

$$\{\texttt{T} = \texttt{Number}, \texttt{Double} <: \texttt{T}\} \uplus$$

$$\{\texttt{LinkedList<? extends Number>} <: \texttt{LinkedList<? super T>}\}$$

we infer T to be Number, and since Double <: Number, the constraints are satisfied. However, the non-atomic constraint is not satisfied, so the method invocation fails to type check.

For a somewhat different example, consider the code fragment in Fig. 28. Because in both cases the names match, and the number of formal parameters matches the number of actual arguments in the call, both methods are considered candidates and will be considered further. Since weak method resolution ignores all generic information, both method signatures are implicitly converted to void bar(Object a, Object b). Because the arguments to the call happen to be of primitive type, weak method resolution will attempt to match the call to a method by means of method invocation conversion (§5.3 of [7]). This results in both methods to be considered applicable. Then the type checking process will consider each method in turn to determine which of these, if any, matches the call.

Let us consider the first definition of bar. Matching the types of the invocation with that of the first definition of bar results in the following constraints, in which the primitive types are automatically promoted to their corresponding reference type:

$$\{\texttt{Character} <: \texttt{T}, \texttt{Double} <: \texttt{T}\} \uplus \emptyset.$$

Because only one type variable is involved, the ordering phase for type variables can be ignored, and we proceed to perform bounds checking. Bounds checking ensures that for all types S with S <: T, that S is a subtype of all the types U that bound T from above. Choices for S in this particular case are Double and Character, the only possibility for

U is Number. The combination Double and Number is fine, but since Character $\not<:$ Number, the method does not match. Notwithstanding, the process does set T equal to the lub of Double and Character. This type is not returned as the type for T, but, instead, used to further uncover potential type conflicts. For example, if there would be another constraint on T, say T <: Integer, then this may help establish more firmly that the types used in computing the lub to obtain T are not the right ones. When we provide an error message to fix the problem, we can then avoid to suggest fixing it in a way that in the next compile a clash with the constraint T <: Integer can occur.

```
class BarUtil{
   static <T extends Number>void bar(T a, T b){}
   static <T extends Integer>void bar(T a, T b){}
   void dummy() {
     BarUtil.bar('0', 3.14);
   }
}
```

```
listings/Listing7.java:5: internal error; cannot instantiate <T>bar(T,T) at
BarUtil to (char,double)
     BarUtil.bar('0', 3.14);
               ^
```
JAVAC

```
1. WARNING in listings/Listing7.java (at line 3)
    static <T extends Integer>void bar(T a, T b){}
                      ^^^^^^^
The type parameter T should not be bounded by the final type Integer. Final
types cannot be further extended
----------
2. ERROR in listings/Listing7.java (at line 5)
    BarUtil.bar('0', 3.14);
            ^^^
Bound mismatch: The generic method bar(T, T) of type BarUtil is not applicable
for the arguments (Character, Double).
The inferred type Object&Serializable& Comparable<?> is not a valid substitute
for the bounded parameter <T extends Number>
```
EJC

```
listings/Listing7.java:5
Method <T extends Number>bar(T, T) of type BarUtil is not applicable for the
arguments of type (char, double), because:
  [*] The type char of the expression ''0'' on 5:18 is not a subtype of T's
      upper bound Number in 'T extends Number'.

listings/Listing7.java:5
Method <T extends Integer>bar(T, T) of type BarUtil is not applicable for the
arguments of type (char, double), because:
  [*] The type char of the expression ''0'' on 5:18 is not a subtype of T's
      upper bound Integer in 'T extends Integer'.
  [*] The type double of the expression '3.14' on 5:23 is not a subtype of T's
      upper bound Integer in 'T extends Integer'.
```

ours

Figure 28. A code fragment with two candidate methods, both of which fail to qualify. JAVAC and EJC provide only one message, but our system provides a diagnosis for both failures.

For the second definition of bar, we similarly obtain an inconsistent set of constraints. In this case U ranges over the set {Integer}, and neither the constraint Double <: T nor the constraint Character <: T can be satisfied. For both method definitions an error message will be provided by our implementation, as seen in Fig. 28. Both EJC and JAVAC give only a single type error message for the invocation. It is not made clear why the method call matches neither, and, in the case of JAVAC it is even not clear to which of the two method definitions the method invocation has been compared.

As an aside, EJC also warns that it makes little sense to have T extend a final class. This is quite similar to one of the heuristics we describe in [2]. However, before we would give such a hint, we make sure that replacing T by its upper bound actually solves the problem. Since that is not the case here, our implementation does not provide such a hint.

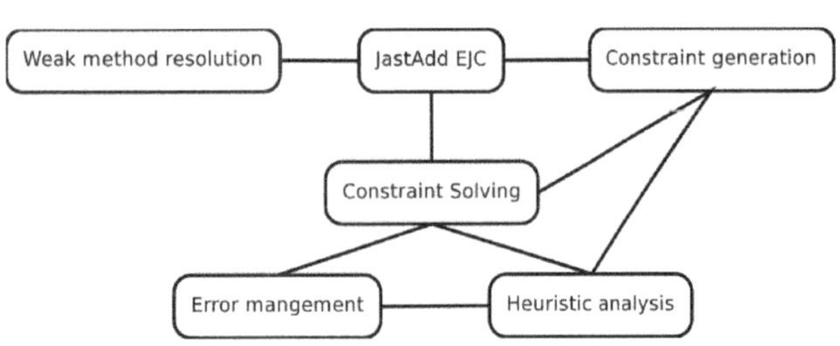

Figure 29. Architecture of our extension to the JastAdd EJC.

IMPLEMENTATION

We have implemented our work as an extension to the JastAdd Extensible Java Compiler (JastAdd EJC) [6], which in turn was built on top of JastAdd [11]. The latter is an attribute grammar compiler that allows specifying compiler semantics in an aspect-oriented way by means of declarative attributes and semantic rules using ordinary Java code. Some more information on this implementation can be found in Appendix.

For the convenience of the weak method resolution, the ordering of type variables and the computation of greatest lower bound have been implemented using JastAdd. We have contributed the module that we have developed for computing the greatest lower bound to the maintainers of JastAdd EJC; it has been added to the repository.

The architecture of the resulting compiler is shown in Fig. 29: the type checker sends a method invocation which fails to typecheck to the weak method resolution which returns a set of methods. The type checker then generates type constraints for the method invocation and each method declaration using the constraint generation algorithm described in Sect. 5. The type checker passes these constraints along to our constraint solver together with the return type of the method declaration under consideration and the type of the value if the invocation appears in an assignment context. The constraint solver will then solve the constraints and return an error message to the type checker if the constraints are unsatisfiable. The error messages returned by the constraint solver are maintained and collected by a separate error manager. This is mainly to facilitate the implementation of a number of heuristics that we use to suggest fixes for the type error [2].

Although we have only discussed method invocations, our extension already gives some limited support for constructor invocations.

RELATED WORK

Thus far, work on improving type error diagnosis has concentrated on strongly typed, higherorder, polymorphic functional languages, such as ML and Haskell. Indeed, one of the reasons we set out to do the current study was to see how far our experience in improving type error diagnosis for Haskell would help us in a different setting.

The PhD thesis of Bastiaan Heeren [12] compiles a number of papers with the second author and includes an extensive bibliography on improving type error messages for functional languages. We mention a few of the more important papers. We omit [34], which was already discussed in the introduction.

Heeren categorises papers based on their approach. The simplest approach to improve type error messages is to change the order in which unifications take place, i.e., constraints are solved, because that will change the unification that will be held responsible for the inconsistency [10, 17, 18, 20].

The second category consists of explanation systems, which in one way or another keep track of how a conclusion about a particular type was derived in order to provide that explanation to the programmer [5, 9, 32, 33, 35]. We make in particular note of Yang et al. [35], because at its basis lies algorithm H, which was inspired by how human subjects (in an experimental setting) perform type checking. In particular, they discovered that human subjects focus on the concrete types derived from the use of literals, and make heavy use of the two-dimensional inspection of code. Contrary to how most algorithms work, humans avoid type variables when explaining the type of an expression.

A potential problem of explanation systems is that explanations can quickly become very verbose, because type information can potentially propagate to all corners of the program. This is less of a problem in the context of Generic Java, because each method invocation is considered in isolation; reasoning is thereby much more localised.

Repair systems try to isolate a particular cause of a problem, suggesting that this part of the program should be changed to remedy the mistake. Particular examples are [2, 9, 21, 31]. The danger of these systems is that they are heuristic: there are always situations where they will suggest the wrong fix. Thus, some researchers prefer to report a set of program locations, usually with some guarantee that no location outside this set can be responsible for the problem. Such a set forms a program slice, and such approaches are said to perform type error slicing [4, 8, 25]. It is still unknown, however, whether such a system can be useful in practice as there is not enough information yet on how large slices can become, and how well the system works in the presence of multiple independent and/or somewhat related mistakes. We believe that the combination of type error slicing with type error repair to be very promising, but we have not yet seen any substantial work in this direction.

A final category consists of systems that allow the programmer to interactively investigate the types of expressions in the program. Such a system can usually give more precise feedback, because from the interaction it may obtain more information from the programmer about his/her intentions. The most well-known attempts in this direction are Typeview [14] and Chameleon [28, 29].

Characteristic of all these attempts is that the authors redesign the type inference process to come up with better error messages. A totally different approach can be found in [19], which uses a Caml compiler as a black box, and presents programmers with complete program fixes for parts of their program. This is done by enumerating variations on the faulty program and submitting these to the compiler to decide on type correctness.

We consider the current paper to belong to the category of explanation systems, although our explanations typically will not be long. Our work also has some elements from [19]: although our work is implemented directly in a Java compiler, we do leave the original type inference process intact.

What sets our work somewhat apart from the literature above is that we need to deal with subtyping and overloading. Because a programmer may be attempting to call any number of methods, our method compares the invocation to multiple method definitions, and for each describes why the call is inconsistent with that method. For the languages that are the subject of the papers above, such a situation never occurs. Moreover, our work is complicated by the fact that instead of the elegant Hindley-Milner type system for the polymorphic lambdacalculus [22], we have to cope with the large, operational specification of Java's type system, which actually coincides with its type checking process.

We are not aware of any other work on improving type error messages for languages besides functional ones, except for el Boustani and Hage [1], which is a shorter version of the current paper, and a follow-up paper that deals with heuristics that can offer suggestions on how to fix the type error [2]. Changes with respect to the former can be summarized as follows: since we have fewer restrictions on length we have recompiled all the programs with the three tools and have included all the outcomes without changing the content of the messages. We made one exception: our implementation also sometimes suggests how to change the program to get rid of a type error. Since these suggestions are the subject of [2], we have omitted these from our messages, and replaced them with (...). We have also added quite a few examples including a realistic one, and a related work section. Finally, we describe more details of the processes involved.

Somewhat related to our work is that of Jadud who performed an extensive study of parse errors and compiler usage for Java [15].

CONCLUSIONS, REFLECTIONS AND FUTURE WORK

We have described how the type checking process of Generic Java can be extended to provide more informative type error messages, particularly for method invocations that involve generics. We have illustrated our work by a sizable number of examples and have made a download available in which our work is implemented as an extension to the JastAdd Extensible Java Compiler.

Our work follows three design principles: Principle number one is to leave the (very complicated) type checking process intact, because any modification of the process risks changing the set of typable programs. The second principle is to avoid acting on what you trust the least, e.g., a major hurdle to obtain good type error messages when following the JLS, is that candidate methods may be disqualified at an early stage of the type checking process. In this paper, we chose to ignore the generic parts of types, based on the assumption that this is where programmers make the most mistakes. The third and final principle is to hold on to type information longer than is necessary for following the JLS. In our particular case, we kept some of the original constraints around to make a more informed decision on the causes of the inconsistencies.

There are plenty of directions for future work. The first is to perform a more global analysis to come up with an even better estimate of what might be the mistake. For example, type inference is highly compartmentalized in the JLS: each method invocation is considered more or less in isolation and independent of others. However, if a lack of understanding of this particular fact is the reason for a mistake, we can only find that out by going beyond these compartments. This is an often observed pattern, and one that makes type error diagnosis significantly more complicated than type checking by itself: to find out what kind of faulty reasoning on the part of the programmer is responsible for a type error, the improved type inference process must be able to distinguish between these forms of reasoning, and therefore be able to maintain and manipulate what, according to the original type system, is inconsistent information.

Beyond method invocations, a particularly interesting and complicated language construct is that of inner classes. In that case, we have the additional problem of dealing with the scope/

shadowing of type variables, and all the mistakes programmers can make in these situations.

Furthermore, although we have weakened method resolution somewhat so that we may determine the method the programmer might have wanted to invoke, there are plenty of variations left unconsidered: why not also consider methods that are not visible or accessible and suggest to modify the program so that they become visible and accessible? There is, in fact, a huge number of possibilities here, and thus far we have barely scratched the surface. To have some idea in which direction to look it would be really helpful to know what kind of mistakes programmers make. Program logging systems like BlueJ might be able to help us there [15]. Having consulted Jadud on the subject, however, we have learned that the programs he has collected do not contain generics. One promising idea, suggested by Pierre-Evariste Dagand in private communication, is to offer our system as a web-based service for Java programmers, and, as part of the service, ask them to rate the output of our system and that of the standard compilers. As a bonus, we obtain a collection of programs that we can use to validate and improve on our work. Recently, we found another valuable source of information which is Angelika Langer's FAQ on Java Generics [16]. Based on this FAQ, we plan to perform a systematic study of the kind of mistakes programmers make, and misunderstandings they might have about Java Generics. As a more labour-intense alternative to the two previous two, the empirically based route followed in [35] could be explored to find out, e.g., what kind of mistakes programmers make, and how they themselves derive the types of expressions in their program. The work presented here can serve to prepare the way for such further studies.

We note that our work takes the JLS as a starting point, and we have yet to consider alternative approaches to combining generics with subtyping, as part of, e.g., Scala [24] and Timber [23]. However, the second author, together with the developers of the Timber language, has recently started to look at the latter language, as an example of a language that adds subtyping to a language based on the polymorphic lambda-calculus.

Finally then, in [27] it is shown how the generics of Java might be "fixed" to obtain a process that is sound and complete. Although soundness and completeness are clearly important issues, we believe that intuitiveness and elegance of the type system is important too, particularly for a language that may well be the first programming language novice programmers encounter. We therefore hope that any fix will take those properties into consideration as well.

ACKNOWLEDGEMENTS

We acknowledge the involvement of Martin Bravenboer during the early stages of this project, and thank the anonymous referees for their suggestions and corrections.

APPENDIX: USING THE SYSTEM

To compile the system you need subversion (http://subversion.tigris.org/) and Ant obtainable from http://ant.apache.org. Once you have these installed on your system, checkout the repository

```
staff.jur.javagenerics/project
```

on the subversion server located at

```
https://subversion.cs.uu.nl/
```

(click on info to get the exact location for the checkout). The README file that you obtain in the process explains how to proceed: run ant in the Java1.5Backend directory, and afterwards proceed to the bin directory where the invocation java JavaCompiler help tells you how the compiler should be invoked. The subdirectory testing contains a large number of example programs on which to try out the compiler. Most of these programs also explain in comments which constraints are generated and how these are used to determine type (in) correctness. Note that many error messages also suggest a problem fix using heuristics; that part of our work is discussed in another paper [2]. The examples in the current paper have all been included in the special subdirectory testing/listings. To compile, e.g., Listing1.java simply write the following at the command prompt while inside the testing subdirectory:

```
java -cp ../bin JavaCompiler -d /tmp listings/Listing1.java
```

REFERENCES

1. el Boustani, N., Hage, J.: Improving type error messages for Generic Java. In: Puebla, G., Vidal, G. (eds.) Proceedings of the ACM SIGPLAN 2009 Symposium on Partial Evaluation and Semantics-Based Program Manipulation (PEPM'09), pp. 131–140. ACM Press, New York (2009)
2. el Boustani, N., Hage, J.: Corrective hints for type incorrect Generic Java programs. In: Gallagher, J., Voigtländer, J. (eds.) Proceedings of the ACM SIGPLAN 2010 Workshop on Partial Evaluation and Program Manipulation (PEPM'10), pp. 5–14. ACM Press, New York (2010)
3. Damas, L., Milner, R.: Principal type-schemes for functional programs. In: Conference Record of the Ninth Annual ACM Symposium on Principles of Programming Languages, Albuquerque, New Mexico, January 1982, pp. 207–212. ACM Press, New York (1982)
4. Dinesh, T.B., Tip, F.: A slicing-based approach for locating type errors. In: 264, Centrum voor Wiskunde en Informatica (CWI), p. 24 (1998). ISSN 1386-369X
5. Duggan, D., Bent, F.: Explaining type inference. Sci. Comput. Program. 27, 37–83 (1996)
6. Ekman, T., Hedin, G.: The JastAdd extensible Java compiler. In: OOPSLA'07: Proceedings of the 22nd Annual ACM SIGPLAN Conference on Object-Oriented Programming Systems and Applications, pp. 1–18. ACM, New York (2007)
7. Gosling, J., Joy, B., Steele, G., Bracha, G.: Java(TM) Language Specification, 3rd edn. Addison-Wesley Professional, Reading (2005)
8. Haack, C., Wells, J.B.: Type error slicing in implicitly typed higher-order languages. In: Proceedings of the 12th European Symposium on Programming (ESOP). Lecture Notes in Computer Science, vol. 2618, pp. 284–301. Springer, Berlin (2003)
9. Hage, J., Heeren, B.: Heuristics for type error discovery and recovery. In: Horváth, Z., Zsók, V., Butterfield, A.

(eds.) Implementation of Functional Languages—IFL 2006, vol. 4449, pp. 199–216. Springer, Heidelberg (2007)
10. Hage, J., Heeren, B.: Strategies for solving constraints in type and effect systems. Electron. Notes Theor. Comput. Sci. 236, 163–183 (2009). Proceedings of the 3rd International Workshop on Views On Designing Complex Architectures (VODCA 2008)
11. Hedin, G., Magnusson, E.: The JastAdd system—an aspect-oriented compiler construction system. Sci. Comput. Program. 47(1), 37–58 (2003). http://www.cs.lth.se/~gorel/publications/2003JastAdd-SCP-Preprint.pdf
12. Heeren, B.: Top quality type error messages. PhD thesis, Universiteit Utrecht, The Netherlands (2005). http://www.cs.uu.nl/people/bastiaan/phdthesis
13. Heeren, B., Hage, J., Swierstra, S.D.: Scripting the type inference process. In: Eighth International Conference on Functional Programming, pp. 3–13. ACM Press, New York (2003)
14. Huch, F., Chitil, O., Simon, A.: Typeview: a tool for understanding type errors. In: Mohnen, M., Koopman, P. (eds.) Proceedings of 12th International Workshop on Implementation of Functional Languages (IFL 00). Aachner Informatik-Berichte, pp. 63–69 (2000)
15. Jadud, M.C.: A first look at novice compilation behaviour using BlueJ. Comput. Sci. Educ. 15(1), 25–40 (2005)
16. Langer, A.: Java generics FAQs—frequently asked questions (2008). http://www.angelikalanger.com/GenericsFAQ/JavaGenericsFAQ.html
17. Lee, O., Yi, K.: Proofs about a folklore let-polymorphic type inference algorithm. ACM Trans. Program. Lang. Syst. 20(4), 707–723 (1998)
18. Lee, O., Yi, K.: A generalization of hybrid let-polymorphic type inference algorithms. In: Proceedings of the First Asian Workshop on Programming Languages and Systems, pp. 79–88. National University of Singapore, Singapore (2000)
19. Lerner, B., Grossman, D., Chambers, C.: Seminal: searching for ml type-error messages. In: ML'06: Proceedings of the 2006 Workshop on ML, pp. 63–73. ACM, New York (2006)
20. McAdam, B.J.: On the Unification of Substitutions in Type Inference. In: Hammond, K., Davie, A.J.T., Clack, C. (eds.) Implementation of Functional Languages (IFL'98), London, UK. LNCS, vol. 1595, pp. 139–154. Springer, Berlin (1998)
21. McAdam, B.J.: How to repair type errors automatically. In: Hammond, K., Curtis, S. (eds.) Trends in Functional Programming, Intellect, Bristol, UK, vol. 3, pp. 87–98 (2002)
22. Milner, R.: A theory of type polymorphism in programming. J. Comput. Syst. Sci. 17, 348–375 (1978)
23. Nordlander, J., Carlsson, M., Gill, A., Lindgren, P., von Sydow, B.: The Timber homepage (2008). http:// www.timber-lang.org
24. Odersky, M.: The Scala homepage (2008). http://www.scala-lang.org/
25. Rahli, V., Wells, J.B., Kamareddine, F.: A constraint system for a SML type error slicer. Tech. Rep. HW-MACS-TR-0079, Herriot Watt University, Edinburgh, Scotland (2010)
26. Russell, S., Norvig, P.: Artificial Intelligence: A Modern Approach, 2nd edn., pp. 137–151. Pearson Education, Upper Saddle River (2003). Chap. 5
27. Smith, D., Cartwright, R.: Java type inference is broken: can we fix it. In: Proceedings of the 23rd Conference on Object-Oriented Programming, Systems, Languages, and Applications (OOPSLA'08), pp. 505–524. ACM, New York (2008)
28. Stuckey, P.J., Sulzmann, M., Wazny, J.: Interactive type debugging in Haskell. In: Haskell'03: Proceedings of the ACM SIGPLAN Workshop on Haskell, pp. 72–83. ACM Press, New York (2003)
29. Stuckey, P.J., Sulzmann, M., Wazny, J.: Improving type error diagnosis. In: Haskell'04: Proceedings of the ACM SIGPLAN Workshop on Haskell, pp. 80–91. ACM Press, New York (2004)
30. Torgersen, M., Hansen, C.P., Ernst, E., von der Ahé, P., Bracha, G., Gafter, N.: Adding wildcards to the Java programming language. In: Proceedings of the 2004 ACM Symposium on Applied Computing (SAC'04), pp. 1289–1296. ACM Press, New York (2004)
31. Walz, J.A., Johnson, G.F.: A maximum flow approach to anomaly isolation in unification-based incremental type inference. In: Conference Record of the 13th Annual ACM Symposium on Principles of Programming Languages, St. Petersburg, FL, pp. 44–57 (1986)
32. Wand, M.: Finding the source of type errors. In: 13th Annual ACM Symp. on Principles of Prog. Languages, pp. 38–43 (1986)
33. Yang, J.: Explaining type errors by finding the sources of type conflicts. In: Michaelson, G., Trinder, P., Loidl, H.W. (eds.) Trends in Functional Programming. Intellect Books, pp. 58–66 (2000)
34. Yang, J., Michaelson, G., Trinder, P., Wells, J.B.: Improved type error reporting. In: Proceedings of 12th International Workshop on Implementation of Functional Languages. LNCS, vol. 2011, pp. 71–86. Springer, Berlin (2000)
35. Yang, J., Michaelson, G., Trinder, P.: Explaining polymorphic types. Comput. J. 45(4), 436–452 (2002)

CHAPTER 15 ETE: A PYTHON ENVIRONMENT FOR TREE EXPLORATION

Jaime Huerta-Cepas, Joaquín Dopazo, Toni Gabaldón

BACKGROUND

Trees are commonly used to represent the results of many bioinformatics analyses. In particular, such type of binary graphs are ideal to describe the hierarchical relationships among a variety of biological entities. Some common examples are the evolutionary analysis of molecular sequences or the clusterization of genes and proteins according to their properties. Besides the information encoded in the topology of trees, branch lengths can also be scaled to provide information on the distances between the different partitions. In phylogenetics, for instance, trees are used to illustrate the evolutionary relationships among species or molecular sequences, considering terminal nodes as extant Operational Taxonomic Units (OTU) and internal nodes as their corresponding ancestors. In such phylogenetic trees, branch lengths are usually proportional to the evolutionary distance among sequences. Other applications, such as the analysis of gene expression, use hierarchical clustering analysis to group genes or experimental conditions according to the similarity of their expression patterns. Likewise, trees are used by many protein classification methods and for the analysis of phylogenetic profiles. Thus, the analysis of tree data structures is a common task in many areas of bioinformatics and there is a need for analytical and visualization tools. In this respect, a number of bioinformatic programs do exist that assist in the exploration of hierarchical trees. Most of them, however, consist of standalone applications that are focused on visualization and, occasionally, on performing specific tests. Some well known examples are TreeView [1], a widely used program for inspecting phylogenetic trees; Cluster Treeview [2], an application for visualizing microarray clustering results; ATV [3], a java program used to explore phylogenies which provides also some editing options; MEGA [4], an evolutionary genetics analysis suite that includes a built-in tree viewer; and many other recent applications [5–8]. While all these programs are very useful to manage single trees, they can hardly be automatized or adapted to specific needs. Thus, when the analysis of hundreds or thousands of trees is required, the use of standalone programs becomes restrictive, because a much higher level of automation is required. In such cases, programming toolkits represent a more adequate framework, since they provide tools and methods to handle data at a lower level. Using toolkits, bioinformaticians can easily create their own analysis pipelines and program custom tasks over large collections of data [9]. Several generic bioinformatic toolkits do exist that cover a wide range of programming languages and scopes, with BioPerl [10] and BioPython [11] being the most extensively developed. Together with a broad range of other features, these toolkits allow certain level of interaction with tree data structures. However, only basic actions are currently supported. Alternatively, the PyCogent [12] and P4 http://bmnh.org/~pf/p4.html python toolkits can be used to extend this functionality, although they are mostly focused on phylogenetic reconstruction. R [13], a general purpose statistical framework, does include several packages to perform statistical tests on clustering and phylogenetic trees. Nevertheless, these packages are focused on performing specific analyses rather than in providing tree handling and manipulation features. Finally, in contrast to the great number of standalone tree viewers, programming toolkits offer few, if any, graphical rendering possibilities. An intermediate alternative between standalone viewers and programmatic tree rendering is that of the TreeDyn program [14], which has support for some scripting options and can be used to create fully annotated tree images.

Citation: Jaime Huerta-Cepas, Joaquín Dopazo, Toni Gabaldón, ETE: A python Environment for Tree Exploration, doi:10.1186/1471-2105-11-24.

In response to these limitations, we present here the Environment for Tree Exploration (ETE), a python programming toolkit to analyze, manipulate or visualize any kind of hierarchical tree. It extends the functionality in other toolkits and allows a high level of customization. ETE›s drawing features, although less exhaustive than in standalone editors, rely on the Python scripting language, which makes possible to combine advanced tree analyses and tree visualization into a single program. The toolkit includes methods to browse and manipulate tree topologies, provides support for the New Hampshire eXtended (NHX) format and allows advanced actions such as node annotation, automatic rooting, cut & paste partitions, tree concatenation, node search, and branch distance related operations. In addition, ETE implements two specific modules to work with phylogenetic and clustering trees. The phylogenetic extension allows trees to be linked to their corresponding multiple sequence alignments, includes two orthology and paralogy prediction algorithms, implements the duplication dating method described in [15] and provides access to the PhylomeDB database [16]. Similarly, clustering trees can be linked to their source data, which allows tree partitions to be analyzed through several validation techniques. Additionally, ETE implements a fully programmable drawing engine that can be used to generate, dynamically, custom tree representations in PDF or PNG formats. This drawing engine is fully integrated with the built-in extensions, thus providing pre-defined visualization layouts for clustering trees and phylogenies. A Graphical User Interface is also included which allows on the fly interaction with trees.

Currently, the ETE toolkit is used in diverse projects, including GEPAS [17], Phylemon [18] and PhylomeDB [15]. ETE package and documentation can be accessed athttp://ete.cgenomics.org

Implementation

ETE is entirely written in Python [19], a programming language that offers a strong support for integration with other languages and tools, and whose popularity is raising among the bioinformatics community [20]. ETE's philosophy is to facilitate the integration with other toolkits as well as to provide a scalable program architecture. Thus, ETE tree objects can be easily imported and expanded by incorporating custom methods and properties. The functionality of the ETE toolkit is divided into several python modules, which can be imported at convenience. A summary of features of the different modules is shown in Table 1.

Table 1: Summary of ETE's features

Module	Description
General trees	Advanced node annotation, tree topology manipulation, automatic tree pruning, cut & paste partitions, trees concatenation, random trees generation, iterate over leaves and descendants, pre and pos-order tree traversal, rooting options, advanced nodes search, get distances among nodes, detect midpoint outgroup, find farthest descendant node, find farthest node in the whole tree, detect first common ancestor among nodes, text mode visualization, newick rendering (several formats), extended newick format integration, built-in python operations: print, len, iter, in.
Phylogenetic trees	Link to multiple sequence alignments, automatic species name detection, check node monophyly, evolutionary events dating, detect orthology and paralogy relationships: species overlap and tree reconciliation methods, complete access API to the phylomeDB database, integrated visualization (show molecular sequences and evolutionary events).
Clustering trees	link to numerical matrices, calculate inter and intra-cluster distances among clusters, calculate Silhouette and Dunn Indexes, integrated visualization (display numerical profiles in several formats).
Tree Visualization	Interactive Graphical User Interface, programmable drawing engine, independent node aspect editing, support drawing node extra features (text or external images), vector graphics rendering using PDF format.

RESULTS

Tree handling Module

ETE's main module allows to read and render trees using the two most common formats: New Hampshire (NH) and New Hampshire eXtended (NHX). Moreover, it allows to generate random trees or create custom tree structures from scratch. In order to increase compatibility with other tools, several newick format standards are currently supported by ETE, both for reading and writing trees (see ETE's extended documentation). ETE's trees are internally encoded as a series of tree node instances connected following a parent-child relationship. Each node is encoded as an independent Python object, which provides many methods to manipulate its connections (i.e. add, remove, delete or detach nodes) and to easily browse its topology (i.e. tree traversal and get terminal, children, sister or descendant nodes). As a consequence, each internal node is treated as a fully featured subtree, thus allowing to analyze different parts of trees separately. ETE's tree object implementation supports multifurcations and can be used to deal with very large structures. As a reference, the NCBI taxonomy newick tree file, with more than 450.000 nodes, could be loaded as an ETE tree object in 40 seconds (Intel Xeon CPU 2.33 GHz).

One of the main advantages of ETE as compared to other toolkits is that nodes can contain additional information other than topology and branch distances. Users are free to associate any external data to the different tree nodes and then use such data in the subsequent analyses, integrate them as part of their tree images or save them using the NHX format. This functionality provides the possibility of creating fully annotated trees.

Finally, a complete set of operations are available to browse, analyze or modify trees: i.e.) pre- and post-order traversing strategies, search nodes or partitions matching specific criteria, midpoint and species-guided automatic tree rooting, calculate distances between branches, detection of common ancestors, random tree building, topology manipulation, tree pruning, tree concatenation, cut and paste partitions, etc.

Tree Rendering and Visualization

The visualization module provides a programmable drawing system to render hierarchical tree structures as dendrograms. The core of this extension consists of an image drawing algorithm that can be controlled by a set of user-defined rules. Such rules can be written as small python functions and are used to determine, dynamically, the aspect of each tree node. This allows, for instance, to vary the aspect of each node according to its internal properties. Moreover, the rendering engine allows not only to draw tree topologies but also to incorporate external graphical information to each node. Thus, external images, graphs or custom text labels can be added to nodes as part of the general tree image. The programatic use of the tree drawing module allows users to control how trees are rendered and what information is shown for the different nodes. Images can be rendered as PNG or PDF files.

In addition to the drawing engine, trees can be interactively visualized using a built-in Graphical User Interface (GUI), which allows on the fly manipulation of trees. Thus, each tree node has its own displaying method that can be used to start the visualization of its specific topology. The GUI is fully integrated with other ETE's features and allows to interact with tree nodes and their properties in a graphical way. Both the GUI and the rendering engine use the last Qt4 programming libraries to increase the performance of large images visualization. Qt4 is available for GNU/Linux, MacOS and Windows, and it is distributed as free software. A complete description of the usage of this module, as well as examples, can be found within the ETE tutorial at http://ete.cgenomics.org.

Phylogenetic Extension

Phylogenetic trees are the result of most evolutionary analyses. ETE's phylogenetic extension implements a special type of tree instances which are focused on the analysis of evolutionary trees. Thus, tree leafs are considered OTUs, while internal nodes are considered their ancestors. By applying different strategies, ETE can automatically assign internal nodes to speciation and duplication events, thereby establishing orthology and paralogy relationships between the OTUs [21]. Two built-in methods are available to predict speciation and duplication events: a species-overlap algorithm that is independent of the species tree [15] and the classical gene-tree/species-tree reconciliation algorithm [22]. Both methods return a list of orthology and paralogy predictions and annotate the original tree nodes according to the detected evolutionary events. Additionally, nodes predicted as gene duplication events can be dated using the topology scanning method described in [15]. Furthermore, molecular phylogenies can be associated with their corresponding multiple sequence alignments, thus establishing a link between each tree leaf and its sequence. This allows the visualization of aligned sequences together with the tree topology, which helps to detect, for instance, linage-specific changes, specific domain composition or conserved regions. As sequences are considered an additional property of tree leafs, they can be combined with the tree browsing capabilities to program analyses such as detecting clades with certain level of sequence conservation or composition.

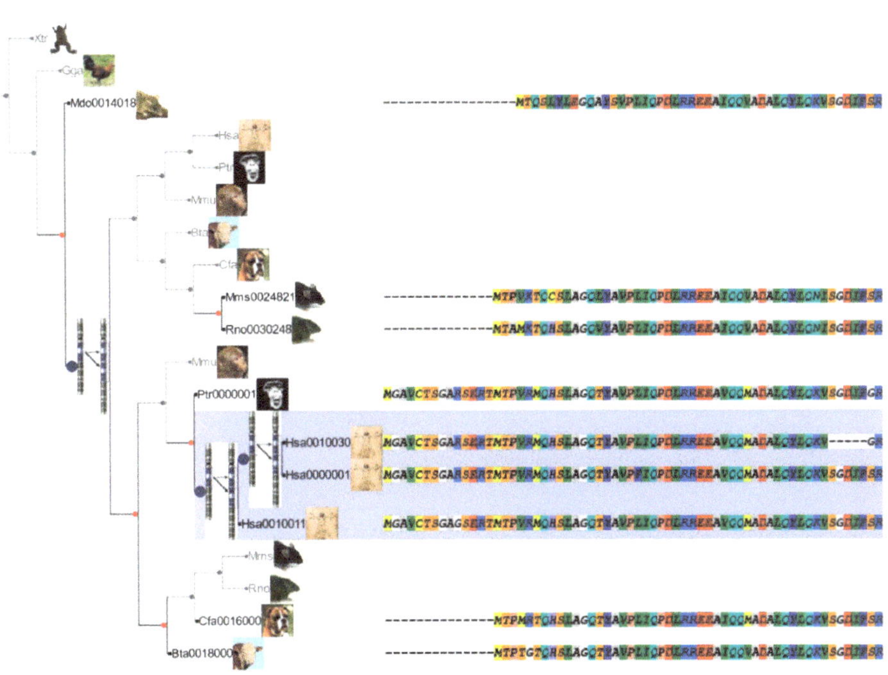

Figure 1: Screenshot of a reconciled phylogenetic tree displayed with ETE. The image shows a portion of a reconciled tree generated using the ETE's strict reconciliation algorithm over an example gene phylogeny. The most accepted tree of life for the species considered was

used for reconciliation. A custom ETE layout function has been used to highlight different aspects of the tree: Grey dashed lines represent the inferred gene losses. Blue nodes indicate duplication events. Red nodes represent speciation events. Each OTU is displayed with their corresponding name and species image. Part of the multiple sequence alignment is displayed with each sequence associated to its corresponding OTU.

This extension is fully integrated with the drawing module, and includes a pre-defined visualization layout to explore trees together with its predicted evolutionary events and the sequences associated to nodes (Figure 1). Other features such as checking the monophyly of nodes, the automatic detection of species names, or the guided selection of outgroups are also available.

PhylomeDB API

PhylomeDB [16] http://phylomedb.org is a database for complete collections of gene phylogenies (phylomes). It currently stores more than 420,000 trees and 120,000 multiple sequence alignments reconstructed using a high-quality phylogenetic pipeline, which includes Maximum Likelihood or Bayesian tree inference, alignment trimming and evolutionary model testing.

ETE provides a complete Application User Interface (API) for accessing phylomeDB. Throughout this API, users can connect to the phylomeDB database and search for pre-computed gene phylogenies, download complete phylomes or obtain the orthology and paralogy predictions provided by the database. The phylomeDB API is fully integrated with the ETE software and trees can be automatically downloaded as phylogenetic tree instances.

Microarray Clustering Trees

Microarray expression data are usually encoded as matrices in which rows represent the expression profile of genes across different conditions (columns). A variety of clustering analyses are used to group genes that respond coordinately to a given set of conditions or, conversely, to group conditions according to their gene expression profiles. In such cases, genes are generally represented by the terminal tree nodes whereas internal nodes represent different levels of similarity among the expression profiles of grouped genes.

ETE's clustering extension can be used to import microarray clustering results and link them to their corresponding gene expression patterns. Thus, the expression profile of any internal tree node (cluster) can be calculated as the mean expression pattern of the grouped leaves (usually representing genes). This allows, for instance, to automate the detection of co-expressed genes in large datasets or to find nodes matching certain expression patterns. Moreover, several clustering validation techniques are implemented that allow to evaluate the goodness of fit of the different tree partitions. Currently, inter- and intra-cluster distances, cluster standard deviation, the Dunn index [23] and the cluster Silhouette index [24] can be calculated. Similarly to the phylogenetic extension, several visualization layouts are also provided for displaying clusters together with their associated profiles (Figure 2).

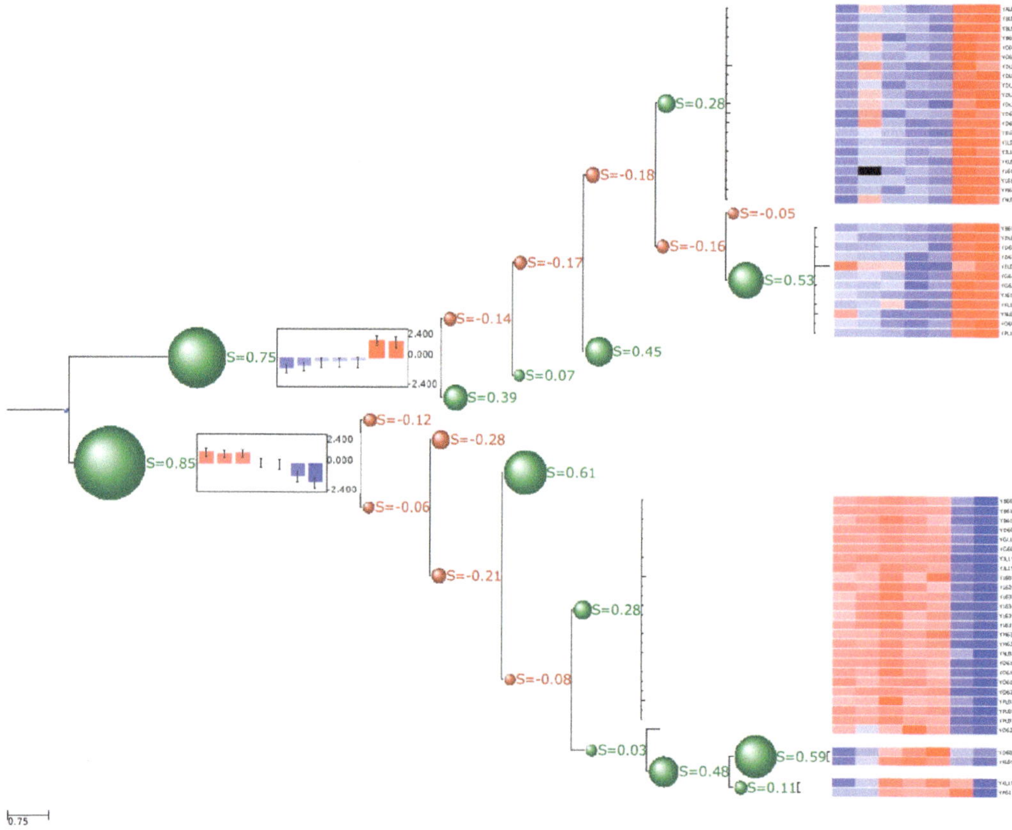

Figure 2: Screenshot of a microarray clustering tree validated and displayed with ETE. Expression profiles of terminal nodes (genes) are shown as a heatmap at the right side of the image. Silhouette indexes were calculated for each internal partition and are displayed in the tree. Size of green and red bubbles is proportional to the silhouette value. Red bubbles stand for silhouette values lower than 0 and green bubbles for silhouettes higher than 0. Two graphs representing the mean expression profile of the two most basal tree branches are also included in the image.

This extension can be further used to handle any other type of trees associated to numerical matrices, such as phylogenetic profiles or protein classification results.

DISCUSSION

Most current tools for tree analysis are standalone applications focused on the visual inspection of trees. However, genomic studies often require the design of specific tests, or to program custom tasks over large collections of data. The Environment for Tree Exploration provides a programming framework to help in the implementation of specific analyses or visualization tasks. ETE's libraries can be imported together with other python toolkits in order to extend the functionality of tree handling operations. Furthermore, using the appropriate python modules, ETE can be connected to other environments such as R (using Rpy [25]), or BioPerl (using PyPerl [26]).

To date, ETE has been used in the automated phylogenomic pipelines employed to reconstruct and analyze complete phylomes [15, 16, 27]. Particularly, the use of ETE has enabled the application of phylogeny-based methods to predict orthology relationships on a genome wide scale [15]. Such approach is closer to the original definition of orthology and it is considered more accurate than classical, pair-wise based orthology prediction methods [28]. In addition, ETE has been used to implement a functional inference pipeline that enabled annotating more than 4,000 genes of the newly sequenced pea aphid genome [29]. This is the first case that such a reliable functional annotation pipeline has been applied to a newly sequenced genome. In addition, as implemented in the phylogenetic extension, ETE allows the use of phylogenetic trees to detect and date gene duplication events, a method that overcomes many of the known drawbacks of methods that are only based on sequence comparisons. Furthermore, ETE is used to provide interactive images of phylogenetic trees in projects such as PhylomeDB [16] and Phylemon [18], and to help in the interpretation of microarray clustering results as implemented in the Gene Expression Pattern Analyses Suite (GEPAS) [17]. Thus, ETE has already proved to be a useful resource in many different applications. By making this tool publicly available we expect that other projects can benefit from it and that ETE continues its expansion through the implementation of additional methods and features. ETE is under continuous development, with new modules and functionalities planned for future releases. We are also open to the possibility of including extensions from the open source community.

CONCLUSIONS

ETE meets the needs of large-scale analyses of hierarchical tree data structures. It has been devised as a highly extensible and programmable toolkit, which has already been used in many different genomic and post-genomic projects. Future releases will incorporate novel analytical methods and extensions, some of which may come from the open source community.

A comprehensive tutorial, a programming guide including the main ETE package structure, and many basic examples are available from the 'Documentation' section athttp://ete.cgenomics.org. Some practical examples are also available from the 'Examples' section at the same web site.

ACKNOWLEDGEMENTS

We thank Leonardo Arbiza, François Serra and Marina Marcet-Houben for their valuable comments and for testing the program. TG received funding from the Spanish ministries of Health (FIS06-213) and Science and Innovation (GEN2006-27784-E/PAT). JHC received funding from the Instituto Nacional de Bioinformática and Genoma España.

AUTHORS' CONTRIBUTIONS

JHC implemented the toolkit and participated in designing the methods and in writing the manuscript. JD participated in designing clustering and visualization modules, and in writing the manuscript. TG participated in designing all phylogenetic methods and the phylomeDB API module, and in writing the manuscript.

REFERENCES

1. Page RD: TreeView: an application to display phylogenetic trees on personal computers.*Comput Appl Biosci* 1996, 12(4):357–358.
2. Eisen MB, Spellman PT, Brown PO, Botstein D: Cluster analysis and display of genome-wide expression patterns. *Proc Natl Acad Sci USA* 1998, 95(25):14863–14868. 10.1073/pnas.95.25.14863
3. Zmasek CM, Eddy SR: ATV: display and manipulation of annotated phylogenetic trees.*Bioinformatics* 2001, 17(4):383–384. 10.1093/bioinformatics/17.4.383
4. Kumar S, Nei M, Dudley J, Tamura K: MEGA: a biologist-centric software for evolutionary analysis of DNA and protein sequences. *Brief Bioinform* 2008, 9(4):299–306. 10.1093/bib/bbn017
5. Santamaría R, Therón R: Treevolution: visual analysis of phylogenetic trees.*Bioinformatics* 2009, 25(15):1970–1971. 10.1093/bioinformatics/btp333
6. Jordan GE, Piel WH: PhyloWidget: web-based visualizations for the tree of life.*Bioinformatics* 2008, 24(14):1641–1642. 10.1093/bioinformatics/btn235
7. Letunic I, Bork P: Interactive Tree Of Life (iTOL): an online tool for phylogenetic tree display and annotation. *Bioinformatics* 2007, 23: 127–128. 10.1093/bioinformatics/btl529
8. Saldanha AJ: Java Treeview-extensible visualization of microarray data. *Bioinformatics*2004, 20(17):3246–3248. 10.1093/bioinformatics/bth349
9. Stajich JE, Lapp H: Open source tools and toolkits for bioinformatics: significance, and where are we? *Brief Bioinform* 2006, 7(3):287–296. 10.1093/bib/bbl026
10. Stajich JE, Block D, Boulez K, Brenner SE, Chervitz SA, Dagdigian C, Fuellen G, Gilbert JGR, Korf I, Lapp H, Lehvaslaiho H, Matsalla C, Mungall CJ, Osborne BI, Pocock MR, Schattner P, Senger M, Stein LD, Stupka E, Wilkinson MD, Birney E: The Bioperl toolkit: Perl modules for the life sciences. *Genome Res* 2002, 12(10):1611–1618. 10.1101/gr.361602
11. Cock PJA, Antao T, Chang JT, Chapman BA, Cox CJ,

Dalke A, Friedberg I, Hamelryck T, Kauff F, Wilczynski B, de Hoon MJL: Biopython: freely available Python tools for computational molecular biology and bioinformatics. *Bioinformatics* 2009, 25(11):1422–1423. 10.1093/bioinformatics/btp163

12. Knight R, Maxwell P, Birmingham A, Carnes J, Caporaso JG, Easton BC, Eaton M, Hamady M, Lindsay H, Liu Z, Lozupone C, McDonald D, Robeson M, Sammut R, Smit S, Wakefield MJ, Widmann J, Wikman S, Wilson S, Ying H, Huttley GA: PyCogent: a toolkit for making sense from sequence. *Genome Biol* 2007, 8(8):R171. 10.1186/gb-2007-8-8-r171
13. R Development Core Team: *R: A Language and Environment for Statistical Computing*. R Foundation for Statistical Computing, Vienna, Austria; 2008. [ISBN 3–900051–07–0]. [ISBN 3-900051-07-0].
14. Chevenet F, Brun C, Banuls AL, Jacq B, Christen R: TreeDyn: towards dynamic graphics and annotations for analyses of trees. *BMC Bioinformatics* 2006, 7: 439. 10.1186/1471-2105-7-439
15. Huerta-Cepas J, Dopazo H, Dopazo J, Gabaldón T: The human phylome. *Genome Biol*2007, 8(6):R109.
16. Huerta-Cepas J, Bueno A, Dopazo J, Gabaldón T: PhylomeDB: a database for genome-wide collections of gene phylogenies. *Nucleic Acids Res* 2008, (36 Database):D491-D496.
17. Tárraga J, Medina I, Carbonell J, Huerta-Cepas J, Minguez P, Alloza E, Al-Shahrour F, Vegas-Azcárate S, Goetz S, Escobar P, Garcia-Garcia F, Conesa A, Montaner D, Dopazo J: GEPAS, a web-based tool for microarray data analysis and interpretation. *Nucleic Acids Research* 2008, 36: W308–14. 10.1093/nar/gkn303
18. Tárraga J, Medina I, Arbiza L, Huerta-Cepas J, Gabaldón T, Dopazo J, Dopazo H: Phylemon: a suite of web tools for molecular evolution, phylogenetics and phylogenomics.*Nucleic Acids Research* 2007, 35: W38–42. 10.1093/nar/gkm224
19. van Rossum G, de Boer J: Linking a Stub Generator (AIL) to a Prototyping Language (Python). *Spring 1991 EurOpen Conference Proceedings* 1991.
20. Bassi S: A Primer on Python for Life Science Researchers. *PLoS Computational Biology*2007, 3(11):e199. 10.1371/journal.pcbi.0030199
21. Fitch WM: Distinguishing homologous from analogous proteins. *Systematic Zoology* 1970, 19(2):99–113. 10.2307/2412448
22. Page RD, Charleston MA: From gene to organismal phylogeny: reconciled trees and the gene tree/species tree problem. *Molecular Phylogenetics and Evolution* 1997, 7(2):231–40. 10.1006/mpev.1996.0390
23. Dunn J: Well separated clusters and optimal fuzzy partitions. *J Cybern* 1974, 4: 95–104. 10.1080/01969727408546059
24. Rousseeuw P: Silhouettes: a graphical aid to the interpretation and validation of cluster analysis. *Journal of Computational and Applied Mathematics* 1987, 20: 53–65. 10.1016/0377-0427(87)90125-7
25. RPy[http://rpy.sourceforge.net/]
26. PyPerl[http://search.cpan.org/dist/pyperl/]
27. Marcet-Houben M, Gabaldón T: The tree versus the forest: the fungal tree of life and the topological diversity within the yeast phylome. *PLoS ONE* 2009, 4(2):e4357. 10.1371/journal.pone.0004357
28. Gabaldón T: Large-scale assignment of orthology: back to phylogenetics? *Genome Biol*2008, 9(10):235. 10.1186/gb-2008-9-10-235
29. Huerta-Cepas J, Marcet-Houben M, Pignatelli M, Moya A, Gabaldón T: The pea aphid phylome: a complete catalogue of evolutionary histories and arthropod orthology and paralogy relationships for Acyrthosiphon pisum genes. *Insect Molecular Biology* 2009, in press.

CHAPTER 16

EVALUATION OF XIS-MOBILE, A DOMAIN SPECIFIC LANGUAGE FOR MOBILE APPLICATION DEVELOPMENT

André Ribeiro, Alberto Rodrigues da Silva

Keywords: Model-Driven Development, Cross-Platform, Mobile Applications, Domain Specific Languages

INTRODUCTION

The mobile computing industry has suffered a great evolution, during the last decade, with the emergence of a great variety of mobile devices, as well as the operating systems that support them [1] . Due to this fact, mobile devices and applications are becoming more present than ever in our lives facilitating our daily tasks. All of this resulted primarily from the efforts made by the major mobile industry companies (e.g. Google, Apple or Micro- soft) to popularize their respective products [2] . However, a certain fragmentation of the mobile platforms has appeared, since each company provides its own platform with specific language, tools and application market. This fragmentation can be an obstacle particularly when someone wants to develop a mobile application for multiple platforms. Moreover, due to the differences between each platform, the development complexity and consequently the costs of producing a cross-platform mobile application have increased, because simply rewrit- ing a mobile application for each target mobile platform is often impractical due to budget and time limitations. Thus, given these problems, the ideal scenario would be to develop the application once and then run it in as many platforms as desired. Fortunately, some work has been conducted over the last years to tackle both prob- lems presented previously: the software development complexity and the mobile platform fragmentation. The use of web technologies (e.g. HTML5, CSS3 and JavaScript libraries), cross-platform tools and frameworks, or approaches based on Model-Driven Development (MDD) [3] [4] , like the one presented in this paper, are exam- ples of solutions focused on solving these problems.

XIS-Mobile [5] has been created precisely with the goal of mitigating these problems. It materializes an idea for the extension of the XIS UML profile [6] [7] , used to model desktop or web interactive applications and generate code for multiple platforms (e.g. Windows Forms.NET and Microsoft ASP.NET). However, XIS re- veals several limitations to model mobile applications, like proper support for the specification of gestures, internet connection, localization and other context-aware issues common in mobile applications. Furthermore, from what have been researched and our knowledge, the smart approach proposed by XIS was never actually implemented, while in XIS-Mobile is implemented, and the support of the XIS language was achieved by a pro- prietary tool that has not been maintained. XIS-Mobile proposes the creation of platform-independent models (PIM) to design mobile applications, using a UML profile, and from them generate native source code for mul- tiple mobile platforms through model-to-model and model-to-text transformations. It is important to emphasize that XIS-Mobile does not intend to replace the role of a developer, but instead represent a helpful tool that ge- nerates the skeleton of mobile applications. Namely, XIS-Mobile helps the developer by generating the repeti- tive and boilerplate code which represents a great percentage of the application's code. Then, the developer can modify the generated code if it does not fulfill all his needs. For instance, he could need to improve the GUI or implement some custom actions attached to certain widgets. XIS-Mobile is suitable for a multitude of mobile apps that are typically business (and form) oriented, e.g., that allow consulting and submitting data; but are not intended for very specific domains such as games. XIS-Mobile has been developed over the last eighteen months following the well-known Action Research Methodology [8] . Over time, it was necessary to evaluate the usefulness and adequacy of XIS-Mobile to the purpose of modeling mobile applications. This evaluation process was

Citation: Ribeiro, A. and Rodrigues da Silva, A. (2014) Evaluation of XIS-Mobile, a Domain Specific Language for Mobile Application Development. Journal of Software Engineering and Applications, 7, 906-919. doi:10.4236/jsea.2014.711081.

done in an iterative and gradual way. Initially, this was done testing subsets of the language, checking the corresponding models and code generated, and then successively adding new language concepts and respective functionalities. Throughout this period, some case study applications were defined and used to analyze the full development process. Furthermore, it was also developed a first version of a code generator for iOS. From this iterative evaluation, several issues and needs were identified and justified the need of a new XIS-Mobile version, more clean and up to date when compared to the one presented in [5] .

The outline of this paper is as follows. Section 2 discusses the related work. Section 3 describes the case study application used throughout the paper to explain the XIS-Mobile language and also used in the session with us- ers. Section 4 presents the XIS-Mobile language, namely its multi-view organization, supported design ap- proaches and main concepts. Section 5 describes the MDD-based framework that supports the XIS-Mobile lan- guage focusing on the usual development process and the technologies used. Section 6 discusses the preliminary results obtained from the creation of the user session. Finally, Section 7 concludes the paper, summarizing its key points and giving directions for future work.

RELATED WORK

Similarly to XIS-Mobile, some works propose and justify the relevance of using UML profiles and MDD to ab- stract the application development, and to achieve platform independency. Unfortunately, none of them re- present a real alternative to XIS-Mobile. For example [9] is more focused on mobile context-aware applications, while MAM-UML [10] targets mobile-agent applications addressing concepts like code mobility.

Phone Gap [11] or Appcelerator Titanium [12] are examples of cross-platform tools for mobile application development, which have appeared in the last years and widely used to overcome the mobile platform fragmen- tation. Surveys like the ones presented in [13] -[15] evaluate several of these tools. Mostly, this kind of tools does not reduce the complexity of implementation and in some cases does not produce truly native applications.

MobiCloud [16] is a textual DSL purposely created to generate mobile applications leveraging the Cloud com- puting paradigm. Besides supporting the automatic generation of mobile applications, it also creates applications that will function as back-end, through the use of Cloud Computing platforms (e.g. Amazon EC2 and Google App Engine). MobiCloud is based on the Model-View-Controller (MVC) design pattern and so has as main components: models, views and controllers. Despite being a textual DSL, MobiCloud is complemented with a tool called MobiCloud Composer that enables the generation of MobiCloud scripts using graphical components. These components can be dragged-and-dropped and interconnected to create the desired configuration. Its Ruby-based syntax represents a shortcoming, because only allows limited constructs. This fact results in generic ap- plications with restrictions in the UI customization and also a limited set of actions supported (only CRUD). While XIS-Mobile only generates code for mobile applications, MobiCloud also generates back-end applications and takes advantage of Cloud Computing.

Unlike XIS-Mobile, MobDSL [17] proposes to achieve portability through the use of a virtual machine (VM) and thus, does not generate native source code, instead interprets the code through the VM. This can represent a drawback, namely on Apple devices, since MobDSL requires the VM to be installed on the device. Moreover, because of being new and textual, it can be harder to develop a mobile application using MobDSL than with XIS-Mobile.

MobiA (Mobile Applications modeler), similarly to XIS-Mobile, proposes a MDD approach to decrease the complexity of developing mobile applications and suggests the use of a high-level model to achieve platform independence. Other points are the use of a visual editor to design the system and the existence of multiple views, like a navigation model and a screen description model, equivalents to XIS-Mobile Navigation Space and Interaction Space views, respectively. On the other hand, MobiA does not use a standard language like UML, but a specific one based on XML. This fact could be a disadvantage not just for introducing less flexibility and expressiveness than a UML-based language, but also, for example, in the rigor of the documentation. In addition, MobiA states is focus on the development of mobile health monitoring applications for non-expert users [18] .

A lot of work has been done based on the Cameleon Reference Framework [19] , being UsiXML4ALL [20] or MARIA [21] some examples. UsiXML4ALL acts as a UI renderer for multiple platforms and connects the UI to application logic code, but requires the manual development of all the business logic code, while XIS-Mobile mainly through its concept of XisAction can generate a considerable part of it. MARIA focuses on service- oriented applications in ubiquitous environments. Like XIS-Mobile, MARIA takes into account notions like ges- tures detection and web service call, but it goes further in ubiquitous environments exploitation, since it sup- ports the migration of UIs from devices (either desktop or mobile) by maintaining their state while the user is moving. Additionally, other initiatives, namely the Google App Inventor [22] , highly abstracted the mobile ap- plication development through the use of building blocks that doesn't require the user to write code and proved its usefulness in introductory programming courses. However, Google App Inventor only supports the genera- tion for Android and has been discontinued by Google and its support was transferred to the MIT Center for Mobile Learning.

CASE STUDY—THE FLIGHT RESERVATION APP

A case study application named "Flight Reservation App" was defined in order to better illustrate and explain the XIS-Mobile language concepts and views throughout Section 4. Additionally, this application was used in the user session, described in Section 6, where the participants had the task of modeling this application using XIS-Mobile.

XIS-MOBILE LANGUAGE

This new version of the XIS-Mobile language introduced new concepts and corrected some others in compari- son to the version presented in [5] , maintaining the multi-view organization and the design approaches. The next sub-sections describe the multi-view organization of the XIS-Mobile language, the dependencies between its views and the design approaches it supports.

Multi-View Organization

XIS-Mobile is organized in four major packages of views: Entities, Architectural, UseCases and User-Interfaces Views. In turn, the Entities View contains the Domain and BusinessEntities Views, while the User-Interfaces View contains the NavigationSpace and InteractionSpace Views. These views depend on each other and that fact influence the design approaches and the transformation stages (see Figure 1). The Domain View does not depend on any other view, since it is the starting point to define the problem domain. In turn, the BusinessEntities View depends on the Domain View, because business entities aggregate domain entities. The UseCases View depends on the BusinessEntities View and the Architectural View, since each use case must be connected to a business entity and/or provider. The Architectural View does not depend on any other view. The Interac- tionSpace and the NavigationSpace Views depend on each other. The InteractionSpace View also depends on the BusinessEntities View, because an interaction space can be associated to a business Entity; and on the Arc- hitectural View, because some widgets can trigger WebService actions defined on that view.

Design Approaches

XIS-Mobile supports two design approaches: the dummy approach and the smart approach. Essentially, the main difference between them is that the smart approach uses model-to-model transformations. By leveraging this kind of transformations, XIS-Mobile avoids the manual creation of the User-Interfaces View package.

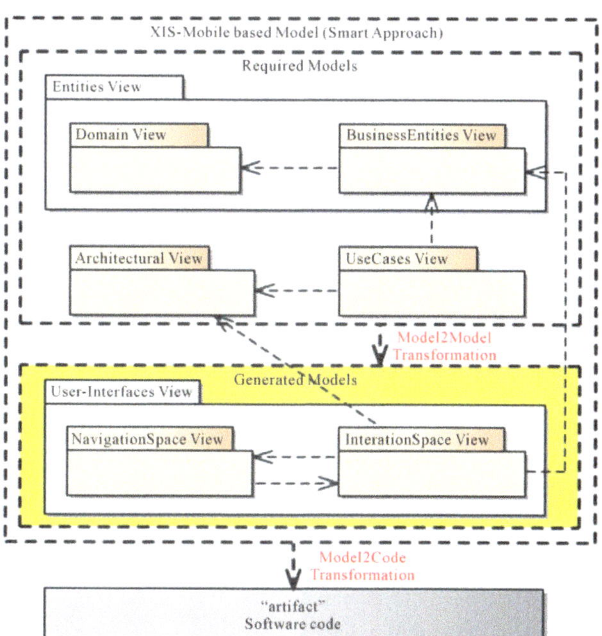

Figure 1: Multi-view organization of XIS-Mobile.

Using the dummy approach, the developer needs to define all views, except the Architectural View that is only required if the application interacts with external entities, like providers or web servers. On the other hand, using the smart approach (see Figure 1), the developer should define only the Domain, BusinessEntities and UseCases Views. Again, like in the dummy approach, the Architectural View is only necessary if the interaction with external entities is a requirement. Then, by leveraging the patterns represented by each use case and the in- formation of the Domain and BusinessEntities Views is possible to perform model-to-model transformations and automatically generate the User-Interfaces View (InteractionSpace and NavigationSpace Views). Then the de- veloper can customize them if he desires so. Therefore, this approach can be much less time-consuming than the dummy approach, since the more complex views are automatically generated. This approach should be used when- ever possible, because it speeds up the modeling process. After defining all these view models either using the dummy or the smart approach, it is possible to generate native source code from them using model-to-text transformations.

Entities View

The Entities View defines the concepts relevant to the problem domain. It is subdivided in the Domain and Bu- sinessEntities Views.

Domain View

The Domain View represents the entities that compose the problem domain as classes, using a traditional Class Diagram. These entities can contain one or more attributes and are related using associations, aggregations or in- heritances. It is also possible to define enumerations and use them as entity attribute types.

The XIS-Mobile language provides the following stereotypes to be applied in this view: 1) XisEntity for classes; 2) XisEntityAttribute for attributes; 3) XisEntityAssociation for associations and aggregations; 4) XisEntityInheritance for inheritances; 5) XisEnumeration for enumerations; and 6) XisEnumerationValue for their values.

Considering the Flight Reservation App's Domain View (see Figure 2), there are three XisEntities: Flight- Reservation, Airport and Passenger. There is also a XisEnumeration named Class with three XisEnumeration- Values: Economy, Business and First. The FlightReservation contains four XisAttributes that specify if the res- ervation is "One Way", its departure and return dates and its class type. The Airport has one XisAttribute re- presenting its name. The Passenger has four XisAttributes for the passportID, name, date of birth and country.

BusinessEntities View

The BusinessEntities View represents high-level entities as classes, known as business entities, using a Class Diagram. A business entity is represented as a class with the stereotype XisBusinessEntity which aggregates one or more XisEntities (from the Domain View). The goal is to provide context to use cases and interaction spaces playing an important role during the transformation stages.

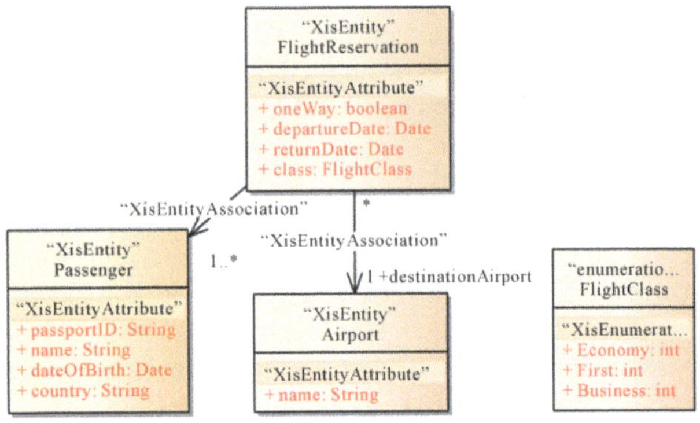

Figure 2: Flight reservation App's Domain View.

A business entity is defined by specifying a domain entity (from the Domain View) as its master entity and, if needed, other domain entities as its detail and reference entities. The definition of the master entity restricts the set of detail and reference entities that can be associated to the business entity in question. Both the detail and the reference entities must be associated to the master entity in the Domain View, through aggregations and associations, respectively. XIS-Mobile provides the following stereotypes to be applied in this view: 1) XisBusinessEntity for classes, 2) XisBE-EntityMasterAssociation, 3) XisBE-EntityDetailAssociation, and 4) XisBE-Entity- ReferenceAssociation for associations connecting business entities to domain entities, identifying their roles (respectively, master, detail and reference). These three associations also contain a tagged value named "filter" that allows the restriction of the domain entity's attributes that can be used in the context of the XisBusinessEntity.

Regarding the Flight Reservation App, we defined three XisBusinessEntities: FlightReservationBE, PassengerBE and AirportBE. The FlightReservationBE has FlightReservation as master entity and Airport and Passenger as references. The PassengerBE has Passenger as master entity and AirportBE has Airport as main entity.

Architectural View

The Architectural View represents the interactions between the mobile application and the external entities, and so, it can also be called "Distributed Systems View". The modeling of this view is performed in a Class Diagram. The mobile application, depicted as a class named XisMobileApp, can be connected to several XisServices, represented as interfaces.

A XisService supplies one or more operations, called XisServiceMethods, and is provided or realized by a class called XisProvider. A XisService is divided in two types: 1) XisInternalService, if it is provided by an enti- ty inside the mobile device; and 2) XisRemoteService, if it is provided by an entity outside the mobile device. A XisInternalService can only be provided by a class called XisInternalProvider. Moreover, a XisInternalProvider has a tagged value that defines its type: 1) Location, which represents the location provider of the device and gives information about its geographical location; 2) Contacts, which allows the access to the contacts of the de- vice; 3) Calendar, which allows the interaction with the calendar of the device; 4) Media, which allows the interaction with the camera, media recorder and media player; and 5) Custom, which is used when the developer wants to create his own provider.

In turn, each XisRemoteService can only be provided by a XisServer, which represents physically a web server, or a XisMobileClientApp, which represents a mobile application running on another device.

The XIS-Mobile language provides the following stereotypes to be applied in this view: 1) XisMobileApp, 2) XisInternalProvider, 3) XisClientMobileApp and 4) XisServer for classes; 5) XisInternalService and 6) XisRemoteService for interfaces; 7) XisServiceMethod for operations; 8) XisMobileApp-ServiceAssociation for asso- ciations between XisMobileApps and XisServices; 9) XisProvider-ServiceRealization for realization relation- ships between XisProviders and XisServices.

Considering the Flight Reservation App, it communicates with one XisRemoteService containing one Xis- ServiceMethod for the operation of synchronizing airports provided by a XisServer named FlightServer.

UseCases View

The UseCases View represents the operations an actor can perform when interacting with the application in the context of a business entity (from the BusinessEntities View) and/or a provider (from the Architectural View), using a Use Case Diagram. This view plays an important role during the model-to-model transformation stages. Namely, according to the use case stereotype, tagged values and the business entity and/or provider associated, a certain type of User-Interfaces View models will be generated based on well defined UI patterns [23] . A use case can have two stereotypes: XisEntityUseCase and XisServiceUseCase.

A XisEntityUseCase represents an operation over a business entity and, consequently, its domain entities. It contains a set of tagged values representing the CRUD (Create, Read, Update, Delete) and the Search operations for the master, detail and reference entities. It was decided to include these set of operations, since it contains the most commonly used operations as it was observed in [24] . In addition to that, a XisEntityUseCase has a tagged value that defines its type: 1) EntityManagement; or 2) EntityConfiguration. A XisEntityUseCase of type Enti- tyManagement will generate interaction spaces (screens are designated as interaction spaces in XIS-Mobile) for managing a list of multiple instances of the master entity (from the associated business entity), while a XisEntity- UseCase of type EntityConfiguration will generate interaction spaces to manage a single instance of the master entity associated. These two types are, in fact, patterns of generation of interaction spaces and in the future the goal is to add new types.

A XisServiceUseCase represents an action that uses the operations provided by a provider. It can also be connected to a business entity, representing that the operations have an effect over the business entity's domain entities. For now, this type of use case generates interaction spaces that use the operations provide by the pro- vider and its associated services. Typically, this type of use case is used as an extension of the XisEntityUseCase. In addition, it is also possible to define actors in this view with the goal, in the future, of specifying the opera- tions an actor are allowed to perform.

The XIS-Mobile language provides the following stereotypes to be applied in this view: 1) XisActor for ac- tors; 2) XisEntityUseCase and 3) XisServiceUseCase for use cases; 4) XisActor-UCAssociation, for associations between actors and use cases; 5) XisEntityUC-BEAssociation for associations between XisEntityUseCases and XisBusinessEntities; 6) XisServiceUC-BEAssociation for associations between XisServiceUseCases and XisBusinessEntities; and 7) XisServiceUC-ProviderAssociation for associations between XisServiceUseCases and XisProviders.

Concerning the Flight Reservation App (see Figure 3), there were defined three use cases: 1) "Manage Flight- Reservations", a XisEntityUseCase of type "EntityManagement" connected to the FlightReservationBE; 2) "Manage Passengers", a XisEntityUseCase of type "EntityManagement" connected to the PassengerBE; and 3) "Sync Airports", a XisServiceUseCase connected to the AirportBE and to the FlightServer used to synchronize the list of airports with that server.

User-Interfaces View

The User-Interfaces View contains the NavigationSpace and InteractionSpace views that are used to define the screens of the mobile application, known as interaction spaces, as well as the navigation flow between them.

NavigationSpace View

The NavigationSpace View represents the navigation flow between the various interaction spaces of the mobile application, using a Class Diagram.

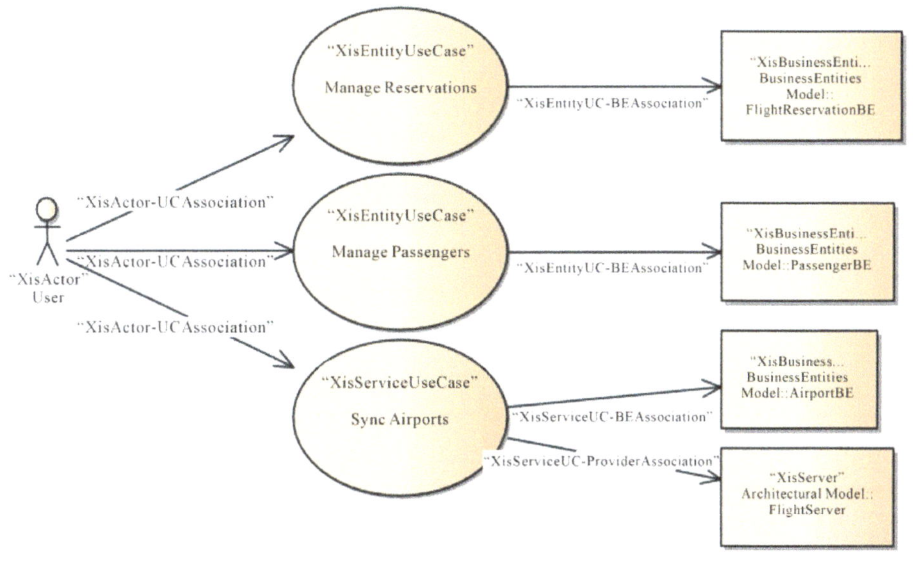

Figure 3. Flight Reservation App's UseCases View.

This navigation flow is represented by directed associations with the stereo- type XisInteractionSpaceAssociation. The XisInteractionSpaceAssociation is the only stereotype provided by the XIS-Mobile language to be applied in this view. Each XisInteractionSpaceAssociation is also responsible to show the event that triggered the navigation between the interaction spaces, because its name must be the same as the event's name. This view provides a good support for documenting the structure of the system and eases the introduction of future corrections and improvements in the mobile application navigation. For simplicity and readability reasons, the details of each interaction space are represented in the InteractionSpace View.

The Flight Reservation App's NavigationSpace View is composed by eight XisInteractionSpaces: 1) HomeIS, which is the home screen of the application; 2) FlightReservationListIS, which lists all the flight reservations; 3) FlightReservationEditorIS, which displays all the information of a flight reservation and allows its edition; 4) PassengerManagerIS, which lists all the passengers associated to a certain flight reservation; 5) PassengerDetai- lIS, which displays the information of a passenger associated to a reservation and allows its edition; 6) Passen- gerListIS, which lists all the passengers; 7) PassengerEditor, which allows the edition or creation of a passenger; and 8) AirportListIS, which lists all airports and allows to synchronize them with a remove server.

InteractionSpace View

The InteractionSpace View represents several details about a certain screen or interaction space of the mobile application, using a Class Diagram. Due to the amount of abstractions it involves, this view is perhaps the hard- est to design and most complex view of the XIS-Mobile language. It is source of several details such as the UI layout, the events a certain UI component can trigger and the gestures that can be performed. All this informa- tion will feed the model-to-text transformations.

Each interaction space is represented as a stereotyped class named XisInteractionSpace. It is the main com- ponent of this view, since it represents an application screen. Each XisInteractionSpace contains one or more XisWidgets, also represented as classes. In addition to that, each interaction space can be connected to a busi- ness entity, through a XisIS-BEAssociation, defining the domain entities that can be bound to the interaction space's inner elements.

A XisWidget represents a UI widget or control that builds up the GUI. It is divided in two major stereotype categories: XisCompositeWidget and XisSimpleWidget. A XisCompositeWidget is a container class that groups other XisWidgets (both simple and composite). As can be noticed, this stereotype follows the well-known Com- posite design pattern [25] . The XisCompositeWidget plays an important role in this view, because it allows the definition of a specific context by associating a domain entity to its "domainEntityName" tagged value. This value should be filled with the name of a domain entity contained in the business entity associated to the interaction space. In addition, whenever this value is filled, all the XisWidgets inside the XisCompositeWidget in- volved have access to the domain entity. Some examples of specializations of XisCompositeWidgets are the XisList, XisForm, XisMenu or XisDialog. In turn, a XisSimpleWidget represents the set of simple controls and cannot contain other elements. Some examples are the XisLabel, XisTextBox or XisButton. A XisSimpleWidget can be bound to a domain entity attribute value through its tagged value "entityAttributeName".

Every XisWidget can have many gestures attached, called XisGestures, but at most only one of each type. The set of gestures supported is: Tap, DoubleTap, LongTap, Swipe, Pinch and Stretch. Then, each gesture can trigger a set of events or actions, the XisActions, which ranges from actions like Cancel or WebService to CRUD operations. A XisAction can also trigger navigation between interaction spaces through the tagged value "navigation" that should be filled with the name of the target interaction space. The XIS-Mobile language also gives users the flexibility to define the stub of a custom operation by providing a XisAction of type Custom. XisGestures are represented as classes, while XisActions are represented as operations. XisGestures can be at- tached to a XisWidget in two ways: through explicit associations and through tagged values that represent the default gestures used with that XisWidget. For example, XisButtons have the gesture Tap as default, because it is the most common gesture when interacting with buttons. Therefore, XisButtons have the tagged value "onTap" that should have the name of the XisAction triggered whenever the Tap gesture is detected.

Moreover, a XisWidget can have a constant value and for that purpose it has the tagged value "value". It is also possible to assign a value from an expression using the tagged value "valueFromExpression".

Regarding the Flight Reservation App (see Figure 4), the FlightReservationListIS is an example of one of its interaction spaces. This interaction space has a XisList, a XisMenu of type "OptionsMenu" and a XisMenu of type "ContextMenu". The XisList is a list of flight reservations and contains one XisListItem with a "Tap" gesture as default that triggers the navigation to the FlightReservationEditorIS.

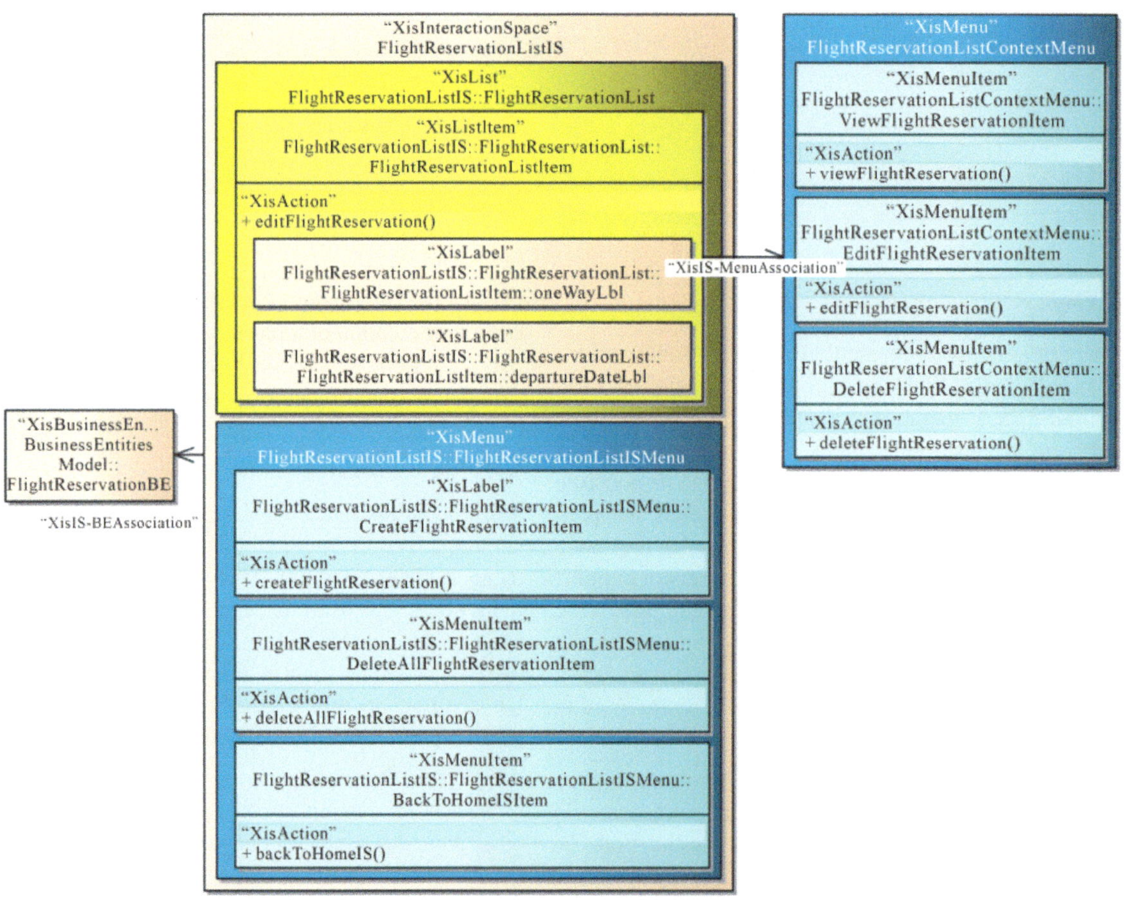

Figure 4: The FlightReservationListIS insteraction space diagram of the flight reservation app

This list item is associated to the context menu, which is opened whenever the list item is long-tapped. The context menu contains three XisMenuItems that allow navigating to the visualization and edition screen of the associated reservation, or instead delete it from the list. The options menu contains three XisMenuItems that allow creating a reservation by navigating to the FlightReservationEditorIS, the deletion of all reservations, and going back to the HomeIS.

XIS-MOBILE FRAMEWORK

The XIS-Mobile language is supported by a MDD-based framework[1] implemented using the Model Driven Generation (MDG) Technologies provided by Sparx Systems Enterprise Architect (EA) along with the Eclipse Modeling Framework (EMF). The use of these technologies leverages the environment they provide, as well as some compatible plug-ins. As shown in Figure 5, the suggested development process of a mobile application using the XIS-Mobile framework consists in four steps: 1) the definition of the required views using the Visual Editor; 2) their validation with the Model Validator; 3) the generation of the User-Interfaces View models with the Model Generator; and finally 4) the generation of the application's source code through the Code Generator. After Step 3), if the designer finds that the model is not yet completed, the process returns to Step 1) for a new iteration. It is important to emphasize that only Step 1) is manual, while the other three are automatic.

First, the Visual Editor is implemented on top of EA through the use of an MDG Technology plug-in. This plug-in technology allowed the definition of UML profiles fully compliant with the OMG specification for UML2, the creation of toolboxes, diagram types, diagram templates and patterns customized to the XIS-Mobile profile.

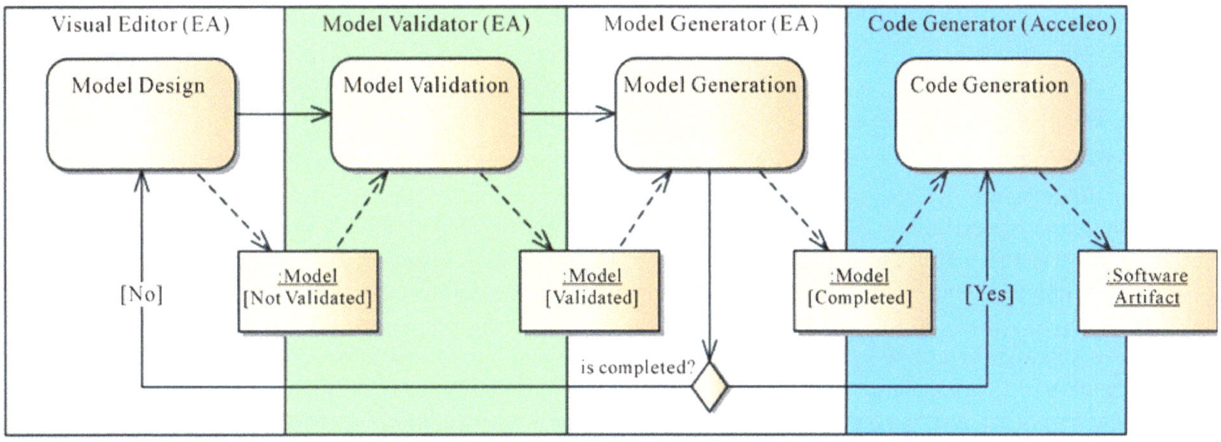

Figure 5: Suggested development process with the XIS-Mobile framework

Second, the Model Validator is implemented as a plug-in using EA's Model Validation API [26] . It plays a crucial role avoiding errors by the designer, improving the quality of the models and, consequently, enhancing the quality of the generated models and code. Despite not being a standard like OCL [27] , this solution allows the definition of custom error messages for each constraint, the assignment of severity levels (error or warning) to them, and the immediate navigation to the element that caused the message.

Third, the Model Generator is implemented as a plug-in leveraging EA's Automation Interface [28] . It per- mits accessing the repository containing the created diagrams and their elements, as well as creating new dia- grams and elements. Thus, the Model Generator performs the model-to-model transformations using the infor- mation of the UseCases, Domain, BusinessEntities and Architectural views. Usually a single instance of each one of these diagrams yields to multiple InteractionSpace View diagrams and a single NavigationSpace View diagram.

Fourth, the Code Generator is based on Acceleo [29] , a template-based code generator framework available as an Eclipse plug-in. Acceleo implements the MOF MTL (Model to Text Language) standard [30] and allows the definition of code templates for any kind of model compatible with EMF. The code templates are composed by regular text (static part of the template) and several annotations (dynamic part of the template) that are replaced by values of the model during generation time. For now, the XIS-Mobile framework supports the generation of applications for Android, and also early versions for iOS and Windows Phone have been developed. An impor- tant point is that whenever the user desires to add support for other platforms, he needs to define the corres- ponding code templates.

EVALUATION

To better evaluate XIS-Mobile, receive feedback from people not directly involved in this work and detect po- tential bugs and user limitations, we decided to conduct a pilot user session. This session involved a group of 9 participants in total with ages ranging from 21 to 48 and with at least a Bachelor of Science degree. All partici- pants had previous knowledge and experience with UML, 5 of them also had experience with mobile application development and 7 had professional experience in the Information Technology area. The user session was con- ducted under the following conditions: tests took place in the laboratory (controlled environment); realization of the task without previous use and learning (for the first time); the user must had a computer running Windows, Java and previously installed Sparx Enterprise Architect (version 7.5, 10 or above); Direct Observation, i.e., while users performed the assigned task, their behavior and performance could be logged; users were free to think out loud and share ideas if they wanted.

Based on these conditions participants received a 40 minutes training explaining the fundamental concepts of the XIS-Mobile language and its framework, as well as a demonstration of the development of a simple case study using XIS-Mobile from model design until code generation. Thereafter, they had a script describing the Flight Reservation App (see Section 3) and were asked to create the corresponding models in XIS-Mobile, vali- date them and launch the code generation for Android in a maximum period of 60 minutes. Finally, participants were asked to fill in a questionnaire to rate: 1) the XIS-Mobile language; 2) its supporting framework; and 3) the overall approach. The answers were classified in a scale of: 0 (N/A-Do not know), 1 (Very Low), 2 (Low), 3 (Medium), 4 (High) and 5 (Very High).

The XIS-Mobile Language aspect included five questions:

QL.1. How suitable is the size (number of concepts) of the language?

QL.2. How easy to use is the notation used (defined as a UML Profile)?

QL.3. How easy to learn is the language without the UI concepts?

QL.4. How easy to learn is the language with the UI concepts?

QL.5. How suitable is the language for the Mobile Apps development domain?

Table 1 summarizes the average score for the answers regarding the language aspect, broken down by ques- tion. In general, we can observe that all questions had a positive score (greater than 2.5) implying some sort of success. Concerning Question 1, we conclude that almost all participants considered the language size suitable (with a score of 4 or 5), while 1 participant considered it inadequate, possibly too large. Questions 2, 3 and 5 were the ones that obtained more favorable answers indicating that XIS-Mobile language notation is easy to use, easy to learn without the UI concepts and suitable for the mobile application development domain, respectively. However, from the answers to Question 4 we can conclude that participants found the User-Interface View more complex and harder to learn than the other views. This can be explained by the degree of detail, specially of the InteractionSpace View that contains a huge set of concepts either for UI widgets, gestures or actions. This is a challenging point that we will take into account in future developments with the goal of improving the represen- tation of each interaction space in a "What You See Is What You Get" (WYSIWYG) fashion. Summarizing, we assume that XIS-Mobile language contains several concepts and initially can be a bit difficult to learn and un- derstand all of them. Despite that we believe from these results that its size, notation and concepts are adequate for the development of mobile applications.

The XIS-Mobile Framework aspect included five questions:

QF.1. How do you rate the usability of EA with the XIS-Mobile plugin?

QF.2. How do you rate the usability of the Model Editor (Stereotypes, Toolboxes, Project template)?

QF.3. How do you rate the usability of the Model Validator?

QF.4. How do you rate the simplicity of the Model-to-Model transformation (Model generation) process?

QF.5. How do you rate the simplicity of the Model-to-Text transformation (Code generation) process?

Table 2 summarizes the average score for the answers to the Framework aspect, broken down by question. Similarly to the previous aspect, we can observe that all answers had a positive score. Question 1 and 2 were the ones that obtained more positive answers and so we can conclude that participants felt highly comfortable with the overall usability of EA with the XIS-Mobile plugin and modeling the Flight Reservation App with the Model Editor. Concerning Questions 3, 4 and 5, it seems that participants found the process of triggering code genera- tion simpler than using the model validation and the model generation process. This can be explained by the fact that the model generation process requires more time to be properly learned, because it highly depends on the use cases that can involve different types, tagged values and associations to business entities and providers.

Finally, the XIS-Mobile General Approach aspect included two questions:

QA.1. How do you rate the productivity with XIS-Mobile comparing to traditional processes?

QA.2. Would you use such a tool on your own Mobile App projects?

Table 1: Questionnaire's average score (in a scale of 0 - 5) by question for the XIS-Mobile language aspect

	XIS-Mobile Language				
	QL.1	QL.2	QL.3	QL.4	QL.5
Average	3.67	4.22	3.89	3.56	4.11

Table 2: Questionnaire's average score (in a scale of 0 - 5) by question for the XIS-Mobile framework aspect

	XIS-Mobile Framework				
	QF.1	QF.2	QF.3	QF.4	QF.5
Average	4.44	4	3.33	3.33	3.56

Table 3 presents the average score for the answers concerning the XIS-Mobile General Approach aspect, broken down by question. We can observe that the score obtained for both questions is highly positive. However, the participants expressed more interest in using XIS-Mobile in mobile app projects than considering the prod- uctivity with XIS-Mobile high comparing to the traditional approach.

Summarizing, as can be seen in Table 4, the results were generally encouraging with positive scores in all three analyzed aspects. Nevertheless, it was observed that the XIS-Mobile Framework and namely its model generation process had the lowest score and possibly need to be refined in order to improve their simplicity. Moreover it was observed that the learnability of the XIS-Mobile language should be improved namely in terms of the InteractionSpace View concepts representation. It can be stated that the number of participants of the ses- sion is relatively small. We believe that number is sufficient to take meaningful conclusions because usability experts have noted that a group of 5 testers is enough to uncover over 80% of the usability problems [31] . Also, since this evaluation focuses on the usability of the language, framework and approach, we believe 9 partici- pants is a reasonable number for an exploratory assessment, at least in order to identify challenges on the usabil- ity of these aspects.

Table 3: Questionnaire's average score (in a scale of 0 - 5) by question for the XIS-Mobile General Approach aspect.

	XIS-Mobile General Approach	
	QA.1	QA.2
Average	4	4.33

Table 4: Questionnaire's average score (in a scale of 0 - 5) for each XIS- Mobile framework aspect.

	XIS-Mobile		
	Language	Framework	General Approach
Average	3.89	3.73	4.17

CONCLUSIONS

In this paper we presented XIS-Mobile, a domain specific language (defined as a UML profile), focused on the development of mobile applications and on mitigating the problems related to the complexity of software de- velopment and mobile platform fragmentation. XIS-Mobile has a multi-view organization and supports two de- sign approaches: the dummy approach and the smart approach. XIS-Mobile has a supporting framework based on Sparx Systems Enterprise Architect MDG Technology and EMF, which intends to generate source code for multiple platforms from a single model specification, through model-to-model and model-to-text transforma- tions. Composed of four major components, this framework suggests developing a mobile application in four steps whenever possible: defining the required views using the Visual Editor, validating them using the Model Validator, generating the User-Interfaces View models with the Model Generator, and finally generating the ap- plication's source code through the Code Generator. This way the developer takes advantage of the MDD bene- fits, namely increasing his productivity by using a single specification of the system with a PIM, by avoiding the implementation of boilerplate code and reducing errors.

XIS-Mobile has been developed over the last eighteen months following the Action Research Methodology and has been evaluated in order to assess its usefulness and adequacy to the purpose of modeling mobile appli- cations. This evaluation process has been done in an iterative and gradual way using case studies applications and a user session. The user session focused on three aspects of XIS-Mobile: the Language, the Framework and the General Approach. During the user session the participants had to develop a case study application using XIS- Mobile and in the end fill in a questionnaire. The questionnaires collected positive results and showed prelimi- nary evidences that demonstrate XIS-Mobile's usefulness and feasibility.

For future work, there are plans to add new use case types and patterns, in order to extend the range of the smart approach and its associated model-to-model transformations. We intend to further evaluate XIS-Mobile, possibly conducting usability tests in the academic field and for teaching purposes.

There is also concern in im- proving the representation of XIS-Mobile stereotypes with the goal of make them more appealing and closer to the final result. The integration with other visual editors represents another interesting future step, aiming to of- fer more portability and flexibility to the users. The design and development of more complex and real-world applications consist in interesting future research directions, to better exercise all language concepts. Finally, some more research has to be done related on how to extend XIS-Mobile to better support scenarios related with the mobile cloud computing (MCC) [32] , context awareness [9] and CMS-based [33] systems.

ACKNOWLEDGEMENTS

André Ribeiro, Alberto Rodrigues da Silva (EXCL/EEI-ESS/0257/2012).

REFERENCES

1. Meeker, M., Devitt, S. and Wu, L. (2010) Internet Trends. Morgan Stanley Research.http://www.slideshare.net/CMSummit/ms-internet-trends060710final
2. Schuermans, S., Constantinou, A. and Vakulenko, M. (2014) Mobile Megatrends 2014, Vision Mobile. http://www.visionmobile.com/product/mobile-megatrends-2014
3. Atkinson, C. and Kühne, T. (2003) Model-Driven Development: A Metamodeling Foundation. IEEE Software. IEEE Computer Society Press, Los Alamitos.
4. Stahl, T. and Volter, M. (2006) Model-Driven Software Development: Technology, Engineering, Management. John Wiley & Sons Ltd., Chichester.
5. Ribeiro, A. and Silva, A.R. (2014) XIS-Mobile: A DSL for Mobile Applications. Proceedings of 29th Symposium on Applied Computing (SAC'14), Gyeongju, 24-28 March 2014, 1316-1323. [Paper reference:3]
6. Silva, A.R., Saraiva, J., Silva, R. and Martins, C. (2007) XIS-UML Profile for Extreme Modeling Interactive Systems. Proceedings of the 4th International Workshop on Model-Based Methodologies for Pervasive and Embedded Software (MOMPES'07), Braga, 31 March 2007, 55-66.
7. Silva, A.R., Saraiva, J., Ferreira, D., Silva, R. and Videira, C. (2007) Integration of RE and MDE Paradigms: The

Pro- ject It Approach and Tools. IET Software Journal, 1, 294-314.

8. Baskerville, R.L. (1999) Investigating Information Systems with Action Research. Communications of the Association for Information Systems. Association for Information Systems, 2, Article 4.
9. Boudaa, B., Camp, O., Hammoudi, S. and Chikh, M.A. (2012) Model-Driven Development of Context-Aware Services: Issues, Techniques and Review. International Conference on IT and e-Services (ICITeS), Sousse, 24-26 March 2012, 1-8.
10. Belloni, E. and Marcos, C. (2004) MAM-UML: An UML Profile for the Modeling of Mobile-Agent Applications. 24th International Conference of the Chilean, Computer Science Society, Arica, 11-12 November 2004, 3-13.
11. Phone Gap Website. http://phonegap.com
12. Appcelerator Titanium Website. http://www.appcelerator.com/titanium/
13. Singh, I. and Palmieri, M. (2011) Comparison of Cross-Platform Mobile Development Tools. IDT. Malardalen Uni- versity, Västerås.
14. Paananen, T. (2011) Smartphone Cross-Platform Frameworks. B.Sc. Thesis, JAMK University of Applied Sciences, Jyväskylä.
15. Ribeiro, A. and Silva, A.R. (2012) Survey on Cross-Platforms and Languages for Mobile Apps. Proceedings of the 8th International Conference on the Quality and Communications Technology (QUATIC), Lisbon, 3-6 September 2012, 255-260.
16. Ranabahu, A.H., Maximilien, E.M., Sheth, A.P. and Thirunarayan, K. (2011) A Domain Specific Language for Enter- prise Grade Cloud-Mobile Hybrid Applications. Proceedings of the Compilation of the Co-Located Workshops on SPLASH'11, Portland, 22-27 October 2011, 77-84.
17. Kramer, D., Clark, T. and Oussena, S. (2010) MobDSL: A Domain Specific Language for Multiple Mobile Platform De- ployment. Proceedings of the 2010 IEEE International Conference on Networked Embedded Systems for Enterprise Applications (NESEA), Suzhou, 25-26 November 2010, 1-7. http://dx.doi.org/10.1109/NESEA.2010.5678062
18. Balagtas-Fernandez, F., Tafelmayer, M. and Hussmann, H. (2010) Mobia Modeler: Easing the Creation Process of Mobile Applications for Non-Technical Users. Proceedings of the 15th International Conference on Intelligent User Interfaces (IUI'10), Hong Kong, 7-10 February 2010, 269-272.
19. Calvary, G., et al. (2002) The CAMELEON Reference Framework. Deliverable 1.1, CAMELEON Project.
20. Trindade, F.M. and Pimenta, M.S. (2007) Prototyping Multi-Platform Software Using the UsiXML4ALL. Technical Report.
21. Patternò, F., Santoro, C. and Spano, L.D. (2009) MARIA: A Universal, Declarative, Multiple Abstraction-Level Lan- guage for Service-Oriented Applications in Ubiquitous Environments. ACM Transactions on Computer-Human Interaction, 16, 1-30.
22. Wolber, D. (2011) App Inventor and Real-World Motivation. Proceedings of the 42nd ACM Technical Symposium on Computer Science Education (SIGCSE'11), Dallas, 9-12 March 2011, 601-606.
23. Neil, T. (2012) Mobile Design Pattern Gallery: UI Patterns for Mobile Applications. O›Reilly Media, Inc., Sebastopol.
24. Langlands, M. (2010) Inside the Oval: Use-Case Content Patterns. Technical Report, Planet Project. http://planetproject.wikidot.com/use-case-content-patterns
25. Gamma, E., Helm, R., Johnson, R. and Vlissides, J. (1995) Design Patterns: Elements of Reusable Object-Oriented Software. Addison-Wesley, Boston.
26. EA's Model Validation API Website. http://goo.gl/XwUvsx
27. Object Management Group: Object Constraint Language (OCL) Specification.http://www.omg.org/spec/OCL
28. EA's Automation Interface Website. http://goo.gl/r9jz0Z
29. Acceleo Website. http://www.eclipse.org/acceleo
30. Object Management Group: MOF Model to Text Transformation Language (MOFM2T).http://www.omg.org/spec/MOFM2T/1.0/
31. Nielsen, J. and Landauer, T.K. (1993) A Mathematical Model of the Finding of Usability Problems, INTERCHI'93.
32. Fernando, N., et al. (2013) Mobile Cloud Computing: A Survey. Future Generation Computer Systems, 29, 84-106. http://dx.doi.org/10.1016/j.future.2012.05.023
33. Saraiva, J.S. and Silva, A.R. (2009) CMS-Based Web-Application Development Using Model-Driven Languages. Proceedings of the 4th International Conference on Software Engineering Advances, Porto, 20-25 September 2009, 21- 26.

CHAPTER 17

BIO:: PHYLO-PHYLOINFORMATIC ANALYSIS USING PERL

Rutger A Vos, Jason Caravas, Klaas Hartmann, Mark A Jensen, Chase Miller

BACKGROUND

Recent years have seen the emergence of the field of *phyloinformatics* [1]. At a practical level this is research where much of the organizational challenge lies in managing *data*, including character state matrices or multiple sequence alignments, phylogenetic trees and the relationships between these, and *metadata*, including cross references to molecular sequence databases, taxonomies, character state descriptions, biodiversity data, and literature references. At the nexus of the relationships between character state data and phylogenies lies the operational taxonomic unit (OTU), i.e. the biological entity on which observations are made (e.g. by measuring morphological traits or by sequencing DNA) and which is placed as a terminal node in a phylogeny.

In the course of a phyloinformatic analysis, data and metadata are collected or generated, transformed, filtered, analyzed and summarized before they can be interpreted to answer meaningful biological questions. Based on first principles of good science such steps should be reproducible; and, in practice, analysis steps often need to be redone by the researcher multiple times [2] and are too error-prone, tedious and time-consuming to perform manually. Hence, environments that allow such analyses to be scripted programmatically can greatly improve the efficiency and reproducibility of phyloinformatics.

Some of these facilities are provided by DendroPy [3], ETE [4] and BioPython [5] for the Python programming language, by the Ape package [6] for the R environment, and by BioPerl [7] for the Perl programming language. However, some of these (DendroPy, Ape), while strong on tree shape simulation and analysis, do not integrate easily in workflows that include external software for sequence alignment and phylogenetic inference or database or web service access, while others (BioPython, BioPerl, ETE) are strong in that respect but are lacking in tree shape simulation and analysis. In addition, none of these toolkits have a facility for managing the syntax and semantics of metadata. This can cause confusion when integrating and sharing metadata from disparate sources. For example, if an OTU is annotated with a taxonomic identifier, where (e.g. which database) does the identifier come from? What is the relation between the OTU and the database record (e.g. is the relationship established by a simple string match or something else)?

The Bio::Phylo toolkit addresses these issues, allowing researchers to read and write previously unsupported data formats, generate and transform data in a variety of ways, compute heretofore unimplemented topological indices, apply heretofore unavailable sampling and resampling algorithms and visualize the results in publication-ready graphics, while allowing phylogenetic knowledge to be managed, represented and shared in ways that preserve its meaning and its relation to metadata, regardless of its origin or context.

Due to its implementation in the Perl programming language and its compatibility with the BioPerl [7] toolkit, the operations supplied by Bio::Phylo are easily integrated in larger analysis workflows that take advantage of the operations supplied by BioPerl and that interface with command-line executables and web services, e.g. for database access or for computationally intensive analysis steps. However, BioPerl is very large and for many users difficult to install, whereas Bio::Phylo has no required dependencies. This makes deployment much easier for users who only require Bio::Phylo's functionality-orientated towards phyloinformatics per se-but not BioPerl's.

Citation: Rutger A Vos, Jason Caravas, Klaas Hartmann, Mark A Jensen, Chase Miller, BIO::Phylo-phyloinformatic analysis using perl, doi:10.1186/1471-2105-12-63.

IMPLEMENTATION

Data and object model

Bio::Phylo's design follows the data model shown in Figure 1. A phylogenetic project (Bio::Phylo::Project object) contains zero or more sets of trees (Bio::Phylo::Forest objects), zero or more sets of OTUs (Bio::Phylo::Taxa objects) and zero or more character state matrices (Bio::Phylo::Matrices::Matrix objects). Each forest object and each character state matrix may refer to a set of OTUs; however, this is not compulsory throughout the life cycle of these objects. For example, a tree parsed from a simple Newick [8] tree description contains terminal nodes-which may imply associated OTUs-but OTUs for these terminal nodes might only be instantiated when the tree is used in a context that explicitly requires them, such as when writing the tree to a file format that uses the OTU concept (e.g. as in NEXUS [9] "taxa blocks").

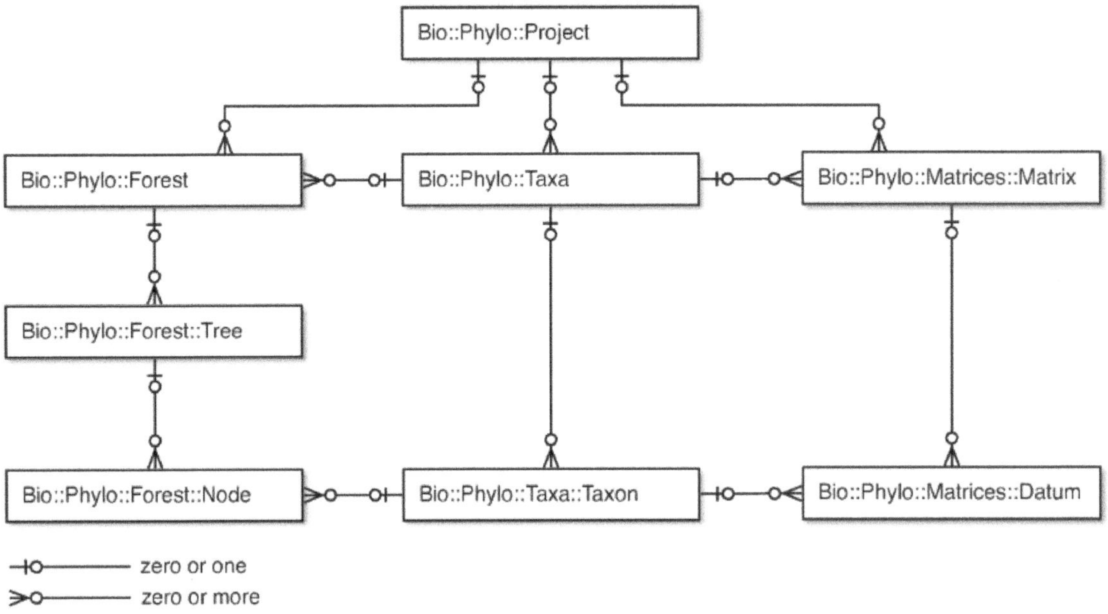

Figure 1: Data model of core Bio::Phylo objects. Cardinality relationships between the objects are shown as "crow's feet" notation; for example, a Bio::Phylo::Project has references to zero or more Bio::Phylo::Forest objects.

Each forest object contains zero or more tree (Bio::Phylo::Forest::Tree) objects, which contain zero or more nodes (Bio::Phylo::Forest::Node). Each of these nodes may have a reference to an OTU (Bio::Phylo::Taxa::Taxon) object, which, conversely, may have references to many nodes. For example, if a NEXUS file with multiple trees for the same set of species is read, the terminal nodes for the same species in the different trees will all hold a reference to the same OTU object, and that OTU object will hold references to all terminal nodes that reference it.

Each character state matrix contains zero or more datum (Bio::Phylo::Matrices::Datum) objects, which represent a character state observation. An observation could be a single character state-such as a morphological state-or a character state sequence, such as a DNA, RNA, amino acid, restriction site, categorical state or continuous state sequence. In addition to holding raw character state symbols, datum objects also manage the semantics of the data, e.g. which symbols are ambiguity symbols for sets of others (as per the IUPAC single character symbols [10]) including "missing" (which means an ambiguity symbol for the set of all possible states) and "gap" (which means an ambiguity symbol for the set of none of the possible states, i.e. "does not apply"). Each of these datum objects may reference an OTU object, which conversely may reference many datum objects.

OTU objects are used in Bio::Phylo to remap the relationships between tree nodes and datum objects from many-to-many to one-to-many from OTU to both nodes and data. This conceptualization is also implied in the NEXUS format and in software projects oriented towards data-management and data-exploration built on top of NEXUS such as Mesquite [11] and TreeBASE [12]. Similarly, containers of OTU objects (the Bio::Phylo::Taxa class) are implemented as objects from which one-to-many relationships exist to character state matrices and to sets of trees.

To implement the functionality implied by the data model (Figure 1) and described here, Bio::Phylo has been designed in object-oriented Perl 5, making use of abstractions and helper classes that have been omitted here for clarity, but which are documented exhaustively in the software release [see http://search.cpan.org/dist/Bio-Phylo].

NEXML

All phylogenetic data objects in Bio::Phylo can be read from, and written to, NeXMLhttp://www.nexml.org, a new XML format that is conceptually similar to NEXUS. The data objects all can hold references to zero or more Bio::Phylo::NeXML::Meta objects, which represent RDFa [13] annotations. This allows Bio::Phylo objects to be serialized as the subjects of "triples" [14] where the predicates and objects can be obtained from any controlled vocabulary or ontology (such as CDAO [15], SKOS [16] or DarwinCorehttp://rs.tdwg.org/dwc/index.htm), providing a flexible, semantic web-ready facility to attach metadata to phylogenetic data objects.

NeXML represents a considerable advance in the structured representation of phylogenetic data because these

RDFa annotations allow phylogenetic data objects to be enriched with flexible predicates and objects, yet constrains these to explicit definitions in controlled vocabularies or ontologies. This is different from PhyloXML annotations and the NEXUS "notes block" because the predicates (or "keys", if viewed from the perspective of key/value annotations) in those formats are based on convention, not explicit definition, which is a situation that can cause ambiguities when integrating data from multiple sources.

A simple example may demonstrate this point: consider reading a file, matching the OTU names read from that file against names in the NCBI taxonomy, then sharing the results of this process. There is no non-ambiguous way to express in machine-readable form in NEXUS or PhyloXML why and how, for example, *Homo sapiens* became associated with the identifier 9606. Using NeXML with RDFa annotations, it can be expressed that the OTU with the name*Homo sapiens* (the subject of the triple) has a match, expressed using, for example, the*closeMatch* predicate from the SKOS vocabulary, with the taxonomy database record identified by http://purl.uniprot.org/taxonomy/9606. The definition of *closeMatch* in the SKOS vocabulary then clarifies unambiguously what the relationship is between the subject (the OTU) and the object (the database record). The key difference between this approach and others in use in phyloinformatics is the usage of formally defined predicates from any knowledge representation to describe the relation between objects and their annotations. (It is for this reason that the TreeBASE project [12] has adopted NeXML as its output format of choice to represent the wealth of metadata that TreeBASE contains.)

Due to NeXML›s OTU-oriented data model, Bio::Phylo, which has a similar model, is a suitable target for NeXML I/O, whereas BioPerl, which lacks a notion of OTUs, is not. In addition, NeXML and Bio::Phylo support categorical and continuous character states, whereas BioPerl does not. By implementing Bio::Phylo with its level of support for NeXML, complex, richly annotated phyloinformatic data objects become amenable to processing in scriptable workflows while persisting more of their context and provenance than heretofore possible.

RESULTS AND DISCUSSION

Object Manipulation and Transformation

Bio::Phylo provides a toolkit for the manipulation of rich phylogenetic data objects. The objects can be annotated and labeled, and have any number of arbitrary other objects attached to them. The objects can be traversed in various ways, including depth-first, breadth-first or level-order traversal of tree shapes and through iterator or visitor access [17] to all objects that are lists of things (e.g. a Bio::Phylo::Taxa object is a list of OTU objects). Traversals can move from node objects to the OTU objects that define them (and back) and from OTU objects to character state observations that were made for the OTU objects (and back). The objects can be tested for various predicates, e.g. whether a tree is rooted, whether it is binary, whether it is ultrametric; whether a set of tips is monophyletic with respect to a given outgroup, whether a set of tips forms a complete clade; whether a node object is a tip, an internal node or the root node; whether it is the ancestor, parent, sibling, child or descendant of another node.

Using these traversal methods and tests, simple calculations are easily implemented. Bio::Phylo provides a number of these, e.g. the sum of all branch lengths on a tree; the average, minimum, maximum and cumulative root-to-tip path length; the amount of redundancy (i.e. the amount of shared, ancestral evolutionary history along all lineages on the total amount of evolutionary history, including along terminal branches). In addition, a number of more sophisticated tree shape methods useful for biodiversity informatics is provided:

- calc_ltt - Calculates lineage-through-time points [18].
- calc_symdiff - Calculates the symmetric difference metric [19] between two trees.
- calc_fiala_stemminess - Calculates stemminess measure [20].
- calc_rohlf_stemminess - Calculates stemminess measure [21].
- calc_imbalance - Calculates Colless's coefficient of tree imbalance [22].
- calc_gamma - Calculates γ-statistic [23].
- calc_i2 - Calculates I2 imbalance [24].
- calc_fp - Calculates the Fair Proportion value [25, 26] for each tip.
- calc_es - Calculates the Equal Splits value [27, 28] for each tip.
- calc_pe - Calculates the Pendant Edge [29] value for each tip.
- calc_shapley - Calculates the Shapley [30] value for each tip.

Likewise, calculations applicable to sets of trees (e.g. split frequencies) and to character state matrices (e.g. state frequencies, G/C content) are provided.

Bio::Phylo also provides methods for the transformation of phylogenetic data objects. For example, phylogenetic trees can be re-rooted, pruned or ultrametricized, nodes can be collapsed or inserted, branch lengths can be exponentiated or log-transformed. Sets of trees can be summarized in consensus trees or represented as pseudo-character-state MRP [31, 32] matrices. Character state data can be manipulated directly, or transformed through bootstrapping and jackknifing [33].

Input/Output

A number of file formats is used for phylogenetic data. The Bio::Phylo::IO module supports the most commonly used ones: trees can be written and read in Newick format [8]; projects, taxa, trees and matrices can be written and read in NEXUS format and in NeXMLhttp://www.nexml.org; character state matrices can be read from CSV, FASTA, PHYLIP and tab-delimited files; trees can be read from the Tree of Life Web Project [34] XML service; trees and character state matrices can be written in the legacy format for the CONTINUOUS [35, 36], DISCRETE [37] and MULTISTATE [37] programs and in PHYLIP format

If BioPerl [7] is present, the wealth of data formats supported by Bio::SeqIO, Bio::AlignIO and Bio::TreeIO is also available because BioPerl objects can be converted to Bio::Phylo objects (using the new_from_bioperl constructors), and Bio::Phylo objects can be passed to thewrite methods of BioPerl. However, different from BioPerl is Bio::Phylo's concept of a "project" object, which is a collection of fundamental data objects (OTUs, trees and matrices) that reference each other. Whereas in BioPerl, NEXUS files are treated as flat containers of records of the same type (i.e. either trees or alignments, which are read sequentially by a tree file reader or an alignment reader, respectively), Bio::Phylo can optionally treat NEXUS and NeXML files as containing a project of related data of different types, in the same way as the informatics-oriented applications Mesquite [11] and TreeBASE [12] do. The compatibility with BioPerl is optional: Bio::Phylo doesn't require BioPerl to be installed or vice versa (they don't share code), but if Bio::Phylo detects BioPerl's presence, it enables a compatibility mode to make trees, nodes, character state matrices and sequences implement the interfaces that BioPerl defines.

Beyond BioPerl, interaction with other toolkits (e.g. ETE, DendroPy, BioPython, Ape) and combination in larger workflows is confined to the extent to which they can read the same data formats as Bio::Phylo. This functionality is usually confined to NEXUS and Newick file exchange, although DendroPy has support for NeXML as well, allowing more fine-grained data and metadata sharing, and similar functionality is in development for BioRuby [38].

Visualization

Bio::Phylo can draw trees where only the branching order and direction, but not the branch lengths are significant ("cladograms"), as trees with branch lengths proportional to time or some other metric such as inferred change ("phylograms") or as trees where branch lengths and distance are significant, but no direction or nesting is implied ("unrooted"). These trees can be drawn with rectangular, curved or diagonal branches. Branch thickness, branch color, node color, node radius and node pie diagrams (e.g. for "likelihood pies" [sensu [39]]) can all be set per node and branch individually. Clades can be represented in a view that shows them collapsed into triangles whose width and color can be set per clade individually. This programmatic access to the visualization of individual objects in large trees allows users to superimpose their data on trees in a variety of ways (for an example, see Figure 2).

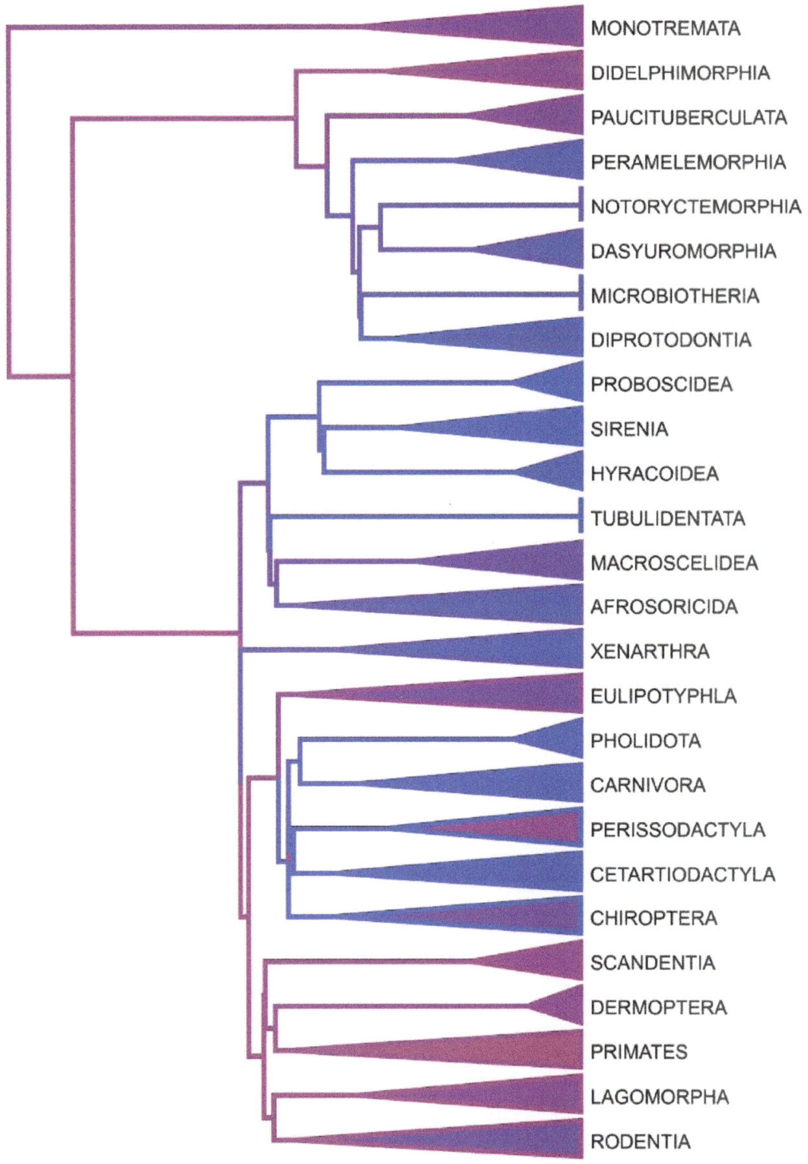

Figure 2: Visualization example: mammal rates. This tree was generated using Bio::Phylo by (i) reading a 3185 taxon phylogeny; (ii) collapsing the major clades; (iii) converting branch-specific speciation rates (read from a separate file, blue indicates low rates, purple and burgundy

indicate higher rates) to RGB color codes; (iv) applying these colors to the branches and the average color within each collapsed clade to the triangles (data and use case kindly provided by Mark Pagel and Chris Venditti).

The visualizations produced by the tree drawer module can be serialized to various bitmap formats (GIF, JPEG, PNG) and vector formats (PDF, SVG, SWF and the new HTML5 Canvas used by modern web browsers and by the iPhone and iPad), some of which can be used to create interactive graphics and animations (SVG, SWF and Canvas). Using the XML-based SVG output format, the resulting serialization can be further processed programmatically, as was done by the authors of a recent study [40] that used Bio::Phylo (Florent Angly, pers. comm.). Any serialization can of course be manipulated further by hand using vector drawing or graphics editing software to prepare it for publication; however, the most useful application of Bio::Phylo's tree drawing capabilities is probably in the creation of interactive graphics for the web, e.g. within the dynamic server environment of a web application that serves trees from a database.

Sampling and simulation

Bio::Phylo can simulate tree topologies under the following models of cladogenesis: pure birth under the model of Hey [41]; pure birth under the Yule model [42]; equiprobable topologies [sensu [43]]; constant rate birth-death, evolving speciation rate and beta binomial models implemented using novel algorithms [44]. The tree sampling interface in Bio::Phylo can also be used to sample from arbitrarily complex user specified models using the algorithms in [44].

CONCLUSIONS

Bio::Phylo is a software library written in Perl 5 that currently consists of about 33,000 lines of code spread out over 59 software modules. A manual that is part of the release provides the principal documentation. On a command line, this manual can be displayed by issuing the command perldoc Bio::Phylo::Manual. (The document is also available onlinehttp://search.cpan.org/dist/Bio-Phylo/lib/Bio/Phylo/Manual.pod). In addition, more documentation - about 14,000 lines as of revision 1204-can be found as embedded documentation in the individual classes of the release. For example, to learn more about reading and writing phylogenetic data, issue the command perldoc Bio::Phylo::IO. Bio::Phylo uses inheritance to a great extent, such that any one object may inherit additional methods from a number of super classes. In such cases, this will be noted in the "SEE ALSO" section of that class's documentation. The Bio::Phylo documentation system rewards the methodical reader who follows these document links.

Because Bio::Phylo implements the same interfaces in its core data objects, it is optionally compatible with BioPerl [7], filling a niche left open for phyloinformatic analysis in Perl. For example, the authors are aware of Bio::Phylo having been used for phylogenomic research [40], cladogenesis simulations [44], and the evaluation of biodiversity metrics [45]. Similar to Bio::NEXUS [46], Bio::Phylo implements more exhaustive implementation of the NEXUS data format than BioPerl does, however, Bio::NEXUS's functionality and use cases are confined to input and output in that format, omitting the object manipulation, annotation, visualization and sampling and simulation features discussed here.

In comparison with open source projects for phyloinformatics implemented in other programming languages, Bio::Phylo most closely resembles the *ape* toolkit for R [6] and the*DendroPy* toolkit for Python [3], however, the language environments of these three projects are obviously different both in actual functionality and in their appeal to differing sense of aesthetics among user communities. Also, the compatibility with BioPerl and the integration with NeXML make Bio::Phylo especially suitable for applications where richly annotated phylogenetic data objects need to be persisted such that the semantics of the metadata are preserved (e.g. between steps in a larger workflow, or as data are serialized for sharing). A simple example of this is shown in Figure 3. In this code sample, two Newick trees are parsed; subsequently, OTUs for the terminal nodes in the trees are annotated with the *skos:closeMatch*predicate that describes the relationship between the OTUs and the respective NCBI taxonomy database records returned by the Entrez web service as best matches for the OTU names. In the final step of the example, the annotated project is persisted to NeXML with the metadata available to other consumers (such as a different script, or a client to a web service) and preserving in machine-readable format *why* the metadata exist.

```
use Bio::DB::Taxonomy;
use Bio::Phylo::IO 'parse';
use Bio::Phylo::NeXML::Meta;

# Assign base URL for NCBI taxonomy entries, assign SKOS namespace,
# instantiate the BioPerl taxonomy searcher, read DATA block
my $ncbi   = 'http://purl.uniprot.org/taxonomy/';
my $skos   = 'http://www.w3.org/2004/02/skos/core#';
my $db     = Bio::DB::Taxonomy->new( '-source' => 'entrez' );
my $trees = do { local $/; <DATA> };

# Parse the newick strings from the DATA block, turn them
# into a Bio::Phylo::Project object
my $project = parse(
    '-format'     => 'newick',
    '-string'     => $trees,
    '-as_project' => 1,
);

# Create OTUs for the terminal nodes parsed out of the newick strings
my $otus = $project->get_forests->[0]->make_taxa;

# Visit the created OTUs
$otus->visit(
    sub {
        my $otu = shift;

        # Add a metadata annotation to each OTU to specify how it
        # matches a record from the NCBI taxonomy, i.e. as a "closeMatch"
        # as per the SKOS vocabulary
        $otu->add_meta(
            Bio::Phylo::NeXML::Meta->new(
                '-namespaces' => { 'skos' => $skos },
                '-triple'     => {
                    'skos:closeMatch' => $ncbi.$db->get_taxonid($otu->get_name)
                }
            )
        )
    }
);

# Add the OTUs to the project, write the result to NeXML
$project->insert($otus);
print $project->to_xml;

__DATA__
(((Homo sapiens,Pan troglodytes),Gorilla gorilla),Pongo pygmaeus);
(((Homo sapiens,Pan paniscus),Gorilla gorilla),Pongo pygmaeus);
```

Figure 3: Code sample: parsing OTUs from Newick tree descriptions and annotating them with NCBI taxonomy database record identifiers using the SKOS vocabulary to describe the relationship between the OTU and the database record (i.e. a close string match).

Future Directions

Bio::Phylo is written in Perl, and while this language has many useful features, it is not very well suited for computationally intensive calculations compared to compiled languages such as C/C++. This means that operations such as maximum likelihood estimation or Markov chains are not usefully implemented in Perl, and so Bio::Phylo does not attempt this. However, Perl can easily make use of applications written in other languages through system calls, which is why it is used as a "glue language" for analysis workflows [2]. This is one of the main use cases for Bio::Phylo. In addition to writing one-off wrappers around command line tools, in this scenario one can also use BioPerl's *bioperl-run* extension, which Bio::Phylo can be seamlessly incorporated into because its objects can, optionally, double as the BioPerl objects that are passed into the wrappers that *bioperl-run* provides. However, this interface is somewhat coarse in the amount of allowed parameterization of wrapped applications, and so novel algorithms are generally difficult to implement this way. Several projects developed in compiled languages-for example HyPhy [47] and BEAGLE [48]-are now being designed so that they can be used as computational back-ends that can be connected to front-ends implemented in scripting languages such as Perl (e.g. using SWIG). Some preliminary tests have shown that it is possible to expose some of HyPhy›s and BEAGLE›s functionality to Bio::Phylo in this way, and this is something that will be explored further in the future, possibly as optional extensions to Bio::Phylo.

Other developments that might affect Bio::Phylo›s future implementation and project organization are some of the new initiatives that are being undertaken in the Perl/bioinformatics community. The BioPerl project has grown to such a size that work is now being undertaken by its core developers to develop a more decentralized and modular architecture. If this results in a model whereby the different components in this new BioPerl ecosystem are decoupled enough that Bio::Phylo can participate in it while continuing to be developed along its original design and API it is the intention to make it part of this ecosystem. The recent decomposition of the BioPerl source code into multiple repositories maintained under the «git» revision control system simplifies this; recent discussions between BioPerl and Bio::Phylo developers point to a solution where Bio::Phylo becomes one such repository (e.g. «bioperl-phylo»). The hope is that this will ensure continued compliance of Bio::Phylo›s implementations of BioPerl interfaces and that it will invite BioPerl users and developers to consider getting involved in Bio::Phylo where it fills niches left open by BioPerl. In fact, Bio::Phylo has been used successfully as an underlying engine for the parsing and production of NeXML format within the BioPerl core code base itself, through the module Bio::Nexml (written by CM). Bio::Nexml is an example of the transparent interoperability of the two toolkits, and a model of how continued cross-fertilization might proceed.

Yet other initiatives in the BioPerl community pertain to innovation in the Perl language itself. For Perl version 5, a new meta-programming extension called Moose greatly simplifies class definitions, and usage of this extension is being explored for BioPerl under the BIOMEhttp://github.com/cjfields/biome project. It has been a guiding principle in Bio::Phylo's development that it does not require any prerequisites that are not part of the Perl core in order to be installed (although some functionality will be unavailable at runtime unless and until optional extensions are installed as specified in the 'Availability and Requirements' section). Since the Moose extension is currently not part of the Perl 5 core, redesigning Bio::Phylo along similar lines as the BIOME project would introduce a prerequisite to installing Bio::Phylo without adding any functionality. At present this makes this an unlikely scenario, but this might change depending on the success of BIOME and inclusion of Moose in the Perl 5 core.

Lastly, an important innovation is the development of the Perl 6 languagehttp://dev.perl.org/perl6/. This new version of the language itself is a break with all preceding ones, with significant differences in syntax and in the object system. The new object system has several useful properties that will promote the development and maintenance of larger, more easily maintainable software projects. However, version 6 is so different from version 5 that adapting Bio::Phylo to it would amount to a port to a new language. Although this is currently being explored for BioPerl, the time investment is not justifiable for Bio::Phylo as long as Perl 6 virtual machines are not installed by default (or indeed available at all) on a great number of operating systems. This, however, is likely to change in the future.

Availability and requirements

- Project name: Bio::Phylo
- Project home page: http://search.cpan.org/dist/Bio-Phylo/
- Source code repository: http://nexml.svn.sourceforge.net/svnroot/nexml/trunk/nexml/perl
- Operating system: platform independent
- Programming language: Perl
- icense: GNU General Public License, version 3
- Other requirements: can all be installed from CPAN, either before or after installation of Bio::Phylo itself. These need to be present to activate certain functionality:

Visualization - any of the following to create the respective serializations: SVG.pm, SWF::Builder, PDF::API2, GD (for bitmap formats).

Tree simulation - Math::Random, Math::CDF

NeXML I/O - XML::Twig (for reading), XML::LibXML (optional, alternate way of creating DOM objects from Bio::Phylo objects).

INSTALLATION

Bio::Phylo is installed like any other CPAN-compliant pure Perl distribution; it requires no compilation, but it does require the *make* (or on Windows, *nmake*) utility, which is freely available on all common operating systems. Bio::Phylo has been successfully installed on a variety of architectures. Installation testing reports collected by CPAN show successful installs on Linux (versions 2.6.26-2-686, 2.6.18-5-alpha-generic, 2.6.26-1-orion5x, 2.6.26-2-amd64 and 2.6.18-4-xen-amd64), Mac OS X (Darwin versions 8.11.0, 8.11.1 and 10.2.0, equivalent to OS X versions 10.4.x and 10.6.x), FreeBSD (versions 6.2-release, 6.4-release, 7.0-release and 8.0-release), NetBSD (version 4.0.1), IRIX (version 6.5), SunOS/Solaris (versions 2.9 and 2.11) and Windows (version 5.00, i.e. "Windows 2000" and Cygwin version 1.5.24(0.15642)). Perl versions upward from 5.8.x are known to work generally, with successful installs using 5.8.6, 5.8.7, 5.8.8, 5.8.9, 5.10.0 and 5.10.1 on threaded and unthreaded perls.

ACKNOWLEDGEMENTS

The authors would like to thank Aki Mimoto and Florent Angly for code contributions and helpful feedback on Bio::Phylo's design. Arne Mooers, Wayne Maddison and Mark Pagel have provided RAV with material support during Bio::Phylo's initial development. Technical and moral support from the BioPerl core development team is gratefully acknowledged. Chris Venditti kindly provided the data and use case for the visualization example in Figure 2. Development was funded by the CIPRES grant (NSF EF-03314953), the Google Summer of Code program and through NESCent hackathons. RAV is supported by a Marie Curie Fellowship (FP7-PEOPLE-IEF-2008/N°237046).

AUTHORS' CONTRIBUTIONS

RAV carried out the initial design of Bio::Phylo and drafted the manuscript. JC, KH, MJ and CM contributed selected parts of the code base and helped draft the manuscript. All authors read and approved the final manuscript.

REFERENCES

1. Cracraft J: The Seven Great Questions of Systematic Biology: An Essential Foundation for Conservation and the Sustainable Use of Biodiversity. Annals of the Missouri Botanical Garden 2002, 89: 127–144. 10.2307/3298558
2. Noble WS: A quick guide to organizing computational biology projects. PLoS computational biology 2009, 5: e1000424. 10.1371/journal.pcbi.1000424
3. Sukumaran J, Holder M: DendroPy: a Python library

for phylogenetic computing. Bioinformatics 2010, 26: 1569–1571. 10.1093/bioinformatics/btq228

4. Huerta-Cepas J, Dopazo J, Gabaldon T: ETE: a python Environment for Tree Exploration. BMC Bioinformatics 2010, 11: 24. 10.1186/1471-2105-11-24
5. Cock P, Antao T, Chang J, Chapman B, Cox C, Dalke A, Friedberg I, Hamelryck T, Kauff F, Wilczynski B, de Hoon M: Biopython: freely available Python tools for computational molecular biology and bioinformatics. Bioinformatics 2009, 25: 1422–1423. 10.1093/bioinformatics/btp163
6. Paradis E, Claude J, Strimmer K: APE: Analyses of Phylogenetics and Evolution in R language. Bioinformatics 2004, 20: 289–290. 10.1093/bioinformatics/btg412
7. Stajich J, Block D, Boulez K, Brenner S, Chervitz S, Dagdigian C, Fuellen G, Gilbert J, Korf I, Lapp H, et al.: The Bioperl Toolkit: Perl Modules for the Life Sciences. Genome Res 2002, 12: 1611–1618. 10.1101/gr.361602
8. The Newick tree format[http://evolution.genetics.washington.edu/phylip/newicktree.html]
9. Maddison D, Swofford D, Maddison W: NEXUS: An Extensible File Format for Systematic Information. Systematic Biology 1997, 46: 590–621. 10.1093/sysbio/46.4.590
10. Cornish-Bowden A: Nomenclature for incompletely specified bases in nucleic acid sequences: recommendations 1984. Nucleic acids research 1985, 13: 3021–3030. 10.1093/nar/13.9.3021
11. Mesquite: a modular system for evolutionary analysis. Version 2.73[http://mesquiteproject.org]
12. Piel W, Chan L, Dominus M, Ruan J, Vos R, Tannen V: TreeBASE v. 2: A Database of Phylogenetic Knowledge. e-BioSphere 2009; London 2009.
13. RDFa in XHTML: Syntax and Processing[http://www.w3.org/TR/rdfa-syntax/]
14. Antezana E, Kuiper M, Mironov V: Biological knowledge management: the emerging role of the Semantic Web technologies. Briefings in Bioinformatics 2009, 10: 392–407. 10.1093/bib/bbp024
15. Prosdocimi F, Chisham B, Pontelli E, Thompson J, Stoltzfus A: Initial implementation of a comparative data analysis ontology. Evolutionary bioinformatics online 2009, 5: 47–66.PubMedCentralPubMed
16. Miles A, Pérez-Agüera J: SKOS: Simple Knowledge Organisation for the Web. Cataloging & Classification Quarterly 2007, 43: 69–83.
17. Gamma E, Helm R, Johnson R, Vlissides J: Design Patterns: Elements of Reusable Software Components. Addison-Wesley Professional; 1995.
18. Nee S, Mooers A, Harvey PH: Tempo and mode of evolution revealed from molecular phylogenies. Proceedings of the National Academy of Sciences of the United States of America 1992, 89: 8322–8326. 10.1073/pnas.89.17.8322
19. Penny D, Hendy MP: The use of tree comparison metrics. Systematic Zoology 1985, 34: 75–82. 10.2307/2413347
20. Fiala KL, Sokal RR: Factors Determining the Accuracy of Cladogram Estimation: Evaluation Using Computer Simulation. Evolution 1985, 39: 609–622. 10.2307/2408656
21. Rohlf F, Chang W, Sokal R, Kim J: Accuracy of Estimated Phylogenies: Effects of Tree Topology and Evolutionary Model. Evolution 1990, 44: 1671–1684. 10.2307/2409346
22. Colless D: Phylogenetics: the theory and practice of phylogenetic systematics. Systematic Zoology 1982, 31: 100–104. 10.2307/2413420
23. Pybus OG, Harvey PH: Testing macro-evolutionary models using incomplete molecular phylogenies. Proc Biol Sci 2000, 267: 2267–2272. 10.1098/rspb.2000.1278
24. Mooers A, Heard S: Inferring Evolutionary Process from Phylogenetic Tree Shape. The Quarterly Review of Biology 1997, 72: 31–54. 10.1086/419657
25. Isaac N, Turvey S, Collen B, Waterman C, Baillie J: Mammals on the EDGE: Conservation Priorities Based on Threat and Phylogeny. PLoS ONE 2007, 2: e296. 10.1371/journal.pone.0000296
26. Redding DW: Incorporating genetic distinctness and reserve occupancy into a conservation priorisation approach. Masters Thesis. In Masters Thesis. University Of East Anglia; 2003.
27. Pauplin Y: Direct Calculation of a Tree Length Using a Distance Matrix. Journal of Molecular Evolution 2000, 51: 41–47.
28. Semple C, Steel M: Phylogenetics. New York, NY: Oxford University Press; 2003.
29. Altschul SF, Lipman DJ: Equal animals. Nature 1990, 348: 493–494. 10.1038/348493c0
30. Haakc CJ, Kashiwada A, Su FE: The Shapley value of phylogenetic trees. Journal of mathematical biology 2008, 56: 479–497. 10.1007/s00285-007-0126-2
31. Baum BR: Combining trees as a way of combining data sets for phylogenetic inference, and the desirability of combining gene trees. Taxon 1992, 41: 3–10. 10.2307/1222480
32. Ragan MA: Phylogenetic inference based on matrix representation of trees. Molecular Phylogenetics and Evolution 1992, 1: 53–58. 10.1016/1055-7903(92)90035-F
33. Felsenstein J: Inferring phylogenies. Sinauer Associates, Inc; 2003.
34. Maddison D, Schulz K-S, Maddison W: The Tree of Life Web Project. Zootaxa 2007, 19–40.
35. Pagel M: Inferring evolutionary processes from phylogenies. Zoologica Scripta 1997, 26: 331–348. 10.1111/j.1463-6409.1997.tb00423.x
36. Pagel M: Inferring the historical patterns of biological evolution. Nature 1999, 401: 877–884. 10.1038/44766
37. Pagel M: Detecting correlated evolution on phylogenies: a general method for the comparative analysis of discrete characters. Proceedings of the Royal Society London Series B 1994, 255: 37–45. 10.1098/rspb.1994.0006

38. Mitsuteru N, Goto N, Nakao M, Kawashima S, Katayama T, Kanehisa M: BioRuby: open-source bioinformatics library. Genome Informatics 2003, 14: 629–630.

39. Schluter D, Price T, Mooers A, Ludwig D: Likelihood of ancestor states in adaptive radiation. Evolution 1997, 51: 1699–1711. 10.2307/2410994

40. Angly F, Willner D, Prieto-Davó A, Edwards R, Schmieder R, Vega-Thurber R, Antonopoulos D, Barott K, Cottrell M, Desnues C, et al.: The GAAS Metagenomic Tool and Its Estimations of Viral and Microbial Average Genome Size in Four Major Biomes. PLoS Comput Biol 2009, 5: e1000593. 10.1371/journal.pcbi.1000593

41. Hey J: Using Phylogenetic Trees to Study Speciation and Extinction. Evolution 1992, 46: 627–640. 10.2307/2409633

42. Yule U: A Mathematical Theory of Evolution, based on the Conclusions of Dr. J. C. Willis, F.R.S. Philosophical Transactions of the Royal Society of London Series B 1925, 213: 21–87. 10.1098/rstb.1925.0002

43. Simberloff D: Calculating Probabilities that Cladograms Match: A Method of Biogeographical Inference. Systematic Zoology 1987, 36: 175–195. 10.2307/2413267

44. Hartmann K, Wong D, Gernhard T: Sampling trees from evolutionary models. Systematic Biology, in press.

45. Redding D, Hartmann K, Mimoto A, Bokal D, Devos M, Mooers A: Evolutionarily distinctive species often capture more phylogenetic diversity than expected. Journal of Theoretical Biology 2008, 251: 606–615. 10.1016/j.jtbi.2007.12.006

46. Hladish T, Gopalan V, Liang C, Qiu W, Yang P, Stoltzfus A: Bio::NEXUS: a Perl API for the NEXUS format for comparative biological data. BMC Bioinformatics 2007, 8: 191. 10.1186/1471-2105-8-191

47. Kosakovsky Pond S, Frost S, Muse S: HyPhy: hypothesis testing using phylogenies. Bioinformatics 2005, 21: 676–679. 10.1093/bioinformatics/bti079

48. Suchard M, Rambaut A: Many-core algorithms for statistical phylogenetics. Bioinformatics 2009, 25: 1370–1376. 10.1093/bioinformatics/btp244

CHAPTER 18 R/PARALLEL – SPEEDING UP BIOINFORMATICS ANALYSIS WITH R

Gonzalo Vera, Ritsert C Jansen, Remo L Suppi

BACKGROUND

In recent years, R [1] has gained a large user community in bioinformatics thanks to its simple but powerful data analysis language. Growing repositories like Bioconductor [2] and CRAN [3] assist bioinformaticians with hundreds of free analytical methods and tools. These user-contributed methods are easily reused and adapted to each particular experiment for analysis of biological data. Examples of often reused and adapted methods are, respectively, the packages tilingArray [4] and affyGG [5]. However, while data generated in experiments previously fitted on a CD-ROM, nowadays, using new equipments, hardly fit on a single DVD-ROM. As a consequence of the post-genomic explosion of data, the demand of computational power is increasing continuously and solutions to keep the *processing pace* of high-throughput devices are required. A common approach in many bioinformatics fields like genomics, transcriptomics and metabolomics, where large sequential data sets are analyzed, is the use of parallel computing technologies [6].

Using R together with parallel computing is not a trivial task as the language does not provide mechanisms to support it natively. To compensate for this lack, several tools have been developed with different degrees of success. Early contributions to parallel computing in R were based on available general purpose parallel computing frameworks like MPI [7] and PVM [8]. Examples of these R libraries are rmpi [9] and rpvm [10]. These libraries provide low level programming interfaces, the complexity of which hinders a wider use of them. In order to hide such complexity, packages like NetWorkSpaces [11], snow [12] or taskPR [13] were created. They provide a higher level of abstraction, encapsulating the previous libraries (i.e. rmpi, rpvm) in simpler libraries and providing sufficient flexibility for the average type of programs coded in R. Additional development has been carried out with the framework pR [14]. It adds several modules to automate the parallelization of any R program. This feature is very important since programmers do not need to think *"in parallel"* when coding their R scripts, and anyone without previous knowledge of parallel computing can benefit from its advantages. However, while the programming model has been simplified during the last years, the dependency on external frameworks and dedicated resources is still a major obstacle for many bioinformaticians (e.g. pR depends on a complex installation to access a cluster of MPI enabled servers). These solutions are well suited for research groups with access to dedicated infrastructures (e.g. computing clusters managed by skilled technicians) and/or enough time to invest in the development of *ad hoc* parallel programs. However, when these requirements are not met, solutions based on self-contained tools (e.g. squid for Perl [15]), capable of running in common desktop computers, are the preferred choice.

In this paper we present an R add-on package for parallel computing: R/parallel. To use it, the programmer does not need to change his algorithm nor install and maintain any additional software as the R/parallel package is self-contained and capable of using current multicore processor desktop computers. It easily and effectively enables the automatic parallelization of loops without data dependencies [16], thus bringing the benefits of parallel computing within the reach of any bioinformatician using R. Its design allows its direct use with current bioinformatics analysis tools such as R/qtl [17], MetaNetwork [18] or affyGG [5] for analysis of genome-wide gene expression data.

Citation: Gonzalo Vera, Ritsert C Jansen and Remo L Suppi, R/parallel – speeding up bioinformatics analysis with R, DOI: 10.1186/1471-2105-9-390.

IMPLEMENTATION

The implementation of R/parallel has been carried out with the objective of increasing the performance of R by means of parallel computing while minimizing the requirements to use it. This section explains the design decisions made to speed up R programs while overcoming the common problems experienced by bioinformaticians with previous parallel computing solutions.

The first aspect taken into account is the desire to minimize user intervention when parallelizing new or existing R programs. The perfect solution should not require any further modification from the programmer. This is achieved with fully automatic parallelizers, which parse the program code, check it for data dependencies and generate a set of independent tasks that can be safely evaluated in separate processors. However, the drawback of this approach is that the parallelizer, *a priori*, does not know the execution time of each independent task. When a set of tasks are running concurrently, additional overhead and delays are introduced due to additional processing steps (e.g. code replication or task coordination). It is quite likely that a sequence of small fast tasks is parallelized and, despite parallel execution, as a result of the transformation process and additional synchronization, the overall processing time can be increased. To avoid this situation, the design decision made is to let the users indicate which code regions (i.e. loops) they need to speed up. With this information, R/parallel will automatically parallelize its execution to increase the performance.

Another aspect to consider when developing parallel programs is the difficult task of debugging when coding errors arise. When multiple processing units are running concurrently at different steps of a program, the identification of the conditions that triggers a bug and the retrieval of the state of each execution thread is a cumbersome task that should be avoided. To minimize this risk, an objective of the design of this package is the ability to run the sequential (and parallel) version of the R programs without changing any further line of code. By running a program sequentially it is possible to test the correctness of the implemented algorithm and debug using traditional tools. The user can activate the parallel execution just by loading the R/parallel package before performing a calculation. This design decision is also supported by the fact that, as the user program is not functionally dependent on R/parallel, it can always be shared with other bioinformaticians without requiring them to install the package or modify a single line of code.

Internally, R/parallel is designed using a master-worker architecture. The master component runs within the main R instance and distributes the work. The workers run in new processes with new R instances and perform the calculations retrieved from the master. The implementation of the package uses R scripts and C++ objects, taking advantage of both programming worlds. Combining low level operating system calls in C++ to manage processes, threads and inter-process communications (IPC) with the intrinsic features of R, like the capability of retrieving or creating functions at runtime (a feature known as "computing on the language" [19]), it has been possible to build a generic solution able to automatically transform a sequential loop and parallelize its execution.

RESULTS

Using the Tool

Figure 1 shows with an example how easy it is to parallelize a loop in R with R/parallel. In this example, a long vector of gene expression data (i.e. traits) is analyzed through a loop to find quantitative trait loci (QTL) underlying variation in gene expression using a multiple QTL model (MQM) approach [20]. Once a programmer has finished coding and testing his function as usual, he only needs to add the lines shown (i.e. the runParallel function and the if-else conditional structure) to run it faster in parallel.

```
qtlMapping <- function( map, genotypes, traits )
{
  result <- NULL
  for( idx in 1:nrow( traits ) )
  {
    tmpResult <- MQM( map, genotypes, traits[idx,])
    result    <- rbind( result, tmpResult )
  }
  return( result )
}
```

```
qtlMapping <- function( map, genotypes, traits )
{
  result <- NULL
  if( "rparallel" %in% names( getLoadedDLLs()) ) {
    runParallel( resultVar="result", resultOp="rbind" )
  }
  else {
    for( idx in 1:nrow( traits ) )
    {
      tmpResult <- MQM( map, genotypes, traits[idx,] )
      result    <- rbind( result, tmpResult )
    }
  }
  return( result )
}
```

Figure 1: Example using R/parallel. To parallelize a loop it is only needed to add an if-else structure. The loop to be parallelized is placed inside the else body and the parallelizer function runParallel inside the if body. The last step is to indicate in runParallel the variable names used to accumulate the partial results and the operations to apply after each iteration. Other arguments like the number of parallel processes (workers) are optional. Detailed documentation and examples can be found on the project web page as well as within the package as R help pages.

Adding the lines explained, the execution time when processing 37685 traits from 73 individuals is reduced, using a quad-core processor, from approximate 4 hours to 1 hour. Another advantage of R/parallel is that it can be used in *batch mode* as well as in *interactive mode*. Moreover, to preserve functionality and allow code sharing, if R/parallel has not been installed and loaded, the if-else instructions added prevent parallelization from taking place and the loop will run sequentially.

Use Cases

Practical applications of parallel computing are to increase the number of finished tasks given a fixed time or to decrease the time needed to perform a long task. To achieve this, a divide and conquer approach is used. The initial problem is partitioned into independent tasks which are computed simultaneously using several processing units.

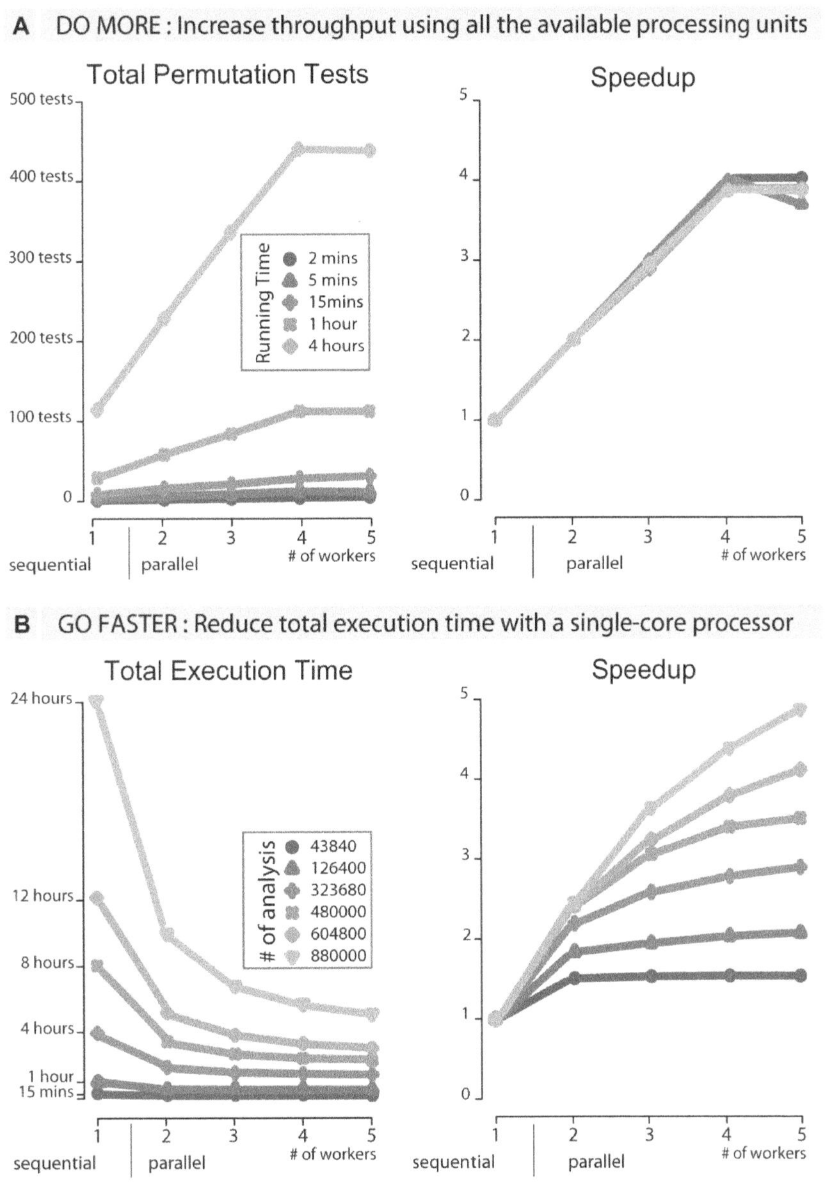

C KEEP WORKING : Control overloading while running calculations

% for **R/parallel**	100%	99%	95%	85%	50%	35%	Sequential
% for other tasks	0%	1%	5%	15%	50%	65%	N/A
Total Exec. Time	1792 s	2096 s	2212 s	2260 s	3419 s	3534 s	3908 s
Speedup	2.18	1.86	1.77	1.73	1.14	1.11	1.00

Figure 2: Performance results. A) The speedup increases linearly with the number of used cores. Setting more workers (5) than existing cores (4) does not improve the results. B)The (super linear) speedup exceeds the theoretical maximum of number of processing units due to faster tasks. C) With a conservative average load of 15% for other tasks, the computer is overloaded when R/parallel claims 100%. By reducing the percentage for R/parallel (with an optional argument) we can recover responsiveness and keep working on other tasks while running our calculations.

With R/parallel, partitioning is applied to loops and data, and multi-processing is used to get access to all the available processing units (i.e. *cores* in current desktop processors). The benefits of partitioning and multi-processing are shown in Figure 2 with three real cases. The observed speedups demonstrate that loops without data dependencies can be executed more efficiently using R/parallel. Obviously, with short calculations the speedup is minimal because of the additional overhead raised by the parallelization.

Typical bioinformatics cases where parallel computations are more often used are permutation tests or heuristic searches of multivariate spaces where, due to time constraints, the best result has to be computed before a deadline. The **case 2A** illustrates the increase of completed analyses (i.e permutation tests) by using all the available processing units. The function qtlThreshold.sma from the package affyGG is used with a quad-core processor to analyze a large number of permuted data sets using the same statistical analysis to compute (approximate) significance thresholds. Incrementing the number of parallel processes (i.e. workers) the usage of more cores has been enabled and therefore the overall performance has increased. The **case 2B** illustrates the decrease of the total execution time after parallelizing a problem. The function qtlMap.xProbe from the package affyGG is used with a single-core processor to compute the same statistical analysis over large data sets. In this case, due to the way memory is managed in R with linked lists and as a result of partitioning, small and faster tasks (with faster data indexing) are created. Therefore, in cases like this, even with a single processing unit, the total execution time is reduced.

The **case 2C**, where the function qtlMap.xProbe is used this time with a dual-core processor, illustrates the problem of processor overloading and how to address it. An inconvenience when the processor load is 100% (i.e. the computer is overloaded) is that ready-to-run processes have to wait for the processor(s) to be run. This delay leads to downgraded response times in interactive programs that makes it hard, if not impossible, to keep working with the computer when simultaneously running intensive calculations. Fortunately, common office applications on today's desktop computers rarely claim more than 1% of the processor [21]. Therefore, by giving up a small percentage of the processor, it is possible to keep using the computer for other tasks, while the ongoing calculation only takes slightly more time.

CONCLUSION

R/parallel, as shown, saves time to bioinformaticians in their daily tasks of analyzing experimental data. It effectively removes the most common obstacles encountered by bioinformaticians approaching parallel computing in R, like complex programming models or external dependencies on hard-to-maintain software frameworks. R/parallel is an easy-to-use R package which allows any programmer to parallelize their loops in a matter of minutes. The results demonstrate that R/parallel efficiently increases the performance of R when running parallel computations in current multicore processor desktop computer. As a consequence, bioinformaticians are able to approach reducing the processing time of a growing number of analytical methods by *N*-fold, *N* being the number of present cores in their computers.

Future work is focused on extending the functional and performance capabilities of R/parallel.

Additional functionalities like support for task parallelism or delayed loading of input data will extend the usability of the package. Additional performance, by expanding R/parallel from a single desktop computer to an office with several desktop computers or even a server farm, is our next milestone to speed up bioinformatics analysis with R.

We encourage any users to share their experiences with the authors to contribute to the extension of R/parallel.

ACKNOWLEDGEMENTS

We thank the members of the Groningen Bioinformatics Centre who have helped us testing R/parallel with their own R tasks and providing valuable comments and suggestions.

Supplementary material

AUTHORS' CONTRIBUTIONS

GV conceived, designed and implemented the software. He wrote an early draft of the manuscript. RCJ provided end user requirements and practical examples to assess the usability of this tool. RLS provided direction and technical advise on the design and implementation. All three authors read, revised and approved the final manuscript.

REFERENCES

1. Ihaka R, Gentleman R: R: A Language for Data Analysis and Graphics. *Journal of Computational and Graphical Statistics* 2005, 5(3):299–314. [http://www.jstor.org/pss/1390807]
2. Gentleman RC, Carey VJ, Bates DM, Bolstad B, Dettling M, Dudoit S, Ellis B, Gautier L, Ge Y, Gentry J, Hornik K, Hothorn T, Huber W, Iacus S, Irizarry R, Leisch F, Li C, Maechler M, Rossini AJ, Sawitzki G, Smith C, Smyth G, Tierney L, Yang JY, Zhang J: Bioconductor: open software development for computational biology and bioinformatics. *Genome Biology*2004, 5: R80. PubMedCentralCrossRefPubMed
3. The Comprehensive R Archive Network[http://cran.r-project.org]
4. tilingArray – Analysis of high-density oligonucleotide tiling arrays[http://bioconductor.org/packages/2.2/bioc/html/tilingArray.html]
5. Alberts R, Vera G, Jansen RC: affyGG: computational protocols for genetical genomics with Affymetrix arrays. *Bioinformatics* 2008, 24(3):433–434. [http://bioinformatics.oxfordjournals.org/cgi/content/abstract/24/3/433]CrossRefPubMed
6. Trelles O: On the parallelisation of bioinformatics applications. *Briefings in Bioinformatics*2001, 2(2):181–194. [http://bib.oxfordjournals.org/cgi/content/abstract/2/2/181]CrossRefPubMed
7. Message Passing Interface (MPI) Forum[http://www.mpi-forum.org/]
8. PVM: Parallel Virtual Machines[http://www.csm.ornl.gov/pvm/]

9. Rmpi: Interface (Wrapper) to MPI (Message-Passing Interface)[http://www.stats.uwo.ca/faculty/yu/Rmpi]

10. rpvm: R interface to PVM (Parallel Virtual Machine) [http://cran.r-project.org/web/packages/rpvm/index.html]

11. NetWorkSpaces for R[http://nws-r.sourceforge.net]

12. Rossini A, Tierney L, Li N: Simple Parallel Statistical Computing in R. *UW Biostatistics Working Paper Series* 2003., 193: [http://www.bepress.com/uwbiostat/paper193]

13. taskPR: Task-Parallel R Package[http://cran.r-project.org/web/packages/taskPR/index.html]

14. Ma X, Li J, Samatova N: Automatic Parallelization of Scripting Languages: Toward Transparent Desktop Parallel Computing. *Parallel and Distributed Processing Symposium, 2007. IPDPS 2007. IEEE International* 2007, 1–6.CrossRef

15. Carvalho PC, Glória RV, de Miranda AB, Degrave WM: Squid – a simple bioinformatics grid. *BMC Bioinformatics* 2005, 6: 197. PubMedCentralCrossRefPubMed

16. Briggs P: Automatic parallelization. *SIGPLAN Not* 1996, 31(4):11–15.CrossRef

17. Broman KW, Wu H, Sen S, Churchill GA: R/qtl: QTL mapping in experimental crosses.*Bioinformatics* 2003, 19(7):889–890. [http://bioinformatics.oxfordjournals.org/cgi/content/abstract/19/7/889]CrossRefPubMed

18. Fu J, Swertz M, Keurentjes JJ, Jansen RC: MetaNetwork: a computational protocol for the genetic study of metabolic networks. *Nature Protocols* 2007, 2(3):685–694.CrossRefPubMed

19. R Development Core Team:*R Language Definition*. The R Foundation for Statistical Computing, Vienna, Austria; 2008. [ISBN 3–900051–13–5] [http://cran.r-project.org/doc/manuals/R-lang.pdf]

20. Jansen RC: Interval Mapping of Multiple Quantitative Trait Loci. *Genetics* 1993, 135: 205–211. [http://www.genetics.org/cgi/content/abstract/135/1/205] PubMedCentralPubMed

21. Gupta A, Lin B, Dinda PA: Measuring and Understanding User Comfort With Resource Borrowing. *13th IEEE International Symposium on High Performance Distributed Computing (HPDC-13 '04)* 2004, 214–224. [http://doi.ieeecomputersociety.org/10.1109/HPDC.2004.21]

CHAPTER 19

OWLCPP: A C++ LIBRARY FOR WORKING WITH OWL ONTOLOGIES

Mikhail K. Levin, Lindsay G. Cowell

BACKGROUND

Ontologies are being increasingly recognized as important information resources that capture descriptive information in a standardized, structured, and computable form. One of the most widely used approaches for representing ontologies is the family of languages referred to as the Web Ontology Language (OWL) [1]. The OWL languages were designed to represent ontologies for use in the Semantic Web and were therefore built on the W3C semantic web stack, which includes XML, XML Schema, RDF, and RDF Schema [2–5].

Working with OWL ontologies involves several common procedures, including parsing ontology documents, storing them as RDF triples and axioms, querying and serializing their in-memory representation, passing the axioms to a reasoner, and performing logical queries. Given the increasing size of ontologies, it is extremely important to have software for working with OWL ontologies that can perform these procedures efficiently.

During the last decade, many open-source libraries useful for working with OWL ontologies written in RDF+XML format have become available. These, however, fail to fully meet the needs of software developers building software for working with OWL ontologies. First, existing libraries do not scale well enough to support ontologies of over a few million triples [6, 7]. In addition, the majority of them are implemented in non-native languages, which are usually less efficient and involve significant overhead when accessed from other languages [8]. For example, the libraries with the most extensive functionality, OWL API [9, 10] and Apache Jena [11, 12], are implemented in Java. Given the difficulties of accessing Java from other languages, it is not surprising that the recent Perl and Python libraries ONTO-PERL [13], RDFLIB [14], and FuXi [15], replicate some of the functionality already present in OWL API and Jena. Redland RDF framework is implemented in C and provides utilities for parsing, storing, and querying RDF triples [16, 17]. Its native code base allows it to more easily expose its API in several other languages and to be usable on virtually any platform, including mobile devices [18]. The functionality of Redland is limited, though, because it does not directly support OWL.

We sought to fill this gap by developing a library with the following key features: (i) supports fast loading and searching of large ontologies, (ii) has a small memory footprint, (iii) provides cross-platform compatibility, and (iv) can be accessed from multiple programming languages. The resulting library, *owlcpp*, is designed to support a common workflow where OWL ontologies written in RDF/XML are loaded from the file system and submitted to a reasoner for processing (Fig. 1). *owlcpp* is implemented in standard C++ and is aimed primarily at C++ and Python software developers. Here we discuss major design features and describe the results of an evaluation in which we compared the loading time, query time, and memory footprint of*owlcpp* and several other libraries across a set of ontologies of varying size and composition (Table 1).

Citation: Mikhail K. Levin, Lindsay G. Cowell, owlcpp: a C++ library for working with OWL ontologies, DOI: 10.1186/s13326-015-0035-z.

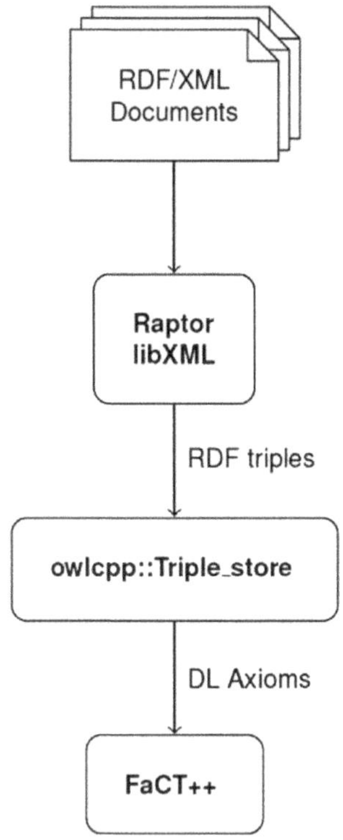

Figure: 1: Workflow of the *owlcpp* library. *Owlcpp* loads RDF/XML documents from the file system, parses them using the Raptor RDF Syntax library, stores RDF triples in a triple store, converts the triples to OWL axioms, and passes these to FACT++ for reasoning.

Table 1: Ontologies used for evaluating *owlcpp*

Name	Size	Terms			Triples	Axioms
	MB	IRI	Literal	Blank		
OBP [29]	3.0	935	2366	5056	25,924	6109
OBI [30]	6.1	4106	10,115	8709	75,666	32,800
Uberon [31]	62.0	32,078	118,935	87,713	579,388	56,956
OpenGALEN part[a]	130.5	45,404	8423	771,980	2,004,170	187,893
VTO [37]	149.2	110,418	502,521	103,801	1,358,341	829,796
MESH [38]	193.8	916,056	249,740	4345	1,667,128	1,654,092
DRON [39][b]	214.8	344,403	322,903	322,902	2,281,817	1,313,110
Biomodels [40]	253.2	232,214	535,725	481,909	2,686,610	1,905,822
OpenGALEN [41]	546.3	127,042	56,469	3,508,389	8,724,486	555,740

[a]OpenGALEN8_DD_2_Chapters.owl and its imports

[b]dron- ndc.owl

IMPLEMENTATION

The design choices in implementing *owlcpp* were based on providing the four key features listed above. Specifically, *owlcpp* is developed in ISO-compliant C++03 [19], which ensures source-level portability, supports generation of language bindings, facilitates creation of concise and expressive APIs [20], and compiles into efficient executables. The API for *owlcpp* was designed to be concise without sacrificing usability and performance. In the interest of clarity and thread-safety, class methods and function arguments were declared const wherever possible.

The compatibility of *owlcpp* with different platforms was verified by compiling the library and executing the unit tests on the following platforms and compilers: Linux, Ubuntu 14.04 64-bit (gcc v4.8, Clang 3.5); Windows 7 64-bit (Microsoft Visual C++ 13); Mac OS X 10.6.8 (i686-apple-darwin10-gcc 4.2.1); Windows XP 32-bit (Microsoft Visual C++ 9, MinGW gcc 4.5.2).

Currently, *owlcpp* comprises three modules, *rdf*, for storing and searching RDF terms and triples; *io*, for loading ontology documents; and *logic*, for converting triples into axioms and passing them to a reasoner. The *io* module depends on the Redland Raptor [21], libXML2 [22], and iconv [23] libraries, and the *logic* module depends on FaCT++ [24, 25]. The *io* and *logic*modules have different external dependencies and can be built and used separately from each other. *owlcpp* also uses many of the Boost libraries, e.g., iterator, multi-index, and file system [26].

The basic features of *owlcpp*, as well as those of other key libraries, are shown in Table 2.

Table 2: Basic features of *owlcpp* and other similar libraries

Feature	***owlcpp***	**Redland**	**Jena**	**OWL API**
Load RDF/XML	√	√	√	√
Serialize RDF/XML	–	√	√	√
Turtle I/O	–	√	√	√
OWL/XML, Functional, Manchester I/O	–	–	–	√
Search RDF triples	√	√	√	–
Convert RDF to axioms	√	–	√	√
Access FaCT++ reasoner	√	–	–	√
Access to other reasoners (Chainsaw, JFact, HermiT, Pellet, RacerPro)	–	–	–	√
Axiom API	–	–	–	√
C/C++ API	√	√	–	–
Python API	√	√	–	–
Java API	–		√	√

rdf module

The *rdf* module implements classes and methods as needed to support the RDF standard. To accommodate the demands of working with large ontologies, the design priorities for the module were compact in-memory representation of RDF terms and triples, and their efficient search and retrieval. The Triple_store class is the main container provided by the module. It supports storing, retrieving, and searching for prefix IRIs, RDF terms, ontology document descriptions, and RDF triples (Fig. 2). The library uses light-weight IDs to point to prefix IRIs (Ns_id), terms (Node_id), and document descriptions (Doc_id). The IDs for prefixes and terms standardized by RDF and OWL are defined by the library as compile-time constants.

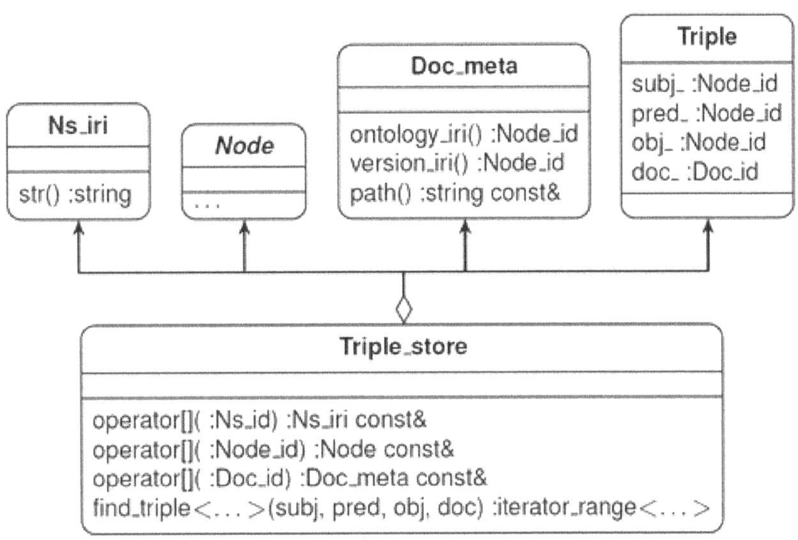

Figure: 2A diagram of the *owlcpp*Triple_store class, objects it stores, and some implemented methods. The Triple_store class serves as a container for prefix IRIs (Ns_iri), different types of RDF terms, which are accessed through the abstract Node interface, ontology document descriptions (Doc_meta), and RDF triples (Triple). Each object can be retrieved through an overloaded square bracket operator by supplying the object's appropriately typed ID.

The RDF standard defines three types of terms implemented in *owlcpp* as the Node_iri,Node_literal, and Node_blank classes (Fig. 3) [4]. These are accessed through the interface defined by the abstract Node class. A Node_iri object represents a prefix IRI with an optional fragment identifier. A Node_literal object stores an ID pointing to a Node_iri defining the datatype (e.g., xsd:date, rdf:PlainLiteral), a value as an appropriate internal type defined by subclasses of Node_literal, and, in the case of a string-valued literal, a language. A Node_blank object stores the ID of the document in which it was defined and an integer uniquely identifying the blank node within the document. In this way, blank nodes from different documents added to the same triple store are always kept distinct.

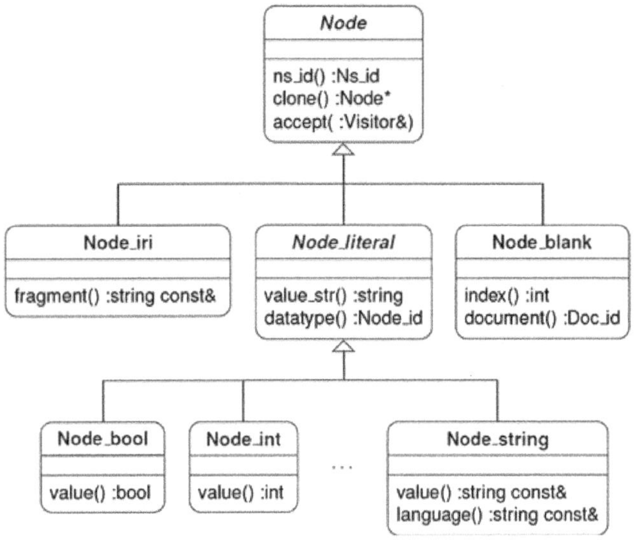

Figure 3: The RDF term type hierarchy as implemented in *owlcpp*. The RDF standard defines three types of terms implemented in *owlcpp* as the Node_iri, Node_literal, andNode_blank classes, which are accessed through the abstract Node interface. The abstract Node_literal class is further subtyped by concrete literal classes that represent the literal values as appropriate internal types, e.g., Node_bool for boolean types, Node_int for integers, etc. String-valued literals may also specify the language of their string values.

The ontology document descriptions (Doc_meta class) store Node_id's for the ontology and version IRIs and for the file system path for the ontology document.

The Triple class represents RDF triples by defining a combination of subject, predicate, and object terms. Since each term may appear in many triples, the Triple class stores a light-weight ID rather than a value for each of the terms. In addition, Triple stores the ID of the source document.

Since term IDs do not distinguish between different types of terms, the Triple class cannot, by itself, enforce the type restrictions on its terms. For example, it is possible to create a triple where the subject term ID refers to a literal or where the predicate term ID refers to a blank node. While such triples will not be created during normal ontology parsing, it should still be noted that the Triple class implements a generalized RDF triple [4].

Searching stored triples is a frequent, performance-sensitive operation. The types of searches are application dependent and may involve matching any combination of subject, predicate, object, and document, while leaving other elements unspecified. To efficiently perform the required types of searches, *owlcpp* stores triples in several indices. Within an index, triples are separated into bins according to one term and sorted within each bin according to the other terms. For example, an index in which triples are binned by subject and sorted by predicate, object, and document can help to efficiently identify the triples matching a subject and a predicate. On the other hand, if matching an object and a predicate is required, an index configured to bin by object and sort by predicate, subject, and document is expected to perform better.

Since the indices have a significant memory footprint, the user can define the number and type of indices during compilation. By default, *owlcpp* uses two indices: (i) bin by subject and sort by predicate, object, and document, and (ii) bin by object and sort by predicate, subject, and document. These defaults were selected because they were empirically found to perform best for axiom generation, as described below.

Searching stored RDF triples is done using the find_triple method provided byTriple_store. The method is designed to automatically select the optimal search procedure based on the type of query and the available triple indices. The results of the search are returned as an iterator range [27], which is both efficient and convenient, because the range can be used to test the success of the search, to obtain the first match, or to iterate over all matching triples.

io module

The *io* module provides several methods for loading RDF/XML ontology documents to a triple store. The documents can be loaded from the C++ Standard Library input streams using method load or directly from the filesystem using load_file. Loading an ontology document involves reading data from a stream, parsing XML structures, interpreting them as RDF statements, converting the statements into RDF terms and triples, and inserting them into a triple store. Currently, the Redland Raptor library is used as an RDF parser [16], which, in turn, relies on libxml [22] for parsing XML and iconv [23] for character encoding support.

The *io* module is designed for early detection of and recovery from errors. The errors may originate at different levels of the document loading process, such as opening a file or parsing XML, RDF, or OWL. An error occurring for any reason during document loading aborts the process by throwing an exception containing detailed information about its causes. In addition, instead of producing a triple store that contains an uncertain number of triples from the document that caused the error, the exception leaves the triple store in a valid state with none of the document's content in the triple store. This behavior allows the user to utilize the existing triple store content or to attempt loading the document again.

OWL documents often import the contents of other documents, identifying them by their ontology IRIs and version IRIs. The *io* module provides a mechanism to automatically load the imports from the file system. To be able to locate the documents, the module implements aCatalog class that stores document descriptions and maps the document, ontology and version IRIs to file system paths. The module also provides a method for scanning file system directories for ontology documents and adding their metadata to the catalog. Supplying aCatalog object to the load or load_file methods causes the module to also load the imported documents to the triple store. Automatically loading documents from the Internet is not currently supported by the module because this feature introduces a significant uncertainty to the success and performance of ontology loading and adds complex operating system-specific dependencies to the library.

logic Module

The *logic* module is responsible for translating RDF triples into OWL axioms and facilitating interaction with reasoners. Translation of triples to axioms is implemented by following the W3C Recommendation [28]. If the triples do not meet some of the stated requirements, the process is aborted by throwing an exception containing detailed information about its causes. Axioms can be generated from the entire store, or from a subset of the triples. Generating an axiom associated with a particular triple usually requires information stored in other triples, which are found by searching the triple store. The axiom generation algorithm searches the triple store by subject, by subject and predicate, and by predicate and object.

Frequent search operations make configuration of triple indices an important factor affecting axiom generation performance. The optimal configuration was identified empirically by comparing axiom generation times using eight hand-picked index configurations and three different ontologies: the Ontology of Biological Pathways (OBP) [29], the Ontology for Biomedical Investigations (OBI) [30], and the Integrated Cross-species Anatomy Ontology (Uberon) [31]. For Uberon, the largest ontology of the three, selecting the best index configuration reduced the axiom generation time by a factor of 2.5 thousand.

Currently, the *logic* module works with FaCT++, which is, to our knowledge, the only open-source C/C++ reasoner library for OWL DL [24]. Logical queries are currently performed directly through the FaCT++ interface.

Concurrency

Although *owlcpp* does not provide explicit support for concurrency, similar to C++ Standard Library containers, it is designed to maximize the number of thread-safe operations without penalizing performance. Operations that do not change the state of *owlcpp* containers (e.g., allconst methods) are guaranteed to be thread-safe. On the other hand, if multiple threads concurrently access an *owlcpp* container object and at least one of the threads modifies its state (e.g., inserts an RDF triple), the behavior is undefined. Therefore the user is expected to ensure that a modifying thread obtains exclusive access to *owlcpp* containers.

Build System

The build system for *owlcpp* is based on Boost.Build and is compatible with both Unix-like and Windows platforms [32, 33]. It is responsible for compilation and linking of static and shared variants of the library, as well as the sample executables according to the configuration provided by the user. The system also builds the required third-party dependencies from their sources, generates a Distutils module of *owlcpp* Python bindings, and produces API documentation using Doxygen [34].

Unit Tests

Unit tests comprise approximately 20 % of the library source code and cover most of its functionality. A separate test suite is implemented for each of the *owlcpp* modules. The tests for the *io* and *logic* modules make use of many small sample ontology documents that are part of the project source tree. Some of the documents are designed to test error detection at the XML, RDF, or OWL level. Some of the sample documents used by the *logic* module tests were adapted from the OWL 2 Test Cases [35]. The tests verify expected consistency of the ontologies and perform more specific logical queries. All unit tests are executed by the build system with a single command.

Python Bindings

The current version of *owlcpp* includes bindings for Python developed using the Boost.Python library. The functionality of the bindings is verified by a separate unit test suite. The bindings and their dependencies are packaged by the build system into a distributable Python module. APIs for other programming languages can also be exposed from *owlcpp* relatively easily and with minimal overhead. In future versions of *owlcpp*, these will be provided with the help of the SWIG library [36].

RESULTS

Evaluation

To evaluate *owlcpp*, we compared the document loading time, triple query time, and memory foot print of *owlcpp* with those of Redland, Jena, and OWL API. Evaluation was conducted using five ontologies of varying size and composition: the Vertebrate Taxonomy Ontology (VTO) [37], Medical Subject Headings ontology (MESH) [38], Drug Ontology (DRON) [39], Biomodels Ontology [40], and OpenGALEN [41]. In addition, a one quarter portion of OpenGALEN (OpenGALEN part) was used. The statistics of the ontologies, including filesystem footprints and the counts for RDF terms, triples, and axioms are listed in Table 1.

To test the ability of the library to process large ontologies on off-the-shelf hardware, the tests were conducted on an underpowered, by current standards, computer. Performance was tested on a laptop with an Intel Core2 Duo T7700 2.40GHz CPU, 3GB of RAM, running Linux Ubuntu 14.04 64-bit. The performance of Java libraries was tested using Oracle Java JDK v1.7.0_51 with a 2 GB maximum memory pool (-Xmx2048m). Unless noted otherwise, *owlcpp* was compiled with gcc v4.8 using the default triple index configuration. Redland v1.0.13 with a hashed in-memory store, Jena v2.12.1 with an in-memory RDF store, and OWL API v4.0.1 were used for comparison, also with their default settings. The source code for performance tests can be found in Additional file 1. All testing was done using *owlcpp* v0.3.5.

Ontology Loading Performance

To evaluate ontology loading performance, each of the six ontologies was loaded into each of the four libraries. Some libraries were unable to load the larger ontologies. Jena was unable to load the complete OpenGALEN ontology, while Redland failed to load the complete OpenGALEN, Biomodels, and DRON ontologies. An attempt to load the complete OpenGALEN into Redland on a system with 32GB of RAM was also unsuccessful. The loading rates (size of the ontology file system footprint divided by the recorded loading time) is shown in Fig. 4a. The ontology loading rate of *owlcpp* ranges from 3.1 to 6.9 MB/s, while the range for the other libraries is from 2.6 to 7.2 MB/s. The *owlcpp* loading rate is faster than that of Jena for the five ontologies Jena could load and faster than that of Redland for two of the three ontologies Redland could load. Redland had a faster loading rate than *owlcpp* for MeSH. In addition, the *owlcpp* loading rate is faster than that of OWL API for four of the six test ontologies. OWL API has a faster loading rate for both OpenGALEN full and part.

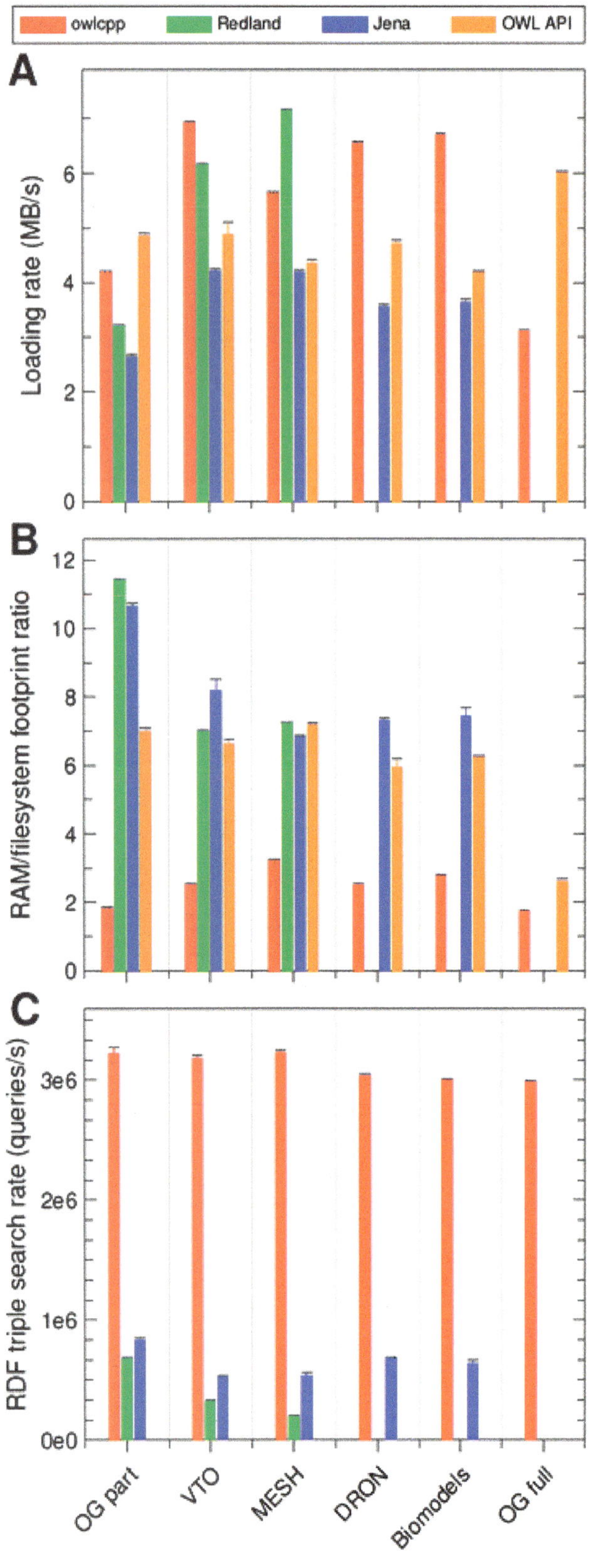

Figure 4: Performance comparison of the *owlcpp*, Redland, Jena, and OWL API libraries. The measurements were done using the following ontologies (by size, see Table 1): part of OpenGALEN (OG part), VTO, MESH, DRON, Biomodels, and complete OpenGALEN (OG full). The *bars* showing performance measurements are color-coded by library and grouped by ontology. The standard deviations of the measurements are shown as *error bars*. The corresponding bars are not shown if ontology loading failed. **a** shows ontology loading rates—ontology size divided by loading time. **b** shows the RAM footprint of each library after ontology loading normalized by the filesystem size of the ontology. **c** shows triple store querying rates. Each query identifies all triples matching a combination of a random subject and a constant predicate. Triple querying rates for OWL API are not shown because this operation is not supported

Memory Footprint

The amount of memory required by each library during ontology loading was estimated by probing the resident set size of the process virtual memory. The peak RAM utilization normalized by the size of the ontology on the file system is shown in Fig. 4b. Of the libraries tested, *owlcpp* had the smallest memory footprint for all ontologies ranging from 1.8 to 3.2 bytes of RAM required for each byte on the file system. The same ratio ranged from 7.0 to 11.5 for Redland, from 6.8 to 10.7 for Jena, and from 2.6 to 7.0 for OWL API.

Triple search Efficiency

Searching by subject and predicate is the most common triples search during axiom generation. Therefore, the triple search performance of the libraries was tested by repeating queries where the subject was selected at random, and the predicate was rdfs:subClassOf. For each query, all matching triples were identified and counted. The number of queries for each test was selected so as to keep the test time at about one minute. The number of queries performed by each library divided by the elapsed time is shown on Fig. 4c. The *owlcpp* library showed significantly higher search rates ranging from 3.0 to 3.2 million queries per second (MQ/s). Jena showed significantly lower rates from 0.53 to 0.83 MQ/s. The rates for Redland ranged from 0.2 to 0.69 MQ/s. Note that OWL API was not included in this evaluation because it stores axioms rather than triples.

Accuracy and error Detection

In addition to evaluating the performance of *owlcpp*, we wanted to assess the accuracy of parsing and axiom generation. This was done using the OWL 2 Test Cases [35], some of which are incorporated into *owlcpp* unit tests. Further testing was done during the development of the Ontology of Biological Pathways (OBP) [29] by executing queries formulated by domain experts and comparing the results with ones from Protégé running with either FaCT++ or the HermiT reasoner plug-in [42]. The results of the queries were always identical.

Strict error checking has proven to be an important feature of *owlcpp*, helping to avoid incorrect semantic interpretation of ontologies and facilitating their development. Examples of errors detected by *owlcpp* but ignored by OWL API and Jena are undeclared property and annotation predicates and misspelled standard OWL terms.

DISCUSSION

owlcpp is a C++ library providing support for storing and searching RDF terms and triples, for loading RDF/XML documents along with their imports into a triple store, for generating OWL axioms based on stored triples, and passing axioms to the FaCT++ reasoner. To the best of our knowledge, *owlcpp* is the first C++ library for working with OWL ontologies.

Our primary goal was to design a library for software developers that would scale well for working with large ontologies. To facilitate use by software developers, we designed *owlcpp* to have a concise and expressive C++ API and an efficient Python API. For example, loading an ontology file into an *owlcpp* triple store can be accomplished with just two lines of code, whereas the same operation through the Redland Raptor library API requires over a dozen lines [43]. The API for RDF triple store search is another example. In *owlcpp*, a single method,Triple_store::find_triple(), can be used to search for triples matching a specific subject, predicate, object, document, or any combination thereof. The search is performed without sacrificing performance by selecting the most suitable triple index at compile time. The result of the search, an iterator range, can be used transparently to determine whether the triple store contains a triple matching the specified condition, to retrieve the first matching triple, or to iterate over all matching triples. On the other hand, the triple stores of both Redland and Jena define over ten different methods for searching triples.

Of critical importance to the utility of *owlcpp* is ensuring its scalability for use with large ontologies. Thus, we designed *owlcpp* to have a compact, in-memory storage of RDF terms and triples, efficient indexing of stored triples, and no virtual machine requirement. The latter facilitates *owlcpp*'s deployment in HPC environments. To evaluate the scalability of *owlcpp*, we compared its memory footprint, ontology document loading time, and triple query time with those of Jena, Redland, and OWLAPI. We found that *owlcpp* has a smaller memory footprint than the other three libraries for all ontologies tested (Fig. 4b), and we find that the ontology document loading time is faster for *owlcpp* than the other libraries for all tests with two exceptions (Fig. 4a): Redland was faster loading MesH, and OWLAPI was faster loading OpenGALEN or a part of OpenGALEN. The lower performance of *owlcpp* with the MeSH ontology is probably due to this ontology's low ratio of triples to IRIs. In MeSH, each IRI appears, on average, in 1.8 triples, whereas in other ontologies this ratio ranges from 6.6 to 69. This property of MeSH increases the relative cost of IRI parsing, while diminishing the benefit of utilizing IRI IDs. Ontology loading by *owlcpp* is slower for OpenGALEN, either full or part, than for the other ontologies. This is probably due to a 50 % greater number of triples per megabyte in the OpenGALEN ontology.

While interpreting the performance measurements of the *owlcpp*, Redland, Jena, and OWL API libraries, it is important to note significant differences in their architecture. *owlcpp* and Redland are natively-compiled libraries, whereas Jena and OWL API run under Java virtual machine and exhibit less deterministic performance and memory footprint due to just-in-time compilation and garbage collection. Furthermore, while *owlcpp*, Redland, and Jena store the documents in memory as a set of RDF triples, OWL API immediately converts the triples into axioms and annotations, which, arguably, can be stored in memory more compactly. Nevertheless, the performance comparison is useful because it helps predict the hardware requirements for a task and reflects on the overall user experience.

There are several limitations of *owlcpp*, which will be addressed in future versions. First, RDF/XML is the only OWL format currently supported by *owlcpp*. Future versions will introduce support for additional syntaxes, particularly Manchester, Turtle, and OWL/XML. Second, *owlcpp* doesn't currently provide a Java API, and is therefore not interoperable with most of the currently available RDF/OWL tools. In future versions, we will provide a Java API. Third, although it is possible to manually add more nodes and triples to an *owlcpp* triple store, it is not currently possible to save the new RDF graph. Another important limitation of *owlcpp*is the lack of a description logic expression and axiom interface for axiom editing. Future versions will include this and will also improve readability of error messages, provide options for less strict parsing and axiom generation, and include a module for batch execution of OWL 2 Test Cases. Finally, future versions of *owlcpp* will provide an axiom-based in-memory data structure.

CONCLUSIONS

owlcpp presents a number of benefits for developers and users. Its compact datamodel and efficient execution make it possible to work with large ontologies using off-the-shelf hardware. As a native library, *owlcpp* does not depend on a virtual machine installation, facilitating its deployment in HPC environments. The C++ and Python APIs of *owlcpp* are concise and expressive and facilitate its integration with other software modules. Currently, *owlcpp* is used in many groups to work with biological ontologies as well as in other fields including virtual reality, robotics, image analysis, and answer set programming.

Any restrictions to use by non-academics: none

ACKNOWLEDGEMENTS

The authors would like to thank Dmitri Tsarkov for help with the FaCT++ library; Alan Ruttenberg and WacŃaw Kuśnierczyk for useful discussions; and Anna Maria Masci, Federico Bozzo, Simone Miraglio, and Andrés Samuel for testing *owlcpp*. This work was supported by an NIAID-funded R01 (AI077706) and a Burroughs Wellcome Fund Career Award to LGC.

AUTHORS' CONTRIBUTIONS

MKL developed the software, tested the performance, and prepared the first draft of the manuscript. LGC provided expert guidance, revised the manuscript, and wrote the final version. Both authors read and approved the final manuscript.

REFERENCES

1. OWL 2 web ontology language structural specification and functional-style syntax. 2nd ed. OWL Working Group. http://www.w3.org/TR/owl2-syntax/ Accessed 11/25/2014
2. Extensible Markup Language (XML) 1.0. 5th ed. http://www.w3.org/TR/2008/REC-xml-20081126/ Accessed 01/23/2015
3. W3C XML Schema Definition Language (XSD) 1.1. http://www.w3.org/TR/xmlschema11-1/ Accessed 01/23/2015
4. RDF 1.1 concepts and abstract syntax. http://www.w3.org/TR/2014/REC-rdf11-concepts-20140225/ Accessed 01/20/2015

5. RDF vocabulary description language 1.0: RDF schema. http://www.w3.org/TR/rdf-schema/ Accessed 11/25/2014
6. Stuckenschmidt H, Klein M. Structure-based partitioning of large concept hierarchies. In: International Semantic Web Conference. 2004. p. 289–303.
7. Janik M, Kochut K. BRAHMS: a workbench RDF store and high performance memory system for semantic association discovery. In: Gil Y, Motta E, Benjamins V, Musen M, editors. The Semantic Web–ISWC 2005. Lecture Notes in Computer Science, vol. 3729. Berlin, Heidelberg: Springer; 2005. p. 431–45. http://dx.doi.org/10.1007/11574620 32.
8. Babik M, Hluchy L. Deep integration of Python with Web Ontology Language. In: Proc. of 2nd Workshop on Scripting for the Semantic Web. 2006.
9. Horridge M, Bechhofer S. The OWL API: a Java API for OWL ontologies. Semantic Web. 2011.
10. The OWL API. http://owlapi.sourceforge.net/ Accessed 1/18/2015
11. Carroll JJ, Dickinson I, Dollin C, Reynolds D, Seaborne A, Wilkinson K. Jena: implementing the semantic web recommendations. In: Proc. of the 13th International World Wide Web Conference. New York, NY, USA: ACM; 2004. p. 74–83. http://doi.acm.org/10.1145/1013367.1013381.
12. Apache Jena. https://jena.apache.org/ Accessed 1/18/2015
13. Antezana E, Egaña M, Baets BD, Kuiper M, Mironov V. ONTO-PERL: an API for supporting the development and analysis of bio-ontologies. Bioinformatics. 2008;24(6):885–7.
14. RDFLib Is a Python Library for Working with RDF. https://github.com/RDFLibAccessed 11/25/2014
15. FuXi, a Bi-directional Logical Reasoning System for the Semantic Web.https://github.com/RDFLib/FuXi Accessed 11/25/2014
16. Beckett D. The design and implementation of the Redland RDF application framework. Comput Netw. 2002;39(5):577–88.
17. Redland RDF Libraries. http://librdf.org/ Accessed 1/18/2015
18. Kim T, Park I, Hyun SJ, Lee D. MiRE4OWL: mobile rule engine for OWL. Computer Software and Applications Conference Workshops 0. 2010. p. 317–22.
19. ISO/IEC 14882:2003: Programming Languages: C++, p. 757. International Organization for Standardization (2003).http://www.iso.org/iso/en/CatalogueDetailPage.CatalogueDetail?CSNUMBER=38110Accessed 11/25/2014
20. Reddy M. API Design for C++. Burlington, MA: Morgan Kaufmann; 2011. p. 472.http://www.apibook.com/ Accessed 9/15/5015
21. Raptor RDF Syntax Library. http://librdf.org/raptor/ Accessed 1/18/2015
22. Libxml, the XML C Parser and Toolkit of Gnome. http://xmlsoft.org Accessed 1/23/15
23. Libiconv–GNU Project. http://www.gnu.org/software/libiconv/ Accessed 11/25/2014
24. Tsarkov D, Horrocks I. FaCT++ description logic reasoner: system description. In: Proc. of the Int. Joint Conf. on Automated Reasoning. Lecture Notes in Artificial Intelligence, vol. 4130. New York, NY, USA: Springer; 2006. p. 292–7.
25. FaCT++ is an efficient description logic reasoner compatible with OWL DL and OWL 2.http://www.fact-project.org/FACT++/ Accessed 01/23/2015
26. Boost C++ Libraries. http://www.boost.org/ Accessed 1/18/2015
27. Boost Iterator Range. http://www.boost.org/doc/libs/release/libs/range/index.htmlAccessed 11/25/2014
28. OWL 2 Web Ontology Language Mapping to RDF Graphs. http://www.w3.org/TR/owl-mapping-to-rdf/ Accessed 11/25/2014
29. Masci AM, Levin MK, Ruttenberg A, Cowell LG. Connecting ontologies for the representation of biological pathways. In: Proc. International Conference on Biomedical Ontology. 2011.
30. The Ontology for Biomedical Investigations. http://purl.obolibrary.org/obo/obi Accessed 01/12/2015
31. Mungall C, Torniai C, Gkoutos G, Lewis S, Haendel M. Uberon, an integrative multi-species anatomy ontology. Genome Biol. 2012;13(1):5.
32. Prus V. The Boost.Build system. In: Proc. 3rd Spring Young Researchers' Colloquium on Software Engineering (SYRCoSE). 2009. http://arxiv.org/pdf/1208.6264.pdf Accessed 9/15/5015
33. Boost.Build V2. http://www.boost.org/build/ Accessed 11/25/2014
34. Doxygen. http://owl.semanticweb.org/page/OWL_2_Test_Cases Accessed 1/18/2014
35. OWL 2 Test Cases. http://owl.semanticweb.org/page/OWL_2_Test_Cases Accessed 9/15/2015
36. SWIG, Simplified Wrapper and Interface Generator. http://www.swig.org/ Accessed 9/15/2014
37. Vertebrate Taxonomy Ontology. http://code.google.com/p/vertebrate-taxonomy-ontology/ Accessed 01/12/2015
38. Medical Subject Headings. http://www.nlm.nih.gov/mesh/meshhome.html Accessed 01/12/2015
39. The Drug Ontology.https://ontology.atlassian.net/wiki/display/DRON/Drug+Ontology+Home Accessed 01/12/2015
40. BioModels Ontology. http://bioportal.bioontology.org/ontologies/BIOMODELSAccessed 9/15/2015
41. OpenGALEN. http://www.opengalen.org Accessed 11/25/2014
42. Gennari JH, Musen MA, Fergerson RW, Grosso WE, Crubézy M, Eriksson H, et al. The evolution of Protégé: an environment for knowledge-based systems development. Int J Hum Comput Stud. 2003;58(1):89–123.
43. Raptor: Parsing Example Code. http://librdf.org/raptor/api/tutorial-parser-example.html Accessed 11/25/2014

INDEX

A

Arithmetic and logical unit (ALU) 22

B

BAM Query Language (BAMQL) 63
Binary Alignment/Map (BAM) 63

C

Coherence rules (CR) 38
Computer-aided design (CAD) 41

E

error diagnosis 118, 128, 138, 139, 141

G

Generic Java 118, 119, 139, 140
Geographic information system (GIS) 41
Geographic information systems (GISs) 43
Graphical user interface (GUI) 58
Graphical User Interfaces (GUIs) 109, 111

H

Health Care and Life Sciences (HCLS) 97

I

Inter-process communications (IPC) 170

J

Java Compiler 118, 138, 139
Java Generics 118, 140
Java Language Specification (JLS) 118
Java Native Interface (JNI) 83
Java Virtual Machine (JVM) 82

K

Knowledge Organization Systems (KOSs) 98

M

Model-Driven Development (MDD) 149
Model-View-Controller (MVC) 150
Multiple Instruction Single Data (M.I.S.D) 20

N

Natural language database (NLDB) 35, 36
Natural language interfaces to databases (NLIDB) 35
Natural language query (NLQ) 35, 36
New Hampshire eXtended (NHX) 144
Nominal group (NG) 36
Non-disclosure agreements (NDAs) 69

O

Object-Oriented (OO) 90
Operational taxonomic unit (OTU) 159
Operational Taxonomic Units (OTU) 143

R

Re-configurable Mesh Computer (RMC) 20
Resource Description Framework (RDF) 97
RGG is available as a stand-alone software (RGGRunner) 111
R GUI Generator (RGG) 109, 111

S

S3DB Query Language (S3QL) 98
Simple Knowledge Organization System (SKOS) 98
Single Instruction Multiple Data (SIMD) 20
Single Instruction Single Data (S.I.S.D) 20
Static random-access memory (SRAM) 69

T

The cancer genome atlas (TCGA) 105

X

Xternal Subroutine (XS) 83